Playful Wisdom

Playful Wisdom

Reimagining the Sacred in American Literature, from *Walden* to *Gilead*

Robert Leigh Davis

LEXINGTON BOOKS
Lanham • Boulder • New York • London

Published by Lexington Books
An imprint of The Rowman & Littlefield Publishing Group, Inc.
4501 Forbes Boulevard, Suite 200, Lanham, Maryland 20706
www.rowman.com

6 Tinworth Street, London SE11 5AL, United Kingdom

Copyright © 2020 The Rowman & Littlefield Publishing Group, Inc.

"Cables To The Ace" by Thomas Merton, from *THE COLLECTED POEMS OF THOMAS MERTON*, copyright © 1968 by The Abbey of Gethsemani. Reprinted by permission of New Directions Publishing Corp.

All rights reserved. No part of this book may be reproduced in any form or by any electronic or mechanical means, including information storage and retrieval systems, without written permission from the publisher, except by a reviewer who may quote passages in a review.

British Library Cataloguing in Publication Information Available

Library of Congress Cataloging-in-Publication Data Available

Names: Davis, Robert Leigh, 1956- author.
Title: Playful wisdom : Reimagining the Sacred in American Literature, from Walden to Gilead / Robert Leigh Davis.
Description: Lanham : Lexington Books, [2020] | Includes bibliographical references and index.
Identifiers: LCCN 2020032671 (print) | LCCN 2020032672 (ebook) | ISBN 9781793626288 (cloth) | ISBN 9781793626301 (pbk) ISBN 9781793626295 (electronic)
Subjects: LCSH: American literature—History and criticism Thoreau, Henry David, 1817–1862—Religion Play in literature Religion and literature
Classification: LCC PS169.P55 D38 2020 (print) | LCC PS169.P55 (ebook) | DDC 810.9/382—dc23
LC record available at https://lccn.loc.gov/2020032671
LC ebook record available at https://lccn.loc.gov/2020032672

For Laurie, always

*In memory of my mother, Fran Davis (1929–2014),
and my friend, Kent Romanoff (1956–2019)*

Contents

Acknowledgments	ix
Introduction: This Is Play	1
1 Play and Attunement: The Spirituality of *Walden*	35
2 Play and Possibility: Emily Dickinson's Theology of Perhaps	69
3 Play and Improvisation: Jack Kerouac's Singing Theology	105
4 Play and Nonsense: Thomas Merton's Last Poem	131
5 Play and Risk: Annie Dillard's Daredevil Faith	159
6 Play and Understanding: Marilynne Robinson's Religious Hermeneutics	189
Bibliography	219
Index	233
About the Author	241

Acknowledgments

In a passage near the end of "Song of Myself," Walt Whitman reminds us that we tramp a perpetual journey and invites us to share the weight as we go: "If you tire, give me both burdens," he says, "and rest the chuff of your hand on my hip." That's how it felt to write this book: a long walk with strong friends. Here are some of their names: Kent Romanoff, Amy Romanoff, Mike Wilcox, Scot Hinson, Lori Askeland, Christina Reynolds, Mimi Dixon, Kent Dixon, Dick Veler, Lynn Brubaker, Wendy Osher, Rick Incorvati, Doug Andrews, Margaret Ann Goodman, D'Arcy Fallon, Mac McClelland, Dan Crump, Robin Inboden, and Mitch Breitwieser—who read an early draft of *Playful Wisdom* cover to cover and helped me see more clearly the shape of my own argument. Mitch may be the most generous and inspiring teacher I've ever known. An earlier version of chapter 4 appeared in *The Merton Annual* 20 (2007), and I want to thank the editors for permission to use that material here.

Playful Wisdom wouldn't exist without the encouragement and support of our daughters, Emily and Hannah, and their husbands Matt Badillo and Karl Berget, and our granddaughter, Izzy, who knows a lot more about play than I do (but would rather not *talk* about it all day). I'm deeply grateful to my students at Wittenberg University for all they've done to make this book possible; and I want to offer special thanks to my spiritual mentor, Reverend Robert E. Jones; Holly Buchanan and Arun Rajakumar, my expert editors at Lexington; and the artist, Geoff Dunlop, who allowed me to use a photograph from his series, THE POND Biophilia 2, on the book's cover. Inspired by his reading of *Walden*, Geoff created the image from a small pool of water near his home in Somerset England. The Somerset pond is barely a "pond," hardly thirty feet across, and yet Geoff found something sacred and beautiful there, which is exactly in the spirit of Thoreau.

Most of all, I want to thank Laurie, who believed in this project from the beginning and who often worked with me on the manuscript in the early mornings as the sun came up over Lake DuBay. Marilynne Robinson said once that "grace has a grand laughter in it." Those mornings seemed like that.

As a final act of acknowledgment, let me tell a story about how this book began. I was living and teaching in Germany some time ago, in a small town near Berlin, and took advantage of a free weekend to visit the famous Gothic cathedral in Nürnberg, St. Lorenzkirche. On the Sunday I attended worship there, the church was welcoming a new Confirmation class. This was a group of thirteen-year-old Nürnberg children who sat in the pew directly behind me and who came up one by one at the beginning of the service to describe an object they'd chosen as their *Konfirmation Zeichen*, their "confirmation symbol"—something that captured for them the meaning of their faith. They brought drawings, flowers, sheet music, and photographs.

Later in the service, with the confirmands behind me, the pastor gave a sermon that involved sheets of white paper included in our worship bulletins. At the start of his sermon, the pastor asked us to fold our papers in half, as he explained how our lives are often divided into parts. And then he made another fold in his paper, which we imitated, and more symbol analysis, and then some paper-tearing, and more explanation, and so on. I was trying to follow all this in rapid German, but things got complicated, and I was pretty sure I'd missed some folds and tears along the way. Which, it turned out, I had. Like most Lutheran churches, St. Lorenzkirche has prayer kneelers along the front of each pew with little desks to hold a worship book. After a great deal of folding and tearing and symbol analysis, the pastor invited us to unfold our papers and spread them out along these benches, starting from the center and moving, in turn, toward the outside aisle, where I was sitting. As people unfolded their papers along the pew, each one turned, magically, into a small, perfectly formed white cross. Right up to me. When I unfolded my paper, however, it didn't turn into a cross but a lopsided "H." So the bench looked like this:

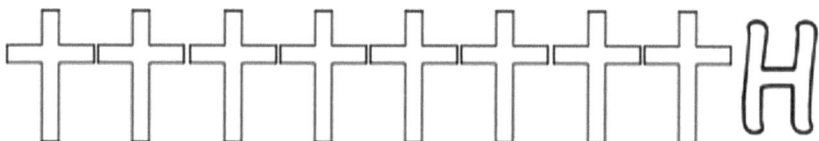

If that wasn't bad enough, as soon as I set my paper on the bench, one of the confirmands behind me said, in perfect English, *Jesus H. Christ*—which cracked up the teenagers, which made me laugh, and which sent a ripple of concern through the church as a whole.

I've kept the "H" since then. It's taped up over my writing desk. It makes me think of Emily Dickinson's depiction of faith as a laughing child; and it helps me remember that grace is surprising and play is holy, turning now to Thoreau, and good things can come from our mistakes.

Introduction
This Is Play

"The mass of men lead lives of quiet desperation," Henry David Thoreau wrote in one of the most famous sentences in American literature. "What is called resignation is confirmed desperation. From the desperate city you go into the desperate country, and have to console yourself with the bravery of minks and muskrats."[1] He would know. By the time Thoreau began writing *Walden* he was out of work; grieving the death of his brother, John; and experiencing the first signs of the tuberculosis that would eventually end his life. And so: the mass of men lead lives of quiet desperation. But what Thoreau goes on to say is equally important: "There is no play in them." By "play," Thoreau means of course no joy, no delight in the adventure of living. But he also means "play" like the play of a hinge: looseness, flex, bend. More than mere frivolity or quirkiness, play serves a higher purpose in *Walden*. It promotes spiritual growth by loosening rigid or compulsive habits of thought and opening the religious seeker to experimentation and creative change. Play is the antidote to spiritual desperation for Thoreau, who associates it with nimbleness, suppleness, the ability to change course, the ability to change the paradigm. He thinks of it almost in physical terms—as a light-handed athleticism of spirit constantly adapting to new perspectives and revising fixed assumptions in the light of fresh experience. And he imagines such play as a form of holiness, a way of living a life of faith: "I can see nothing so holy as unrelaxed play and frolic in this bower God has built for us."[2]

Thoreau despised organized religion—and signed off from the Unitarian First Parish in Concord when he was twenty-three. But Thoreau's thinking about holy play resonates with what I see as a distinctive kind of piety in American literature, one not based on religious ideologies or institutions but rather on experiences of the sacred that release people from the "walled-in" boundaries of an encapsulated ego (a pun Thoreau enjoyed) and connect them with something larger and more enduring than themselves. I've chosen to call that spirituality "playful wisdom," a phrase Thoreau used to describe what he loved about the *Hitopadeśa*, a collection of Hindu animal fabliaux, and contrast such wisdom with Thoreau's analysis of modern despair, a quiet desperation he found in his neighbors and in himself. Play is a symbol of God's freedom and creativity for Thoreau, the divine Artist "sporting on this bank," as he says in the "Spring" chapter of *Walden*. But it's also an experimental mode of religious devotion tuned to divine presence like the exquisite responsiveness of the pond. "In enthusiasm," he wrote in his *Journal* in 1840, "we undulate to the divine spiritus—as the lake to the wind."[3]

My claim is that Thoreau explored a particularly intense and timely version of religious play in *Walden*, which influenced several later American writers who both affirm and critique his religious ideas. Admittedly, the writers I've chosen are all over the religious map: a New England transcendentalist (Thoreau); a religious iconoclast (Emily Dickinson); a beat mystic (Jack Kerouac); a Trappist monk (Thomas Merton); a one-time Presbyterian (Annie Dillard); and a devoted Congregationalist (Marilynne Robinson). This diversity of religious traditions suggests an unlikely gathering of writers. Yet all were influenced by Thoreau; all deploy tropes of game and play to represent a life of faith; and all share with Thoreau an improvisational "looseness" or "mobility" in their thinking about the sacred, a sense that sacred experience unsettles fixed belief and alters the very shape of the perceiving self. And then requires that newly altered self to wait patiently for the next *altering*, the next soul-loosening God-storm that will pull the anchor pins and make possible a nimbler and more responsive faith. From this perspective, what matters isn't unswerving orthodoxy as much as agility and poise, a gift for responding to unstable moments of spiritual illumination that come and go in time—forming belief, then erasing it, then reforming it again in a spiritual practice Dickinson called "nimble believing" and Thoreau named "holy play." Thoreau's *Walden*, several of Dickinson's religious poems, Kerouac's *On the Road*, Merton's *Cables to the Ace*, Dillard's *Pilgrim at Tinker Creek*, and Robinson's *Gilead* are all versions of this ludic faith, I'll argue, experimental works of spiritual witness that identify doubt not as an obstacle to spiritual practice but as itself a kind of sacred vocation or holy calling.

It follows then that the view of play I develop has little to do with competitive sports and games that sample uncertainty briefly before sorting out winners and losers in stabilizing categories, a major theme in modern play studies.[4] Nor does play create islands of aesthetic form in the midst of life's chaos (as in Friedrich Schiller's *On the Aesthetic Education of Man*); or offer compensatory experiences of symbolic mastery and ego control (as in many psychoanalytic accounts of play); or rehearse competitive skills of public achievement that fit children to their proper roles (as in Johan Huizinga's

Homo Ludens); or fashion a heterodox American culture into a uniform model of corporate discipline (as in William A. Gleason's *The Leisure Ethic: Work and Play in American Literature, 1840–1940*).

Instead, Thoreauvian play subverts normative control and fosters flexible modes of interaction and reframing. Play's habitat is multidimensional and multivocal, crisscrossed with different voices and perspectives, a living ecology. As a form of communication, play sends mixed messages and contradictory signals and invites us to operate on more than one level at once. Play isn't a specific setting or relationship but a way of designating settings and relationships, drawing a chalk circle around them and stepping inside. It's possible to play with anything, as children know, improvising on odd little bits close at hand: making a doll out of grass stems or turning someone's math homework into a paper airplane. In short, play isn't an activity but a context or disposition, what Thoreau calls a "yard" ("it depends on how you are yarded"). Play is a way of setting brackets around something and saying, *inside* these brackets anything can happen. *Here*, we can suspend our disbelief.

Responding to play's multiplicity was something of a holy calling for Thoreau, a way of being faithful to the "sporting" God of *Walden*'s spring. But Thoreau doesn't essentialize play as an all-purpose category of social and spiritual liberation. Instead, play emerges as a specific response to the situation Thoreau found himself in at the dawn of the industrial age. Kenneth Burke said once that "critical and imaginative works are answers to questions posed by the situation in which they arose. They are not merely answers, they are *strategic* answers, *stylized* answers . . . [that] size up the situations, name their structure and outstanding ingredients, and name them in a way that contains an attitude towards them" (original emphasis).[5]

Play is Thoreau's strategic answer to the quiet desperation of American modernity. It emerges not as a liberating alternative in all places and at all times but as a reply to a particular set of historical circumstances, what Thoreau analyzed as the hegemony of the American marketplace. The key attribute of that marketplace is its ability to collapse multiple realities into a single unquestioned view, what both Thoreau and Merton call the "common mode" or the "common sense." That perspective depends on a set of premises Thoreau walks on continually in *Walden*: that the common sense is natural and inevitable; that it denotes the things people know instinctively, know without having to articulate or defend; and that such knowing is uniform and intersubjective, shared by all and available to all.[6] If that's the source of modernity's spiritual desperation, a toxic but unquestioned common sense, then it makes sense that Thoreau will cherish a capacity for living in two worlds at once, like the Walden loon, or reframing experience from a different angle, like the Walden Hermit. For Thoreau, religious play undermines reigning orthodoxies and opens the religious seeker to alternative points of view, an idea that also occurred to Merton: "There are times when it seems that fidelity to God is *not* compatible with mere obedience to an external norm, where fidelity to God requires something else: certainly not revolt nor disobedience but a presentation of alternative and deeper views" (original emphasis).[7]

The presentation of alternative views is central to my project in *Playful Wisdom* and the key to Thoreau's influence on the play theologies of American literature. If the effect of modern consciousness is to produce a small set of privileged sensations and perspectives (the approved prospect or the normative view), then Thoreau's response is to stretch perception toward a fuller sensory and interpretive array and to embrace play as a mode of thought open to what he does not already know: meanings and feelings not preformulated for him by the common sense. Walden Pond means many things to Thoreau—it's an ecology, a companion, a sacred space, a higher self—but the pond is also a parallax device of liberating estrangement, a lens or prism that allows him to experience objects from multiple standpoints or approach ideas through different frames of mind. This is Thoreau's signature maneuver as a religious writer. He brackets, abstracts, re-positions, and re-yards virtually everything he encounters, shifting the frames he uses to organize his experience and recovering what he calls the "sufficient distance" of perspectival knowing (152). Calling this way of thinking, *playful*, suggests that there can be a corresponding joy in life's uncertainty (rather than only anguish and disorientation). And calling it, *wisdom*, evokes the metacognitive dimensions of play, the hope that we can become more fully awake and self-conscious through these practices and reclaim our role as co-players or co-creators in a world we help bring into being (rather than accept passively like unthinking machines).[8]

This bracketing or contextualizing aspect of play relates it to dream, art, religion, fantasy, metaphor, and madness—the emotional DNA of human experience. But this is also something we share with many animals according to Gregory Bateson, who argued that animal play is not reflexive or hardwired (the "behavioral" bias of 1950s psychology) but instead improvisational and adaptive.[9] Animals who can spot the cue, *This is play*, suspend fixed responses in favor of a new set of behaviors and codes. Bateson's play theories began with a visit to the Fleishhacker Zoo in San Francisco in 1952, where he watched young monkeys play-fighting with one another. The monkeys knew they were playing. Bateson knew they were playing. But the differences between real-fighting and play-fighting were subtle and depended on the monkeys' ability to use basically the same expressive vocabulary in completely different ways, altering *bite* to mean one thing today (aggression) and something else tomorrow (affection, flirtation, boredom, dominance—sometimes all at once). Play thrives on this creative reframing and depends on people and animals who can pick up the cue and respond accordingly, not reacting mindlessly to the mood signals of another but reading those signals as *signals*, which can be denied, amplified, trusted, interpreted, or corrected.[10] In play, the old rules are suspended for a time and a different set of interpretive procedures kicks into gear, one that relies on metaphor, irony, paradox, and a flair for the subjunctive (pretend this is a bite; act as if this were a bite—which it *isn't*).

What interested Bateson and his coworkers was how this subjunctive framing loosened hard-and-fast rules of communication:

> My personal interest in the abstract problem of play is a desire to know about those processes whereby organisms pull themselves up by their bootstraps. And they do it, as far as I can see, by loosening up on the rules of communication—the onionskin structures within which they are operating. They play with these structures or rules and thereby move forward to new rules, new philosophies, etc.[11]

Bateson uses the word "abstract" meticulously in his play discussions, "the *abstract* problem of play," to accent the ability to move up a conceptual step in communication sequences (from activity to frame or message to category)—a level jump Bateson often signals with the prefix, *meta*: metamessages or metacommunication. Play is above all a metacognitive process for Bateson, a way of framing experience that allows players to exist in two dimensions at once: both playing a game and *aware* that they're playing a game (and so able to recall themselves from their roles). In Bateson's vocabulary "meta" means critical distance or conceptual detachment, an idea that will emerge often in *Playful Wisdom*. (*Meta* is literally Annie Dillard's middle name.) Meta indicates the ability to stand apart from concepts and convictions and view them from the side or from above. "With thinking we may be beside ourselves in a sane sense," Thoreau says in *Walden*. "By a conscious effort of the mind we can stand aloof from actions and their consequences; and all things, good and bad, go by us like a torrent" (145). Metacognitive thinking is flexible and polysemic. It "carries us beyond" literal meaning (*meta-phora*) and requires a form of nonattachment Bateson associates with the sacred in his later writings. Faith is metacognitive (aware of two worlds at once). Humor is metacognitive (based on hidden possibilities). And for Bateson and Thoreau, so is animal play. It's worth remembering that Thoreau's thinking about "playful wisdom" emerged in response to his reading of the *Hitopadeśa*, a collection of Hindu animal tales used as a teaching manual for wise statecraft but which Thoreau admired not for its platitudes but for its self-awareness, which struck him as a model for his own writing: "A playful wisdom which has eyes behind as well as before, and oversees itself. This pledge of sanity cannot be spared in a book—that it sometimes reflect upon itself—that it pleasantly behold itself—that it hold the scales over itself."[12]

Like Bateson, Thoreau often pictures metacognitive play as a kind of theatrical self-consciousness, an ability to look down on oneself as "the scene, so to speak, of thoughts and affections" (145–46). Although he's less certain than Bateson that animals actually *understand* this process, Thoreau stresses a version of this theatrical doubleness in his scenes of animal play, so that the squirrels, loons, and partridges in *Walden* always seem to be "performing" in the presence of an audience, as in this scene from "Winter Animals":

> Usually the red squirrel (*Sciurus Hudsonius*) waked me in the dawn, coursing over the roof and up and down the sides of the house, as if sent out of the woods for this purpose.... All day long the red squirrels came and went, and afforded me much entertainment by their manoeuvres. One would approach at first warily through the shrub-oaks, running over the snow crust by fits and starts like a leaf blown by the wind, now a few paces this way, with wonderful speed and waste of energy, making inconceivable haste with his "trotters," as if it were for a wager, and now as many paces that way, but never getting on more than half a rod at a time; and then suddenly pausing with a ludicrous expression and a gratuitous somerset, as if all the eyes in the universe were fixed on him,—for all the motions of a squirrel, even in the most solitary recesses of the forest, imply spectators as much as those of a dancing girl,—wasting more time in delay and circumspection than would have sufficed to walk the whole distance,—I never saw one walk,—and then suddenly, before you could say Jack Robinson, he would be in the top of a young pitch-pine, winding up his clock and chiding all imaginary spectators, soliloquizing and talking to all the universe at the same time. (296–97)

Critics usually interpret this scene as an anthropomorphizing self-portrait, Thoreau's way of ascribing his own self-consciousness to the animals at the pond and making the squirrels bear the symbolic burden of his ideas.[13] But Bateson's research reverses the developmental sequence and suggests that animal play precedes human self-consciousness and that in performing their extravagant maneuvers the squirrels remain *squirrels*, not mini-Thoreaus, and just as capable of responding playfully and creatively to their environment as he is. Thoreau has no way of representing squirrel play on its own terms, so he imports odd-fitting words like "somerset" or "soliloquy" to accent the subjunctive reframing and suggest that nothing in the scene is all that stable. We're in the magic circle now, where squirrels can look like gymnasts (as well as leaves, race horses, dancing girls, and stage actors). Thoreau begins the scene with his schoolroom voice, informing us that the squirrel's scientific name is *Sciurus hudsonius*. But by the end of the scene, *Sciurus hudsonius* isn't a bedrock designation either, only one name among many, taking its place in a spectacular display of mixed metaphors and paradoxical frames. Thoreau doesn't develop the religious implications of animal play here; he saves that for the loons, but waking up "in the dawn" is a loaded phrase in *Walden*. If there's a higher purpose to this scene, as Thoreau suspects, it may be that the squirrels open his eyes to a kinetic world of astonishing mobility. Plato believed that play begins in the need of young creatures to "leap." Thoreau spins this idea into a gymnastic catalog of fast-twitch play: squirrels leaping, running, trotting, frisking, dancing, somersaulting. In watching the squirrels, Thoreau wonders if such play manifests an equally active mind: "a mind not made up whether to get [the ear of corn] again, or a new one, or be off; now thinking of corn, then listening to hear what was in the wind" (298). Thoreau will explore what good might come from "a mind not made up" and how we might develop that mobile subjectivity into a form of athletic piety or gymnastic devotion, modeling our lives on the playful wisdom of the squirrels.

Bateson's observations about animal play became the foundation for his subsequent theories of sacrament, deutero-learning, and the ecology of mind—all of which depend on the mind-bending ability to say *yes* and *no* at the same time and understand something that both *is* and *is not* itself: "The playful nip denotes the bite," Bateson writes, "but it does not denote what would be denoted by the bite."[14] For Bateson, play's paradoxical framing allows for the ongoing nature of social communication, "a self-experiment out of which the player discovers new possibilities for thinking," and suggests the moment in our ancient pre-history when irony, metaphor, and literature were born.[15] But this also suggests the moment when religion, ritual, and sacrament were born, subjunctive ways of thinking and feeling that also depend on doubled or paradoxical states of mind.[16] The charioteer standing beside Arjuna both *is* and *is not* his old friend and teacher (in the *Bhagavad Gita*). The man walking beside Cleopas on the road to Emmaus both *is* and *is not* a stranger in Jerusalem (in the Gospel of Luke). And being able to sense that shift or "give" in ordinary perception is being able to play. "Buoyancy, freedom, flexibility, variety, possibility"—these are the characteristics of the sacred for Thoreau, the "qualities of the Unnamed."[17] And these are also the hallmarks of religious play.

The implications of this theory of play are profound. Bateson thought of it as having eaten the fruit of the Tree of Knowledge. When a jackdaw learns to imitate its own mood signals, for instance, then virtually anything can become play, including "play," and things spiral out from there: fixed meanings, automatic responses, and one-dimensional communication go right out the window. We must watch carefully now for shifting cues, moving nimbly through different symbolic registers and deploying and discarding different interpretative frames. Biologically, this flexibility reinforces "the organism's variability in the face of rigidifications of successful adaptation," Brian Sutton-Smith writes, offering a quasi-Darwinian definition of play.[18] But if Bateson's right that play is the origin of metaphor and paradox, then play's reframing may have religious implications as well, changing the way we think about the divine. If religious devotion means consolidating and protecting a privileged set of beliefs, then it makes sense to picture faith as something adamant and unyielding, like Luther's mighty fortress or St. Paul's armored warrior (Eph. 6:10–17). But if devotion means being attuned to a world that's changing by the hour, as it was for Thoreau, then it requires a different style of religious wisdom, one that holds its ideas lightly, holds its "faith" in quotation marks, in responsive attunement to the infinite variability of the divine. Bateson describes such faith as "a floating devotion" or a commitment to "a floating creed"[19]—a religious stance that's more relational than private, more focused on improvisation than on predetermined response, and more rhetorical than literal or unaware. It's this metacognitive, highly rhetorical play that interests Thoreau and shapes the theological legacy I'll explore in *Playful Wisdom*. When Thoreau imagines divine creativity as a sport or game in the sandbank scene in *Walden*, for instance, he avoids the mystical language of direct report, which he sometimes uses in his *Journal*, or the creedal language of established confession, which he almost never uses, and relies instead on the *as-if* language of subjunctive play:

> What makes this sand foliage remarkable is its springing into existence thus suddenly. When I see on the one side the inert bank,—for the sun acts on one side first,—and on the other this luxuriant foliage, the creation of an hour, I am affected as if in a peculiar sense I stood in the laboratory of the Artist who made the world and me,—had come to where he was still at work, sporting on this bank, and with excess of energy strewing his fresh designs about. (331)

Critics often associate the complex figurality of this passage with Emerson's theory of the symbol. But this image of *deus ludens*, the playing God of Walden Pond, owes as much to the *līlā* tradition of divine play in the *Harivaṃśa* and the *Vishnu Purāṇa* as it does to *Nature* and "The Poet." I'll defer a discussion of the sporting Artist until the next chapter, except to point out what Bateson would call the "play signal" of this passage, the subjunctive *as if*. The moment God appears to Thoreau as a sort-of Artist, play's metacognitive loosening has already begun. We are now in a world of "luxuriant" possibility where multiple realities morph and meld: work and sport, spontaneity and design, artist and Artist. Thus, it's tempting to put quotation marks around everything: "creation," "bank," "world," and so forth. And Thoreau's changing too, melting as fast as the sandbank. Within this play space, God both is and is not an Artist; the world is and is not a laboratory; and this is and is not Thoreau—at least not a definitive, frozen-in-place Thoreau. In play, nothing is frozen in place; a bite can mean ten different things, so it seems right to put quotation marks even around "Thoreau" and so keep attention on high alert, ready for the moment when the scene shifts and something else comes into view. ("The Scene-shifter saw fit here to close the drama, of this day," Thoreau says in the "Sunday" chapter of *A Week*, "without regard to any unities which we mortals prize.")[20]

In this regard, the opposite of play is not seriousness, industry, work, or labor—a point Thoreau stresses many times. Divine "work" and divine "sporting" exist side by side in the sandbank passage, as Gleason points out, separated by the faint pause of a comma.[21] Instead, the opposite of play is literality, reification, dogmatism, or single-mindedness—what Herbert Marcuse called "one-dimensional thinking" (bleached of multiplicity and contrast) and which felt to Marcuse like being trapped within one set of interpretative procedures.[22] It's possible to work that way just as it's possible to pray and worship that way: the activity isn't the point; the framing is the point, the *as-if* awareness of possibility and change. When we're open to that possibility, we're playing, even if what we're doing is extremely difficult. When we're not open, we're not playing, even if what we're doing sounds pleasant, like looking at spring flowers. Bateson's example of anti-play is Wordsworth's Peter Bell, who sees a yellow primrose as a yellow primrose, nothing more. No play, slippage, luxuriance, reframing—just a primrose, period.[23] As Stephen Nachmanovitch has shown, much of Bateson's work was devoted to contesting that dead-end literalism by challenging linguistic and perceptual habits that reify not only primroses but also people and relationships, turning them into inert things we can "have" or "possess."[24]

Where Bateson calls these reifying habits "dormitive principles," Thoreau calls them simply "the common sense"—the ready-made set of scripts and responses designed to stabilize the everyday lifeworld and place "play" (and the creatures associated with play: squirrels, loons, loafers, dreamers, children, non-workers) in a special sorting category designed to protect the common sense from confusion, the category of "nonsense."[25] Like play, the common sense is not a specific activity but a way of framing and thinking about activities, marking them off as serious and necessary. The activity itself may look ridiculous from the outside (Thoreau could supply a hundred examples here: paying the poll tax, inheriting property, fixing elaborate dinners), but from a commonsense point of view, these things are indispensable. Thoreau's basic religious point is that our frames are variable—life changes them; time changes them—and everything depends, then, on how we're yarded, which is the metacognitive message of play.

I'll come back to the common sense in a moment and consider two "play" scenes from two different religious traditions: Mary's encounter with the risen Christ in John's gospel and Arjuna's encounter with the revealed Krishna in the *Bhagavad Gita* (a key source for Thoreau's thinking about the "nextness" or "neighboring" of the divine in *Walden*). But let me pause here to offer an example of how play reveals what the common sense keeps hidden: its provisionality, its dense but fragile constructedness. The scene I have in mind occurs in the first few pages of "Brute Neighbors" in *Walden*, a chapter that answers Thoreau's most prescriptive religious chapter, "Higher Laws," with one of his most playful ones. The scene begins with a contemplative Hermit just settling down to his mid-day meditations when his friend, the Poet, drops by with the suggestion that they spend the day fishing. Once that happens, which is to say, once "play" happens, the Hermit loses his original orientation and must think his way back into frames of mind that now feel less secure. Here's how Thoreau tells the story, just after the Poet's interruption:

> *Hermit alone.* Let me see; where was I? Methinks I was nearly in this frame of mind; the world lay about at this angle. Shall I go to heaven or a-fishing? If I should soon bring this meditation to an end, would another so sweet occasion be likely to offer? I was as near being resolved into the essence of things as ever I was in my life. I fear my thoughts will not come back to me. (245)

The point of Thoreau's irony is not to mock the Hermit's bewilderment or recruit him to a new gospel of outdoor recreation. (Later, he'll undermine *that* Thoreau's devotion to the sacrament of fishing.) Instead, the point is to make the "frames" and "angles" show—with meditation here, with fishing later. Moreover, Thoreau chooses to do that in the Hermit story, surprisingly, by turning the scene into a *scene*, a little piece of *Walden* theater—complete with a script, a soliloquy, and an odd little Shakespearean flourish, *methinks*. The theatricality of the scene causes the Hermit to acknowledge the artifice and contestability of his way of framing the world, which becomes *this* frame, one among many. If Thoreau's teaching us something about religious wisdom here, the lesson may have to do with the doubleness of a contemplative point of view and the resulting ability to both occupy and critique a particular frame of mind—the way Walt Whitman, in a similar mood, thought of himself as being "both in and out of the game, and watching and wondering at it."[26] When Thoreau caps his theater piece with a series of ontological questions— "Why do precisely these objects which we behold make a world? Why has man just these species of animals for his neighbors; as if nothing but a mouse could have filled this crevice?" (245–46)—he allows play's loosening effect to spread like ripples on the pond, raising possibilities the common sense would rather ignore: What are we missing then? Why *this* world? Who else is out there?

Once these questions get started, it's hard to make them stop. The goal of commonsense economies is habit and efficiency, not having to raise all sorts of ontological questions that scatter attention and slow the pace of automatic response. Thoreau's pace is not automatic or efficient in *Walden*, not the straight-line plot of traditional narrative, but a dilatory plot of hesitating, pausing, backtracking, reconsidering—which expresses the hope of Thoreau's religious sensibility: that both world and mind are active, unstable, multiple, and open at the edges. When Thoreau stresses the "play" of nondesperate forms of wisdom or the "frolic" of his religious practice at the pond, he's not trivializing religion so much as aligning it with the deep plurality of a changing world. "Thank Heaven, here is not all the world," he says at the end of *Walden* (347)—reminding us that *this* world, this particular arrangement of power and perspective, is not the only world and that accepting this instability can be a fundamentally religious act, a blessing worthy of praise.

The common sense resists this and keeps people who think that way on the outside, in the nonsense box, in order to convey the impression that its perspective is *not* constructed but necessary and inevitable and so beyond the scope of conscious thought and revision. Commonsense modes of thinking are strategic and efficient. (In this sense, they are "work" economies, as Alfred Schutz stresses.) They streamline attention by creating hard boundaries between what matters and what doesn't in order to protect awareness from paralyzing swarm. A world unsorted by clear distinctions between "sense" and "nonsense" threatens to swamp attention with too many possibilities. But play thrives on possibility, creating a space where a silly game with a loon can suddenly feel sacred, as it did to Thoreau. Or a backyard cedar she's seen a hundred times can suddenly be transfigured, as it was for Dillard. There's an implicit aesthetics to this frame play in the *trompe l'oeil* tradition of perspectival illusion (an idea Thoreau explores in *A Week*), but there's also an implicit theology.[27] When Mary arrives at the empty tomb in John's gospel, for instance, she mistakes the risen Christ for the gardener, who's not what she expects or needs, not someone important, until "the gardener" calls her by name and the frames shift—and suddenly it's Easter morning. "Christ plays in ten thousand places," Gerard Manley Hopkins wrote in this spirit, savoring a world where Easter could happen anywhere and Christ could appear under any guise.[28]

The gospels delight in stories of the shape-shifter Christ present but undetected by those who overvalue the literal surface. To the rabbis in the synagogue, Jesus is a twelve-year-old boy. To Pilate, he's a delusional revolutionary. To Mary, he's a gardener. To the disciples on the road to Emmaus, he's a stranger—and the only person in Jerusalem who doesn't know what just happened. Each scene frames "Jesus" according to a pre-established point of view that's true but incomplete: *boy, revolutionary, gardener, stranger*. And each scene invites us to embrace the irony of a Christ who is more than himself, more than he first appears, and who stands beside us even though we fail to see him. The gospels position us as "insiders" in these recognition scenes, initiates who know what others do not: that the boy is Christ, the gardener is Christ, and so forth. Moreover, they tend to present that dramatic irony in visual terms, as a problem with the *eyes* of the eyewitnesses: "Their eyes were kept from recognizing him" (Luke 24:16). There's often a muted humor in such scenes, as when the disciples on the road to Emmaus presume to lecture Jesus about *Jesus*, telling the hidden Christ at some length what he told them and what he himself had just endured. But even though the gospel writers position us as insiders in these scenes, they warn us about any form of presumptive knowing that would "hold" Christ to a rigid frame. If the very people who knew him best were wrong, our insider knowledge is fragile at best, precious but incomplete. "Do not hold on to me," Christ says to Mary in the garden scene, refusing even the tender regard of a grieving friend as a sufficient and stabilizing point of view (John 20:17).

Thoreau says little about frame play in the gospels, except to point out that Christ's deliberate unwisdom exposes the flimsy constructions of church tradition ("an ancient and tottering frame with all its boards blown off").[29] But he was fascinated by stories of divine neighboring and proximity in many faith traditions—Hellenic, Hebrew, Zoroastrian, and Hindu. The *Bhagavad Gita*, for instance, is told from the point of view of two people standing next to one another: the Kuru warrior, Arjuna, and his charioteer, the Lord Krishna in disguise. Arjuna and Krishna stand side by side in the chariot, but their social positions are not equal: a charioteer's status is far below the social rank of the warrior he serves, in the same way the servant status of a gardener is below that of a Jerusalem family who could afford a tomb. To "see" the Lord Krishna in his most exalted form in the *Gita* requires a perceptual suspension of ordinary notions of rank and class, an eye that can "abstract" and reframe. Arjuna's despair in the opening scenes of the *Gita* is associated with his inability to see any alternative to a sequence of historical events leading inevitably toward war. Krishna responds to that despair by altering Arjuna's frame of perception and allowing him to see the world with different "eyes": "But these things cannot be seen with your physical eyes," Krishna tells Arjuna in the climactic revelation of Book 11; "therefore I give you spiritual vision to perceive my majestic power."[30] Divine presence is prismatic and refractive in the *Gita*, as it is in *Walden*, a kaleidoscopic proliferation of "faces" that fractures one-dimensional perception into compound planes of awareness: "Having spoken these words, Krishna, the master of yoga, revealed to Arjuna his most exalted, lordly form. He appeared with an infinite number of faces, ornamented by heavenly jewels, displaying unending miracles and the countless weapons of his power."[31] The "heavenly jewels" name both the gemlike multiplicity of divine presence in the *Gita* and the kind of "eye" that can receive and cherish that presence. To see with spiritual vision, the *Gita* suggests, is to see the world cubistically, to see with diamond eyes, and to cultivate an inner multiplicity receptive to a God "whose face is everywhere."[32] The *Gita* describes this multiplicity as a form of spiritual understanding, "manifold wisdom."[33] And the *Vishnu Purāna*, another key scripture for Thoreau, describes it as a form of divine ontology, "manifold being."[34] In both cases, divine encounter offers no philosophical bedrock, no final or definitive point of view.

In the next chapter, "Play and Attunement," I'll say more about how Thoreau cultivates this inner multiplicity as a contemplative practice in *Walden*, but for now let me summarize my argument. In his animal research, Bateson defines play semiotically as metamessages passing back and forth in an open-ended communication sequence. Play is a form of interactive framing that loosens the ordinary rules of communication and prevents creatures from becoming locked into one set of interpretive habits, thus protecting them when their environments become unstable. Play teaches animals to tune themselves to the variability of a changing world. Thoreau anticipates and extends this theory of play by stressing the variability of a changing God, a divinity "whose face is everywhere," and by exploring styles of thought and writing responsive to that unstable truth. Thoreau thus imagines play not only as a matter of interpretive flexibility, as Bateson does, but also as a form of religious devotion, as it is in the Hindu scriptures. Multiplying perspectives and altering frames is not an end in itself for Thoreau. The liberation *from* rigid frames of meaning is also a liberation *for* new possibilities of religious thinking and relationship. It can be difficult to find the right word for this relationship (Thoreau tries several: sympathy, communion, resonance, correspondence), in part because it names a bond that's "closed" and "open" at the same time, committed and changing, connected to God and unsure of God in the same complex response. What makes Thoreau important for modern notions of spirituality is that his piety has less to do with gathering and protecting a consistent set of religious practices or ideas (which change chapter by chapter in *Walden*) and more to do with tuning himself to the play of Holy Spirit in the world. In this regard, Thoreau sought to internalize the responsive delicacy he observed in the pond and become in effect a mini-Walden, one of the *Waldenses*, as if consciousness itself could become a quivering, rippling, vibrating surface—what the Greeks called "mental waters" and cherished as the highest gift of the gods.[35]

A DIFFERENT LEGACY

This is bound to seem strange at first. Despite the pioneering work on Thoreau's religious imagination by Jonathan Bishop, Frederick Garber, Malcolm Young, Alan Hodder, and others, most readers do not see Thoreau as a particularly religious writer, much less the source for anything so grand as a theological legacy. As Hodder has shown, we tend to think of Thoreau as a nature writer, cultural critic, and iconoclastic literary artist—and construct his legacy accordingly, a fact that has more to do with the secularization of *Walden* in literary textbooks and postwar academic criticism than with Thoreau's reception by his original audience. Moreover, my view of play as the presentation of alternatives suggests a very different approach to what William Gleason calls the "actual *ethic* of play" in American literature as well as an alternative account of play's relation to social control.[36] Because of the importance Gleason ascribes to Thoreau as the preeminent theorist of modern play in American literature, let me consider *The Leisure Ethic* briefly here and then suggest its affinity to another important study of modern play, Johan Huizinga's *Homo Ludens*.

Gleason's book is about play and power. He argues that play served as a substitute source of fulfillment for people estranged from work by the degradation of labor in modern capitalism. As the Protestant work ethic began to look increasingly suspect to people clocking in at unfulfilling factory jobs in mid-nineteenth-century America, play and leisure became alternative sources of community, spirituality, and self-esteem, what Richard Cabot called a new "gospel of play."[37] The key theme in that gospel, Gleason argues, is cultural assimilation. Motivated by intense anxieties about social control in an increasingly diversified America, turn of the century play theorists mirrored Thoreau's nativist anxiety about cultural and racial "outsiders," Irish immigrants in particular, and followed Thoreau in imagining leisure as a tool of cultural instruction, a way of melding a heterodox population into what George Lipsitz calls "the normative self of industrial culture."[38] For Gleason, the nativist anxiety at the heart of Thoreau's play theory in *Walden* makes visible the problematic ethic of leisure reform: its transcendental celebration of spontaneity and freedom on the one hand, play as liberation, and its anxieties about social management and corporate discipline on the other, play as norming. For Gleason, God's "work" and "sporting" blur in the sandbank scene of *Walden* not because Thoreau is adapting the play theologies of classical Hinduism to modern modes of faith but because "work" and "sport" are geared to the same corporate goal: transforming unruly bodies (children, women, non-workers, the Irish) into well-adjusted and well-functioning citizens. In this account, Thoreau's alternatives to the quiet desperation of industrial capitalism turn out to be infected by the same hegemonic values he sought to escape. And the liberating hope of democratic pluralism in *Walden* founders on nativist anxieties that will influence play and leisure theory for many years to come.

What's missing from this account is the role of irony in Thoreau's self-presentation. The liberating hope of the *Walden* project has less to do with the exemplary achievement of a fully realized multicultural hero and more to do with the experimental promise of adaptation and growth. Indeed, Thoreau invites us several times to ignore his *example* and cherish his *experiment*, as he continually tests and reframes his experience from different points of view. This experimental reframing is the fundamental meaning of play in *Walden*, a self-correcting practice that leads him not only to document his failures and blind spots but also to revalue error as the creative incentive for genuine change. That Thoreau fails to live up to the promise of his own book should come as no surprise to readers accustomed to the rhetoric of failed experiment central to Thoreau's project as a whole. The *Walden* hero misunderstands *everything*—the pond's depth, color, shoreline, natural history, social history. Misunderstanding the Irish is not the only or most damaging mistake in a book filled with mistakes, a book determined in fact to foreground misunderstanding as a form of salutary bewilderment. It's hard to think of a single philosophical or ethical premise that Thoreau doesn't walk on at some point (including his own most cherished assumptions). This does not excuse Thoreau for the nativist anxieties displayed in his writing about the Irish (or misogyny in his writing about women or primitivism in his writing about Native Americans). But it does shift the focus from a fully realized democratic hero in *Walden*, an ideal Thoreau clearly fails to achieve, to the hope of an uncertain and still evolving future.

Gleason's history of work and leisure applies to American literature a respected and long-standing philosophical tradition that identifies play as an instrument of social control, an idea central to Huizinga's *Homo Ludens*. Like most Western philosophers of play, Huizinga sought to rationalize play as contributing something positive to modern society and thus challenge the tradition in Puritan rhetoric that saw play as the *opposite* of Christian civilization, its unholy twin, and the very thing we're compelled to renounce in response to God's heavenly call. Indeed, renouncing play in one form or another was the standard trope of Puritan conversion narratives, as Michael Oriard has shown, which have a clearly delineated before-and-after structure (where scenes of play and mirth occur on the *bad* side of the divide). Setting the pattern for later writers, John Bunyan recounts his enthusiasm for "cat," an early form of baseball, before God convicted his game-loving heart with the sinful state of his soul (convicted him literally between the first and second swings of his bat). The games change in different versions of this story, but the basic lesson is the same: "God sent you not into the world as into a

Play-house, but a Work-house," the Puritan cleric, John Bailey, declared in 1689.[39]

There's little difference between playhouse and workhouse in *Homo Ludens*. For Huizinga, play does not spin loose from culture as a threatening subversion. Instead, play restricts and consolidates social power by rehearsing in children the roles and values they'll later assume as adults, thus ensuring "the *fitness* of the citizen for his tasks in the *polis*" (original emphasis).[40] "The struggle to win is itself holy," Huizinga argues, not because wealth or success are necessarily sacred but because competitive play is a microlesson in hierarchy, subordination, and social acclaim.[41] Successful cultures depend on and enforce these hierarchies, which gives play its sacred and all-pervasive role. In response to the approaching chaos of World War II, Huizinga sought to reorient the study of play from the biological functionalism of earlier play theorists like Karl Groos, where play serves as a training ground for animal survival, to a kind of cultural functionalism, where play provides the training ground for the survival of European civilization. For Huizinga, the elegant orderliness of well-fought games and well-argued law cases offered a redemptive alternative to a world slouching grimly toward a fascist apocalypse. (Huizinga wrote *Homo Ludens* in the northern Dutch city of Groningen in 1938 and was arrested by the Nazis the following year.) Catherine Bates mentions that whenever Huizinga gave a visiting lecture on "The Play-Element of Culture," his hosts wanted him to change the "of" in his title to "in"—as if play were one component of something larger.[42] But culture is not larger than play for Huizinga. Instead, culture is competitive play extended and proliferated into dozens of different realms (law, literature, religion, sports, music)—each reinforcing the interlocking order of the whole: "Inside the play-ground an absolute and peculiar order reigns. Here we come across another, very positive feature of play: it creates order, *is* order. Into an imperfect world and into the confusion of life it brings a temporary, a limited perfection. Play demands order absolute and supreme."[43] In an earlier work, *The Waning of the Middle Ages*, Huizinga describes in rich detail the mannered world of late medieval culture in which every aspect of human life—tournament, heraldry, costume, love, manners—was "regulated like a noble game."[44] Huizinga brings that sensibility to a theory of sacred play in *Homo Ludens* in which the law court, card table, temple, and stage orchestrate and strengthen impulses toward cultural order on which, for him, so much depends.

My book traces an alternative tradition of religious play in American literature by emphasizing a process theology of attunement, improvisation, and change. When Jack Boughton turns to his godfather and namesake, John Ames, and asks to hear his views on the doctrine of predestination, in Marilynne Robinson's *Gilead*, it's not because Jack wants to have a theological discussion with the old pastor, but because he's trying to save his life and the life of his family. And the first step toward that salvation for Jack is to decide whether or not severely damaged people can change. It's as if Jack had asked, *do you think people can be different from what they've always been? Do you think some people are irretrievably lost? Could you tell me how to grow?* Only Jack doesn't speak in that direct way, and so he asks his godfather those questions in code by asking him about the doctrine of predestination. When she hears the unspoken need behind Jack's question, Ames' wife, Lila, answers gently, "A person can change. Everything can change."[45]

Lila's name means "play" in Sanskrit, and I take her answer as the motto of *Playful Wisdom*. I don't see play as the essence of world religion, as David Kinsley has argued in his study of Hindu theologies of play, nor as the essence of Christian ritual, as James H. Evans suggests in his study of African-American play theology.[46] Play seems anti-essentialist to me, averse to grand theories of any kind, even about itself. But play does provide a fresh point of intersection in the study of literature, culture, and religion and a new context for understanding the history of modern American spirituality. Typically, historians tell the story of that spirituality around binary categories: Calvinist or Emersonian, dweller or seeker, conservative or liberal. One version of this well-known argument is that experimental thinkers like Thoreau and Dickinson helped drive the liberal "loosening" of Puritan orthodoxy in mid-nineteenth-century America by emphasizing the radical otherness of God and recovering the subjective dimension of religious experience. In this account, *Walden* was part of a major re-examination of American spirituality taking place across the religious left: by Emersonian transcendentalists, radical Unitarians, reform-minded Jews, inner-light Quakers, Vedantists, Spiritualists, Whitmanians, and all manner of "restless souls," as Leigh Eric Schmidt names this stream of American religious thought.[47] The restlessness Schmidt identifies with reform impulses on the religious left in the nineteenth century gave rise a century later to the "seeker" mentality Robert Wuthnow describes in his sociological analysis of American spirituality since 1950 (and contrasts with a "dweller" mentality drawn to the cradle-to-grave security of an established church, mosque, or synagogue).[48]

The key issue in this way of framing American religious history is the status of doubt. In more conservative traditions, doubt and faith can seem like mutually self-canceling conditions, to have one is not to have the other.[49] In more liberal traditions, doubt and disbelief are not contaminating impurities purged from faith's integrity but the source of its lively and various fluctuation. The fracture point between these two positions is usually located with Emerson, whose theory of consciousness as flux or flow revalued religious doubt as the engine of creative growth. Thus for James McIntosh, "Emerson (perhaps above all others) helped make poetically minded New Englanders aware that they faced an 'abdication of Belief,' while at the same time he claimed to give them the wherewithal to deal with it—the self-reliance, the intuitive faith in spirit."[50] And for Schmidt, the "Emersonian turn" in American religion liberated spirituality from church and synagogue, inspired the eclectic piety of many strands of modern and postmodern faith, and now "is worthy of serious consideration as an important variety of American liberalism."[51]

This is somewhat problematic for my project. Aside from Kerouac, none of the twentieth-century writers I consider held much regard for Emerson, whose thinking about the status of play as a mode of religious reflection was ambivalent and whose criticism of Thoreau's attempt to live in that mode was severe. It's possible to argue that these twentieth-century writers took their Emerson "in translation"—that is, through Thoreau and Dickinson's reinterpretation of transcendentalism. But it's also possible that the traditional categories we use to organize the history of American religion—Calvinist or Emersonian; conservative or liberal—are somewhat misleading, especially if it slants spiritual experimentation toward the New Left and portrays traditionally religious people as somehow shielded from questions about the existence of God or immune to experiences of religious doubt. Schmidt makes this slant explicit by opening his book with a quotation from the right-wing commentator, Laura Ingraham, whose contempt for religious experimentation is allowed to stand unchallenged as the voice of the "other" side, what a conservative (not doubting or seeking) spirituality sounds like. Part of the ambition of my project is to show that experimental theologies of play exist on *both* sides of this divide—inspiring two of the most unorthodox thinkers in American religion, Thoreau and Dickinson; two writers whose relationship with organized religion was ambivalent, Kerouac and Dillard; as well as two writers deeply committed to established faith communities, Merton and Robinson.

I don't mean to diminish Emerson's importance to the loosening of Calvinist orthodoxies in the history of American religion. Instead, I want to suggest that responding to the mysterious play of divine love is just as difficult in a church or synagogue as by a pond or on the road and that this difficulty is an important feature of both traditional and non-traditional religious writing. To take a recent theological example, consider Michael Fishbane's study of sacred attunement in Judaism. Orthodox Jewish theology is a narrative of rupture and repair, Fishbane argues, the story of a divine call that breaks in to normative consciousness, waking the prophets from "the mindlessness of habitude" and turning them off a familiar path.[52] Bending down or stepping aside are embodied responses to divine call for Fishbane, the sign of a person inflected by the solicitation of God and turning toward that call in humility and readiness, as when Moses "turns aside" to the burning bush (Exod. 3:1–6). This turning off or stepping aside is repeated in dozens of scriptural call narratives and constitutes an intense form of spiritual attunement for Fishbane, a "covenant attentiveness" ever-ready to step off the path of religious habit in response to sacred rhythms that "break the veil of our daily stupor."[53] Moses learns that attentiveness in the wilderness, by tuning himself to divine voice in the loneliness and terror of Mount Sinai. Others learn that attentiveness by reading scripture and allowing the tropes and turns of exegetical hermeneutics to tune the reading mind to diverse grammatical and rhetorical rhythms and thus stir attention from habit to alertness, doctrine to relationship. Both prophet and reader maintain a subject position of vigilant awareness, Fishbane argues, hyper-alert to the rhetorical play of divine language in both scenes, wilderness and synagogue, and open to the diverse modes of attention such play inspires. Theology is not a set of doctrinal beliefs or interpretative procedures; it is this "multiform spiritual awareness" for Fishbane, this style of variable attention. Thus, in Judaism: "Alertness is all."[54]

This model of responsive attention is also a key feature of Jürgen Moltmann's Protestant theology of play. Moltmann reverses the emphasis on rational management in the play theorists of his generation and recovers a biblical model of playful wisdom in the figure of Sophia, the feminine Wisdom Child of Proverbs 8:

The Lord begot me, the beginning of his works,
    the forerunner of his deeds of long ago. . . .
When he fixed the foundations of earth,
    then I was beside him as artisan;
I was his delight day by day,
    playing before him all the while,
Playing over the whole of his earth,
    having my delight with human beings. (Prov. 8:22–31; NABRE)

The image of Wisdom playing "beside" God, the nextness or along-sidedness Thoreau will also stress in his narratives of divine encounter, offers theology several insights. First, Sophia's play alters dominion. She is a child rather than a conqueror and so her wisdom is playful and vulnerable, not the imperial wisdom of ineluctable law. Sophia has no throne or palace but plays instead through the whole of creation, which is the expression of her artistic delight. Second, as a free creation, the world does not reveal the necessary unfolding of an already perfected plan but suggests instead an eschatology of the possible for Moltmann, where the future remains "an *open process*" and human creativity co-participates with God to bring that future into being, as Sophia does.[55] And third, Moltmann aligns Sophia with other classical and

Christian images of *deus ludens*—the child playing drafts in Heraclitus, for instance, or the Harlequin Christ of medieval theology—to pose a religious alternative to the pervasive rationalization of Western culture and the various power rhetorics they rehearse:

> The one-sided emphasis on the dominion of God in the Western church, especially in Protestantism, has subjected Christian existence to judicial and moral categories. Theology describes Christ as prophet, priest, and king, but of doxology and the "transfiguration of Christ," which is of central importance to the Eastern church, little has remained. The aesthetic categories of the new freedom have given way to the moral categories of the new law and the new obedience.[56]

By choosing to be a childlike player rather an all-powerful judge, God chooses against those legal categories—with their corresponding virtues of temperance, obedience, autonomy, and heavenly reward. The image of divine Wisdom in Proverbs 8 sets to one side what we might call the steadfast virtues of judicial religion and emphasizes instead the improvisational virtues of creative play, which Moltmann identifies as lightness, limberness, responsiveness, rejoicing, and dance-like rapport. Indeed, the Hebrew word for "play" in Proverbs 8 occurs in two other scriptural passages describing David's dancing before the Lord (2 Kings 6:5, 21).

At the heart of this theology of play is Moltmann's emphasis on the "all-quickening" power of divine grace. Such quickness produces a surprising mobility in the life of faith, the "constant *changing* of existing conditions," as if God could break out at any moment and in any way.[57] As we unlearn the power rhetorics of modern life, which treat others as a means to an end, play emerges as a contemplative discipline for Moltmann, a way of preparing ourselves for divine encounter: "We are playing in the world and with the world, and we are trying through free play to make ourselves fit for the totally-other."[58]

Hugo Rahner's Catholic theology of play develops around a similar set of themes. To say that divine intentionality "plays" in the world is to understand creation as God's freely chosen, rather than necessary or compulsory, activity. Divine creativity is compelled by nothing and answers to nothing other than the expressive freedom of its own joy.[59] It thus requires in people of faith a "nimbleness of mind" attuned to that freedom.[60] In Rahner's view, human beings are not fallen sinners but co-players or co-fashioners in an open-ended game of faith, Moltmann's "game of the totally-other." Play is not a unique or occasional feature of divine intentionality but a continuous process of creative renewal. Existence *is* play, in this view, which is permanent rather than occasional and privileged rather than low status. To be in a covenant relationship with the divine requires a person whose creative multiplicity imitates God's creative hand, Rahner stresses, someone whose faith is a continual process of "indefatigable tinkering." In this sense the life of a Christian resembles the life of an artist, someone "who is never completely satisfied with his work and who 'as one in play' must ever be starting and experimenting anew."[61] Sometimes such play looks like singing or dancing in the classical, patristic, and medieval sources Rahner studies. Sometimes it looks like tossing a ball back and forth or playing a game of draughts or constantly adjusting or refocusing something. But sometimes sacred play seems like stuttering or stammering to Rahner, like trying to affirm and deny something at the same time or trying to say *yes* and *no* in the same breath—an idea that also occurred to Bateson and Thoreau.[62]

If God is more like a divine player than a divine judge, and if religious devotion is more like a freely chosen game than a work-a-day obligation, then this is a game that values responsive alertness, a willingness to welcome disruption in "ready adaptability" (*bona conversio*) to the play of spirit in the world.[63] What matters to Rahner is this theological nimbleness, a version of Fishbane's "covenant attentiveness," which remains ever alert to the deadening effects of religious habit and gifted with talents for adjustment and change. To picture this responsiveness, Rahner adapts a term from Aristotle's *Nicomachean Ethics*, "eutrapelia" (*well-turning* in Greek), which accents the gift for troping or turning Rahner discovers at the core of Christian theologies of play.[64] This does not, however, suggest a spiritual life of endless wandering. Rahner's sources are traditional, even orthodox Christian thinkers: Augustine; Clement of Alexandria; Gregory Nazianzen; Notker, the stammering monk of St. Gall; Maximus the Confessor; Mechtild of Magdeburg; Teresa of Lisieux; Thomas Aquinas; and others. But this does suggest an open process of spiritual revision and restatement, a life of indefatigable tinkering, which Rahner offers as a corrective to faith's tendency to harden around a fixed set of religious habits. That, for Rahner, is the most un-Catholic thing imaginable, an idea that occurred to Thomas Merton at about the same time.[65]

This does sound like the religious orientation I'm calling "playful wisdom"—a style of religious devotion that's both committed and searching, simultaneously settled and on the road. Hybrid concepts like "eutrapelia" in Catholic play theology or "multiform spiritual awareness" in Jewish attunement theology evoke the religious thinking of writers like Emerson, Dickinson, and Thoreau. But they also evoke the stories all sorts of people tell about their faith. "It is possible to be a believer and a listener at the same time," Krista Tippett writes about the collection of faith narratives she gathered from scientists, educators, rabbis, farmers, and physicians for her NPR program, *Speaking of Faith*. "It is possible to be both fervent and searching, to nurture a vital identity and wonder at the identities of others." This conclusion leads Tippett to "trace a powerful and creative and humbling line between theology and human experience—between religious ideas and real life."[66]

The writers in my study walk that line. They fluctuate between conviction and doubt and explore forms of religious faith that are traditional and experimental at the same time, which felt to Kerouac like a good jazz improvisation and felt to Thoreau like traveling widely in his hometown. If play's anything, it's liminal, existing on the threshold between tradition and rupture, continuity and change. The tendency to pull these categories apart and frame American spirituality around one or the other—Calvinist (fervent) or Emersonian (searching)—simplifies faith's liminal richness and ignores the stuttering and hesitation of faith confessions occurring within the bounds of organized religion: Moses' halting tongue (in Judaism) or Notker's faltering speech (in Catholicism). That stammering confession is not exceptional in the history of Catholic theology for Rahner, which says "Yea" and "Nay" at the same time. Nor is it exceptional in the history of Jewish theology for Fishbane, which says "Yes" and "No" in the same moment and for the same reason.[67]

I stress this point to suggest that playful wisdom is not necessarily conservative, confessional, or nostalgic. Nor is it necessarily radical, post-secular, or postmodern. It does not exist on one or the other side of these traditional divisions of American religion; nor does it privilege *doubt* (as the sign of religious tolerance) or *conviction* (as the sign of religious fervor). These are constitutive rather than self-canceling conditions, bound together like the yes-and-no confessions of Catholic monks and Jewish prophets and just as integral to the faith story Merton tells in a Catholic hermitage as the one Thoreau tells at the pond. This does not mean, however, that playful wisdom is all things to all people. Its wisdom depends on what Bateson discovered at the Fleishhacker Zoo: play dwells in possibility. It cherishes reframing. When we welcome that reframing and say with Lila, a person can change, everything can change, we affirm faith's open horizon and embrace its play. When we deny that change and assure the broken-hearted that their fate is sealed and probably deserved, we ignore that wisdom and take our place with Peter Bell, staring blankly at a primrose; or the Thoreau of "Baker Farm," staring blankly at an Irish infant (and barely able to hide his contempt). If we can't make that frame budge, nor imagine anything beyond its reifying and reductive gaze, we're not playing anymore, even if we have our fishing gear in hand.

My point is that the reifying gaze can come from anywhere—religious radicals, religious conservatives, non-religious people—and that the conditions of play and possibility can also come from anywhere. What's important isn't the standpoint but the alertness, the "covenant attentiveness." That covenant may involve an established religious tradition and a monotheistic God as it does for Merton and Robinson. Or it may involve a covenant with "life" or the "real"—as it does for Thoreau, who collapses the distinction between loving God and loving the pond in the same way Jesus collapses the distinction between loving God and loving one's neighbors. What matters is the way such love disables imperial fantasies of power and control and makes possible a religious faith based on humility, humor, responsiveness, and joy. Theological doctrines and traditions can help form that awareness through sacred stories of faith: the story of Mary in the garden, for instance; or the story of Krishna and Arjuna standing side by side in the chariot. But that awareness can also be formed by the aesthetic imagination, as we'll see, by stories of faith from our literary and philosophical "neighbors," as Thoreau said about Plato's dialogues, standing a few shelves over from the *Bible* or the *Bhagavad Gita* and yet "addressed to our condition exactly" (115).

THE PLURALITY OF PLAY

Let me say a word about those neighbors now. Despite their differences in temperament and style, Dickinson and Thoreau are both philosophers of interruption who prize an "outside" zone of wilderness or darkness just beyond the mind's control. Moreover, both writers stage scenes of intrusion when an occasional visitor from the wilderness zone steps into thought's domain and unsettles its ordinary, self-validating procedures.[68] Thoreau names these ordinary procedures "quiet desperation," and Dickinson calls them our "dread," but in both cases the interruption raises the possibility of redemption by offering a chance for change, a less dreadful or desperate way of being in the world. Whether an upsurge of the unconscious or an encounter with wild nature or the call of a mysterious God, these encounters expand the subject's range of feeling and quicken her inner life, revealing a pluralistic consciousness Dickinson studies carefully in her play poems. Where play often serves a managerial role in the philosophical discourse of Dickinson's era, centering and streamlining the developing self, play decenters consciousness in Dickinson, rendering it less stable and secure. Play reveals and exaggerates subjective pluralities in Dickinson's players, an identity faceted like the face of a gem in "We play at Paste" or proliferated into multiple forms like "myriad Daisy"[69]—as if the facets and fractures of consciousness are precisely what enigmatic encounter demands, as Megan Craig has argued, a unique capacity to adjust and attend, rising to the possibilities of the present moment (rather than deploying a preformed response) or answering the notes of an immediate call. The religious self is "myriad" in Dickinson not because she's splintered by loss or insufficiently trained to her adult role but because she responds to a divine spirit that is itself multiple and changing and so requires a corresponding agility in the faithful heart.

We can learn that agility, Jack Kerouac believed, through music. In his 1957 novel, *On the Road*, Kerouac foregrounds a series of "jazz skills" in the life of faith: giving space to the other through alert responsiveness, for instance, or accepting and reframing failure. Most of all though, learning to "play" or "sing" theology, as Jeremy Begbie has argued, means acknowledging the role time plays in music and using that temporality to critique theology's penchant for essentialism and abstraction—which is exactly where Sal Paradise prefers to dwell. Like Jay Gatsby, a character with whom he has much in common, Sal "sees archetypes, not persons," as John Leland points out, movie posters where a human being might be.[70] But like Fitzgerald, Kerouac uses jazz not to sustain timeless illusion but to tear right through it with the ungraspable sound of a temporal occasion, "an arrangement of notes that will never be played again," as Nick says of Daisy's voice.[71] For Kerouac, jazz represents "the sound of surprise," the title of Whitney Balliett's study of improvisational jazz, an irruptive call piercing the veil of Sal's inattention and provoking a fresh, ad hoc response. Sometimes the irruptive call comes from nature, as in Thoreau and Dickinson, but often the call comes from suffering children, like the baby in the Gregoria brothel whose cry wakes Sal from his reifying and pornographic dream of Mexico. It feels strange to compare a baby's wail to a saxophone cry, but this is how jazz works for Kerouac. Jazz creativity depends on discord and disruption, the wrong note or odd phrase that's jarring at first and then reveals new possibilities of meaning and sound. Sal's spiritual growth occurs in breakthrough moments when he sheds his prefabricated ideas in favor of spontaneous dialogue and temporary rapport, tuning himself to the social environment he actually occupies (rather than the one he's created in his mind).

My next chapter, "Play and Nonsense," is about Thomas Merton's book-length poem *Cables to the Ace*. Merton was interested in the relationship between play and religion from the beginning of his career. He cherished the truth to power courage of holy jesters in several religious traditions—Zen fools, Catholic clowns, and Russian *yurodivye*—and thought that the ability to laugh at oneself was the surest sign of God's grace. He read Ananda Coomaraswamy's essays on Hindu epistemology as a student at Columbia in the 1940s. He read *Homo Ludens* and *One-Dimensional Man* and taught a class to first-year monks at Gethsemani that included many of the patristic and medieval writers Rahner studies in *Man at Play*. He was intrigued by references to sacred play in classical and pre-classical philosophy and wrote an essay connecting the logos of Heraclitus with the Tao of Lao-Tse and the Word of St. John: God is "the Logos, the Wisdom," he wrote, "not so much 'at work' in nature but rather 'at play' there."[72] These interests coalesced for Merton in 1965, when he moved from Gethsemani to St. Mary of Carmel, a cinderblock hermitage set on a small hill near the monastery where the monk began reimagining his life in self-conscious dialogue with Dickinson and Thoreau. He came to feel "that the whole world runs by rhythms I have not yet learned to recognize, rhythms that are not those of the engineer."[73] And so he began looking for ways to de-engineer his imagination: writing poetry again after a long hiatus and creating artistic assemblages and mixed-media collages from grass stems, postage stamps, seed pods, and pieces of broken wood. Merton was reading and translating the Latin American surrealists in this period and adapted what he called the creative "nonsense" of Nicanor Parra's *Poems & Antipoems* to his last complete work, the anti-poem *Cables to the Ace*. Composed in eighty-eight spontaneous verse and prose fragments, *Cables* is a debris poem, an absurdist collage, and its verbal play is the *anti* by which rigid categories are subverted and rebuilt. Nonsense antagonizes cultural norms and brings to attention the lives of socially marginal people, as Susan Stewart argues. Nonsense is the voice of "those on the peripheries of everyday life: the infant, the child, the mad and the senile, the chronically foolish and playful."[74] Nonsense is an aesthetic practice for Merton, a way of releasing his poetry from the dominant rules of academic formalism, but it's also an ethical and contemplative practice, a way of opening his imagination to the folly of God. "No man can see God except he be blind," he writes in *Cables*, quoting from Meister Eckhart, "or know him except through ignorance, nor understand him except through folly."[75] Such folly is anathema to the American cult of order and efficiency, which Merton saw as the four-square gospel of modern life. From his *Walden*-like position outside the mainstream, Merton shuffles the "lenses" we use to make sense of experience—"Lenses discover blue flame / In the mouths / Of fatal children"—allowing us to glimpse spirit-killing norms obscured by custom and the common sense.[76]

Annie Dillard began shuffling the lenses as soon as she could draw, as she reports in *An American Childhood*, sketching her baseball mitt over and over from different angles and at different times of day. When Bateson quotes William Blake's famous prayer, "May God us keep from Single Vision & Newton's sleep," he hints at how such perceptual reorientation might become a religious practice.[77] In *Pilgrim at Tinker Creek*, Dillard explores dozens of strategies to put in question the complacency of Single Vision and un-see or un-know shopworn notions of the divine. She switches background and foreground in her nature descriptions and cherishes experiences of disorientation, dizziness, vertigo, and mirage, what Roger Caillois termed *ilinx*-play. She looks at things in the "wrong" way, inside out or upside down. She observes the creek through a camera lens, a butterfly wing, and a sheet of ice—running perception through a yoga-like practice of nimble reframing, which she offers as an alternative to more aggressive and reifying ways of knowing the world. Thoreau said once that walking with and without a gun changed the way he saw the "woods"—focusing his attention on the one hand and unfocusing it on the other. Dillard imagines what it would be like to walk in the woods without a gun, without a fixed and predetermined aim. Like Thoreau, she identifies such relinquishment as a form of contemplative unselving and stresses the danger such play presents to ingrained habits of egoistic control.

My final chapter is about conversation, porch swings, theology, and playing catch. Marilynne Robinson's *Gilead* is built around binary pairs and structural oppositions. Its focus fluctuates between home and away, inside and outside, member and non-member, the stay-at-home pastor and his prodigal godson. And in that vacillation Robinson suggests an emblem for a dialogic theology that will, in time, allow Ames to welcome the stranger in his midst, welcome and bless his godson. That change doesn't happen all at once but develops slowly from the rhythm Ames enjoys in his own gentle play: the to and fro of porch swings and the back and forth of playing catch. In Hans-Georg Gadamer's theory of play and hermeneutics, this to-and-fro rhythm elucidates the very process of human understanding—the complex interplay of reading, thinking, preaching, conversing, interacting with other people, interacting with different traditions. Ames studies scripture in exactly this manner in *Gilead*, often on walks with Robert Boughton where their theological conversations recreate the back and forth they enjoyed while playing catch together as boys. This dialogic perspective evokes the double focus of Bateson's play theories, but it also models our relationship with the divine. When Gadamer opens *Truth and Method* with a poem from Rainer Maria Rilke about playing catch with God—"when you're suddenly the catcher of a ball / thrown by an eternal partner"—he suggests that faith too can be a form of play, a back-and-forth game that draws us out of ourselves in reply to a partner we can interact with but not command: "why catching then becomes a power," Rilke continues, "not yours, a world's."

So, let me sum up where we're going. Play is not a "top-down" strategy of normative discipline, shaping people to their social roles. Nor is it a "bottom-up" celebration of literary disruption, the freeplay of language endlessly deferring. Instead, playful wisdom names a religious disposition of agile responsiveness and practiced rapport. Play loosens frames and stretches horizons, opening toward the unknown. That opening requires an attitude of receptiveness and hospitality, turning out of oneself to receive the other (even when that other is in fact *us*, Thoreau would add, a sudden mood or unbidden insight that makes us stand "beside ourselves in a sane sense"). The question that intrigues the writers in my book is how we might adjust ourselves to that neighboring multiplicity and imagine that "adjustment" as a form of spiritual devotion, a way of being faithful to the varieties of religious experience.[78] Their answers are not singular, collapsing play into a reductive uniformity, but they are consistently practical and ethical, what the *Bhagavad Gita* calls "wisdom in action." Such wisdom matters because it changes things, us most of all. For Thoreau, it dials down the voice of the solitary ego and tunes the mind to the rhythms of the real. For Dickinson, playful wisdom opens a space of possibility, contingency, plurality, and change. For her, play means movement or "ecstasy" (*ek stasis*)—not stuck or stopped. For Kerouac, playful wisdom reveals the warping logic of our self-protective dreams and frees us to acknowledge and reframe our failures. Play means improvisation, using our mistakes to create new meaning. For Merton, playful wisdom antagonizes cultural routines that diminish true spirit and offers a parable of possibility to the fatal children with their mouths on fire. Play means listening to nonsense voices beyond the pale. For Dillard, playful wisdom reveals the provisionality of what our culture takes for the real and dispels the illusion of our environmental and epistemological control. Play means risk and exposure, an experimental hermeneutics rigged for trouble. And for Robinson, playful wisdom interrupts an ego-centered subject secure in its own skin or steady in its own stance and sets the moral focus just beyond the nucleus of the private self, displacing attention from center to edge, self to neighbor. Play means dialogue, surrendering our autonomy to the back and forth of a game we don't need to win.

In short, these are the key themes of my book: play as attunement, possibility, improvisation, nonsense, risk, and dialogue. And this is my principal thesis: play's interactive framing reorients us from our imaginary place at the center of the world to our rightful place in a larger community, neighbored by others we can interact with but not govern, and unsettled by a God we can commune with but not comprehend. When Thoreau declares that play is holy, he's calling attention to this dimension of religious wisdom, the variability of a God who plays in ten thousand places, and he's recruiting the power of play to stir attention from complacent hegemony and monocular vision. This argument draws on discussions of play in several disciplines (literature, music, anthropology, folklore, philosophical hermeneutics, and several strands of classical and postmodern theology). And it has at least four implications for further scholarship. First, it changes the way we read *Walden* and the way we construct Thoreau's legacy in American literature. (He becomes what he said he was, religious above all.) Second, it complicates the too-neat framing of American religious history as the story of two feuding families: restless liberals and settled conservatives. Neither family has a monopoly on dogmatic orthodoxy nor an exclusive claim to covenantal faith. Third, *Playful Wisdom* impacts play studies by shifting attention from sports fiction, game theory, language theory, and the socialization of outsiders, standard themes in the field, to the meaning of play as a theological practice and mode of religious devotion. Fourth, my book challenges traditional associations of the sacred as something precious, rare, or unprofaned and explores instead a piety of the humble and the mere. Inviting us to surrender our narcissistic illusions, religious play resembles the ancient practices Thoreau discovered in his study of world religions, what Christian and Hindu traditions call *upekṣa*, *kenosis*, and *Gelassenheit*, but which sounded impossibly remote and melancholy spelled out that way. So, Thoreau experiments with a style of religious devotion oriented toward reverence and rapport, like the ancient traditions, but one that identifies the tools of that devotion as common, foolish, unmarketable, and near at hand, the very things we've been doing since we were children (but set aside in our maturity): day-dreaming, huckleberrying, playing with words, playing with nonsense, playing with animals. Most of all: being awake enough to pick up the sacred signal, *this is play*, and turning out from ourselves in reply.

NOTES

1. Henry D. Thoreau, *Walden*, ed. Jeffrey S. Cramer (New Haven: Yale University Press, 2006), 7. Subsequent references to *Walden* will refer to this edition and be cited in the text by page number.

2. Henry D. Thoreau, *The Journal of Henry D. Thoreau*, gen. ed. John C. Broderick, vol. 1 (Princeton: Princeton University Press, 1981), 350.

3. Thoreau, *Journal*, 1:206.

4. On writers who stress the power of play to isolate experiences of uncertainty in order to control them, see Catherine Bates, *Play in a Godless World: The Theory and Practice of Play in Shakespeare, Nietzsche and Freud* (London: Open Gate, 1999), 1–41.

5. Kenneth Burke, *The Philosophy of Literary Form: Studies in Symbolic Action* (Berkeley: University of California Press, 1973), 1.

6. The central characteristic of the common sense for Clifford Geertz is this "obviousness," this air of inevitability, what any right-thinking person would surely know. The common sense doesn't need to express or defend its premises, Geertz stresses; it has no "premises." It's not constructed. It's just *there*, the way things naturally are: "Religion rests its case on revelation, science on method, ideology on moral passion; but common sense rests its on the assertion that it is not a case at all, just life in a nutshell. The world is its authority." See his "Common Sense as a Cultural System," 1975; repr. *The Antioch Review* 67, no. 4 (Fall 2009): 772.

7. Patrick Hart and Jonathan Montaldo, eds., *The Intimate Merton: His Life from His Journals* (San Francisco: HarperOne, 1999), 202. Patrick F. O'Connell connects this theme in Merton directly to Thoreau: "Thus for Merton Thoreau is a counterforce to 'the consuming image' issuing forth from 'the box,' the image of the contented consumer presented by the mass media but also the image that itself consumes all other images so as to present a single unchallenged interpretation of reality." See his "Keeping Pace With His Companion: Thomas Merton and Henry Thoreau," *The Concord Saunterer* N. S. 7 (1999): 131.

8. This theme in Thoreau anticipates what Martin Heidegger will later identify as the key feature of Western modernity, what he calls *Gestell*, "Enframing." In ordinary German *stellen* means to place or set, but Heidegger uses the term to name a horizon of possibility through which reality reveals itself. That horizon is impossibly narrow in modern technological societies, Heidegger argues, limiting the real to one and only one form of disclosure: utilitarian value. Technology is not just a tool or tactic for Heidegger. It's a frame of mind or form of revealing, a window through which reality becomes present. *Gestell* turns or twists that reality toward us, toward human needs and desires, so that things show up as *things* in this enframing, work-ready resources available for our manipulation and use. When *Gestell* holds sway, it drives out every other possibility of revealing, every view but its own, turning the world into a gigantic petrol station, as he said famously. Moreover, *Gestell* twists us too, turning us into users and consumers in a wholly transactional world. On *Gestell* as the "essence" of modernity, see Martin Heidegger, *The Question Concerning Technology and Other Essays*, trans. William Lovitt (1977; repr. New York: HarperPerennial, 2013), 3–49. On how play and festival free thought from utilitarian enframing and open new horizons of disclosure in Heidegger, see Kevin Aho, "Recovering Play: On the Relationship Between Leisure and Authenticity in Heidegger's Thought," *Janus Head* 10, no. 1 (2007): 217–38.

9. Bateson develops his theory of play in two major essays from the 1950s: "The Message 'This is Play,'" in *Group Process: Transactions of the Second Conference*, ed. Bertram Schaffner (New York: Josiah Macy, Jr. Foundation, 1955), 145–243; and "A Theory of Play and Fantasy," first published in *A. P. A Psychiatric Research Reports* 2 (Dec. 1955): 39–51; and then reprinted in *Steps to an Ecology of Mind* (1972; repr. Chicago: University of Chicago Press, 2000), 177–93.

10. Bateson, *Steps to an Ecology of Mind*, 178.

11. Bateson, "The Message 'This is Play,'" 216. This relationship between play and creativity has had a major impact on anthropologies of children's play. Helen B. Schwartzman, for instance, follows Bateson in stressing the framing and metacommunicative aspects of play as a resource children use to separate "figure" from "ground" and experiment with innovative manipulations within their environments. See her *Transformations: The Anthropology of Children's Play* (New York: Plenum, 1978). Thomas S. Henricks summarizes how play constitutes framing behavior not only in cultural anthropology but also in cognitive psychology and theories of social encounter. See his *Play and the Human Condition* (Urbana: University of Illinois Press, 2015), 68–89.

12. Thoreau, *Journal* 2:40. See also, Henry David Thoreau, *A Week on the Concord and Merrimack Rivers*, ed. H. Daniel Peck (New York: Penguin, 1998), 118.

13. See for instance John D. Barbour's reading of this passage in *The Value of Solitude: The Ethics and Spirituality of Aloneness in Autobiography* (Charlottesville: University of Virginia Press, 2004), 105–6.

14. Bateson, *Steps to an Ecology of Mind*, 180.

15. Bateson, "The Message 'This is Play,'" 216.

16. Victor Turner has written extensively about this aspect of play, connecting its subjunctive mood with the performative liminality of religious ritual: "Just as the

subjunctive mood of a verb is used to express supposition, desire, hypothesis, or possibility, rather than stating actual facts, so do liminality and the phenomena of liminality dissolve all factual and commonsense systems into their components and 'play' with them in ways never found in nature or in custom." See his *The Anthropology of Performance* (New York: PAJ Publications, 1986), 25. Selva J. Raj and Corinne G. Dempsey apply Turner's ideas about play to their analysis of ritual in South Asian religious traditions. See *Sacred Play: Ritual Levity and Humor in South Asian Religions*, ed. Selva J. Raj and Corinne G. Dempsey (Albany: SUNY Press, 2010), 4.

17. Thoreau, *A Week*, 109.

18. Brian Sutton-Smith, *The Ambiguity of Play* (Cambridge: Harvard University Press, 1997, 2001), 231.

19. Gregory Bateson and Mary Catherine Bateson, *Angels Fear: Towards an Epistemology of the Sacred* (Toronto: Bantam, 1988), 68.

20. Thoreau, *A Week*, 92.

21. William A. Gleason, *The Leisure Ethic: Work and Play in American Literature, 1840–1940* (Stanford: Stanford University Press, 1999), 44.

22. Herbert Marcuse, *One-Dimensional Man: Studies in the Ideology of Advanced Industrial Society*, 2nd ed. (Boston: Beacon Press, 1991).

23. Bateson develops this idea in his 1974 essay, "The Creature and Its Creations," where he quotes from Wordsworth's "Peter Bell"—"A primrose by a river's brim / A yellow primrose was to him, / And it was nothing more"—to exhibit an alienated consciousness unable to sense the vast ecological processes which brought the primrose into being. Bateson names these processes "an ecology of mind" and stresses the humility required to recognize ourselves as participants in the same ecological systems. See his *A Sacred Unity: Further Steps to an Ecology of Mind*, ed. Rodney E. Donaldson (New York: Cornelia and Michael Bessie Book, 1991), 263–64.

24. Stephen Nachmanovitch, "This is Play," *New Literary History* 40, no. 1 (Winter 2009): 13.

25. "In everyday discourse, nonsense is used as a category that is both negative and residual," Susan Stewart argues. "Like its companion categories of Fate, Chance, Accident, Miscellaneous, and even *etc.*, it gives us a place to store any mysterious gaps in our systems of order." See her *Nonsense: Aspects of Intertextuality in Folklore and Literature* (1978; repr. Baltimore: Johns Hopkins University Press, 1989), 5.

26. Justin Kaplan, ed., *Walt Whitman: Complete Poetry and Collected Prose* (New York: Literary Classics of the United States, 1982), 30. Let me also note how Krishna's discussion of wisdom in the *Gita* resembles the metacognitive play of *Walden* and *Leaves of Grass*. Picturing personality as a field of forces, *gunas*, Krishna invites Arjuna to cherish the interplay of different strands of the self without becoming trapped within any single mood, voice, sensation, or stance. "Wisdom" names this state of transcendental detachment in the *Gita*, this ability to remain both in and out of the game, as in these verses from Book 13: "[Wisdom] dwells in all, in every hand and foot and head, in every mouth and eye and ear in the universe. Without senses itself, it shines through the functioning of the senses. Completely independent, it supports all things. Beyond the gunas, it enjoys their play." *The Bhagavad Gita*, trans. Eknath Easwaran (Tomales, CA: Nilgiri Press, 1985, 2007), 217–18.

27. Thoreau delights in perceptual experiments that invite us to reframe the "same" scene by studying varying levels of visual depth: focusing on the surface of the river to see twigs and grass passing by, for instance, and then on the river bottom to notice sand and weeds, and then to the surface again to contemplate the mirrored heavens. We can "intend" this flexible reframing, he suggests in *A Week*, by allowing vision to flatten along the river's surface, then penetrate to its watery depth, then lift off toward opaque heavens: "Wherever the trees and skies are reflected, there is more than Atlantic depth, and no danger of fancy running aground. We notice that it required a separate intention of the eye, a more free and abstracted vision, to see the reflected trees and the sky, than to see the river bottom merely; and so are there manifold visions in the direction of every object, and even the most opaque reflect the heavens from their surface." To rigidify response within one interpretive frame is unnatural for Thoreau, not appropriate to the flow of time and the river, but it's also irreverent, draining the universe of wonder and ignoring opaque but ever-present intimations of the divine. Alan Hodder connects these experiments in perceptual reframing to the soteriological ambition of Thoreau's work, his attempt to live in two worlds at once, and thus sense the presence of heaven in the mirroring surface of the everyday. See Thoreau, *A Week*, 39; and Alan D. Hodder, *Thoreau's Ecstatic Witness* (New Haven: Yale University Press, 2001), 191–99.

28. Gerard Manley Hopkins, "As Kingfishers Catch Fire, Dragonflies Draw Flame," in *Poems and Prose of Gerard Manley Hopkins*, ed. W. H. Gardner (1953; repr. London: Penguin, 1985), 51.

29. Thoreau, *A Week*, 56.

30. Easwaran, *The Bhagavad Gita*, 195.

31. Easwaran, *The Bhagavad Gita*, 195. In the edition Thoreau read, Charles Wilkins translates Sanjay's speech this way: "The mighty compound and divine being *Haree*, having O *Raja*, thus spoken, made evident unto Arjoon his supreme and heavenly form; of many a mouth and eye; many a wondrous sight; many a heavenly ornament." See *Bhagvat-geeta*; or *Dialogues of Kreeshna and Arjoon* (London [n.p.], 1785), 65.

32. Easwaran, *The Bhagavad Gita*, 195.

33. Wilkins, trans., *Bhagvat-geeta, or Dialogues of Kreeshna and Arjoon*, 88. Thoreau quotes this sentence from Book 10 in a *Journal* entry from 1846: "But what, O Arjoon, hast thou to do with this manifold wisdom?" Thoreau, *Journal*, 2:258.

34. *The Vishnu Purāna: A System of Hindu Mythology and Tradition*, trans. H. H. Wilson (1840; repr. Calcutta: Punthi Pustak, 1972), 396.

35. See Roberto Calasso, *Literature and the Gods*, trans. Tim Parks (New York: Vintage, 2001), 32.

36. Gleason, *Leisure Ethic*, 5.

37. Richard C. Cabot, *What Men Live By* (Boston: Houghton Mifflin, 1914); quoted in Gleason, *Leisure Ethic*, 1.

38. George Lipsitz, *Time Passages: Collective Memory and American Popular Culture* (Minneapolis: University of Minnesota Press, 1990), 64; quoted in Gleason, *Leisure Ethic*, 18.

39. John Bailey, *Man's Chief End to Glorific God*, 64; quoted in Michael Oriard, *Sporting with the Gods: The Rhetoric of Play and Game in American Culture* (Cambridge: Cambridge University Press, 1991), 360.

40. Johan Huizinga, *Homo Ludens: A Study of the Play-Element in Culture* (1950; repr. Mansfield Centre, CT: Martino Publishing, 2014), 64.

41. Huizinga, *Homo Ludens*, 82. As Roger Caillois points out, it's difficult to reconcile Huizinga's claim that play's primary motivation is to win "pomps, applause, and ovations" with his declared interest in forms of religious play that have no relation to competitive contests. Since play is "nearly always spectacular or ostentatious" in *Homo Ludens*, Caillois argues, it has no relationship to divine mystery and cannot be meaningfully linked, then, to the sacred. See his *Man, Play and Games*, trans. Meyer Barash (1961; repr. Urbana: University of Illinois Press, 2001), 4, 5.

42. Bates, *Play in a Godless World*, 19.

43. Huizinga, *Homo Ludens*, 10.

44. Johan Huizinga, *The Waning of the Middle Ages*, trans. F. Hopman (Harmondsworth: Penguin, 1955); quoted in Bates, *Play in a Godless World*, 19.

45. Marilynne Robinson, *Gilead* (New York: Picador; Farrar, Straus and Giroux, 2004), 153.

46. David R. Kinsley, *The Divine Player: A Study of Kṛṣṇa Līlā* (Delhi: Motilal Banarsidass, 1979), x; and James H. Evans Jr., *Playing* (Minneapolis: Fortress Press, 2010), 75.

47. Leigh Eric Schmidt, *Restless Souls: The Making of American Spirituality*, 2nd ed. (Berkeley: University of California Press, 2005, 2012).

48. Robert Wuthnow, *After Heaven: Spirituality in America Since the 1950s* (Berkeley: University of California Press, 1998).

49. See Wuthnow, *After Heaven*, 8.

50. James McIntosh, *Nimble Believing: Dickinson and the Unknown* (Ann Arbor: University of Michigan Press, 2004), 16.

51. Schmidt, *Restless Souls*, xv, xii.

52. Michael Fishbane, *Sacred Attunement: A Jewish Theology* (Chicago: University of Chicago Press, 2008), 52.

53. Fishbane, *Sacred Attunement*, 52, xiii.

54. Fishbane, *Sacred Attunement*, 35, xiii.

55. Jürgen Moltmann, *Theology of Play*, trans. Reinhard Ulrich (New York: Harper and Row, 1972), 21.

56. Moltmann, *Theology of Play*, 39.

57. Moltmann, *Theology of Play*, 36, 44.

58. Moltmann, *Theology of Play*, 16.

59. On this, see also David Kinsley's discussion of divine freedom in the Hindu scriptures: "The gods are entirely complete. They need and desire nothing. Their activity, therefore, is appropriately called *lilā*. And *lilā* is different from, or 'other' than, the world of here and now that is dominated by cause and effect, where man is forced to act out of necessity." *The Divine Player*, xi.

60. Hugo Rahner, *Man at Play*, trans. Brian Battershaw and Edward Quinn (New York: Herder and Herder, 1967), 2.

61. Rahner, *Man at Play*, 33.

62. Rahner, *Man at Play*, 40.

63. Rahner, *Man at Play*, 101.

64. Rahner, *Man at Play*, 2, 91–105.

65. Let me note here both the danger and opportunity of the kind of inter-faith dialogue I hope to inspire in *Playful Wisdom*. The danger is obvious: bringing Jewish, Catholic, Protestant, Hindu, and transcendental theories of play into conversation with one another risks flattening the cultural and linguistic particularity of theological discourse and ignoring the embeddedness of that discourse in specific religious histories. While acknowledging that danger, Michael Fishbane also stresses the neglected value of what he calls "general theology," which opens new possibilities of ecumenical dialogue and theological self-critique. By seeing how notions of "play" and "attunement" develop within various religious communities, we discover opportunities for difference and growth, allowing the reframing effect of play to alter our own embedded understandings. "Every actual theology must thus appear in a specific cultural language," Fishbane notes. "In this way, life is infused with an inherited intimacy of purpose and vision. But this said, it must never be forgotten that *theology* itself, as a 'discourse about God,' has the primary duty of serving God alone—not some particular religious formulation or tradition. This means helping make the world 'God-real' or God-actual (in Buber's terms) by thoughtful realizations of the many modalities of divine effectivity." *Sacred Attunement*, 39. My hope is that it's possible both to honor the inherited intimacy of specific theological traditions and to enrich those traditions with a deeper awareness of play's diversity. Wisdom is plural in the Hebrew scriptures. She plays with God and beside God from the beginning of time, and her play reveals the manifold presence of the divine. My goal is not to offer a comprehensive treatment of sacred play within a single religious tradition but to tell play's story from six different perspectives and reclaim that multiplicity as the playful wisdom of modern faith.

66. Krista Tippett, *Speaking of Faith* (New York: Viking, 2007), 3, 2.

67. Fishbane, *Sacred Attunement*, 35.

68. On this theme in *Walden*, see Stanley Cavell, *In Quest of the Ordinary: Lines of Skepticism and Romanticism* (Chicago: University of Chicago Press, 1988), 16, 9.

69. Emily Dickinson, *The Poems of Emily Dickinson*, ed. R. W. Franklin (Cambridge: Harvard University Press, 1999), 282, 108.

70. John Leland, *Why Kerouac Matters: The Lessons of "On the Road"* (New York: Penguin, 2007), 14.

71. F. Scott Fitzgerald, *The Great Gatsby* (1925; repr. New York: Scribner, 2004), 9.

72. Thomas Merton, *The Behavior of Titans* (New York: New Directions, 1961), 79.

73. Thomas Merton, *Raids on the Unspeakable* (New York: New Directions, 1966), 9.

74. Stewart, *Nonsense*, 5.

75. Thomas Merton, *Cables to the Ace*; or *Familiar Liturgies of Misunderstanding* (New York: New Directions, 1968), 28.

76. Merton, *Cables*, 11.

77. This quote occurs often in Bateson's writings. Its original source is Blake's letter to Thomas Butts, November 22, 1802, *Letters of William Blake*, ed. Geoffrey

Keynes (New York: MacMillan, 1956), 79. Nachmanovitch discusses the importance of the Blake quote in "This is Play," 12–14.

78. Although Thoreau plays a minor role in William James' *The Varieties of Religious Experience*, I find James' definition of "religion" especially congenial to my project: "Were one asked to characterize the life of religion in the broadest and most general terms possible," James writes, "one might say that it consists of the belief that there is an unseen order, and that our supreme good lies in harmoniously adjusting ourselves thereto. This belief and this adjustment are the religious attitude in the soul." What we're adjusting ourselves to is uncertain in James: a "something more" or "something there," which turns thought in a new direction and makes a difference in the way people live. What matters to James is not how we define that "something more," nor exactly where we experience it (as an object present to the senses or as an intuition present in the mind). Instead, what matters is the *turning*, the change in moral behavior. See his *The Varieties of Religious Experience: A Study in Human Nature*, ed. Martin E. Marty (1902; repr. Harmondsworth, Middlesex: Penguin, 1987), 53.

Chapter 1

Play and Attunement
The Spirituality of Walden

LIVING IN CONCORD

So far, I've argued that play is more an attitude than an activity for the writers in my study, a flexible stance or receptive orientation that encourages us to see things from more than one perspective and to feel them through different shades and gradations of tone. In animal play, these shadings replace one-dimensional communication, bite as bite (now and always), with shifting and multivalent meanings, bite as "bite" (so be ready). In this sense, play is a mode of adaptive attunement for Gregory Bateson, a way of being in sync with the changing moods and behaviors of others. The words "game" and "play" seem to imply established rules and stable relationships, as in chess or canasta. But for Bateson, play is more improvisational than that, "an evolving system of interaction," where the rules and roles can change suddenly and the game itself is a kind of living creature (like the croquet match in *Alice in Wonderland*, where the mallets are nervous flamingos and the ball is a moody hedgehog, who might just walk off on his own).[1] There's a survival advantage to this flexibility: animals that can't play don't last very long in the wild because they can't abstract and reconfigure, adjusting their responses to the changing demands of the moment. Both animals and human beings have automatic reactions, Bateson acknowledges, like the grip reflex in very young children, but the real advantage is being able to tune one's responses to subtle differences in the physical environment as well as equally subtle changes in the temper and disposition of other creatures.[2]

This delicate self-tuning was one of Thoreau's most important religious ideas. Religion for Thoreau was never propositional, an affair of creeds and church statements, and it was never dogmatic, a life-binding orthodoxy or "ligature" (the root word of *religion*, as he liked to point out).[3] When

Thoreau uses theological language to express his spiritual life, he contrasts the "dogma" of theology and philosophy with what he calls "a newer testament,—the gospel according to this moment" to emphasize life's astonishing capacity for change.[4] Thoreau thought of that change not as random or disordered but as the expression of nature's own spiritual life, what he called the divine law of undulation: "The subtlest and most ideal and spiritual motion is undulation."[5] Thoreau witnessed that law often and with delight: in the flights of birds and insects, in the motions of stars and planets, in the bodies of cats and fish, and in the rippling action of water and sand. Rippling undulation is the signature of spirit in *Walden* and the expression of a divine Intelligence Thoreau sought not so much to comprehend or analyze as to commune with in sympathetic resonance, tuning himself like an exquisitely sensitive conducting surface to the play of spirit in the world.[6]

In her master's thesis on Thoreau, Annie Dillard used the image of the oscillograph, an instrument for measuring the fluctuations of electrical currents, to describe this spiritual responsiveness—first in *Walden*, the subject of her Hollins College thesis, and later as a figure for her own spirituality in *Pilgrim at Tinker Creek*, as I'll say more about in chapter 5.[7] Like Dillard's oscillograph, Thoreau's images of spiritual attunement are often mechanical, like the "divining rod" used to detect the presence of hidden springs.[8] Or the "Realometer" he describes in "Where I Lived, and What I Lived For"—a device keyed to the rhythms of the actual world (and only those rhythms) in a culture drenched to drowning in human delusion (104). We need these spiritual tools because the artificial rhythms of consumption and accumulation in a market economy threaten to exaggerate the ego's importance and throw its appetites out of scale. The antidote is a different kind of "drumming"—not salesmanship and exploitation but the living rhythms of actual things: wind, waves, pulsebeats, wing beats, the natural cycles of inspiration and respiration, growth and decay—all of which restore and rescale the self within the larger ecology of the pond. Thoreau's famous line about marching to the music of a different drummer is not meant to mock his desperate neighbors with his own iconoclastic liberation but to suggest that our *rhythms* are wrong, that we've scaled our lives to the wrong score. In contemplation, Thoreau could feel life's pulse in his wrist and breath and sense what he called "kindred vibrations" in the outside world: the insect hum of crickets and wasps; the throaty rattle of wood ducks; the voiced rhythms of good writing; and the distant drumming of partridges, pond waves, and summer rain (the inspiration for Thomas Merton's response to Thoreau, "Rain and the Rhinoceros").

Honoring the differences in his readers and the diversity of his own inner life, Thoreau pictures this attunement in several ways. Religious faith is largely a private concern for Thoreau, not something he can make public very easily or explain to someone with any hope of understanding. "What is religion?" he asks in his *Journal* in 1858. "That which is never spoken."[9] And so Thoreau doesn't talk about his spirituality directly in *Walden*, but secretly or cryptically, hinting at things he can't express in any other way: "I will only hint at some of the enterprises which I have cherished" (16). Thus, faith is like a Realometer tuned to the pulse of the natural world or a divining rod vibrating to sacred springs. But faith is also like an Aeolian harp whose strings are "swept by the divine breath."[10] Or an upside-down ax, its head resting on the bottom of the pond and its helve gently waving in invisible currents (195). Most of all though, faith is like the pond, whose infinitely sensitive surface responds to every fish, breeze, insect, cloud, gun shot, leaf fall, paddle stroke, and ray of light: "Not a fish can leap or an insect fall on the pond but it is thus reported in circling dimples, in lines of beauty, as it were the constant welling up of its fountain, the gentle pulsing of its life" (205). Thoreau's phrasing is biblical, not a sparrow falls to earth, because his theme is religious.[11] Thoreau uses the same word to describe the responsiveness of the pond—"it is thus reported"—that he used earlier in *Walden* to describe his calling as a religious writer: to be the faithful "reporter" of divine spirit. When Thoreau makes subtle distinctions in that report in *Walden*—by pointing out, for instance, that the ripples caused by pickerel are different than the ripples caused by insects—he suggests not only the devotion of his religious calling but also the rigor of its love. In a similar spirit, Gary Snyder writes, "Ripples on the surface of the water— / were silver salmon passing under— different / from the ripples caused by breezes."[12]

In a more orthodox religious tradition, such loving attention would be called "reverence" or "worship"—words that Thoreau resists using to avoid associating faith with the special province of a religious tradition or the special powers of a holy mystic. Noticing the differences between the ripples caused by insects and those caused by fish or wind doesn't pull people out of ordinary life into the special realm of a transcendent God. It roots them more deeply in *this* life and teaches them to become more faithful by teaching them to become more like the pond. The pond is the model for the artist on whom nothing is lost. But the pond is also the model of spiritual attunement for Thoreau, perfect spiritual pitch, and it stands out, then, as the goal of his religious practice. Which is still *perseverance*, being faithful, but being faithful not to a religious doctrine set in stone, nor to a salvation story of one-time redemption, but faithful instead to the undulating presence of a divine spirit that is infinitely variable and infinitely free and that comes and goes in time.

Thoreau encountered an intense version of this religious view in the play theologies of South Asia. Beginning in the summer of 1840, when Emerson loaned him his copy of *The Laws of Manu* and asked him to excerpt passages for publication in *The Dial*, Thoreau studied several key texts in the *līlā* tradition of Hindu spirituality.[13] A late Sanskrit word that means "sport" or "play," *līlā* refers to the idea that God is a free artist who creates and governs the world through the spontaneous outpouring of divine joy. Divine creativity is not motivated by acquisitive desire (*kāma*) or the consequences of past actions (*karman*), which would suggest that God lacks something or is compelled by something. Instead, divine creativity is an end in itself in the *līlā* literature, like a game played for the love of the game or a work of art created for its own sake. "There is nothing in the three worlds for me to gain, Arjuna," Krishna explains in the *Bhagavad Gita*, "nor is there anything I do not have; I continue to act, but I am not driven by any need of my own."[14] Although the word, *līlā*, does not appear in the *Gita*, Krishna's emphasis on free or spontaneous divine action is at the heart of this theological tradition. In the *līlā* literature, "a joyful, ever-creative God is continually revealing himself in the play of natural forces and in the interactions of human beings," Norvin Hein writes.[15] In this view, existence *is* play, top to bottom, which is both continuous and continuously changing. More nuanced than the word "play," *līlā* expresses that creativity in several ways. As a verb, *līlayati* means rocking or swinging, like the back-and-forth play of waves and trees. As a noun, *līlā* conveys notions of liveliness, lightness, and agility as well as theatrical illusion and the *as-if* mood of subjunctive possibility, things that appear like other things (*gājendralīla* is a man who seems like an elephant, literally "elephant-play-man").[16] As a term in Hindu theology, *līlā* can refer to the weaving and unweaving of the universe by the successive incarnations of the divine (*avatāra* and *līlāvatāra*) as well as the contemplation and enjoyment of that play. Technically, *Manu* is a legal text (*dharma-śāstra*), a repository of Hindu moral guidance, which is separate from the *līlā* literature. But Manu draws on that literature in his creation narratives, as in this verse from Chapter One: "The Epochs of a Manu are countless, and so are the emissions and reabsorptions (of the universe); as if he were playing, the Supreme Lord does this again and again."[17]

In the *Harivaṃśa Purāna*, a work Thoreau borrowed from the Harvard College Library on November 5, 1849, *līlā* sets off a different set of associations by accenting the freedom of divine creativity from cultural precedent and moral code (exactly the calibrated regulation of human life Manu aimed to create in Bengali society). Divine rhythms are less wave-like than jarring and unpredictable in the *Harivaṃśa*, which transforms the morally earnest Krishna of the *Bhagavad Gita* into a ludic figure of daring transgression: playing tricks, stealing food, kicking over wagons, disobeying his mother, flirting with the *gobis*. As Hein says, "The age of Kṛṣṇa as sportive being— as a doer of *līlās*—had begun."[18] Reveling in Krishna's boyhood antics, his human play (*manuṣyalīlā*), the *Harivaṃśa* does not explore the theological implications of a sporting god. That would come later in the *Vishnu Purāna*.

Instead, the *Harivaṃśa* describes the boy-god's playful refusal to curb his desires and become dutiful and self-sacrificing, the cardinal virtues of the *Bhagavad Gita* and the moral foundation of the brahmanical code. As that code expanded and intensified in the Gupta age, "the tightening of the bolts on a structure of steel," Hein calls it, the *Harivaṃśa*'s Krishna became immensely attractive as a figure of social and religious liberation. The *Gita*'s Krishna seeks to save a disintegrating world from chaos. The *Harivaṃśa*'s Krishna is the source of creative chaos. The music of his flute crashes in from the woods like an unearthly sound, rattling old mentalities and shaking life to its core (thus creating the conditions for new growth). In his extended discussion of the *Gita* in the "Monday" chapter of *A Week*, Thoreau qualifies his enthusiasm for the epic by stressing the paralyzing bondage of the Hindu caste system: "The Brahman never proposes courageously to assault evil, but patiently to starve it out. His active faculties are paralyzed by the idea of cast, of impassable limits, of destiny and the tyranny of time. Kreeshna's argument, it must be allowed, is defective."[19] There are no impassable limits in the *Harivaṃśa*, whose Krishna offered a democratizing counter-voice to the suffocating strictures of caste and code in the Gupta Empire.[20] That idea must have intrigued Thoreau, so much so that when he composed his own version of the divine player "sporting on this bank" in *Walden* (a formulation that went through several revisions), his final phrasing looks like a sly homage to the *Harivaṃśa*, where "once on a time Lord Bhava was sporting on the bank of a charming river."[21]

Several of these themes converge in Horace Hayman Wilson's translation of the *Vishnu Purāna*, a work well known in Concord by the 1840s. (Emerson used the *Vishnu Purāna* as the basis of his 1846 poem, "Hamatreya.") Thoreau borrowed the *Vishnu Purāna* from the Harvard College Library in 1850 and again in 1854; quoted a passage from its discussion of spiritual liberation in "Walking"; quoted another passage on the duties of hospitality in "Former Inhabitants"; and adapted the *Vishnu Purāna*'s image of spiritual awakening to the ending of *Walden*: "all intelligences awake with the morning."[22] In addition, the *Vishnu Purāna* offered Thoreau a compendium of Hindu theologies of play and attunement. Like *Manu*, it presents *līlā* as the simultaneous making and unmaking of the cosmos by divine *avatāra*. And like the *Harivaṃśa*, it retells the tales of Krishna's boyhood play as his *manuṣyalīlā*, his human sport. But the *Vishnu Purāna* also stresses the graceful or dance-like aspects of *līlā*, an important precedent for Thoreau's divine law of undulation. When Parāśara raises the question of how the divine can be imagined—"Who can describe him who is not to be apprehended by the senses: who is the best of all things"?—Parāśara responds by depicting divine creativity as playful frolic, as it is in the *Harivaṃśa*: "Vishnu being thus discrete and indiscrete substance, spirit, and time, sports like a playful boy, as you shall learn by listening to his frolics."²³ The *Vishnu Purāna* renders that frolic not as anarchic or transgressive, the frame-shattering music of Krishna's flute, however, but more like the rising and falling tempos Thoreau experienced at the pond. David Kinsley describes this tempo in the Hindu scriptures as "God's rhythmical dance of creation and his ongoing pulse in the preservation of the world," which Parāśara pictures as the undulating rhythm of ocean waves: "The multifarious forms of that manifold being encounter and succeed one another, night and day, like the waves of the sea."²⁴

Tuning himself to those rhythms felt religious to Thoreau, but religion without church or creed, where what matters isn't fixed doctrine or unswerving belief but a capacity for living in tune with what he called the "vibrating music" of the world.²⁵ Sometimes that music is awesome and terrifying and inspires reactions that are unmistakably religious. But sometimes the vibrations are more subtle than that and require nuanced forms of contemplative listening: "If I listen, I hear the peep of frogs which is older than the slime of Egypt," Thoreau writes in *A Week*, "and the distant drumming of a partridge on a log, as if it were the pulse-beat of the summer air."²⁶ Such listening is one of Thoreau's worship practices, his way of keeping the Sabbath. There is no divide in him between reading scripture and listening to the partridges. They are continuations of the same sacred rhythm, which he sought to experience in his daily walks and record in his daybooks and journals. Thoreau's goal as a religious writer is to live "in concord" with that sacred code ("I have travelled a good deal in Concord"), and thus tune himself to the divine rhythm of reality, as in a verse Raimon Panikkar quotes from the conclusion of the *Rig Veda*:

Let us be in harmony in our intention,
in harmony in our hearts
in harmony in our minds
that we may live in concord.
—according to the divine and cosmic
rhythm of reality.²⁷

Thoreau experienced that divine rhythm both inside and outside the thinking self: as the pulsebeats of inspiration and mood, on the one hand, and the drumbeats of wild nature, on the other. Thoreau's goal is to match and balance both sides—mind and nature, subjectivity and the pond—and so experience himself in a dynamic state of dance-like attunement. Those rhythms had to be real to *him*, not forced on him from the outside at the expense of his own personality and temperament (what he hated about the Concord church). But those rhythms had to be *not him* at the same time, not created in his own imagination to rescale the world to the pinched economy of his own need.

Panikkar emphasizes this delicate "strain" or "tension" in his study of sacred rhythm:

> Rhythm is outside me; I do not invent it. I have only to listen, to obey (*ob-audire*, listening) the beats of the real, and in order to listen I need to be silent, to silence my egocentrisms, my *ahamkāra*. More, I need to be pure. In addition, rhythm is also inside me. My reception is indispensable, and my identification is a requirement. It is not superimposed on me. I discover it in myself by means of the drums from outside. Serenity, *upekṣa*, *Gelassenheit*, all these similar virtues consist in discerning the rhythm of life by being attuned to it.[28]

At the heart of this faith practice is a capacity for responsive attunement Panikkar discovers in the root, *div*, which gives us another Sanskrit word for play, *divyati*, as well as the noun *Devī* (Goddess, Divinity). Panikkar traces this notion of divine play through several branches of Hindu theology—Indic *rasa* theory, the Sanskrit idea of *samanvaya*, and the dance of the universe in the *Rig Veda*—but he finds similar notions in Hellenic, African, Christian, and Zoroastrian cosmogonies, all of which emphasize musical or rhythmic views of the divine.

As Panikkar's references to *ahamkāra* and *Gelassenheit* suggest, none of this begins with *Walden*. What seems distinctly Thoreauvian at first, "his repeated efforts to 'tune' his moods to match the pitch of the world," in Robert B. Ray's phrase, expresses in fact what Augustine described as the origin of Christian theology, what Thoreau's New England ancestors considered the true spirit of Protestant worship, and what the classic texts of Hinduism identify as the goal of devotional practice.[29] Moreover, when Thoreau pictures that attunement as a kind of vibrating sensitivity, like the skin of a drum or the surface of the pond, he's adapting theologies of attunement present in many religious traditions to the aesthetic mood of his generation. The literature of Thoreau's period is filled with drum-tight souls primed to vibrate at the slightest touch of the beloved. Thoreau walks that jumpy subjectivity outside and reworks notions of romantic sensitivity into a faith stance of spiritual attunement. Thoreau's "beloved" is importantly non-human most of the time, but he discovers in the audible vibrations of birdsong and the insect hum of the wasps who shared his bed some nights the same half-thrilling, half-terrifying intimacy. ("They never molested me seriously, though they bedded with me," he joked about the wasps.)

Strange as it sounds, sleeping with the wasps is a kind of faith practice for Thoreau—not because he's reinventing medieval rites of corporeal penance but because God is nonhuman too: not subject to our domesticating fantasies, not an "object" of conscious thought and comprehension, and thus every bit as wild to our frame of reference as the wasps. "[T]he Almighty is wild above all," Thoreau wrote in his *Journal*,[30] as if to make explicit what he felt intuitively about his "brute neighbors" at the pond: that these were sacred and enchanted creatures, the loons most of all, whose unearthly laughter sounded to him like prayer. How then do we relate to all that buzzing, laughing, stinging, vibrating otherness? We can join its play, Thoreau thought. We can unlearn the utilitarian wisdom of the Concord marketplace (which collapses value to profit) and form nonviolent relationships of reciprocity and attunement with a world we do not own.

NIMBLE BELIEVING

That kind of play is harder than it looks. Sometimes Thoreau was uncomfortable with the key terms of his own religious vocabulary—frolic, leisure, Sabbath, nooning—and he tended to slip the qualifier, *unrelaxed*, into his play formulations: "I can see nothing so holy as unrelaxed play." He used that kind of phrasing not only to indulge his taste for paradox (and annoy his friends) but also to distinguish the contemplative discipline of his spirituality from an anything-goes mentality of religious whim. Thoreau understood that a faith practice based on play is easily mistaken for laziness or indifference. And he also knew that his religious calling to be a reporter of pond ripples looked ridiculous to most people, Emerson for one, but even his Aunt Maria had her doubts: "I wish he could find something better to do than walking off every now and then."[31]

Thoreau felt the sting of these judgments—precisely because he was proposing nothing less than a reversal of reigning religious values: play for duty, responsiveness for doctrine, and spiritual astonishment and gratitude for work-a-day norms of religious habit. He knew that this "curious world which we inhabit is more wonderful than it is convenient; more beautiful than it is useful; it is more to be admired and enjoyed than used," as he said in his 1837 Commencement essay.[32] But he also knew that this kind of reversal requires extraordinary inner work, as he said about play's wisdom: "The mass of men lead lives of quiet desperation. . . . There is no play in them, for this comes after work" (7). With this in mind, Thoreau begins *Walden* by counting the costs of spiritual adventure, down to the ¼ cent, and being as clear as possible about the sacrifices or "necessities" a life of faith will require. And there are several. A life of faith will require a more focused life practice, living deliberately, and a streamlined relationship with commodity culture. Faith will depend on contemplative habits of stillness and solitude that allow the mind to settle more deeply into the body, returning to the senses. It will entail a different understanding of holiness and miracle and a different relationship between leisure and work. Most of all, a life of faith will develop a talent for religious adjustment and improvisation, which is sometimes a visual discipline in *Walden*: the ability to stretch perception into multiple, almost cubistic points of view. And sometimes a musical discipline: the ability to march to the beat of a different drummer. And it's different every time, so faith requires a gift for experimenting or maneuvering, what Dillard calls "tinkering" (*Pilgrim at Tinker Creek*)—which surrenders the privilege of a fixed or dogmatic point of view.

That may be the hardest one of all. In some ways, it's difficult to imagine a *less* playful or spontaneous human being than Henry David Thoreau. He didn't like being touched or surprised. He didn't play games with other people and was so withdrawn and serious that his childhood nickname was the "Judge." He held his friends to impossibly rigid standards (and often abandoned them when they fell short). He didn't like being questioned or contradicted. He boasted more than once that he'd never changed his mind about *anything*, that he in fact believed the same things at forty that he did at fourteen, and that the course of his life was a razor-straight line of undeviating conviction. It wasn't—but the appeal of that self-image never lost its allure. Nathaniel Hawthorne thought that Thoreau had a "certain iron-pokerishness" about him, "an uncompromising stiffness" in his character, and that he was "the most unmalleable fellow alive."[33] And Hawthorne *liked* him. Thoreau loved to be right, perhaps more than most people, and he was never more at home than when he found himself defending a position against all comers, the one righteous person in the room.

Of course, this is part of *Walden* too. Thoreau may say that his spirituality is playful or that he's not "prescrib[ing] rules to strong and valiant natures" (15). But *Walden* is chockablock with rules and prescriptions—about the right books (classics), the right clothes (old), the right bread (unleavened), the right way to prepare a bean field (without manure), the right way to bait a fishhook (earthworms only). Moreover, when other people break his rules for righteous living, as John Field does when he baits his hook with pieces of fish, Thoreau's as willing as anyone to ridicule and condemn. I stress these moments not to judge Thoreau but to emphasize the rigor of his religious calling, what Dietrich Bonhoeffer would call the cost of this discipleship, and to suggest that Thoreau's lifelong quarrel with dogmatic Christianity was also a lifelong quarrel with a deep quality in himself.

Let me consider one part of that quarrel now. As a child Thoreau attended both the Unitarian and Trinitarian churches in Concord, but the Puritan God of the Trinitarian church seemed to have made the strongest impression and inspired some of Thoreau's most intense religious writing. In the "Sunday" chapter of *A Week*, for example, Thoreau calls the Calvinist God, "Jehovah," and contrasts the unyielding sovereignty and masculine bullying of that deity with the playfulness and youthful erring of the Greek Pantheon. Unlike Jove,

Jehovah has no sisters or lovers. Unlike Pan, he doesn't walk in the woods with his daughter, Iambe, or his wood nymph, Echo. Jehovah has no jester or fool, as Momus was for Jove. He doesn't "sport" anywhere. His worship is not playful but "bigoted," "inflexible," "intolerant," and "wholly masculine."[34] He embodies what Thoreau considered the *worst* part of human personality, a need for overwhelming authority, at the expense of a fuller range of religious experience. Why, then, are we stuck with him? Thoreau wonders. How did *that* God become America's God? The choice seemed entirely arbitrary to Thoreau, given the diversity of world religions, the uncertainty of sacred knowledge, and the intolerable presumption of anyone who claims to speak in God's name. "The perfect God in his revelations of himself has never got to the length of one such proposition as you, his prophets, state," Thoreau writes in a withering tirade addressed to the religious authorities of his day:

> Have you learned the alphabet of heaven and can count three? Do you know the number of God's family? Can you put mysteries into words? Do you presume to fable of the ineffable? Pray, what geographer are you, that speak of heaven's topography? Whose friend are you that speak of God's personality? Do you, Miles Howard, think that he has made you his confidant? Tell me of the height of the mountains of the moon, or of the diameter of space, and I may believe you, but of the secret history of the Almighty, and I shall pronounce thee mad.[35]

From the point of view of sacred mystery, Thoreau suggests, what other sort of religious wisdom is possible but a *playful* one? The mystery of a universe in constant change was the central fact of Thoreau's cosmology, and he writes *Walden* with that principle in mind, so that whatever he says about the subjects that concern him (God, nature, other people, other books, his own thoughts) is not stone-tablet revelation but nimble and temporary belief. Not a truth to the end of time but barely a truth to the end of the chapter. Indeed, the mobile play of these temporary truths is the characteristic of Thoreau's style in *Walden*: his "extra-vagant maneuver" (Joseph J. Moldenhauer); "wariness and adaptation" (Frederick Garber); "drama of adjustment" (Robert Milder); and "shifting stance" (James McIntosh).[36] In this mood, Thoreau cherishes the railroad as a metaphor for transporting spirit and disdains it as a sign of contaminating commerce. He vows to "fish and hunt far and wide" one day and admits that he "cannot fish without falling a little in self-respect" the next (226, 233). Weeds are a symbol of wickedness at the beginning of "The Bean-Field" and a sign of God's blessing by the chapter's end. Ants represent craven meanness in "Where I Lived, and What I Lived For" and epic heroism in "Brute Neighbors." Simplicity is the characteristic of spiritual clarity in "Economy" and the sign of an immature imagination still stuck in the fourth grade in "Reading." The pond is hard-bottomed then no-bottomed. Measurable then not measurable. A space without change and a space of ceaseless change. It's a lower heaven and the source of the river Styx, which makes sense because Thoreau sees both angels and ghouls at the pond and writes that paradox into the undulating rhythms of his prose. For every gem-like scene of diamond sameness, Thoreau writes a countervailing scene of liquid change. For every hard-rock refuge, a muddy melting. For every ice-pure winter, an excremental spring. Such a world is alive in all its details and changing in all its details, so that any stated version of its mystery is already out of date in the flash and fin of this next new thing.

It's common to point out these contradictions as evidence of Thoreau's narcissistic self-involvement (Perry Miller); artistic incompetence (Vincent Buranelli); fractured personality (Richard Bridgman); or personal crises (Philip Abbott).[37] But presenting a unified personality is less important to Thoreau than cultivating a playful spirit of responsiveness and detachment, one that allowed him to move through different moods and positions in his life at the pond, assuming and then discarding different standpoints, without allowing any single perspective to define the work as a whole. Neither God nor the earth is "a mere fragment of dead history" for Thoreau, but a live force of creativity and quickening, which calls out a corresponding lability in its observer (334).

The problem with religion, Thoreau argued, is that it tends to fix this mobility into rigid systems of belief:

> Every author—be he ancient lawgiver or modern philosopher—writes in the faith that his book is to be the final resting place of the sojourning soul and sets up his fixtures therein as for a more than oriental permanence. . . . The universe will not wait to be explained. Whoever seriously attempts a theory of it is already behind his age. His yea has reserved no nay for the morrow. The wisest solution is no better than dissolution.[38]

Sometimes Thoreau welcomed the loss of religious "fixtures" as the advent of a new spirituality of experimentation and self-trust, "a wild yea-saying overburst of American joy," as Sal Paradise puts it in *On the Road*. Sometimes Thoreau felt that way. But sometimes he drew back from the prospect of an unfixed faith subject to fluctuating sensations of exhilaration and loss, one after another, like the belly-tipping turns of a roller coaster. One minute you're "Indra in the sky" and the next you're "driftwood in the stream," as he puts it in "Solitude" (145). One minute God appears at your door like a "wise and humorous friend" and the next minute he "keeps himself more secret than ever did Goffe or Whalley" (148). Keeps himself more secret, that is, than the political assassins who killed King Charles I and fled to America (hiding not far from Walden Pond). This sort of unfixed faith undermines stable forms of thought and subjectivity, but this is how we know ourselves in relation to an ever-changing reality, not as fixture but as flux and thus the site of shifting and contradictory sensations: hope and despair; conviction and doubt; sure of God, not sure of God; sure of ourselves, not sure of ourselves—a hundred times an hour, as Emily Dickinson said: "On subjects of which we know nothing, or should I say *Beings* . . . we both believe, and disbelieve a hundred times an Hour, which keeps Believing nimble."[39]

Thoreau practices a form of nimble believing not only in his relationship with a God "who keeps himself more secret" but also in his day-to-day life at the pond. Whatever Thoreau stops to consider in *Walden*, wherever he allows his attention to linger, he discovers hidden facets, levels, edges, dimensions, and tricky little diamond bevels that all flash differently in the sun, as he turns (and turns and turns) each new thing over in his writing. As Markus Poetzsch has argued, Thoreau's habit of framing and then reframing his nature descriptions expresses his attempt to come to terms "with the very slipperiness of lived experience" and with its "almost willful resistance to the tools of empirical knowledge."[40] As an example of this disposition, Poetzsch cites a passage in "The Ponds" where Thoreau describes the color of the pond's water—which Thoreau sees as "clear and deep green," initially, but then, depending on his perspective and the time of day, becomes many other colors as well: *blue*; *dark slate*; *yellowish*; *light green*; *vivid green*; *greenish blue*; *light blue (like sword blades)*; *darker blue*; *blue mixed with the yellow of the sand*; *cerulean alternating with the original dark green on the opposite sides of the waves*; and finally, *colorless* (193–94).

This kind of limber positioning is beautiful, like the brilliant dance of the sandbank. But it's also extraordinarily demanding, like the hardest yoga session in the world. Who hasn't read *Walden* and had the impulse to say, at least once, it's just *water*. And in those same moments, who hasn't sensed that perhaps our impatience is the problem, our need for fixed designations, and that maybe we've lost more than we know. Or maybe we haven't lost enough yet, because Thoreau cherishes bewilderment as a liberating confusion.[41] For all his talk about stillness, *Walden* is a very nervous book, because the bevel flash can come from anywhere. And for all his talk about leisure, *Walden* is a very busy book—which allows thought to run out long and hard, exhausting all its categories, using up all its ideas—and *then* allowing the mind to settle and be still. Not sleepy, exactly the opposite of sleepy, but poised, responsive, playful, nimble.

The threat to this responsive poise is not only slavish conformity to received doctrine but also the mind's tendency to frame the world according to an a priori intention and then "discover" in nature a confirmation of one's own ideas, thus seeing in nature whatever one expects to see or wants to see and foreclosing, then, any possibility of surprise. This is what consciousness does best, as Frederick Garber points out: it "transform[s] the world into images of itself."[42] And this is also what religion does best, as Thoreau argued in *A Week*: "What man believes, God believes."[43] It may seem childish or perverse to see the ants as mean one day and heroic the next—unless that way of thinking distances "ants" from *any* projective identification, good or bad, and so prevents us from subjecting the world to our own instrumental designs. That narrow self-projection, rather than doubt or disbelief, is the real threat to religious faith for Thoreau. Our gods act and think like us, he argues (anticipating the argument Ludwig Feuerbach will develop in *The Essence of Christianity*). Our need for overwhelming authority is magnified in the story of Jehovah just as our vulnerabilities are mythologized in the story of the crucified Christ. It's human personality on a cosmic scale. Which is a real problem if what we'd like to escape, ultimately, is a closed and quietly desperate subjectivity, one that turns everything and everyone (including God, including the ants) into versions of itself. "Every people have gods to suit their circumstances," he argues; "the Society Islanders had a god called Toahitu, 'in shape like a dog; he saved such as were in danger of falling from rocks and trees.'"[44] It's a powerful critique: we turn our gods into our dogs, domesticated to serve our needs through the same instrumental logic we use in the Concord marketplace, where nature and other people exist *for us*, tailor-made to our satisfactions.

In *A Week*, this projective fantasy is something *other* people do: Society Islanders, dogmatic Christians. But in *Walden*, Thoreau sees the same tendency in himself: a self-protective impulse to wall out the wild or the real and create, in its place, an imaginary enclave unnicked by the predations of time and strictly off-limits to the meanness and moiling of other people: "I have, as it were, my own sun and moon and stars," he writes in "Solitude," "and a little world all to myself" (141). Emerson called this sort of thing an "excluding sanctity," and like Thoreau he knew that church people weren't the only ones prone to its allure. Indeed, *A Little World All to Myself* sounds like a course on canonical American literature, so important is this theme to the male writers in our tradition. Loving a self-protective "imaginary" is the characteristic of slave owners, Frederick Douglass argues, people whose Christianity has no earthly relation to the way things actually are and is astonishing in its self-referential completeness. Loving the imaginary is what Ahab does, his mind fixed on a "bigotry of purpose" and his bone leg stuck in a stationary standpoint drilled in the Pequod's deck. Loving the imaginary leads to the doll-like palaces Poe's artists create in the bereavement stories and the doll-like palace Gatsby creates on Long Island to hold his doll-like version of Daisy Fay.

The challenge facing people of faith, Thoreau argues, is to surrender that self-protective imaginary and face a God who is not subject to domesticating fantasies and not included in the inventory of our doll-like possessions. If that's the situation we find ourselves in, then the hiddenness of a God who keeps himself more secret than Goffe and Whalley begins to make a sort of backhanded sense. By defeating at every turn our attempts to comprehend divine nature—through its fluctuating and enigmatic appearances, its otherness to human systems of classification and control—the sacred saves us from *ourselves*. It releases us from dogmatic standpoints framing the world to a self-serving perspective and disables our fantasies of grandeur and power. (In that sense the sacred is a kind of regicide.) The hiddenness of the divine prevents us from trying to "own" everything—"I have my own sun and moon and stars"—and thus imprison life within the narrow limits of our own subjectivity. Thoreau rejoices in the unpredictability of simple things—weeds that are a blessing one day and a curse the next—because such mysteries liberate us from what William Connolly calls "the hegemony of the modern project of mastery," which is one source of our spiritual despair.[45]

In *Walden*, losing that despair will involve growing "down" in our relationship with nature, growing "smaller," and recovering a sense of our true scale in a natural ecology that is wilder and more extravagant than we can know. From this point of view, we don't need to choose between loving God and loving the world, as much of the theology in Thoreau's culture claimed. Loving the pond in its particularity and mysterious depth was a kind of secret religion for Thoreau, a version of what Simone Weil calls an "indirect or implicit love of God"[46]—precisely because loving nature accurately and deliberately and over a long period of time empties the self of its egoistic illusions and replaces larger-than-life fantasies of kingship and control with exact humility and restorative scale. Such love causes the self to voluntarily "withdraw," a key word for Thoreau, not in cringing servitude to an overpowering Jehovah (as in some strands of Puritanism), nor in astonished terror in the face of an alien sublime (as in some strands of romanticism), but as an act of spiritual kenosis and self-surrender, which Thoreau frames as an act of religious courtesy: choosing to be quiet enough to allow something else to speak; or choosing to hold back enough to allow something else to come forward.[47]

CONTEMPLATIVE *SOLVO*

In this way, kenosis and attunement go hand in hand for Thoreau, as Panikkar argued about sacred rhythm: "Rhythm is outside me; I do not invent it. I have only to listen, to obey (*ob-audire*, listening) the beats of the real, and in order to listen I need to be silent, to silence my egocentrisms, my *ahamkāra*."[48] *Ahamkāra* is a Sanskrit word that means "ego" or "egotism." (In the *Gita*, Krishna tells Arjuna that his *ahamkāra* must be removed: "stay free from the fever of the ego.") Occasionally, Thoreau is explicit about his debt to Hindu spirituality in *Walden*, but more often he keeps his religious reading in the background and practices his faith obliquely or secretly in order to avoid identifying his spirituality with the tenants of any particular religious tradition. It requires no special knowledge of *Gelassenheit* (in Christianity) or *ahamkāra* (in Hinduism) to bath in the pond in the mornings or listen carefully to birdsong. And yet these practices may achieve the same ancient goal: diminishing obstructive egocentrisms and restoring the religious self to the redemptive rhythms of the real.

It's in this spirit that Thoreau presents his various ice experiments as a form of religious contemplation: "Ice is an interesting subject for contemplation" (321). When he studies his reflection in air bubbles trapped in the ice in "House-Warming," for instance, the scene suggests a cleansing ritual of contemplative humility. Thoreau gently marks the scene as religious: the ice bubbles look like "a string of beads" (269), that is, like sutras or Upanishads. But he's less indirect about the risk. To get to the ice bubbles you must "lie at your length on ice only an inch thick, like a skater insect on the surface of the water" (268). What he sees in that precarious position is himself, his own face, but reduced and reframed into dozens of tiny "Thoreaus":

> [W]hile the ice is as yet comparatively solid and dark, that is, you see the water through it. These bubbles are from an eightieth to an eighth of an inch in diameter, very clear and beautiful, and you see your face reflected in them through the ice. There may be thirty or forty of them to a square inch. There are also already within the ice narrow oblong perpendicular bubbles about half an inch long, sharp cones with the apex upward; or oftener, if the ice is quite fresh, minute spherical bubbles one directly above another, like a string of beads. (268–69)

Sometimes Thoreau felt exalted and godlike at the pond, an imperial ego of magnificent proportion. But in this scene Thoreau allows the pond to refract and diminish him, like an infinity mirror in which each reflection grows smaller than the last. This kind of metacognitive awareness is what Thoreau prized about the playful wisdom of the *Hitopadeśa*, as we saw in the Introduction: that a book "sometimes reflect upon itself—that it pleasantly behold itself—that it hold the scales over itself." The ice mirrors do just that, as Thoreau becomes for a moment the object of his own measuring gaze. In that reflection, Thoreau sees a different and lesser version of himself, not the pond's author or spokesman but something more fleeting and fragile, like a bubble hanging in the void as the sutras say. The pond acts like a kind of visual "solvent" in this sense (from the Latin *solvo*: I unfasten, I untie), which loosens the grip of commonsense realism and releases the religious self from an exaggerated but ingrained egocentrism. Strangely enough, Thoreau receives that instruction with gladness. The ice bubbles seem precious and beautiful to him—"like silvery coins poured from a bag" (269)—precisely because such mirroring introduces an alternative scale of value. These are coins of a different realm, like the pearl of great price. Thoreau begins the ice story by comparing himself to an insect—you must "lie at your length on ice only an inch thick, like a skater insect"—as if only in this posture of risk and humility can he participate in the larger ecology of wild nature and achieve its wider view.

As we recover our true scale in the wild ecology of the pond, which is a fraction of our "normal" size, the world becomes increasingly extravagant and mysterious. But discovering that wider view is not, strictly speaking, something we achieve for ourselves. The familiar notion of Thoreau as an angry hermit isolating himself at the pond neglects how important feelings of sociability and neighborliness are to his experience of the sacred. For Thoreau, religious truth is not an abstract theory or theological proposition but a specific happening in real time, an event or encounter that draws him out of himself, or partway out of himself, and into relationship with "something other." It sounds vaguely gothic to put it that way, but this is what spirituality feels like for Thoreau. It's like sensing something out of the corner of your eye or being aware of something next to you, neighboring you, which you know is there but can't pin down and can't see directly. Indeed, Thoreau stresses these goose-bump sensations whenever he writes about God: "Nearest to all things is that power which fashions their being. *Next* to us the grandest laws are continually being executed. *Next* to us is not the workman whom we have hired, with whom we love so well to talk, but the workman whose work we are" (144–45, original emphasis). This wild neighboring may be frightening in some moods (edging toward the uncanny) or desirable in others (edging toward the erotic)—but either way, it disturbs thought's sleepy self-repose with the provocation of a living encounter. The French philosopher Gilles Deleuze has a way of phrasing this that might be helpful for understanding such moments in Thoreau:

> Something in the world forces us to think. This something is an object not of recognition but of a fundamental *encounter*. What is encountered may be Socrates, a temple or a demon. It may be grasped in a range of affective tones: wonder, love, hatred, suffering. In whichever tone, its primary characteristic is that it can only be sensed. In this sense it is opposed to recognition (original emphasis).[49]

Opposed to recognition: that's important for Thoreau. From a different point of view, the purpose of religious thinking is clarity and control, answering a theological question or sorting out an ethical dilemma. But Deleuze imagines something quite different: thought's encounter with what doesn't fit its categories, something that can be sensed but not comprehended and so something that feels more like encountering a stranger than solving a problem. Indeed "encountering a stranger" is a good way to describe Thoreau's experience of the sacred in *Walden*, the feeling of being close to someone who's real and alive without knowing precisely who that someone is. And *not* knowing is strangely liberating for Thoreau, a reminder that the world abounds with nonhuman purposes and intelligences he can sense but not fully share.

Thoreau stages this kind of Deleuzean encounter in the game he plays with the Walden loon, which acts like another "solvent," a contemplative exercise of egoistic deflation and recovered scale. This story takes place at the end of "Brute Neighbors" just after Thoreau had been thinking about different sorts of hybridity in nature: winged cats, flying squirrels—creatures that live in two worlds at once. The prime example of such hybridity is the loon, a creature that is equally at home in water and air, living above the surface of the pond like a bird and below its surface like a fish. Living in two worlds at once is what people of faith do, Thoreau implies, and so he again gently marks his scene as religious, as he did with the ice sutra in "House-Warming." Thoreau sees the loon as an "ungainly visitor from another sphere"; describes its laughter as a kind of "prayer"; and wonders if perhaps the loon is "omnipresent." Thoreau conducts several thought experiments in *Walden*, where he tries to enter the mind of a wild animal, usually an owl or a thrush, but the failure of that identity exchange is revealed here. Unable to anticipate the loon's maneuvers or in any way think its thoughts, Thoreau decides instead to play along, surrendering himself to outcomes he cannot control and allowing the wildness of the loon to shape his zigzag course:

> As I was paddling along the north shore one very calm October afternoon, for such days especially they settle on to the lakes, like the milkweed down, having looked in vain over the pond for a loon, suddenly one, sailing out from the shore toward the middle a few rods in front of me, set up his wild laugh and betrayed himself. I pursued with a paddle and he dived, but when he came up I was nearer than before. He dived again, but I miscalculated the direction he would take, and we were fifty rods apart when he came to the surface this time, for I had helped to widen the interval; and again he laughed long and loud, and with more reason than before. He manoeuvred so cunningly that I could not get within half a dozen rods of him. (255)

This goes on for the better part of an afternoon. Calculating the loon's course like a math problem doesn't work. It doesn't help to divine the loon's thoughts in an identity exchange or strain his eyes in a feat of athletic perception. These procedures yield success in other encounters but not here. So Thoreau stops trying to predict the loon's course and returns to a contemplative posture of humility and waiting, a state of unrelaxed play: "I found that it was as well for me to rest on my oars and wait his reappearing as to endeavor to calculate where he would rise; for again and again, when I was straining my eyes over the surface one way, I would suddenly be startled by his unearthly laugh behind me" (256–57).

This sort of play looks foolish from a commonsense point of view, as an exasperated St. Paul told the church at Corinth: "Has not God made foolish the wisdom of the world?" And it felt pretty foolish to Thoreau as well: "He was indeed a silly loon, I thought" (257). But like the playful wisdom of the crows and jackals in the animal fables of Hindu mythology or the trickster wisdom of rabbits and coyotes in Native American spirituality, the loon's play is both silly and dangerous. The loon lives in different depths or dimensions—sometimes in the air, sometimes on the pond's surface, sometimes eighty feet down—and shape-shifts among different animal forms: bird, fish, wolf. The danger of playing games with such a creature is that it reveals the pretensions of human mastery and mocks Thoreau's various claims to be the pond's prophet, surveyor, saint, parable-maker, or "Lord Warden himself" (272). The loon game balks that privileged status and returns Thoreau to his rightful position as a tiny figure in a vast landscape, neighbored by mysterious creatures he can interact with but not understand.

Deleuze mentioned that we grasp our encounter with otherness "in a range of affective tones" and that affective range is evident in the loon game, which changes from something "pretty" and "silly" to something "demoniac" and "unearthly":

> It was surprising to see how serenely he sailed off with unruffled breast when he came to the surface, doing all the work with his webbed feet beneath. His usual note was this demoniac laughter, yet somewhat like that of a water-fowl; but occasionally, when he had balked me most successfully and come up a long way off, he uttered a long-drawn unearthly howl, probably more like that of a wolf than any bird; as when a beast puts his muzzle to the ground and deliberately howls. This was his looning,—perhaps the wildest sound that is ever heard here, making the woods ring far and wide. (257)

The loon's howl is "unearthly" not because it issues from a higher plane of heavenly transcendence but because it contradicts the wisdom, ideology, dreamlife, and power relations of human beings living in this particular set of circumstances on this particular (and arbitrary) earth. *This* earth, as it looks to people who measure value by the dollar, shape their gods to their own self-interest, kill wild loons for sport, and "rake the tongues of bison out of the prairie grass" (259). The loon's "unearthly howl" speaks for that mute desolation and compels the same contemplative reframing Thoreau experiences with the ice mirrors. The wisdom of that reorientation is clear but hard to swallow: we need to grow *smaller*. We need to *withdraw*. That sort of religious wisdom would indeed appear "demoniac" to the utilitarian values of the Concord marketplace. It contradicts conventional notions of the "sacred" (which looks to heaven as the source of highest value) as well as conventional notions of the "secular" (which treats the earth as a commodity to be managed and used).[50] The spiritual comedy of the loon game loosens the ligatures of both forms of devotion and shows the wisdom of the world to be arbitrary and violent and the fool's way then to be a path of truth.

SACRED SOUND

The final solvent I'd like to consider is the famous Cut Bank passage of "Spring," which connects both views of play we've seen so far: play as responsive attunement (vibrating to the rhythms of the real) and play as kenotic rescaling (deflating the imperial mind). Sometimes attunement is visual in *Walden*, the ability to perceive natural analogies in nature (wave, wing, ripple, fin). And sometimes it's closer to dance or yoga, like the impromptu game Thoreau played in the woods one day, picturing the snow-bent shapes of pine and willow trees as the figures of religious reformers (Jesus, Tecumseh, George Fox) and trying to match their postures pose for pose.[51] But as Gordon V. Boudreau has shown, what first interested Thoreau about the Cut Bank wasn't its shape but its *sound*, an audible hum passing through a series of telegraph poles planted on the west side of the bank.[52] Built in the 1840s by the Fitchburg Railroad, the Cut Bank was a railroad cutting bisecting a small hill between Concord and Walden Pond. Thoreau walked back and forth along that line for years, but he gives it only glancing reference in his poetry and only one sentence in the first draft of *Walden*.

That changed in September 1851 when a telegraph wire was installed along the track. At that point, Thoreau's wide-ranging interests in spiritual attunement found an intense convergence:

> To the Three Friends' Hill over Bear Hill. Yesterday & today the stronger winds of Autumn have begun to blow & the telegraph harp has sounded loudly. I heard it especially in the deep cut this afternoon. The tone varying with the tension of different parts of the wire. The sound proceeds from near the posts where the vibration is apparently more rapid. I put my ear to one of the posts, and it seemed to me as if every pore of the wood was filled with music, labored with the strain—as if every fibre was affected and being rearranged according to a new & more harmonious law—every swell and change or inflexion of tone pervaded & seemed to proceed from the wood the divine tree or wood—as if its

very substance was transmuted.... When no music proceeds from the wire—on applying my ear I hear the hum within the entrails of the wood—the oracular tree acquiring accumulating the prophetic fury.[53]

This is another Thoreauvian play circle, signaled as Bateson would say by the subjunctive *as if*—"as if every pore of the wood was filled with music." Although Thoreau calls this core-altering rhythm "music," it seems more elemental than that, a vibratory "hum" passing through the wooden post and changing it in the process, making it more active and unstable. The vibrations confound rigid dualisms: the difference between male and female (the vibrating pole is both phallic and feminine, laboring with hidden life); the difference between tree and flesh (the wood has pores and entrails); and the difference between sacred and secular, which is the most surprising one of all. Literally, Thoreau has his ear pressed to the wood of a manufactured telegraph pole installed along a rail line whose primary purpose is to facilitate the commodification of labor in Western Massachusetts, magically turning raw materials into marketable commodities in the factories in Lowell and Boston (and mystifying the physical presence of the laborers in the process). This sort of industrial alienation repelled Thoreau and inspired some of his most impassioned sermons about desecrated groves and the loss of the holy. But this wood is sacred to Thoreau, a "divine tree." Moreover, Thoreau experiences this divinity not by observing or thinking about it but by actually pressing his ear to the wood, entwining himself in the object (and so sharing the vibration). If the telegraph scene is another parable of attunement, like the Realometer or the upside-down ax, its blessing comes through the body, what Panikkar terms a "participatory awareness in reality"[54]—not standing above or apart from the other in a position of epistemological security but rather yielding to the rhythm in the wood and moving with it in sympathetic rapport.

In the Vedic literature, the universe is composed of a divine vibration coursing through and transforming the phenomenal world, making it tremble like a field of strings (a concept also found in quantum physics). The universe is a sound creation in the Hindu cosmology, in which existence is set in motion by the vibration of a sacred syllable, *Om* or *AUM*, which the *Vishnu Purāna* calls "a low murmuring sound, like the chanting of the *Sáma Veda*."[55] That originating murmur is not a one-time burst of divine speech but a constantly renewing rhythm, like a heartbeat, which is pre-verbal and pre-human, a "rudiment of sound" existing from the beginning of time.[56] We can hear that original force (the *Prana*) in the chanting of the Vedas and feel it in the vibrations of wind and waves—precisely because the universe preserves the divine singing at its core, as if every fiber of existence were "filled with music," as Thoreau said. Hindu worship affirms and internalizes that divine vibration through its mantras and incantations, which tune the body of the worshipper to the elementary rhythms of the cosmos. Although Thoreau didn't have access to the Vedic hymns themselves, he encountered a version of this idea in *Manu*, which describes the worshipper's embodied attunement with unusual detail:

> He should always say, "Om!" at the beginning and at the end of (reciting) the Veda, for (the recitation) slips away without "Om" before it and dissolves (without "Om") after it. Sitting (on sacrificial grass) with the tips pointing east, purified by the purifying (grasses) and by suppressing his breath three times, he is fit to say, "Om!" The Lord of Creatures milked out of the three Vedas, the syllables "a," "u," and "m," and (the exclamations) "Bhūḥ!," "Bhuvaḥ!," and "Svaḥ!". . . All the Vedic rituals, the oblations and the sacrifices, perish, but it should be realized that the syllable does not perish; it is ultimate reality and the Lord of Creatures.[57]

These verses turn on a complex pun: in Sanskrit, *aksara* means both "syllable" and "non-perishing" and names the vibrational core of existence, its acoustic prototype. By chanting *Om* at the beginning and ending of each mantra, the Brahmin allows the syllable to form in the body's core, just above the abdomen, before passing up through his chest and skull (vibrating old mentalities off their cranial foundation on its way through). The syllable then passes on through the throat and lips and back into the world, completing the circle. *Om* is a wordless affirmation of that interconnection, a syllable of permission and yielding. And what it permits is *flow*, the passage of the seed syllable through the variable forms of existence—planets, ponds, books, bodies—in a way that reconciles and unites them. Unlike *Logos*, which is articulate discourse, worded meaning, *aksara* precedes meaning and makes it possible, like the vibration under the music or the hum before the words.[58] "Only the lull I like," Whitman writes in a similar spirit, "the hum of your valvèd voice."[59]

Whitman experienced that sacred hum in the wordless resonance between lovers. Thoreau experienced it in nature: "Nature always possesses a certain sonorousness," he wrote in 1841, "as in the hum of insects—the booming of ice—the crowing of cocks in the morning and the barking of dogs in the night—which indicates her sound state. God's voice is but a clear bell sound."[60] "Listening" seems too passive a word for Thoreau's response to the sonorous. Instead, he internalizes the hum, drinks it in, sleeps with it (when the wasps arrive), and allows the sonorous to penetrate and quicken his inner life. Thoreau doesn't control the booming and crowing, which disturb his self-repose and draw him out of doors, toward a world that's larger than the circle of his attention. To be listening is to be open to the voices of insects and ice and to allow the sonorous to break down the walls of the private self, an acoustic penetration Thoreau often associates with the sacred, "God's voice." To be listening is to be receptive, undefended. Thus, the sonorous "offers itself as open structure," Jean-Luc Nancy argues in his phenomenology of listening, not only because the ear is an open organ (the one a child cannot close, as Freud pointed out) but also because sound arrives as a "cut" or break in unresponsive neutrality: "To be listening is to be inclined toward the opening of meaning," Nancy writes, "hence to a slash, a cut in un-sensed [*in-sensée*] indifference."[61] Nancy studies the way sounds arrive from the "outside," interrupting the self-generating tempo of the isolated, non-listening ego. This acoustic cut is messy and unstable in Nancy, as it is in Thoreau's Cut Bank, a vibratory resonance that loosens fixed forms and opens the listening subject to a cross-pressured, polyrhythmic world (an idea Kerouac will develop in relation to jazz as we'll see). Unlike the visual, which favors clean lines and tends toward the mimetic, the sonorous favors undulating lines and tends toward the "methexic" (i.e., having to do with sharing or mixing).[62] In this sense the sonorous also tends toward the "sacrificial," toward the transformation of the isolated ego, as Manu emphasizes: "Sitting (on sacrificial grass)," the Brahmin relinquishes his egocentrism, his skin-encapsulated *ahamkāra*, by allowing the holy syllable to tune him to the rhythms of the world, not once but continually. In *Manu*, the divine syllable is as far down as we can go, the world's "sound bottom," as Thoreau would say. But Nancy wonders if even that's far enough. Or if in fact there's a murmur below the syllable, an undifferentiated sound prior to language or time, which is the sound of "a vanishing of difference" for Nancy, like the *il y a* of Emmanuel Levinas: the toneless hum of impersonal existence.[63]

From the beginning of his career, Thoreau marked these auditory cuts as sacred, so that the theology of divine sound in the Hindu scriptures confirmed what he had experienced first-hand in nature, which is the basic test of religious knowledge in *Walden*: Does it move the needle on the Realometer? When Thoreau develops these ideas in "Sounds," he'll stress the difference between listening and understanding (where "listening" is prior and preconceptual). And he'll conduct a series of acoustic experiments designed to recover what he calls "original sound" (132)—the rhythmic vibration of baying dogs and rumbling wagons *before* his mind recognized and categorized the sounds as distinct entities, that is, before the sounds had meaning. These sound experiments resemble the contemplative unknowing of the ice mirrors, but this time Thoreau is not trying to "un-see" a socially constructed self-image but rather to "un-hear" a socially constructed soundscape, one built up from deeply ingrained preferences and prejudices.[64]

Thoreau often practices this deep listening with birdsong, as when he tries to hear the click of larynx bones in a whippoorwill's throat, which he calls "that singular buzzing sound" at the end of each note (133). This is birdsong after it stops being "birdsong," a body murmur below the music. And he tries a similar experiment with the Concord church bells, which from a sufficient distance don't sound like church bells but something more basic than that: "a certain vibratory hum" (132). This is church music with both the "church" and the "music" filtered out, as if strained through a fine natural mesh of pine needles and air: "a melody which the air had strained" (132). Through this straining, Thoreau sought to release his imagination from the traditional music of Protestant New England and experience sacred rhythms not fully possessed by any religious heritage. Sometimes Thoreau thinks of that original vibration as a universal language, "the language which all things and events speak without metaphor" (119). And sometimes he thinks of it as a universal music, "a vibration of the universal lyre" (132). But either way, he sought to tune himself to those rhythms like a telegraph wire strung tight as a fiddle string and singing in the wind.

This exquisite self-tuning is on full display in the final version of the Cut Bank passage, which like the church-bell scene in "Sounds" is spiritual but not doctrinal, not necessarily connected to any particular faith tradition. The featured word in that scene, *lobe*, has sacred associations in Hinduism: it means "tongue" in the *Taittiriya Upanishad*, for instance, as it vibrates in religious chant.[65] And the *Chandogya Upanishad* makes the same association between "syllable" and "leaves" that Thoreau does.[66] But *leaf* and *lobe* are less recognizably religious than *logos*, *Om*, or *aksara*—which allowed Thoreau to evoke the spiritual possibilities of his scene playfully or non-coercively, in the spirit of its sporting God. It's not necessary to read the sandbank passage as a distinctly Hindu (rather than Hellenic, Christian, transcendental, or Zoroastrian) meditation. Indeed, it's not necessary to read the sandbank passage as religious at all. In fact, most commentary on the scene sets religious questions to the side in order to consider Thoreau's libidinal regression and infantile "orality" (in the psycho-biographical criticism). Or to explore his adaptations of key texts in botany (Linnaeus' *Philosophia Botanica*); anatomy (James John Garth Wilkinson's *The Human Body and Its Connection with Man*); linguistic theory (Charles Kraitsir's *Glossology*); or romantic form (Goethe's *Metamorphosis of Plants*).[67] And yet Thoreau's unusually intense and muscular performance of the word, *lobe*, resembles the rendering of the divine syllable in Hindu chant:

> When I see on the one side the inert bank,—for the sun acts on one side first,— and on the other this luxuriant foliage, the creation of an hour, I am affected as if in a peculiar sense I stood in the laboratory of the Artist who made the world and me,—had come to where he was still at work, sporting on this bank, and with excess of energy strewing his fresh designs about. I feel as if I were nearer to the vitals of the globe, for this sandy overflow is something such a foliaceous mass

as the vitals of the animal body. You find thus in the very sands an anticipation of the vegetable leaf. . . . *Internally*, whether in the globe or animal body, it is a moist thick *lobe*, a word especially applicable to the liver and lungs and the *leaves* of fat, (λείβω, *labor*, lapsus, to flow or slip downward, a lapsing; λοβος, *globus*, lobe, globe; also lap, flap, and many other words,) *externally* a dry thin *leaf*, even as the *f* and *v* are a pressed and dried *b*. The radicals of *lobe* are *lb*, the soft mass of the *b* (single lobed, or B, double lobed,) with the liquid *l* behind it pressing it forward. In globe, *glb*, the guttural *g* adds to the meaning the capacity of the throat. The feathers and wings of birds are still drier and thinner leaves. Thus, also, you pass from the lumpish grub in the earth to the airy and fluttering butterfly. (331–32)

I've quoted two passages from a much larger scene to accent the way Thoreau internalizes sacred sound, takes it into his body. Thoreau makes that change vivid by balancing the visual focus of the first sentence, *When I see*, with the subjective emphasis of the second, *I feel*. The fulcrum of that pivot is *Walden*'s sporting God, whose *līlā*-play introduces the possibilities of the subjunctive (I am affected *as if*; I feel *as if*), and whose creativity converts a place so banal Thoreau barely noticed it for years into a site of extraordinary transformation. That transformation is continuous (the Artist is still creating); conciliatory (overcoming the alienation between "world" and "self"); sonorous (taking place in a reverberating and rhythmic soundscape); and slippery (with respect to monolithic, hegemonic, or exclusively American frames of reference). One part of the "global" emphasis of the sandbank scene is the multicultural range of its allusions, as Thoreau's critics and biographers have demonstrated. If the performance of a seed syllable *sounds* Hindu, the passage nonetheless *looks* Hellenic, one source of Thoreau's thinking about spiritual attunement. In Heraclitus and Plato, for instance, ultimate reality is dynamic and rhythmic, an ordered flow (the Greek root of rhythm, ῥέω, means, *to flow*). We experience that rhythm not only in abstract thought, as in philosophy and mathematics, but also in embodied participation, like the child playing draughts in Heraclitus or the dancing philosopher in Plato's *Laws*.

In both cases, Hellenic and Hindu, what matters is responsive participation. Thus, Thoreau abandons his initial stance of passive spectatorship, looking down at sand forms taking shape at his feet, in favor of intimate involvement. Moreover, he draws us in too, until we find ourselves *inside* the wet cave of his mouth, a resonating chamber issuing pulse after pulse of *glbs, lbs, fs*, and *vs*. Thoreau has been preparing us for this moment by modeling his complex reaction to the *hums, clicks, buzzes,* and *tr-r-r-oonks* washing over him at the pond. The cry of a screech owl, for instance, sets off a whole chain of feelings and associations for Thoreau (to hymns, threnodies, suicidal lovers, mourning women, night-walking ghosts) that are meaningful but nonverbal and nonexclusive: lovers, ghosts, witches, and owls all mixed together like the hybrid product pooling at his feet. Thoreau favors and enters into that methexic messiness, which overtops conceptual containers and remains elusive or "slippery." As a noun, *labor, laboris*, means work or toil, as William Gleason points out, but as a verb, *labor, labi, lapsus sum*, means to glide, skate, play, slip, or fall away.[68]

To enact that sacred play, Thoreau's language glides in and out of different linguistic sites: a Greek word (λείβω); a Latin word (*labor*); a set of associated words in English (*lap, flap*); even parts of words (the *glb*s and *lb*s)—as if what matters isn't conceptual stability but looseness, slipperiness, word play, and the ability to adopt and discard different acoustic and linguistic categories as the experience unfolds in real time. The meaning of the sandbank is this unfolding, the generative friction of different things flowing with and into one another: sand and leaves, coral and lichen, Greek and English, Hindu and Hellenic. In the color of water scene, Thoreau helps us see what this kind of process-meaning might look like: a rapid-fire progression of color tones experienced one after another. Here, he explores what that process-meaning might sound like: a multicultural polyglot of words and syllables issuing from the bank on the one side and from his own mouth on the other.

I find it difficult to read the second half of the sandbank passage silently. Indeed when Thoreau mentions the physical sensations involved in pronouncing the word *lobe*—"The radicals of *lobe* are *lb*, the soft mass of the *b* (single lobed, or B, double lobed) with the liquid *l* behind it pressing it forward"—he invites us to *feel* as well as *see* the letters and so internalize the syllable as a physical experience. With the word *globe*, that experience begins with an in-drawn breath (the lungs); then moves to the back of the throat (the guttural *g*); then to the rounded palate (the long *o*); and finally to the closed lips of the explosive *b* and the expelled breath. This is the basic inside-out rhythm of Hindu chant, which slows and elongates the seed syllable in a process Manu calls "milking" the sound, so that we experience each component in different parts of the body (*a, u, m*) before allowing the vibration to pass back into the world. Thoreau makes that emancipatory send-off especially vivid by allowing the syllable to pass from the *l*s and *b*s inside his mouth to the wings of birds and butterflies in the woods, returning the vibration to the world. This emancipation frees the syllable from Thoreau (he doesn't create or control it). But it also frees the syllable from human language altogether, making it global and transhuman, as in the Hindu scriptures.

This butterfly effect is present all through the sandbank passage, where nothing exists in isolation, as a little world all to itself. Sometimes Thoreau uses visual "rhymes" to suggest the interrelationships: lichens, coral, brains, all resemble one another. And sometimes he uses acoustic echoes to the same effect, creating sound puns and slant rhymes to help us hear the interconnection. Thoreau doesn't use Bateson's phrase "ecology of mind" to name these interlocking systems (although he's moving in that direction by placing brains next to coral, as if natural ecologies were capable of intelligent and self-regulating thought, as Bateson argued). While this global or ecological view is not necessarily religious, Thoreau leaves that possibility open by placing his most explicit reference to the *līlā* literature in the middle of this scene, the *Harivaṃśa*'s sporting God, and by practicing another form of contemplative *solvo*, this time in his treatment of language. Like the sound experiment with the church bells, which turns a hymn into a hum, Thoreau decomposes the word "globe," milking it down to the consonants (*glb, lb, l, b*), to put us in the same acoustic register as the "low murmuring sound" of the *Sáma Veda* or the vibratory "hum" of the telegraph pole. Thoreau's attention to radical sound at the sandbank, "the radicals of *lobe* are *lb*," thus shapes a view of transformation near to the heart of his Hindu sources but equally close to what he actually observed in nature, as Boudreau has argued: "The conversion of lobe into leaf that occurs in nature finds its parallel in a hypothetical conversion of the word *lobe* into the word *leaf*. When these two words are considered as stages of a continuum of oral expression—'lobe' gliding to 'leaf'—the original *l* is a radical, permanent letter, abiding through the change."[69] This glide or "give" in ordinary perception is not restricted to the sandbank, however. Boudreau points out that when Thoreau observes the sun-lit hawk later in the chapter—"it sported with proud reliance in the fields of air; mounting again and again with its strange chuckle" (343)—he invites us to hear the wild laughter of the Walden loon, now playing overhead, and to sense the sporting presence of Walden's God, neighboring us the whole time.

God's sport is sonorous, methexic, transhuman, and still evolving—which suggests a powerful point of convergence in the sound theologies of several religious traditions. Moreover, as hum, chant, music, and laughter, sacred sound poses an alternative to what Thoreau saw as the muteness of religious despair, his culture's quiet desperation. Divine vibration rattles that quietly desperate self out of its *ahamkāra*, its egocentric isolation, allowing it to resume its rightful place in a larger community of living creatures. And if there's a kind of kenosis in such play, as Panikkar suggests, it's not that Thoreau dissolves into nothing, bequeathing himself to the dirt, but that he dissolves into his true stature, his harmonized proportion, tuned precisely to the sacred music of the pond.

THE SECRET LOVE OF GOD

It seems right that there's a ludic God in the middle of all this, not because religious experience is trivial but because it contradicts the common sense—as desert saints and barefoot prophets have always done. Jeremiah wore a wooden yoke around his neck like an ox. St. Simeon Salus tied a dead dog to his leg. The Hindu saint Chaitanya ate dirt, danced himself into frenzies, and seemed to most people like the town drunk. Jesus was said to be "beside himself" by the religious authorities of his culture (Mark 3:21)— beside himself without Thoreau's mental health disclaimer: "With thinking we may be beside ourselves in a sane sense" (145). Stretching out on an ice sheet to contemplate air bubbles or spending the day chasing a loon (and not trying to kill it) or chanting *lobe, lobe, lobe* at the foot of a melting snowbank are not the signs of Thoreau's narcissistic self-indulgence but the ecstatic witness of a religious reformer withdrawing from the culturally obvious.[70] Thoreau didn't invent the terms of that critique, which exist in the religious folklore of many cultures, but he keeps the old saints and fools offstage in *Walden* in order to present his religious experience indirectly, almost secretly, not in overtly religious language but in everyday scenes so close at hand it seems strange to call them sacred.

Let me close, then, by returning to Weil's notion of implicit religion as a way of understanding what Thoreau calls holy play in his *Journal* but keeps largely under wraps in *Walden*, hinting at things he cherishes but does not express outright, as he warns us about from the start: "There are more secrets in my trade than in most men's" (16). If by trade, Thoreau means his spiritual business, his commerce with the Celestial Empire, then *Walden* may indeed suggest an instance of what Weil terms a secret love of God—a love of God that doesn't look like "the love of God" and doesn't name or think of itself that way. This love emerges, Weil argues, whenever the soul withdraws from relations of domination and force and allows the other to emerge not as a "thing" to be used but as an independent presence in its own right, that is, as a "neighbor," the same word Thoreau uses. Like Thoreau, Weil describes this withdrawal as a form of kenotic unselving. Moreover, she imagines spiritual exercises that train the soul to this effacement, but which have nothing to do with organized religion. Weil doesn't mention ice mirrors, loon games, or melting sandbanks, of course, but her example of implicit spirituality is just as surprising. Weil was interested in how certain kinds of *schoolwork* achieve this result, especially working at math problems that won't budge or spending half a day translating a passage of Greek that balks the student's every effort and just stays *Greek*. Such schoolwork rehearses habits of playful attention, Weil believed, an ability to loosen rigid frames and hover lightly over the material, letting the answer come when it chooses to come rather than forcing it to do our will. And the not forcing part is incredibly valuable for people of faith, precisely because it teaches us to receive our experience as a gift, an act of unmerited grace. Thus, for Weil, spiritual attention consists of "suspending our thought, leaving it detached, empty, and ready." Spiritual attention means "waiting, not seeking anything, but ready to receive in its naked truth the object that is to penetrate it."[71] The important thing about school exercises is that the solution to the math problem seems to come when we're *not* looking at it directly, the way some kinds of stars only appear when we see them out of the corners of our eyes. This suggests to Weil that some people pray without *trying* to pray. That is, they receive their lives as a gift, as an act of grace, without thinking of that reverence as esoteric or other-worldly or even necessarily religious.

Thoreau, it seems to me, was that sort of person. Weil's not trying to be sly or manipulative about this, renaming the math problem "religious" and so roping in all sorts of unsuspecting "believers" (who were really just trying to get their homework done). But both Thoreau and Weil share a sense that head-on religion has its dangers and that pursuing God directly leads to any number of ego traps and dogmatic confusions that could just as well be avoided by looking at God the way we see those stars, not face to face but from the side, and then throwing ourselves into a religious vocation by throwing ourselves into the secular duties close at hand: loving our day jobs, loving our schoolwork. Which for Thoreau meant loving the pond heart and soul and loving his brute neighbors heart and soul, even when they refuse to acknowledge that love and make him rest on his oars and wait, as the loon did. And that may be a good place to leave Thoreau for now. For this is the stance of spiritual readiness in *Walden*, the sacred play of a religious writer who sought to receive the gift of life in all its forms, in every alphabet, and who loved his wild God extravagantly and in secret.

NOTES

1. Gregory Bateson, *Steps to an Ecology of Mind* (1972; repr. Chicago: University of Chicago Press, 2000), 192, 30.

2. On attunement in Bateson, see Edmond Wright, "Gregory Bateson: Epistemology, Language, Play and the Double Bind," *Anthropoetics* 14, no. 1 (Summer 2008), http://anthropoetics.ucla.edu/ap1401/1401wright/.html (accessed May 12, 2018).

3. Henry David Thoreau, *A Week on the Concord and Merrimack Rivers*, ed. H. Daniel Peck (New York: Penguin, 1998), 52; and Henry D. Thoreau, *The Journal of Henry D. Thoreau*, gen. ed. John C. Broderick, vol. 1 (Princeton: Princeton University Press, 1981), 153.

4. Thoreau, *Journal*, 1:159; and "Walking," in *Walden and Other Writings of Henry David Thoreau*, ed. Brooks Atkinson (New York: Modern Library, 1992), 662.

5. Thoreau, *Journal*, 1:206.

6. One of Thoreau's most explicit formulations of this idea is also in "Walking": "My desire for knowledge is intermittent; but my desire to bathe my head in atmospheres unknown to my feet is perennial and constant. The highest that we can attain

to is not Knowledge, but Sympathy with Intelligence. I do not know that this higher knowledge amounts to anything more definite than a novel and grand surprise on a sudden revelation of the insufficiency of all that we called Knowledge before,—a discovery that there are more things in heaven and earth than are dreamed of in our philosophy." Thoreau, "Walking," 657.

7. Annie Dillard, "Walden Pond and Thoreau" (master's thesis, Hollins College, 1968), 18; and *Pilgrim at Tinker Creek* (1974; repr. New York: HarperPerennial, 2007), 79.

8. Henry D. Thoreau, *Walden*, ed. Jeffrey S. Cramer (New Haven: Yale University Press, 2006), 105, 307. Subsequent references to *Walden* will refer to this edition and be cited in the text by page number.

9. Henry David Thoreau, *Letters to a Spiritual Seeker*, ed. Bradley P. Dean (New York: Norton, 2004), 16.

10. Thoreau, *Journal*, 1:50.

11. Matt. 10:29.

12. Gary Snyder, "Ripples on the Surface," in *No Nature: New and Selected Poems* (New York: Pantheon, 1992), 381.

13. In stressing the importance of the *līlā* literature for Thoreau's thinking about religious play here, let me also note that his reading about play extended well beyond the Hindu scriptures and included works like Richard Chenevix Trench's *On the Study of Words* (1851); Victor Cousin's *Introduction to the History of Philosophy* (1832); Friedrich Schlegel's *Lectures on the History of Literature* (1818); Horace Bushnell's *Work and Play* (1848) and *God in Christ* (1849); and James John Garth Wilkinson's *The Human Body and Its Connection with Man* (1851). On this, see Michael West, "Scatology and Eschatology: The Heroic Dimensions of Thoreau's Wordplay," *PMLA* 89, no. 5 (October 1974): 1043–64.

14. *The Bhagavad Gita*, trans. Eknath Easwaran (Tomales, CA: Nilgiri Press, 1985, 2007), 106–7.

15. Norvin Hein, "Līlā," in *The Gods at Play: Līlā in South Asia*, ed. William S. Sax (New York: Oxford University Press, 1995), 19.

16. On the etymology of *līlā* and its denotative range, see Ananda K. Coomaraswamy's essays, "Līlā," *Journal of the American Oriental Society* 61, no. 2 (June 1941): 98–101; and "Play and Seriousness," *The Journal of Philosophy* 39, no. 20 (September 24, 1942): 550–52. See also Johan Huizinga, *Homo Ludens: A Study of the Play-Element in Culture* (1950; repr. Mansfield Centre, CT: Martino Publishing, 2014), 32. For a more comprehensive discussion of *līlā* in Hindu religious practice, see David R. Kinsley, *The Divine Player: A Study of Kṛṣṇa Līlā* (Delhi: Motilal Banarsidass, 1979), and William S. Sax, ed., *The Gods at Play*.

17. *The Laws of Manu*, trans. Wendy Doniger with Brian K. Smith (New York: Penguin, 1991), 12. For Thoreau's comments on *Manu*, see *Journal*, 1:173–74, 178, 311–12; and *A Week*, 118–20. For a fuller discussion of Thoreau's interest in Asian thought, see Arthur Christy, *The Orient in American Transcendentalism: A Study of Emerson, Thoreau, and Alcott* (1932; repr. New York: Octagon Books, 1972); Carl T. Jackson, *The Oriental Religions and American Thought: Nineteenth-Century Explorations* (Westport, CT: Greenwood Press, 1981); Arthur Versluis, *American Transcendentalism and Asian Religions* (New York: Oxford University Press, 1993);

David Scott, "Rewalking Thoreau and Asia: 'Light from the East' for 'A Very Yankee Sort of Oriental.'" *Philosophy East and West* 57, no. 1 (January 2007): 14–39; Robert Kuhn McGregor, "Henry David Thoreau: The Asian Thread," in *Thoreau's Importance for Philosophy*, ed. Rick Anthony Furtak, Jonathan Ellsworth, and James D. Reid (New York: Fordham University Press, 2012), 201–17; and Alan D. Hodder, "'Ex Oriente Lux': Thoreau's Ecstasies and the Hindu Texts," *Harvard Theological Review* 86, no. 4 (October 1993): 403–38; his "Concord Orientalism, Thoreauvian Autobiography, and the Artist of Kouroo," in *Transient and Permanent: The Transcendentalist Movement and Its Contexts*, ed. Charles Capper and Conrad Edick Wright (Boston: Massachusetts Historical Society, 1999), 190–228; his further development of these ideas in *Thoreau's Ecstatic Witness* (New Haven: Yale University Press, 2001), 174–217; and his later essay "In the Nick of Time: Thoreau's 'Present' Experiment as a Colloquy of East and West," *Religion and the Arts* 9, nos. 3–4 (Sept. 2005): 235–57.

18. Norvin Hein, "A Revolution in Kṛṣṇaism: The Cult of Gopāla," *History of Religions* 25, no. 4 (May 1986): 296.

19. Thoreau, *A Week*, 112–13.

20. On this, see Sax, "Introduction," *The Gods at Play*, 6–7; and Hein, "A Revolution in Kṛṣṇaism"; and his "*Līlā*," in *The Gods at Play*, 15–16.

21. *Harivamsha*, trans. Manmatha Nath Dutt (Calcutta: Elysium Press, 1897), 744. The tropes, *sporting by the waters* or *sporting on the bank*, occur in dozens of stories in the *Harivaṃśa*. It applies to the *līlā*-sport of Krishna's play but also to any number of Hindu gods, kings, and heroes, including Karkotaka, Haryashura, Baladeva, and the sons of Vasudera. Thoreau's first reference to divine play in the melting sandbank occurs not in the manuscript version of *Walden* (1846–47) but in a journal entry in the spring of 1848: "Here is an artist at work—as it were not at work but a-playing designing" (*Journal*, 2:383). In a later revision, Thoreau changed the artist to a God: "Here is that God who is reputed to have built this world 6000 years ago still at his work,—freshly this spring day sporting on this bank." Thoreau, "Selected Later Revisions," *Journal*, 2:577. By capitalizing the word "Artist" in the final version, "the Artist . . . sporting on this bank," Thoreau drew on both sets of associations while maintaining the original phrasing of the *Harivaṃśa*.

22. *The Vishnu Purāna* is a major compendium of Hindu mythology, with chapters on cosmogony, cosmic cycles, Vishnu and his avatars, and the genealogy of gods and kings. In January 1850, Thoreau read the English translation by H. H. Wilson, published through the Asiatic Society of Bengal, and then began working his way back through earlier Vedic literature, including John Stevenson's 1842 translation of the *Sáma Veda*, a work the *Vishnu Purāna* cites in its account of cosmic creation through sound.

23. *The Vishnu Purāna: A System of Hindu Mythology and Tradition*, trans. H. H. Wilson (1840; repr. Calcutta: Punthi Pustak, 1972), 8, 9.

24. Kinsley, *The Divine Player*, 7; *The Vishnu Purāna*, 396.

25. Thoreau, *Journal*, 4:92.

26. Thoreau, *A Week*, 122.

27. Raimon Panikkar, *The Rhythm of Being: The Unbroken Trinity* (Maryknoll, NY: Orbis, 2013), 49.

28. Panikkar, *The Rhythm of Being*, 49.

29. Robert B. Ray, *Walden x 40: Essays on Thoreau* (Bloomington: Indiana University Press, 2012), 87. On Augustinian attunement, see Nathan Crawford, *Theology as Improvisation: A Study in the Musical Nature of Theological Thinking* (Leiden: Brill, 2013), 159–92. On attunement in Puritan theology and autobiography, see Elisa New, *New England Beyond Criticism: In Defense of America's First Literature* (Chichester, West Sussex: Wiley Blackwell, 2014), 23–46. On Hindu theologies of play and attunement, see Panikkar, *The Rhythm of Being*, 34–50; Kinsley, *The Divine Player*; and Sax, *The Gods at Play*.

30. Thoreau, *Journal*, 5:458.

31. Maria Thoreau to unknown correspondent, September 7, 1848, Thoreau Society Archives, Henley Library; quoted in Laura Dassow Walls, *Henry David Thoreau: A Life* (Chicago: University of Chicago Press, 2017), 259.

32. Henry David Thoreau, *The Writings of Henry David Thoreau*, vol. 6 (Boston, 1906), 9; quoted in Walter Harding, *The Days of Henry Thoreau: A Biography*, 2nd ed. (New York: Dover, 1982), 50.

33. The Hawthorne passages are from F. B. Sanborn, *Hawthorne and His Friends* (Cedar Rapids, IA: Torch Press, 1908), 28 and the Nathaniel Hawthorne Manuscripts in the New York Public Library; all are quoted in Harding, *The Days of Henry Thoreau*, 237, 243.

34. Thoreau, *A Week*, 54, 52.

35. Thoreau, *A Week*, 57.

36. Joseph J. Moldenhauer, "The Extra-Vagant Maneuver: Paradox in *Walden*," in *Critical Essays on Henry David Thoreau's Walden*, ed. Joel Myerson (Boston: G. K. Hall, 1988), 96–106; Frederick Garber, *Thoreau's Redemptive Imagination* (New York: NYU Press, 1977), 30; Robert Milder, *Reimagining Thoreau* (Cambridge: Cambridge University Press, 1995), xii; and James McIntosh, *Thoreau as Romantic Naturalist: His Shifting Stance Toward Nature* (Ithaca: Cornell University Press, 1974).

37. Perry Miller, *Consciousness in Concord: The Text of Thoreau's Hitherto "Lost Journal" (1840–1841) Together with Notes and a Commentary* (Boston: Houghton Mifflin, 1958); Vincent Buranelli, "The Case Against Thoreau," *Ethics* 76, no. 4 (1957): 257–68; Richard Bridgman, *Dark Thoreau* (Lincoln: University of Nebraska Press, 1982); Philip Abbott, "Henry David Thoreau, the State of Nature, and the Redemption of Liberalism," *Journal of Politics* 47, no. 1 (1985): 182–208.

38. Thoreau, *Journal*, 1:428, 122.

39. Emily Dickinson, *The Letters of Emily Dickinson*, ed. Thomas H. Johnson, vol. 3 (Cambridge: Harvard University Press, 1958), 728.

40. Markus Poetzsch, "Sounding Walden Pond: The Depths and 'Double Shadows' of Thoreau's Autobiographical Symbol," *American Transcendental Quarterly* 22, no. 2 (June 2008): 390, 393.

41. As Thoreau writes in *Walden*, "Not till we are lost, in other words, not till we have lost the world, do we begin to find ourselves, and realize where we are and the infinite extent of our relations" (187). I'll develop Emily Dickinson's explorations of liberating bewilderment as a feature of play in chapter 2.

42. Garber, *Thoreau's Redemptive Imagination*, 26.

43. Thoreau, *A Week*, 53.

44. Thoreau, *A Week*, 53.

45. William E. Connolly, *Identity/Difference: Democratic Negotiations of Political Paradox* (Ithaca: Cornell University Press, 1991), 155.

46. Simone Weil, *Waiting for God*, trans. Emma Craufurd (1951; repr. New York: HarperPerennial, 2009), 83.

47. On this, see Thoreau's 1850 letter to Harrison Blake: "Let God alone if need be. Methinks, if I loved him more, I should keep him,—I should keep myself rather,—at a more respectful distance. It is not when I am going to meet him, but when I am just turning away and leaving him alone, that I discover that God is." Thoreau, *Letters to a Spiritual Seeker*, 53.

48. Panikkar, *The Rhythm of Being*, 49. For a similar argument about attunement and humility, see Paul K. Moser, *The Elusive God: Reorienting Religious Epistemology* (New York: Cambridge University Press, 2008), 113–23.

49. Gilles Deleuze, *Difference and Repetition*, trans. Paul Patton (New York: Columbia University Press, 1994), 139. J. Heath Atchley develops the implication of Deleuze's notion that philosophical thought emerges through encounter rather than through recognition. See his *Encountering the Secular: Philosophical Endeavors in Religion and Culture* (Charlottesville: University of Virginia Press, 2009).

50. On this, see John A. McClure, *Partial Faiths: Postsecular Fiction in the Age of Pynchon and Morrison* (Athens: University of Georgia Press, 2007), 14–15.

51. Thoreau, *Journal*, 1:205.

52. Gordon V. Boudreau, *The Roots of "Walden" and the Tree of Life* (Nashville: Vanderbilt University Press, 1990), 136–38.

53. Thoreau, *Journal*, 4:89–90.

54. Panikkar, *The Rhythm of Being*, 36. I emphasize these scenes of embodied attunement to answer a common critique of spiritualties based on play: that they're speculative, theoretical, disembodied, or gnostic. "Surprisingly, play theology is not very body-conscious," Bjorn Krondorfer argues in this vein; rather, it treats play as "a disembodied construct to enhance theological thinking." Such thinking "idealizes the play mode," he continues, "dichotomizes it into categories of good and bad, and presents the nature of play as harmless and harmonious." Thoreau does stress the relationship between play and harmonious attunement in *Walden*, but that attunement comes at a considerable risk, the epistemological security of the religious self. See Bjorn Krondorfer, "Play Theology as a Discourse of Disguise," *Journal of Literature and Theology* 7, no. 4 (December 1993): 366. For a philosophical account of embodied attunement, see Shigenori Nagatomo, *Attunement through the Body* (Albany: SUNY Press, 1992).

55. *The Vishnu Purāna*, 27.

56. *The Vishnu Purāna*, 15.

57. *The Laws of Manu*, 25–26. See also Manu's discussion of the threefold Veda, 276–77.

58. Guy L. Beck distinguishes between sacred sound in Hindu theology and the Word of God in Christianity somewhat differently: "Whereas in Hinduism language and sacred sound are intimately bound up with the divine, in Christianity any special

kind of sacred language or sacred sound is ultimately suspect, since only the person of Jesus Christ is defined precisely as the Word of God." See his *Sonic Theology: Hinduism and Sacred Sound* (Columbia: University of South Carolina Press, 1993), 15.

59. Walt Whitman, *Walt Whitman: Complete Poetry and Collected Prose*, ed. Justin Kaplan (New York: Literary Classics of the United States, 1982), 30.

60. Thoreau, *Journal*, 1:277.

61. Jean-Luc Nancy, *Listening*, trans. Charlotte Mandell (New York: Fordham University Press, 2007), 8, 27.

62. Nancy, *Listening*, 10.

63. Nancy, *Listening*, 25.

64. For a more complete discussion of the importance of sound to Thoreau's inner life, see Sherman Paul, "The Wise Silence: Sound as the Agency of Correspondence in Thoreau," *New England Quarterly* 22, no. 4 (December 1949): 511–27; and his *The Shores of America: Thoreau's Inward Exploration* (New York: Russell and Russell, 1958), 64–68; Kenneth W. Rhoads, "Thoreau: The Ear and the Music," *American Literature* 46, no. 3 (November 1974): 313–28; and Hodder, *Thoreau's Ecstatic Witness*, 70–101. Typically, Thoreau's sound experiments are associated with Western theories of acoustic rapture and musical harmony (in Plato, Pythagoras, Sir Thomas Browne, and Wordsworth). But Paul and Hodder also stress the influence of South Asian literature on Thoreau's thinking about spirituality and sound. See especially Paul, *The Shores of America*, 70–71; and Hodder, 185–86.

65. *The Upanishads*, trans. Eknath Easwaran (Tomales, CA: Nilgiri Press, 2007), 248.

66. See Beck, *Sonic Theology*, 42.

67. For a detailed casebook of academic commentary on the sandbank passage through the 1980s, see Boudreau, *The Roots of Walden*, 117–34.

68. William A. Gleason, *The Leisure Ethic: Work and Play in American Literature, 1840–1940* (Stanford: Stanford University Press, 1999), 44. Ananda K. Coomaraswamy makes a similar argument about the *līlā* literature: "And so extremes meet, work becoming play, and play work." See his "Līlā," 99.

69. Boudreau, *The Roots of Walden*, 111.

70. This in fact is the fundamental "quasi-quality" of the common sense for Clifford Geertz: its "naturalness," its "air of of-courseness": "Common sense represents matters—that is, certain matters and not others—as being what they are in the simple nature of the case. An air of 'of-courseness,' a sense of 'it figures' is cast over things—again, some selected, underscored things. They are depicted as inherent in the situation, intrinsic aspects of reality, the way things go." See his "Common Sense as a Cultural System," 1975; repr. *The Antioch Review* 67, no. 4 (Fall 2009): 782.

71. Weil, *Waiting for God*, 62.

Chapter 2

Play and Possibility
Emily Dickinson's Theology of Perhaps

THE ACRES OF PERHAPS

Play can mean so many different things to Emily Dickinson that it's tempting to see it not as a category or activity but more like a fugitive trace or carnivalistic negation, as Victor Turner said about play.[1] Dickinsonian play is notoriously hard to pin down. It's associated with childhood on the one hand ("We play at Paste") and death on the other ("She lay as if at play").[2] It can be nostalgic one moment ("Let Us play Yesterday" Fr754) and spooky the next ("Untarnished by the Sepulchre, / The Mouldering Playmate comes" Fr337). At various points, Dickinson imagines play as *liberating* ("God permits industrious Angels - / Afternoons - to play " Fr245); *sacred* ("Meek at whose everlasting feet / A myriad Daisy play" Fr108); *secular* ("God . . . cannot bear to see / That we had rather not with Him / But with each other play" Fr1752); *erotic* ("Hid, Lip, for Thee - / Play it were a Humming Bird - / And just sipped - me" Fr380); and profoundly *cruel* (as when God plays with a dying Moses Fr521). Some of Dickinson's players maintain social conventions ("I play at Riches - to appease" Fr856), while others carnivalize those conventions, like one of Thomas Merton's holy fools ("God be with the Clown" Fr1356). Play is what fops and clowns do and so it has low status. And yet play is what God and the angels do and so it has high status. All of which raises questions like, what is Dickinsonian play, exactly? And what sort of religious wisdom does it offer? If play is more like a mood than an activity, more like "playfulness" than the strategies and mindset of a particular game, then what would it mean to live and think in a light-handed, play-begotten mood? And how would that shape our relationship with God?

Instead of a definition, let me offer in effect two scenarios: when we enter a liminal zone where things are "more" than themselves—more figurative than literal, more like a poem than a declaration of fact—then our thought is playful, subjunctive, provisional, and "weak" (or weak-bold, as Turner said about play, "an infantine audacity in the face of the strong").[3] When we allow indicative realities to claim the whole discursive field, collapsing the future into the present as its predictive destiny or subordinating the possible to the actual as its superior form, then we're not playing anymore. Dickinson reserves the designation *prose* for that indicative landscape and *poetry* for the "more numerous" zone of the possible:

I dwell in Possibility –
A fairer House than Prose –
More numerous of Windows –
Superior – for Doors – (Fr466)

Later theorists will imagine play's "more" in bio-mechanical terms, thinking of play as a steam vent for excess energy, which cultures can turn to their advantage, designing games that rehearse and strengthen social norms (this was Huizinga's position). Dickinsonian play is closer to Turner's view: a critique of "presentness" and an enemy of the status quo.[4] Play's surplus reveals counter-environments or counter-myths that undermine existing legitimacies (by making them seem funny or ludicrous), even as it generates a storehouse of future possibilities, dreams, and fantasies that don't exist and perhaps can't exist, or at least can't exist in the way things are now (which makes the "now" seem less final). Play doesn't compete with indicative realities, it's too weak for that, but it compels the indicative to draw its boundaries, to say what it is and what it's not, which allows a discursive space of contingency, figurality, and conjecture to appear, what Dickinson calls "the Acres of Perhaps" (Fr725).

In *The Insistence of God*, John Caputo shows how "a theology of perhaps" quietly answers onto-theologies of sovereignty and power by offering a different, weaker, and more eschatological view of God.[5] For Caputo, whatever we might say about God is framed by the subjunctive: perhaps this is God or suppose this is God or act as if this were God (which it *isn't*). With this, we enter the same present-but-absent milieu the play theorists study, interacting with something that both *is* and *is not* itself, like Bateson's bite or Derrida's track, a sign that's also "more" than itself, because it bears the mark of its own negation, the trace of what it does not mean.

For Caputo, this surplus has less to do with the creative extravagance of a gifting God, as in Paul Ricœur and Stephen H. Webb, and more to do with the futural horizon of what we can't see coming, an event that's always arriving but never revealed (and so never fully itself). "Perhaps" doesn't mean agnostic indecision for Caputo but interpretive vulnerability and religious risk, our openness to the unforeseen. This is how Derrida puts it in a quote Caputo uses at the beginning of *The Insistence of God*:

> "Perhaps"—one must *(il faut)* always say *perhaps* for God. There is a future for God and there is no God except to the degree that some event is possible which, as event, exceeds calculation, rules, program, anticipations, and so forth. God, as the experience of absolute alterity, is unpresentable, but God is the chance of the event and the condition of history.[6]

The structural openness of Derrida's *perhaps* prevents time from collapsing in on itself and becoming an eternal present, a nonfuture or hopeless future Annie Dillard calls the fixed. Instead, a theology of perhaps foregrounds a God of movement and process, possibilizing the present from out of the future and undermining the prestige (or terror) of the status quo. Like the category paradoxes the play theorists study, a God of the possible is both here and not here, both imminent and transcendent, because still arriving from a future we can't know. The temporal possibilities of the *to come* enliven a settled present with "the chance of the event," creating an open-ended game of faith.

Dickinson anticipates this idea by creating a poetic voice that speaks "against" or "away from" whatever she just said (*apo phasis*), both affirming and denying at the same time, sometimes in the same breath: "that Diviner thing / Disclosed to be denied" (Fr1291). What prompts Dickinson's apophatic unsaying is not the impossible remoteness of divine alterity, a God we can't reach with words, but the fact that divine revelation occurs in time, undermining secure possession with "that Diviner thing" now appearing. And then undermining *that* new thing as well. Thus, whatever she might say about God is temporary, subjunctive, playful—good for the moment perhaps but subject to what Thoreau would call the "newer testament" of the coming day. *This* world, Dickinson stresses in a similar mood (this arrangement of power and privilege, this perspective on God and faith), is not conclusion. A theology of perhaps cherishes that temporal insecurity and presents a corresponding view of religious faith as agility or adjustment, what Caputo terms *attunement* and Dickinson calls *poise* (Fr546). Which is exactly what "Faith" looks like in "This World is not conclusion": a young girl who accepts that "Sagacity, most go"—that is, must move, change, evolve—and she moves with it, dancing on the surface of a rolling world: "Faith slips - and laughs, and rallies" (Fr373).

The critical commentary on Dickinsonian play usually tips the balance in the other direction, aligning play not with vulnerability but with power. In this view, play defends and strengthens human consciousness by bringing contingency (death, alterity, uncertainty) under the mind's control. For many, that's the point of Dickinsonian play: to achieve "mastery of her suffering" by making "even grief a plaything" (George Whicher)[7]; or "to reduce more threatening natural phenomena to manageable terms" (Nancy Walker)[8]; or to use humor as "a way of accessing power, of maintaining playful, symbolic mastery" (Martha Nell Smith)[9]; or to use play as "a means for overcoming the panic and terror that pervades the darkest poems on death, turning them instead into strategies for ordering that which cannot be ordered" (Domhnall Mitchell).[10] If play is indeed a technique of symbolic mastery, then it fits a poet who often presents herself as the sovereign empress of her own domain, advancing on chaos and old night one poem or one thought at a time. "Dickinson finds just such dominion," Renée Tursi argues. "Her forward-moving mind seizes and conquers, shaping the continents of her own unwritten worlds as she goes."[11]

My goal is not to dispute Dickinsonian sovereignty, a role she clearly cherished, but to foreground instead forms of thought and encounter in her work that have nothing to do with seizing and conquering and that have much to contribute, then, to a religious "hermeneutics of play."[12] Here, the task of religious thought is not to come to grips with unknown or unwritten worlds, not to seize them, but to move as the spirit moves, exactly as Dickinson's "Faith" does: slipping and rallying (and slipping and rallying) as we do our best to stay in play with mysteries that elude our grasp.

If this is an unusual way of thinking about Dickinson, as a theologian of perhaps, it's also an unconventional way of thinking about play, at least according to the authoritative philosophical traditions of her day. Dickinson doesn't marginalize play as mere "fancy," an immature form of the imagination, as in Coleridge. Nor does she secularize play as a strictly human phenomenon, as Emerson does in *Nature*, a disposition that has nothing to do with God.[13] Nor does she recruit play into a totalizing model of culture building, as does the German poet and philosopher Friedrich Schiller, whose *On the Aesthetic Education of Man* was one of the most influential philosophies of play in Dickinson's era. Because of Schiller's importance to modern play theory, let me summarize the *Aesthetic Education* briefly here and point out how Dickinson turns that theory upside down.

For Schiller, play is a branch of German *Bildung*, developmental self-formation, where the competing drives of a fractured self are brought into productive alignment, like a perfectly orchestrated symphony. That orchestration is what Europe might have achieved if the French Revolution hadn't ended in such chaos. For Schiller, play steps into the political breach to offer what we might call a "subjective correlative" for democracy—and the last best hope for political reforms shot to pieces in the Reign of Terror (Schiller wrote the *Aesthetic Education* in 1795). Play is democracy turned *inward* for Schiller, a beautiful city of the soul, and the foundation then for reforming a broken world.

The problem with that world, as Schiller saw it, is that human personality is caught between two warring extremes, the subjective sensations of early childhood and the abstract forms of mature thought, heart and head divorced from one another and each vying for control. Play resolves the conflict by rebalancing the sides, allowing thinking people to dip into the inchoate flux of childhood sensation and feeling people to reclaim the rational principles of order and law. Play holds a mediating or managerial role for Schiller: easing the tension on one side, tightening it on the other, continually tuning and retuning human personality like a musical instrument. If this has a slightly Freudian feel, it's because the mediating role Schiller assigns play in the *Aesthetic Education* anticipates the function Freud will assign the ego in his own drive theory of human personality. Schiller names the drives differently, but the conflict is basically the same: a sense-drive of primal feeling and a form-drive of abstract reason—hyper-sensual on one side, hyper-intellectual on the other—and both devoted to the same goal: bringing the other to heel, which was exactly the state of tyrannical control Schiller witnessed after the French Revolution. Play reconciles the drives. It steps in as a third way, a third drive, not to compete with the others (and add a new tyrant to the mix), but to weave the various parts of the self into a smooth-running whole, in precisely the same way artists bring the different components of their media—sound, tempo, texture, character, color, shape—into elegant and unforced accord.

Ideally for Schiller, games, poems, symphonies, citizens, and nation states are like fractals, perfectly nested Russian dolls. Moreover, this fractal nesting is a mode of learning for Schiller, an aesthetic education, where each new step in the developmental sequence absorbs or incorporates what went before: chaos into play; play into aesthetics; aesthetics into beauty; beauty into civil law; civil law into higher law—and from there to the divine. Each step is exactly consonant with what precedes it, "a reliable link in the causal concatenation of forces."[14] And each step is a "step," an occupied moment of time, which transforms raw sensation into temporal sequence and thus organizes a primal swarm. Schiller names this incremental self-surmounting, *aufgehoben*—to disappear into a higher form—which turns his aesthetic education away from Kantian theories of judgment, where Schiller's thinking about play began, and toward Hegelian theories of totalizing spirit (as Hegel immediately recognized).[15]

Dickinson reverses and reroutes the developmental sequence. Playful wisdom doesn't move *forward*, toward mature sagacity. If anything, it moves *backward*, toward refreshing bewilderment. Thus, play is not a technique for managing contingency, as it tends to be in the critical commentary on Dickinson. Nor is it a technique for organizing the developing self, as in Schiller's theories of aesthetic education and Freudian and Eriksonian theories of ego-formation (ideas that were partly inspired by Schiller). Where play brings the competing drives into harmonious accord for Schiller, so that we are most ourselves in play, most fully human, play has an *unselving* effect in Dickinson, which brings it closer to religious experiences of ecstasy and transcendence. Play makes us *less* like ourselves—that is, less like the version of ourselves we find most accommodating and secure. Play causes things to drift loose from their moorings. It defamiliarizes them, and it defamiliarizes *us* at the same time, altering the body habits and perceptual norms we use to orient ourselves in a stable, ego-centered world. Dickinson's players are not all that well regulated. Instead, they're a rogues' gallery of tramps, ghosts, dogs, clowns, carps, tricksters, bee-chasers, Sir-teasers, fence-jumpers, and straying children: "With bolder Playmates straying" (Fr1588).[16]

In what follows, I'll stress the "thrown" quality of Dickinsonian play, its close kinship with bafflement and surprise, which tends to block or delay the developmental progress Schiller stresses in the *Aesthetic Education*. Spirit is a mobile force for Dickinson, as it is for Hegel and Schiller, but there's no way to plot that force on a stable axis. Spirit "bloweth where it listeth" for her (John 3:8), like the zigzag course of her bees and squirrels or the impossible to predict routes of the Walden loon. Dickinson's just as interested in growth and learning as Schiller. Indeed that's the theme of the four poems she sent to Thomas Wentworth Higginson in April 1862, her poetic debut and "first public reading," as Jim von der Heydt terms it.[17] But Dickinson puts a playful spin on reigning notions of aesthetic growth by writing poems of balked wisdom or failed sagacity in order to picture growth not as developmental progress but as negative capability, where we know that we don't know—and so turn in wonder toward encounters we can't summon or script. This is what makes play blessed for Dickinson, as she told her cousins: "Blessed are they that play, for theirs is the kingdom of heaven."[18]

My argument is that play is the ninth Beatitude for Dickinson not because it reduces the world to manageable proportions but because it prepares the heart for religious surprise, prepares it to be *unprepared*. Like Thoreau, Dickinson values the "quickness" and "slipperiness" of play, which is the most complete expression of her religious imagination: living in a state of watchful readiness for the uncanny appearance of her human and nonhuman neighbors (and not trying to manage them once they arrive). Because play dwells in possibility, it suggests a way of interacting with a God who may be or could be, but we don't know for sure. Play trains us in the wisdom of not being sure, not immediately and irritably reaching after fact and reason but instead "letting" the other emerge in its own way and on its own terms and granting God the same religious courtesy, the same distantiation and withdrawal. This does not mean that facts and reasons don't exist for Dickinson but that they exist as opportunities for creative reply, a chance to see what else those "realities" might yield. Nor does this mean that Dickinson welcomes otherness for its own sake, a vague openness to the Unknown. If play is a mode of encounter in her work then this is a covenant connection with a world outside the self and a testimony to a life interwoven with the lives of others, whole hosts of others, which she can acknowledge and respond to but not control.

COULD YOU TELL ME HOW TO GROW?

On April 15, 1862, Dickinson wrote a letter to Thoreau's friend and admirer, Thomas Wentworth Higginson. She had just read Higginson's "Letter to a Young Contributor," the lead article in the April edition of the *Atlantic Monthly*, where Higginson offered advice for would-be writers, including the rather arch suggestion that they not publish for as long as possible: "Such being the Majesty of the Art you presume to practice, you can at least take time before dishonoring it."[19] Dickinson loved that sentence and could quote it from memory fifteen years later. But she was also intrigued by a challenge Higginson posed in an earlier issue of the *Atlantic*, in September 1861, where Higginson wondered if all the art and literature of the world had made the slightest progress "towards describing one summer day." Higginson had been writing in this vein for years, turning out nature essays devoted to seasonal changes and local plants, and in the earlier *Atlantic* piece, "My Outdoor Study," he singled out Thoreau for exclusive praise, saying that before *Walden*, "absolutely nothing in Nature had ever yet been described."[20]

Higginson enjoyed that sort of extreme pronouncement, Dickinson did too, and so she rose to the *Walden* challenge and sent Higginson four poems, including *her* description of "one summer day," "I'll tell you how the Sun rose" (Fr204), along with "The nearest Dream recedes - unrealized" (Fr304); "We play at Paste" (Fr282); and "Safe in their Alabaster Chambers" (Fr124). Gary Lee Stonum said once that a large number of Dickinson poems are not self-contained units of meaning but responses in an ongoing conversation, "reply poems," where we hear only one side of a dialogue (and have to reconstruct the rest).[21] Dickinson's first bird of spring poem, "I dreaded that first Robin, so" (Fr347), may be a reply to the first bird of spring scene in *Walden*, as I'll say more about later. But in the poems Dickinson sent Higginson, this notion of poetic reply is explicit and intended, which raises important questions about influence, belatedness, newness, and growth, the very questions uppermost in Dickinson's mind in her correspondence with Higginson: "I fear my story fatigues you," she wrote him a few days after sending her poems, "I would like to learn—Could you tell me how to grow?"[22]

Dickinson frames her relationship with Higginson as a dialogue between a teacher and a student by signing many of her letters to him, "Your Scholar";

adopting the faux-naivete of a schoolgirl ("I enclose my name—asking you, if you please—Sir—to tell me what is true?"); and making the question of growth central to the poems she chose for him to read.[23] Higginson knew that the teacher/student relationship was more or less a writing device for Dickinson, a performative fiction, and that he had little to teach her about poetry. Dickinson raises the question of growth not because she doesn't know how people grow but because this is the theme of her "published" anthology, which is especially important because Dickinson almost never does this.[24] Ten poems and one letter were published in her lifetime, but even the published poems offer virtually no help for readers trying to decide which of the nearly 1800 poems go together. No help, that is, other than the Higginson anthology, in which Dickinson not only handpicks the poems for her public debut but also suggests how those poems should be read: as responses to the question of growth. Let me begin then with that summer day:

I'll tell you how the Sun rose -
A Ribbon at a time -
The Steeples swam in Amethyst -
The news, like Squirrels, ran -
The Hills untied their Bonnets -
The Bobolinks - begun -
Then I said softly to myself -
"That must have been the Sun!"
But how he set - I know not -
There seemed a purple stile
That little Yellow boys and girls
Were climbing all the while -
Till when they reached the other side -
A Dominie in Gray -
Put gently up the evening Bars -
And led the flock away - (Fr204)

There's a horizontal line (in the fascicle but not in the Higginson version) separating the first eight lines of the poem from the second. Above the line, the speaker is more or less in command of her own power. She knows how the sun rose and can tell us about it. What does dawn look like? It looks like bright ribbons unfurling one by one. Or to change the figure, it looks like "news" arriving from a distance. And what does that look like? It looks like running squirrels (except that these squirrels are made of a very special kind of light that we can read or hear). What do the hills look like when that happens? They look like women untying their bonnets; only now the ribbons of light are actually ribbons of shadow, the last strips of enclosing night. As the literary figures proliferate, Dickinson's speaker calms the burgeoning energies of dawn with one clear thought: "That must have been the Sun."

That she needs to tell herself this is a measure of how unruly things are becoming. Even the church is swimming: "The Steeples swam in Amethyst," which is unusual because amethyst is a purple form of quartz, rock-hard. What should be immovable and enduring, the First Congregational Church of Amherst, is melting in sunlight and swimming in crystal, just as the "news" of that day, the good news, if this is a Sunday morning, runs like color on a wet page. If the yellow boys and girls in the second stanza are play figures for Dickinson, doing what her playmates often do, climbing over a fence, then the first poem of the Higginson anthology would foreshadow the third, "We play at Paste." And if that's true, then play appears to dissolve hard things—gems into loose sand in "We play at Paste," amethyst into liquid color here—and what we thought we understood grows less secure as we enter a space where things run together: light into ribbons, hills into bonnets, bobolinks into children, steeples into flowing stone. This is the opposite of Schiller's play-drive, which organizes primitive confusions by making them "conformable with law."[25] But this in fact is what play often does: it creates what D. W. Winnicott calls a "potential space" where solid objects soften and transform, so that an everyday tangle of string can become a nested cradle for sleeping toys one moment and a symbolic umbilical cord the next.[26] In play, objects are simultaneously real and imaginary, both found (as external) and created (as internal) in a way that requires play theorists to invent non-binary vocabularies to describe what they see, like Winnicott's subjective object or Carl Jung's imago or Heinz Kohut's self-object.

Dickinson's potential space is liminal in just this way, a metaxic zone of subjunctive possibility, which makes the Amherst steeples look playfully unchurch-like. Dickinson defamiliarizes one of the most recognizable features of a New England landscape, a steepled church, in the same way William Carlos Williams will unbottle a bottle in *Paterson* and Annie Dillard will try to unpeach a peach in *Pilgrim at Tinker Creek*, breaking and melting static form. We're so accustomed to thinking of religious faith as something rock-like and unyielding, "On this rock I will build my church" (Matt. 16:18), that the metaphorics of melting can seem irreverent and subversive, the opposite of Calvinist rigor, which may be why Thoreau centered his most intense spiritual experience on a melting sandbank. But if Elisa New's right about the extravagant figurality of Puritan preaching, its "mixings and meltings,"[27] then this poem may be Dickinson's way of walking the sacred outside the church and applying the rhetorical tradition of her religious heritage to the natural world, which is just what the preaching would have urged her to do. Metaphor is not only a favored device of Puritan homiletics, New shows, but also an emblem for the action of divine grace itself, which turns and transports the faithful soul into ever-fresh perceptions of God. In her view, the graced soul habitually acts against itself, against its own fixed integrity, as metaphor does, creating new possibilities of relationship and thought from the unlikely marriage of tenor and vehicle:

> Following Dickinson's lead, here I use "metaphor" in this most general sense to describe a linguistic realm where phenomena discover and catch their truest likenesses by entertaining unlikenesses. The poetic vehicle's contravention of identity is key to that identity's truer realization, as something other than, more alive than, its mere self.[28]

Similarly, in Puritan preaching the vehicle is *vehicular*, New stresses, constantly changing, as in a passage she quotes from John Cotton: "It is a mighty power of the Spirit of Grace to turn itself so many ways."[29] Cotton could be talking about the sky in Dickinson or the grass in Whitman—as if divine spirit is best thought of as a poem, an idea that also occurred to Caputo.[30] Indeed trope means *turn*, so that the figurative play of Puritan preaching, its remote and precious metaphors, as John Donne would say, its third heavens of hyperboles, is not an obstructive ornament to the plain meaning of the text but its exact rhetorical purpose, what the preaching is meant to do: train the soul in a style of variable attention New calls "adjustment" or "transposition":

> Unlike the self, this soul has, in place of identity, a knack for what Jonathan Edwards calls consent—which is to say a gift for living doubly, contrapuntally, responsively: or, to invoke a favorite Protestant figure for this adjustment, musically. The graced soul is that gifted with talents for modulation and transposition: in place of an identity it has—and we want to use this word spatially and musically—*range*.[31]

The transfiguring God New discovers in Cotton's preaching, Edwards' theology, and Sarah Pierpont's faith practice suggests a Puritan version of the nimble spirit Dickinson discovered in nature and explored in her poems, a piety that's "more play than regimen."[32]

As we draw closer to Dickinson's "Dominie," in the second stanza, a titled figure of religious authority, the rhetorical play becomes increasingly unstable, as if the poem is untying itself, like the hills: "The Hills untied their Bonnets." Are the yellow children made of flesh or made of light? Is the Dominie a human pastor, a natural process, a sign of God's presence, a sign of God's absence? Now things *seem* rather than are—"There seemed a purple stile"—and we've crossed into the Acres of Perhaps. Perhaps the stile is a gap in the hills changing color at sunset. Or perhaps the stile is a set of steps allowing passage over a farmer's fence. Or perhaps the stile is the purple "style" of a poem flamboyant in its metaphors. As the yellow children cross to the other side of knowing we witness two final transformations: first the children turn into a flock of animals and then they turn into nothing, into darkness. But Dickinson's speaker isn't certain about that, she's only guessing about the flock, because the Dominie lowers the bars and she's left wondering and unsure, a mood that will link all four poems in the collection. It's possible that this kind of uncertainty prompted Dickinson's question to Higginson, could you tell me how to grow? But it seems more likely that this is what growth actually means for Dickinson and the very place her Dominie is leading her: into a cloud of unknowing where fixed ideas loosen and swim.

From this watery perspective, religious wisdom seems transitive and insecure, *running* like the streaming tropes of this poem or *going* like the sagacity "Faith" encounters in "This World is not conclusion": "Sagacity, must go." There may be other, more permanent forms of knowledge, but that kind of truth is inaccessible and inhuman, as Dickinson stresses in two other Higginson poems, where sagacity is locked up in the plush tombs of dead saints in "Safe in their Alabaster Chambers"; or carried off by a playful bee in "The nearest Dream recedes - unrealized" (Fr304). In that poem, the bee teases a pursuing schoolboy in an aerial version of the game Thoreau played with the loon. But unlike Thoreau, Dickinson foregrounds the Christian implications of play by comparing the schoolboy's pursuit of the bee to her readers' pursuit of heaven. Both forms of pursuit are based on proximity, what's nearest to us. And both quests remain unrealized, as they would be in a theology of perhaps. If this is a parable not only about our relationship with nature but also about our relationship with God, our "nearest Neighbor" as she said (Fr723), then the bee's wildness may be a spiritual tonic for the schoolboy, a cure for what Dickinson calls his homesickness, which is the boy's desire to make reality match his own prior experience (and so not change or grow). That even a child endures this sickness suggests how deeply our dreams of heaven are embedded in static remembrance and how redemptive then is the wild presence of this bee:

The nearest Dream recedes - unrealized -
The Heaven we chase -
Like the June Bee - before the School Boy -
Invites the Race -
Stoops - to an easy Clover -
Dips – evades - teazes - deploys -
Then - to the Royal Clouds
Lifts his light Pinnace -
Heedless of the Boy -
Staring - bewildered - at the mocking sky -

Homesick for steadfast Honey -
Ah - the Bee flies not
That brews that rare variety! (Fr304)

Dips, evades, teazes—makes sense enough. This is a wild creature that stays wild. But *deploys* suggests that there's something strategic about the teasing, something the schoolboy would do well to learn. If that's true, then bewilderment may actually be the honey, the nourishing gift, freeing the boy from nostalgic longing and curbing his desire for fusion and power. In that sense, Dickinson may be offering a lesson in *negative* growth, learning in its deconstructive phase, in which bewilderment provides a liberating confusion.[33]

Whether the schoolboy would ever see it that way is an open question, but it seems unlikely. The disillusioned schoolboy is Faith's precise counterpart ("Faith" as the young girl in "This World is not conclusion"). He is what Faith would look like if she couldn't laugh and rally. Hurt by the teasing, the schoolboy sees only mockery in his disappointment, a "heedless" heaven that should have protected him from just this predicament. If heaven *invites* the predicament, as the June Bee invites the race, then bewilderment may have a role to play in the child's moral growth, as Thoreau suggested in *Walden*: "Not till we are lost, in other words, not till we have lost the world, do we begin to find ourselves, and realize where we are and the infinite extent of our relations."[34] If losing ourselves is a necessary step toward that true neighboring—a way of meeting without totalizing or interacting without *aufgehoben*—then the roots of a less violent religious sensibility may exist in the games we played as children. Moreover, rather than being heedless of the schoolboy, heaven may be seen as merciful and instructive, providing the exact inspiration for the child's spiritual growth in the playful flight of a summer bee.

The teasing bee elaborates an idea Dickinson had been writing about for years. Dickinsonian play deflects and undermines the will to power of all sorts of schoolboys—including the grown-up schoolboys who appear in her poems as Sir, Despot, Master, and Signor. Play doesn't respect imperial titles, it pokes fun at them, which opens these relationships to reformulation and growth. "Which is the Despot, neither knows," a teasing speaker says in "I make His Crescent fill or lack" (Fr837). "Which, Sir, are you, and which am *I*," another speaker asks in a poem written three years before the Higginson anthology, "In lands I never saw - they say" (Fr108). Play doesn't confront power directly in these poems but obliquely or teasingly, as Suzanne Juhasz writes:

> Tease is habitually Dickinson's response to patriarchal power, something that simultaneously attracts, angers, and frequently frightens her. With tease rather than direct attack, Dickinson questions and negotiates power relationships as

they are traditionally structured in terms of hierarchies and dominance. Teasing is defense as well as invitation, and it provides a space—in Dickinson's case, the space is the poem—in which renegotiation as well as critique is possible."[35]

If Dickinson merely reverses the hierarchies and claims for herself the Master's title, then she offers little help in understanding a religious faith oriented toward the unknown. But if religious wisdom is different from the power ploys of subordination and dominance, then it sets thought on a new footing and recovers unexpected possibilities of mutuality and rapport: "We hold a Mutual Disc - / And front a Mutual Day," as the speaker of "I make His Crescent fill or lack" says (Fr837).

This is not what playful wisdom typically means either in the critical commentary on Dickinson's play poems or in the philosophical discourse of her milieu. When Schiller tries to imagine wisdom in the *Aesthetic Education*, for instance, Athena in full armor springs to mind: "It is not without significance that the old myth makes the goddess of Wisdom emerge fully armed from the head of Jupiter; for her very first function is warlike."[36] If the goal is to defeat error and defend truth, as it is for Schiller, then the warrior goddess is theology's best emblem. But if the goal is to interact with "subjects of which we know nothing," as it is for Dickinson, and so approach religious questions obliquely and playfully, through a theology of perhaps, then the myriad Daisy of "In lands I never saw" may be better suited to Dickinson's disposition as a religious writer and better adapted to the needs of her cultural moment. Insofar as playful wisdom suggests a shift from violent to nonviolent forms of thought, from sovereignty to neighboring, perhaps, or from power to mutuality, then it suggests a peaceable intervention in a culture at war. What that peaceable kingdom might look like is far from clear: it exists "in lands I never saw," Dickinson says, which means that it exists as possibility, the signature of her theopoetics. What is clear is that to realize that possibility requires a stance of epistemological modesty and vulnerability—what I've been calling "weak thought," in the manner of Gianni Vattimo,[37] but which Dickinson pictures as meekness, echoing the language of the Beatitudes:

In lands I never saw - they say
Immortal Alps look down -
Whose Bonnets touch the firmament -
Whose sandals touch the town;

Meek at whose everlasting feet
A myriad Daisy play -
Which, Sir, are you, and which am *I* -
Opon an August day? (Fr108)

The setting seems important here. Daisy plays at the foot of snow-capped mountains, whose peaks touch the firmament and whose base reaches a town. This is another liminal zone, Winnicott's potential space, where the mountains exist between earth and heaven, touching both, and where they are both external (in the world) and internal (in the mind): a real place, the actual Alps, and an imaginary place (with feet, sandals, and bonnets). Furthermore, the mountains exist both within and beyond human time, anchored in the present, one August day, and yet "immortal" and "everlasting," evoking the divine.

That basic scene, a female character playing in the presence of the everlasting, has a long religious history. In Egyptian mythology, for instance, the goddess, Maat, the cosmic source of justice and order, plays before her Father, the creator god Re. And in biblical tradition, Sophia, the Wisdom Child of Proverbs 8, plays in the presence of God, as I mentioned in the Introduction. Sophia is God's companion and co-creator, and her play sustains the renewal of the world:

When he fixed the foundations of earth,
    then was I beside him as artisan;
I was his delight day by day,
    playing before him all the while. (Prov. 8:29–30; NABRE)

In this view, divine Wisdom is feminine, creative, delightful, and continuous.[38] Like Krishna and Siva, Sophia's play sustains existence, *creatio continua*. She is still and always at play. Religious sophiology is less a gnostic quest for eternal truths and more an expression of the multiplicity of Wisdom's creative presence in the world, which biblical tradition names *multiformis sapientia* (multiform wisdom).[39] As Walter Brueggemann argues, such wisdom is the opposite of craven idols and static codes:

> The wisdom tradition asserts that the ethical realities of God's world are not as one-dimensional and settled as sometimes thought with reference to the traditional commandments given in revelation. Ethics cannot be so fully settled in a world that refuses to be decoded. . . . The wisdom tradition attests that all of the data is not in, and therefore ethical judgments and conclusions are endlessly provisional and open to reformulation.[40]

Brueggemann's view is that Wisdom exposes faith to multiple viewpoints, leaving it vulnerable to critique, and thus more like a playing child than a conquering king. Because no single stance or interpretive judgment comprehends Sophia's play, she creates a surplus, a theological "more." Indeed, her presence as God's creative companion pluralizes Old Testament monotheism: "It may be suggested that the theological adventuresomeness of Prov. 8:22-31, in its originary utterance, served to create theological room inside the house of 'covenantal nomism,' which at times was surely constrictive."[41] Dickinson would have enjoyed that image: a theological house more numerous of windows and superior for doors.

Dickinson replies to the Wisdom literature by placing one of her avatars at the feet of the everlasting—she often signed her letters, *Daisy*—and by incorporating the multiform wisdom of religious play into her own self-presentation: she is *myriad Daisy*. Moreover, the plurality of Daisy's play loosens and restructures her relationship with patriarchal power. When Daisy asks, "Which, Sir, are you, and which am *I*," she implies that he too is myriad, not fully revealed by his title and credentials, not inarguably himself. His *Sir-ness* is a construct, one reality among many. She's teasing now, hinting at dips and reversals, as if the sun-lit bee were talking to the schoolboy, or talking to Sir as if he were a schoolboy, and urging him to cherish a confusion he would otherwise fear.

Such liberating confusion is keyed to the presence of a "beyond" for Dickinson's speaker, a land she's never seen, which frames and relativizes human experience, rendering it less conclusive. Dickinson didn't need to bring in the Alps to picture daisies growing at the foot of the mountains or Daisy playing guessing games with Sir. That happens in New England. But the existence of that other realm inspires Daisy's playful pluralism. We *need* that beyond, Dickinson suggests. It accents the variability of this summer world and motivates the time stamp in the poem's last line, one "August day." The presence of the everlasting suggests that whatever happens that day is temporary, provisional, deconstructible, which holds open the futural possibilities of the unknown.

This is how I interpret Daisy's meekness. She bows to that futural horizon—not to Sir or God or the Alps but to the unpredictable otherness of what's still to come, *tout autre*, an advent she cannot predict (which would include her *own* advent, the myriad Daisies she may yet become). Caputo stresses "the coming of what we cannot see coming" as the leading idea in a theology of perhaps.[42] Dickinson relishes that incompleteness as the enabling condition of both religion and literature. Not knowing what the future will hold or how the game will end sustains what she once called the "unfinished pleasure" of the unknown.[43] If this world is not conclusion, then neither is this *Sir, I, game, day, firmament, landscape,* or *poem*—which condemns us to bewilderment from one perspective, the schoolboy's, or releases us into it from another, Daisy's.

It makes sense then that Dickinson would use Christ's voice in the Beatitudes to describe play to her cousins, "blessed are they that play," precisely because the Beatitudes picture a world where up is down, poverty is wealth, and vulnerability is a genuine strength. Dickinson understood the revolutionary potential of that wisdom, which destabilizes worldly hierarchies and frees thought from the reigning ideologies of Master and Sir. She understood that biblical wisdom blesses the gap between the everlasting truth of holy mountains and the fallible perceptions of this August day. Go into that *gap*, Dickinson seems to tell her readers, as Ezekiel urged the true prophets of Israel (Ezek. 22:30). This is the potential space of creative possibility, where Sophia, Faith, and Daisy play. This is how we grow.

In "We play at Paste," Dickinson helps us glimpse what that growth might look like:

We play at Paste -
Till qualified for Pearl -
Then, drop the Paste -
And deem Ourself a fool -
The Shapes, tho', were similar,
And our new Hands
Learned Gem Tactics
Practising Sands - (Fr282)

The "paste" in the first line may be costume jewelry, what a girl in Dickinson's era might wear in imaginary games of courtship and marriage. If that's the case, then the purpose of play isn't bewilderment but norming, preparing girls to take their place in an adult world. Once she's been "qualified" for pearls, the symbol of female maturity, the woman can stop pretending, leaving the paste play behind with her dolls and toys, which now seem foolish. Indeed, for the gender norming to work the paste play *must* seem foolish, not real in the way the pearls are. Otherwise, the gender symbols will lose their expressive authority and become a prop or disguise, another form of dress-up. Once play crosses the line from childhood to maturity, so that the woman is not fully revealed by her public symbols but is instead still playing or pretending, femininity becomes pluralized and subversive. Dickinson raises this possibility with the curious pronoun *ourself*, as if to accent the speaker's sense of her own multiplicity. In cultures that qualify female maturity with clearly specified rituals and symbols—confirmation, betrothal, marriage, childbirth, and so on—the before-and-after differences need to be sharply defined. Whatever futural possibilities existed for the playing child are curtailed the moment she accepts her membership as a qualified adult. From there, the possible collapses into the actual, the contours of this particular life, which she accepts as the true measure of her calling. (Dickinson writes several poems about this process.) The hint of "play" in the woman's pearls, however, the way they resemble the costume jewelry of her childhood, blurs that hard line and raises the possibility of gender play *after* her maturity, as if beneath the pearls she's still that playing child. In "She rose to His Requirement," *pearl* conveys just this sense of childhood imagination and amplitude, a secret life hidden beneath the public requirements of a woman's adult role. "Pearl" is a figure of weedy depth and mysterious transformation in that poem, a sign for the very thing social orthodoxies can't control and prefer not to mention, like Pearl in *The Scarlet Letter*. If the "we" in the first line of "We play at Paste" refers to a community of girls undergoing an identical norming process, then the poem appears to comment on how play organizes and streamlines social identity, exactly as Schiller claimed in the *Aesthetic Education* and Huizinga argued in *Homo Ludens*. The sign of this norming is the repetition of the word *paste* in the first and third lines, which is less a verbal rhyme than a visual representation of what happens in normative play: different things come out the same. From this point of view, the pearl is the reward for social compliance, the proof that the now-grown child has dropped the "Playthings of Her Life" and risen, successfully, to his requirements (Fr857). But if *we* refers to the poem's speaker—who was plural then, when she played at paste, and is plural now, as she wears her pearls—then play disrupts that streamlining effect with a hint of destabilizing uncertainty, which is exactly where Dickinson brings all the speakers of the Higginson sequence: into a potential space of liberating confusion.

The adult speaker of the second stanza seems to realize this possibility—and put it to good use as a working poet. If "We play at Paste" ended with the word *fool*, it would restate the plot of "The nearest Dream recedes - unrealized," where the schoolboy feels mocked and foolish but can't imagine what to do with those feelings (except retreat into an imagined past, into homesickness). But in "We play at Paste" the speaker embraces her foolishness, makes it part of her adult self-image, and builds a ludic aesthetics from there. What connects childish and mature play for Schiller is conformity to law, learned early in the games we played as children and carried forward into increasingly authoritative public realms (education, religion, aesthetics, civil governance). Each step in Schiller's sequence cancels and absorbs what went before it, growth through *aufgehoben*, which creates a totalizing dialectic. What connects childish and mature play for Dickinson is foolishness, the corrective and liberating power of play, which is also learned early in childhood games of light-watching, bee-chasing, and paste play but which we never outgrow.

This doesn't mean that we can't make progress. The gem play in the second stanza is prismatic and possibilizing, which is the true measure of the poet's growth. Gem play reverses the organizing and streamlining function Schiller and Huizinga assign to play and reveals instead unexpected faces or facets of a world we thought we knew. Gem play courts creative multiplicity.

It fractures one-dimensional knowing into compound planes of attention, like Sophia's multiform wisdom in Proverbs 8 or Krishna's self-revelation in the *Bhagavad Gita*. Dickinson claims this prismatic vision for her ludic poet. The moment we duck below the line and enter the second stanza, things begin to swarm: *shapes, hands, tactics, sands*, as if play pluralizes experience, multiplying its possibilities, like a gem turning white light into dazzling spectrum. Moreover, the poet does this tactically, as the desired outcome of her play: "our new Hands / Learned Gem *Tactics*." No single face expresses the whole of a gem and the working poet cherishes that beveled dimensionality, which she acquires not only through philosophical aesthetics, Schiller's mode, but also through the concrete sensations of handmade poems: the scratch of her pen on paper or the pull of her thread through a fascicle: "our new *Hands / Learned*." The poet learns gem tactics on forgiving surfaces, sand or glass (high-silica sand), and then applies her skills to topics that require diverse modes of thought: questions of growth, religion, perception, power, and gender—the subjects of the Higginson anthology. Thus, the working poet turns the compound *ourself* of childhood, both singular and plural, into an aesthetics perfectly suited to a world of spangled complexity. Thoreau tried to see nature like an arthropod, with "insect-view" precision.[44] Dickinson writes poems that feature bees, spiders, crickets, and beetles—creatures whose compound eyes are layered with obliquely angled lenses. Gem poets have insect vision. They practice an art of faceted attention. They see the world with diamond eyes. To do less is to risk stasis and selfsameness, the opposite of growth, as I'd like to consider now: not myriad Daisy but a mind stuck in place: *paste, paste*.

ECSTATIC PLAY

Let me return then to 1862, the date of the Higginson anthology, to consider one last form of Dickinsonian play: play as movement or transcendence, an "ecstatic" turning of traumatized consciousness toward the world. As we've seen so far, Dickinson construes the ludic possible in terms of metaphoric surplus, play's figurative "more." Further, I've argued that this view of play is closer to Dickinson's Puritan ancestors than her philosophical peers, Schiller in particular, where play is a tool of epistemological mastery, a way of bringing experience under the mind's control. As Elisa New has argued, Puritan figurality reveals how little we really know about God and the world, which nurtures a faith in the unforeseen, a spirit that turns itself in so many ways. As the troping poet reveals those other ways, she cocreates with a transfiguring God, as playful Wisdom does in the biblical tradition. The resulting uncertainty can be terrifying, as it often is in Puritan preaching, but it can also be refreshing and pleasurable, a source of creative delight, as it often is in Dickinson's play poems.

But there's another way to understand Dickinsonian play. Questions of growth and change are important to her in the Higginson anthology not only because she was a poet at the beginning of her career but also because she was a poet at the beginning of the Civil War. From very early on Dickinson saw herself as writing after an apocalypse: an earth-scorching, god-wounding cultural cataclysm that was partly the Civil War and partly the literary and epistemological wars she fought in her second-floor bedroom. Both wars had the same effect: they reduced religious experience to bare essentials and raised the question of what survives the cataclysm, what theological terms and tools might a religious poet still use. Starting from there, Dickinson looks for signs of greening and growth, and it doesn't much matter whether those signs look traditionally religious or traditionally secular. What matters is the "quickness," the capacity for live response. The most important distinction in her religious vocabulary is not the difference between the saved and the damned but the difference between "the quick and the dead" (1 Pet. 4:5). And it's possible in an Emily Dickinson poem to be dead and *still* quick, changing or turning in the grave. Just as it's possible to be alive and *not* quick, not a living person but a spiritual corpse. In this poem, written during the last year of the Civil War, Dickinson's speaker is caught halfway between, still alive but barely, as her body turns to marble under her own astonished eyes:

I've dropped my Brain - My Soul is numb -
The Veins that used to run
Stop palsied - 'tis Paralysis
Done perfecter in stone -

Vitality is Carved and cool -
My nerve in marble lies -
A Breathing Woman
Yesterday - endowed with Paradise.

Not dumb - I had a sort that moved -
A Sense that smote and stirred -
Instincts for Dance - a caper part -
An Aptitude for Bird -

Who wrought Carrara in me
And chiseled all my tune
Were it a witchcraft - were it Death -
I've still a chance to strain

To Being, somewhere – Motion - Breath -
Though Centuries beyond,
And every limit a Decade -
I'll shiver, satisfied. (Fr1088)

Most of the quickness is gone from this speaker, who remembers that her veins "used to run" and that she was a "Breathing Woman / Yesterday." She remembers sensations she no longer feels and an instinct for play she can no longer fully express. She calls that instinct the "caper part" and an "Aptitude for Bird." But her brain is "dropped," so it's hard for her to understand what's happening, what silenced her voice or numbed her soul, whether it was death or some kind of "witchcraft." We're close to the spirit of *King Lear* in this poem, the final scene, where life is reduced to the essentials of breath and motion, a father holding a feather to his daughter's lips and praying that she stirs. *Breath, motion, shiver, stirred*: these are Dickinson's words too. But unlike the dead Cordelia, who stirs nothing, Dickinson's speaker pushes back against encroaching stone with a life-instinct Dickinson names, the *strain to Being*: "I've still a chance to strain / To Being, somewhere - Motion - Breath."

If this is indeed a "play" poem, one that explores what dance and caper might look like under emergency conditions, then play seems rooted for Dickinson in the idea of motion, which becomes synonymous with life itself: "Motion - Breath," as if the dash were an equals sign. The dance theorist Maxine Sheets-Johnstone points out that we are born into the world not as consciousness, which comes later, but as bodies in motion. We *move* our way into being, infused with an "original kinetic spontaneity" that defines our aliveness and creates our concepts and categories. Indeed, that kinetic spontaneity creates *us*, our bearing in the world.[45] What Sheets-Johnstone calls "the primacy of movement" in her study of dance is also at the heart of several play theories. Huizinga found notions of rapid movement in the designations for play in a dozen Indo-European languages. Roger Caillois thought that the word *jeu* conveyed a sense of looseness or latitude, an ease of movement. Hans-Georg Gadamer identified the to-and-fro motion of play as the rhythmic shape of reading, thinking, conversation, and philosophical hermeneutics. Working from a different set of premises, Dickinson's relationship with Puritanism, transcendentalism, and the discourses of sentimental piety, James McIntosh stresses the primacy of movement to Dickinson's religious imagination, which he calls her "kinetic spirituality." To believe, as Dickinson did, in the otherness of divine spirit suggests a religious discipline not of static virtue but of responsive quickness—the "nimble love" Dickinson stressed in her relationship with nature and the nimble believing McIntosh emphasizes in her relationship with God (Fr163). McIntosh shows that rather than committing herself to a consistent set of religious doctrines or practices,

Dickinson put her faith in uncanny moments of transformation and transport, experiences of rich inner motion, and she used her poetry not to recollect those experiences in tranquility but to record them as they were happening to her in real time.[46]

In the poems of marbling and paralysis, these movements are impossibly small, sometimes as minimal as breathing, shivering, slipping a little, standing up, raising a pen a few inches, raising one's gaze a few inches, turning to face something or hear something in the distance—as if motion itself becomes precious in these conditions, the sign of a still-quickened spirit: "It was not Death, for I stood up" (Fr355). Megan Craig writes about this when she charts "the effort required to turn or to prance," in Dickinson's trauma poems, "to stand in the sunrise and rise to the day," which she interprets as a form of ethical self-transcendence: "The self is ever opening and moving toward something other than the self—transcending toward the world."[47] In "I've dropped my Brain," the motion isn't rapid or easy, as in Huizinga and Caillois, but barely there at all, little more than a shiver, and yet that's the surviving hope of the poem: the speaker's capacity to turn toward the world a little, turn toward Being somewhere, which is kinetic spirituality *in extremis*.

It seems odd to call that motion *redemptive* especially in a poem where the church words—perfecter, Paradise, Soul—feel so cold. But this is what transcendence might feel like from the inside. Dickinson trained herself to use the aggressive evangelism of her Calvinist culture as a theatrical performance, so that she became the characters she studied in the Bible and tested scriptural ideas on her pulse. In this way, she merged elements of Calvinist Christianity with the romanticism of Emerson and Thoreau and learned to transform biblical scenes into the drama of her own interior life, as the romantics did with nature. Biblical stories of miraculous resurrection—Lazarus rising from the tomb at Bethany (John 11:38-44); a twelve-year-old girl rising from the dead in Galilee (Mark 5:35–43); Christ's resurrection in Jerusalem (Matt. 28:1–10, in Dickinson's favorite gospel)—thus become *her* stories, the drama of her own Easter. In this poem, Dickinson removes the decorative elements to make the story more her own, not only the white light, linen cloth, and dazzling angels of the gospel narratives but also the rococo filigree of choirs and cherubs added by several centuries of Christian art. Dickinson strips off those features until all that's left is the marble and the straining, as if this is transcendence in its most basic form: being able to sense something beyond the self and turn toward that something with all one's might.

This doesn't sound much like "ecstasy," which suggests a flashy, all at once release from human limitation as the liberated soul takes flight. The flights that concern Dickinson are often smaller than that, an "Aptitude for Bird" that may be as modest as turning toward a window. But these turns of attention are extraordinarily precious to Dickinson, even redemptive, precisely because they reveal a vitality not yet "carved and cool." This is ecstatic spirituality under emergency conditions and a much-reduced theology of transcendence. The threat to such transcendence is not atheism or impiety but thickness, numbness, marbling, soldering, petrifying, turning off the valves of one's attention, cramping down around an emotional or spiritual wound.

This is one way Dickinson's spirituality differs from Thoreau's. Divine encounter causes the self to grow smaller in *Walden* and to recover a sense of humanizing limit and ecological scale, as we saw in chapter 1. The self is *already* small in many Dickinson poems. Several of her speakers start out that way, so diminished that their world ground threatens to bury them alive, as in a scene from a Beckett play. Dickinson specializes in showing people standing on the lip of a grave just before they go down. One of her speakers is a girl who imagines her mouth filling up with ice—*while* she's still speaking (Fr923). Such speakers are like traumatized soldiers who've survived wars of consciousness, gender, history, and religion every bit as consequential as the wars fought on battlefields. In that sort of world, it's good to stay small, limit your exposure. The veterans in Dickinson's poems are young and old, male and female, blasphemers and Christians, but nearly all of them adopt the same survival strategy: they filter sensation through narrow apertures and wall out as much of the world as they can. For one of her speakers, it's all she can do to face the sliver of landscape visible between a window frame and a draped curtain (Fr578). For another, the song of one spring robin is too much to bear (Fr347).

Though it may strike us as surprising, Dickinson's religious poems are often "pastoral" or consoling in these situations. But her view of consolation is quite different from familiar notions of religious salvation. The world ministers to people by *not* becoming a sanctuary for their suffering minds. God cares for them by not satisfying preset notions of spiritual care—"Of Course - I prayed - / And did God Care?" (Fr581)—and not answering their prayers for safety and success. Out of that disappointment, new possibilities take root. Dickinson invites us to make peace with recurring disappointment, accepting and using exactly those sensations of incomprehension and loss that religion, in other contexts, would be expected to relieve. In this, she remains a devout Calvinist. Her God ministers to people by remaining *other* for them, immune to religious tactics of domestication and control and unmoved by pleas for stillness, numbness, security, and narcotics. "Narcotics cannot still the Tooth," as she says in "This World is not conclusion," leaving Faith's disappointment unrelieved (Fr373). Instead, Dickinson's Calvinist God specializes in the shock of the new: sending shouts when we ask for silence (Fr347); or "Silence" when we ask for mild religious talk (Fr525). This is a rough consolation but perhaps just what's needed by a culture that responded to the trauma of the Civil War by building grand myths of monolithic union:

systematic theologies; risk-free corporate economies; philosophical and scientific systems of ontological hierarchy, determinism, and fixed result.

Nothing is fixed in Dickinson's religious imagination. If the spirit truly bloweth where it listeth, then a theology of perhaps "bends in the winds of what insists without existence," as Caputo writes, "of what withdraws from presence, pointing like the arrow of a weathervane in the direction of the promise, of the flickering possibility of what neither is nor is not."[48] The mercy of God, the authority of the Bible, the existence of heaven: Dickinson offers no definitive answers to these questions, as if having one's questions answered is less important than developing a capacity for growth and change, a negative capability that tolerates loss and confusion and remains quickened by encounters it does not control. Hers is a spirituality of astonishment and gem play (not only outside the self but also *inside* the perceiving mind, that hodge-podge bundle of angled mirrors). Hers is a world in which everything and everyone is unknowable and mysterious. Even the speakers of her poems are unfixed, drawing attention to themselves not as a perceiving center or a controlling consciousness but as a temporary excursion of expressive thought, like "a voice thinking"—a phrase Marilynne Robinson used to describe the persona she admires in William James.[49]

What her speakers come up with on these voice excursions isn't really doctrinal, a message about the existence of God, which we could then use to prove or disprove something. The religious messages vary and contradict one another poem by poem, as if the proof we need has little to do with schools and creeds and everything to do with our capacity to transcend ourselves in small, sacred acts of attention: lifting awareness a few degrees to acknowledge a bird coming down the walk or answer the salute of the bees, those holy messengers calling us deeper into the world. Perhaps if we were less damaged, we'd go outside more and answer the world's salute with brave shouts and hallelujahs. But many of Dickinson's speakers are terribly damaged, so that changing the direction of their gaze a few inches requires extraordinary effort, like lifting marble.

This is the subject of "I dreaded that first Robin, so" (Fr347)—which strikes me as a reply to the famous "first sparrow of spring!" passage in *Walden*. When Thoreau tells his first sparrow story (in "Spring," *Walden*'s Easter moment), *everything* ascends in joyous resurrection. Thoreau plays the scene like grand opera, the choir in full voice. Grass, rivers, fish, birds, the squirrels mating under his floorboards, the lyricism of the prose itself—all rise to this new day: "Walden was dead and is alive again." I'll come back to the squirrels in a moment, but the Easter scene itself deserves quotation:

> The first sparrow of spring! The year beginning with younger hope than ever! The faint silvery warblings heard over the partially bare and moist fields from

the blue-bird, the song-sparrow, and the red-wing, as if the last flakes of winter tinkled as they fell! What at such a time are histories, chronologies, traditions, and all written revelations? The brooks sing carols and glees to the spring. The marsh-hawk sailing low over the meadow is already seeking the first slimy life that awakens. The sinking sound of melting snow is heard in all dells, and the ice dissolves apace in the ponds. The grass flames up on the hill-sides like a spring fire. . . . It is glorious to behold this ribbon of water sparkling in the sun, the bare face of the pond full of glee and youth, as if it spoke the joy of the fishes within it, and of the sands on its shore,—a silvery sheen as from the scales of a *leuciscus*, as it were all one active fish. Such is the contrast between winter and spring. Walden was dead and is alive again.[50]

Thoreau interweaves several strands of biblical witness here. The muscular lifting and pushing of landscapes recalls Ps. 68: "Why leap ye, ye high hills?" The imagery of a world united under the sign of the fish—"as it were all one active fish"—borrows from the earliest visual representations of Christ, the *ichthus*. And Thoreau casts the whole thing as a scene of natural resurrection, an Easter moment in real time.

Just before the birdsong, Thoreau presents himself as absorbed in winterish thought, busy "reading or writing" in the cabin (busy, presumably, reading or writing *Walden*), and annoyed, then, by the "chirruping and vocal pirouetting" of sex-mad squirrels under his floor.[51] Thoreau tries to silence the squirrels by arguing with them and stamping on the floorboards. But the squirrels answer his foot-stamping with a "strain of invective," which Thoreau translates from Squirrel Idiom as "No you don't—chickaree—chickaree."[52] Then suddenly, the scene turns. The strain of invective becomes a strain of music, the first birdsong, which turns Thoreau's attention outside himself, beyond the limits of his thinking mind. There's no time for books in that living worship and no occasion for bookish thought, which would objectify the music into chronologies and histories and miss the *right now* of the living thing, Walden rather than *Walden*.

In "I dreaded that first Robin, so," Dickinson picks up elements of the *Walden* story, but slows everything down. Her speaker is also preoccupied with thought, *dread*, in fact, and also experiences a kind of redemptive unselving when her mind opens to a nonhuman "word," a call from outside. Dickinson borrows ideas and tropes from Thoreau, but again her scale is different. The Easter moment is tiny in Dickinson, the lifting of a quill pen a few inches. But the tomb is huge. It's almost *all* tomb in Dickinson's poem, all encapsulating thought. Thus, the ecstatic turning out of consciousness, when it happens, is as minimal and precious as the marbled woman's straining toward being or the little girl's straining to speak, even as her throat fills with ice:

I dreaded that first Robin, so,
But He is mastered, now,
I'm some accustomed to Him grown,
He hurts a little, though -

I thought if I could only live
Till that first Shout got by -
Not all Pianos in the Woods
Had power to mangle me -

I dared not meet the Daffodils -
For fear their Yellow Gown
Would pierce me with a fashion
So foreign to my own -

I wished the Grass would hurry -
So when 'twas time to see -
He'd be too tall, the tallest one
Could stretch to look at me -

I could not bear the Bees should come,
I wished they'd stay away
In those dim countries where they go,
What word had they, for me?

They're here, though; not a creature failed -
No Blossom stayed away
In gentle deference to me -
The Queen of Calvary -

Each one salutes me, as he goes,
And I, my childish Plumes,
Lift, in bereaved acknowledgment
Of their unthinking Drums - (Fr347)

    The first stanza evokes a speaker determined to control her fear of a changing world by treating it like an intellectual challenge, as the schoolboy would, something to be "mastered." The robin's cry is already in the past, a remembered wounding, as we move deeper into the season, when flowers are in bloom and the bees are out. The bird's shout "hurts a little" she says—presumably because it makes her think about the passage of time (spring beginning and then passing). But she's halfway to mastering that strangeness by calling it a "shout," what people do, rather than a call or cry, the defiant *chickaree*. Thoreau presents nature's otherness as comic and playful in the *Walden* scene, the squirrels busy with "their mad pranks, defying humanity to stop them." Moreover, Thoreau doesn't stop the squirrels so much as join them, discovering his own squirrel-nature in the process, so that their pirouetting and his floor-stamping blend into the same ice-cracking Easter dance.

Dickinson's speaker moves carefully toward a similar convergence, but stopping or controlling the shock is on her mind first. What her speaker does to master her world is narrow and focus her perception, the survival strategy of Dickinson's veterans. Dickinson sometimes pictures consciousness as an aimed cylinder, like a gun pointed at the world or a listening tube adjusted to the pitch of one voice or note (and no more). Her speakers often fear swarm, dissonance, too much happening at once, and so they narrow their focus to a tiny sliver of landscape or a narrow band of sound. Dickinson knows that we can "close" our lives before we die—"My life closed twice before it's close" (Fr1773)—and that this is a survival tactic for people in pain.

Closing her life this way, Dickinson's speaker draws down her consciousness, admitting less and less of the world. She projects that violence outside herself (in the mangling of the pianos and the piercing of the daffodils) but dread does this mangling, as she well knows. She mentions the "Pianos in the Woods" not only to suggest the full-voice soundscape of uncensored nature, Thoreau's creation choir, but also to picture the expressive scope of a fully living, fully functioning human being, what Elisa New stressed as Dickinson's aesthetic and spiritual range. This speaker can't imagine living that way. Instead, she actively dims her world in a form of violent self-limiting Dickinson associates with crucifixion. The speaker's fear of not being able to turn wild shouts into human meaning, and her dread of losing control of perception in the face of too much swarm, commits her to a life of perpetual self-wounding. She is the "Queen of Calvary," a mistress of self-crucifixion, and only by relinquishing that imperial title will she discover another way of being in the world. Dickinson hints at that other way in the daffodil stanza, when the speaker senses that it may be possible to "meet" rather than "master" the world. But her speaker no sooner thinks that thought than recoils from the daring such an encounter would require:

I dared not meet the Daffodils -
For fear their Yellow Gown
Would pierce me with a fashion
So foreign to my own –

To meet the world this way suggests a different kind of Golgotha: not being sealed in a self-made tomb but being wounded by otherness, pierced by "a fashion / So foreign to my own." The Queen of Calvary recognizes and rejects that sort of meeting and adopts instead a strategy of acute self-protection, an idea Dickinson explores in several religious poems. In "My period had come for Prayer," for instance, Dickinson shows how religion can become a kind of tactical fantasy, a set doctrines or practices designed to minimize the self's exposure and limit how much divinity gets through. Before considering the ecstatic play of "I dreaded that first Robin, so," let me quote the first and final stanzas of that poem:

My period had come for Prayer -
No other Art - would do -
My Tactics missed a rudiment -
Creator - Was it you? (Fr525)

Before meeting her Creator, this speaker makes several assumptions, none of them all that controversial. She believes that God can be located in space (above her); that she can approach that space intentionally (through prayer); and that what she'll find on her spiritual errand will be a kind and "Curious Friend" (Fr525). But she also senses that something's missing from all that, a "rudiment" below her expectations and maneuvers. And she knows, further, that embracing that rudimentary worship would require the courage of a live encounter: "Creator - Was it you?"

Dickinson's phrasing corresponds almost exactly to the language Thoreau uses to make the same point: that the foundation of religious experience is a meeting in the dark: "Walden, is it you?" Thoreau asks,[53] stirred from sleep by the intimate proximity of what Dickinson would call his nearest neighbor. Dickinson shares Thoreau's goal of encountering the other this way, meeting in unguarded personhood, but Dickinson depicts that experience not as secretly religious, as Thoreau does, but as the undisguised rudiment of the spiritual life. In the final stanza of "My period had come for Prayer," Dickinson's speaker does indeed meet her Creator, but the encounter is so different from what she expected that the word "prayer" doesn't come close. Here's the last stanza:

The Silence condescended -
Creation stopped - for me -
But awed beyond my errand -
I worshipped - did not "pray" - (Fr525)

The speaker in "I dreaded that first Robin, so" wants nothing to do with that sort of experience. On the contrary, she's in full retreat from meeting the other on any but her own guarded terms. Thus, she builds a fictional counter-world that's quieter, safer, dimmer, and less exposed. In her dream garden, the grass grows faster than usual, screening her from view. There, the bees stay on their side of the line, in their "dim countries," responding with courtesy to her suffering mind. Dickinson's speaker builds that walled-in garden, and then abandons it, suddenly, with a simple three-beat line: "They're here, though."

That's the ecstasy, the first sign of spring. It doesn't look like much at first, certainly not like the Hallelujah Chorus in *Walden*, but this is an answered prayer for Dickinson's speaker, her prayer for continued *life*: "if I could only live," as she says in the second stanza. And it changes things. Nothing keeps its distance now, and she realizes that the little world she'd built for herself is a hill of crosses, a home-made Calvary. With that recognition, she allows the aimed corridor of traumatized consciousness to rotate and open, turning crosswise to her standpoint and presenting in full display the temporality of living creatures passing by:

Each one salutes me, as he goes,
And I, my childish Plumes,
Lift, in bereaved acknowledgment
Of their unthinking Drums – (Fr347)

The temporality of a changing world isn't the shock of the new. The speaker senses that temporality from the first "shout"—and builds her protective garden from there. The real shock is the discovered gift for growth and pluming, an "Aptitude for Bird" not marbled after all. Like Thoreau dancing with the squirrels, Dickinson's speaker finds in herself what she feared in the world, something primal and wild, and that discovery feels like being born again. Like any new creature, she's born vulnerable, childlike, born into a world that's not framed by the limits of her mind. Indeed, that's the blessing of it, the indifferent drumming, for what she needs is resurrection on a *non*human scale: not more but less self, less siting of the imperial mind at the center of its domain. What she finds outside her mind *is* a kind of generous music, wave after wave of living sound, but orchestrated to a completely different score. None of the pianos in the woods are subject to her dominion. None of them began to play when she started listening and none will fall silent when she's gone. What's remarkable is that she feels the bereavement of her unselving and yet raises her pen in reply, saying *yes* to the cosmic and divine rhythms of the world, what Raimon Panikkar called "the drums from outside."[54] Thoreau ends his winterish retreat by joining the play of the Walden squirrels. Dickinson's Easter dance is different and smaller, one raised hand, but even that minimal gesture is a sign of freshness and growth, the childish plumes of a new creation.

FAITH'S BLUSH

As we've seen, the playful wisdom of Dickinson's poems has different faces or facets, like her gems. It means figurative surplus in the Higginson anthology, play's possibilizing "more." And it means movement in the poems of marbling and dread, a kinetic spirituality *in extremis*. In addition, play often means teasing, parody, slapstick, sarcasm, and a distinct style of religious humor for Dickinson, as many commentators have noted.[55] Dickinson's niece, Mattie, remembers playing games with her aunt—Gypsy and Pirate, Hide and Seek, the Battle of Bunker Hill—and Dickinson plays games with God too. Who but Emily Dickinson would think of lightning as the dropped fork of a clumsy deity (Fr1140)? Or threaten to take God to court for freezing her flowers with an early frost (Fr101)? Or sum up Christianity as "Him - and Holy Ghost - and all" and decide that she'd rather *not* go to heaven because it's always Sunday there (Fr437)? Dickinson's humor liberates people not only from quiet dread but also from loud pomposity, the "Strong Hallelujahs" of authoritarian religion (Fr373). Against that strength, Dickinson proposes a counter-notion of weak thought or ludic faith, which advertises its own naivete. In this view, weak is *good*, an alternative to religious doctrines that divide the world into believers and nonbelievers and pave the way for sectarian violence (something of an Amherst specialty).[56] A playful religion prefers experimental risk to unthinking conformity, as Dickinson said about Christ's spirituality: "Faith - The Experiment of Our Lord" (Fr191). It chooses childish pluming over marbled tombs and bewildered thinking over totalizing aesthetics. Play is the enemy of priggish philosophy, humorless preaching, hellfire revivals, strong doctrine, and "prima" donnas of any kind (Fr381).

This kind of piety can appear wasteful and unproductive, at least from the outside—precisely because it's working underground to unlearn religious habits of power and dominion and meet the other as a neighbor or person. This unlearning takes place in secret for Thoreau and Dickinson, as it does in the contemplative tradition of unknowing. "My practice is 'nowhere,'" Thoreau said, not something he can make public very easily or use to bolster his authority as a religious writer.[57] Thus, playful wisdom is what religion looks like when it's off duty, not gaining ground or power. Playful wisdom cherishes Sabbath-moods of wondering and wool-gathering and takes as its heroes *ingénues* of many sorts: children, provincials, tramps, powerless people, people who don't accomplish very much, at least according to the utilitarian standards of the day, like the non-praying mystic of "I have a King, who does not speak" (Fr157) or the non-dancing dancer of "I cannot dance upon my Toes" (Fr381). It makes sense, then, that Dickinson would find something neighborly about Concord's famous layabout, Henry David Thoreau, who could have been a captain of politics or industry but chose instead to be "the captain of a huckleberry-party," as Emerson said, cruelly, at Thoreau's funeral.

This sort of faith looks foolish and weird, even to someone like Emerson. But that foolishness expresses the core paradox of Christianity for Dickinson, that folly (*moria*) is wisdom and vulnerability is strength and "this world"—this particular framing of human life, this set of assumptions about work and play and faith—"is not conclusion." That sounds orthodox enough if Dickinson's proverb points faith's gaze toward the metaphysical, toward heaven rather than the earth. But the proverb becomes more radical if she means *any* conclusion, any of the hundreds of doctrines and dogmas we use to stabilize religious experience and deny the volatile truth of a mysterious God. How would anyone practice a faith without creeds and conclusions? No predictive thinking of any sort. No tactical rituals or self-protecting filters. Indeed, Dickinson presents the religious self as vigilant and vulnerable, available to whatever comes walking over the mountain and brave enough to face it when it comes: surges of spiritual gladness and fear that felt to Dickinson like the flash and click of lightning storms (Fr901). Or pulses of thought so intense it seemed like her pen could take flight like a pluming bird. Living that way means *letting* the pen take flight, which is the proper stance of a poet "who felt herself to be simultaneously subject to, and representative of, an overwhelming force," as Linda Freedman says, just as it is the proper stance of a person of faith subject to the mysterious call of an unknown God.[58]

The cost of this discipleship is different but still demanding. It has nothing to do with public confessions of Christian belief, as required by Hannah Porter and Mary Lyon in the Mount Holyoke Revivals Dickinson endured when she was seventeen. Nor does it require drawing up and signing a one-time religious contract, as Dickinson's father did when he joined the Amherst church. Instead, Dickinson's faith means cultivating an aptitude for spiritual growth that's continually offered by the world's abundant greening and continually blocked by self-protective habits of fear. Dickinson's faith demands "quickness," as James McIntosh, Elisa New, and Megan Craig have shown: a knack for moving, prancing, playing, capering, breaking inertia and turning toward whatever's coming down the walk (with no guarantee about what that visit might bring). As an experimental religious writer, Dickinson explores what it would mean to practice a nondogmatic religion, one that's skeptical of institutional authority; alert to the deadening effects of religious habit; indifferent to boundary-creating schools and doxa; immune to binding interpretation; and light enough in its shoes to respond to a divine spirit that has no fixed address but comes as it comes, different every time: "The Spirit never twice alike, but every time another—that other more divine."[59] Living this way is extraordinarily difficult, Dickinson knows, maybe impossible, especially for people trained to think of religion as a life-binding ligature of authoritarian doctrine and no-nonsense rules. If that's *not* what religion means, we may need some guidance. And so

Dickinson offers a four-line snapshot of a weakened but irrepressible faith in her description of a laughing young girl named, helpfully, "Faith":

This World is not conclusion.
A Species stands beyond -
Invisible, as Music -
But positive, as Sound -
It beckons, and it baffles -
Philosophy, dont know -
And through a Riddle, at the last -
Sagacity, must go -
To guess it, puzzles scholars -
To gain it, Men have borne
Contempt of Generations
And Crucifixion, shown -
Faith slips - and laughs, and rallies -
Blushes, if any see -
Plucks at a twig of Evidence -
And asks a Vane, the way -
Much Gesture, from the Pulpit -
Strong Hallelujahs roll -
Narcotics cannot still the Tooth
That nibbles at the soul - (Fr373)

It's hard to miss the sarcasm. "Much Gesture" from the preacher, "Strong Hallelujahs" from the choir: it's just "Narcotics" for the aching soul. Which is the opposite of Dickinson's shock of the new God, who sends the robins and bees to draw us back into the world and release us from the numbing effects of our dread. Faith (as the laughing child) accepts this insecurity and models the agility we'll need to practice a different and more playful religion. She's not singing in the choir or listening to the sermon. She's not puzzling out the riddles with the scholars. It doesn't look like she's trying to "gain" anything: "To gain it, Men have borne / Contempt." Thus, when she slips, she laughs and begins again. If turning toward the bees is the minimal sign of ethical transcendence for Dickinson, as Megan Craig argues, then this may be the minimal sign of religious improvisation, the ability to slip and rally. To practice this sort of faith, we don't need strong theology, scholarly sagacity, or an appetite for conquest and control. We need resiliency and self-deprecating humor. We need to become like children again, as Jesus kept telling the representatives of "strong" religion in his faith tradition. Comfortable in her weakness, Faith knows that she doesn't know. Dickinson has her pluck "at a twig of evidence," to gain a little foothold perhaps, but footholds are nothing compared to her knack for quickened, blushing response.

It's possible to see Faith's "blush" as another sign of the sarcasm, which hits its targets one by one: scientific epistemology (that might categorize the "beyond" as a species); scholarly expertise (forced to jump through the hoop of a riddle); verbal sophistication ("Philosophy, dont know"); evangelical fervor (the strong hallelujahs); and then faith itself, which appears as a hotly embarrassed child. From this point of view, the poem remains an agnostic negation from start to finish, which would make it "safer" than the poems I've considered, not exposed like the pluming poet. Agnostic negation commits to nothing and so risks nothing and is free then to mock whatever it sees: science, literature, philosophy, and religion. "Both the poetic and religious leap end as a hobble," Linda Freedman argues, "but that is preferable to the misguided skipping of 'Faith' or the foolish stridency of the church."[60]

I don't mean to defend Faith from criticism, precisely because Dickinson seems interested in what an undefended faith might look like, one that's embarrassed and vulnerable and *knows* that about itself. If that's true, then embarrassment doesn't disqualify religious faith but reveals it, bringing forward a fundamental insecurity at the heart of the religious life and making that insecurity self-aware. Embarrassment means we know we look ridiculous, a metacognitive awareness blocked by more secure or authoritative modes of thought. Moreover, the child's blush can appear deeply human and humanizing, especially in contrast to the "coolness" of the anxiety poems: throats icing up, spirits turned to stone. Darwin thought of blushing as the quintessential human expression, the sign of self-consciousness and "self-attention."[61] Keats associated blushing with emotional and creative risk, a life of negative capability, and believed that being uncertain and being embarrassed went hand in hand.[62] Erving Goffman valued blushing as a sign of hope. By showing embarrassment we hold open the prospect of difference and growth and claim the chance to achieve in the future what eludes us for now.[63] In Goffman's terms, blushing means Faith has failed at something she aspires to, that she's not what she should be or wants to be. Which means that she too is not conclusion, not fully revealed by what we see today. Like myriad Daisy, she's not finally and inarguably herself.

Thus, it seems unfair to criticize Faith for being misguided if Dickinson's exploring a religious witness that has no strong guidance and looks foolish, then, from more orthodox points of view. Faith's blush is exactly the point. This is how playful wisdom appears in public: without authority or credentials, like the captain of a huckleberry party. Faith offers a positive alternative to agnostic negation not because she resolves theological disputes but because she changes their character and tone, from stridency to laughter or intransigence to play. The elusive "slipperiness" of the sacred was one of Thoreau's most important ideas—*labor, labi, lapsus sum*—which names a theological style on the one hand, a mode of writing and thinking, and a potent force of real-world transformation on the other. To be in covenant relation with the sacred, to be quickened by it, requires a shifting stance of perpetual adjustment, one that's never settled, never really in control, like skating on thin ice. Dickinson compresses that idea into a six-word line and creates a religious personification appropriate to that sliding world. Faith slips, it's one of the few things we know about her, and she rallies afterward, which suggests a capacity for growth strikingly absent from the other, stronger figures in the poem. If that's the case, then we may need to bracket our conclusions about her: faith becomes "faith," just as prayer becomes "prayer." This is how religion appears to Dickinson on the Acres of Perhaps. It bends in the winds of the possible, as Caputo said, "pointing like the arrow of a weathervane in the direction of the promise." Faith seems fine with that: she "asks a Vane, the way." She's not homesick like the schoolboy or armored like Athena or self-crucified like the Queen of Calvary. She laughs at her mistakes, recovers after loss, and lifts her blushing face to the presented opportunities of an ever-changing world. What could be more faithful than that?

NOTES

1. "As I see it," Turner wrote in one of his last published essays, "play does not fit in anywhere particular; it is a transient and is recalcitrant to localization, to placement, to fixation—a joker in the neuroanthropological act." See his "Body, Brain, and Culture," *Zygon* 18, no. 3 (September 1983): 233.

2. Emily Dickinson, *The Poems of Emily Dickinson*, ed. R. W. Franklin (Cambridge: Harvard University Press, 1999), 282, 412. Subsequent references to Dickinson's poems will refer to this edition and be cited in the text by poem number.

3. Turner, "Body, Brain, and Culture," 235.

4. Turner, "Body, Brain, and Culture," 236.

5. See John D. Caputo, *The Insistence of God: A Theology of Perhaps* (Bloomington: Indiana University Press, 2013); and *The Folly of God: A Theology of the Unconditional* (Salem, OR: Polebridge Press, 2016).

6. Jacques Derrida, "Force of Law: 'The Mystical Foundation of Authority,'" trans. Mary Quantaince, in *Acts of Religion*, ed. Gil Anidjar (New York: Routledge, 2002), 257; quoted in Caputo, *The Insistence of God*, 8–9.

7. George Frisbie Whicher, *This Was a Poet: A Critical Biography of Emily Dickinson* (New York: Scribners, 1938), 109.

8. Nancy Walker, "Emily Dickinson and the Self: Humor as Identity," *Tulsa Studies in Women's Literature* 2, no. 1 (Spring, 1983): 60.

9. Martha Nell Smith, "The Poet as Cartoonist," in *Comic Power in Emily Dickinson* (Austin: University of Texas Press, 1993), 92.

10. Domhnall Mitchell, *Emily Dickinson and the Limits and Possibilities of Critical Judgement* (PhD diss., Trinity College, Dublin, 1989), 218; quoted in *Comic Power in Emily Dickinson*, 145n7.

11. Renée Tursi, "Emily Dickinson, Pragmatism, and the Conquests of Mind," in *Emily Dickinson and Philosophy*, ed. Jed Deppman, Marianne Noble, and Gary Lee Stonum (New York: Cambridge University Press, 2013), 174.

12. John D. Caputo, *Radical Hermeneutics: Repetition, Deconstruction, and the Hermeneutic Project* (Bloomington: Indiana University Press, 1987), 213.

13. Emerson writes, "God never jests with us, and will not compromise the end of nature, by permitting any inconsequence into its procession." See his *Nature*, in *Ralph Waldo Emerson: Essays and Lectures*, ed. Joel Porte (New York: Library of America, 1983), 32. Mitchell Breitwieser sees the loon game in *Walden* as Thoreau's direct reply to that claim. See his *"Walden* and the Spirit of Capitalism: Presence, Damage, and Cultural Revival." The teasing play of many of Dickinson's nature poems may suggest a similar rejoinder.

14. Friedrich Schiller, *On the Aesthetic Education of Man*, trans. Reginald Snell (1954; repr. Mineola, NY: Dover, 2004), 31.

15. Schiller, *Aesthetic Education*, 88n.

16. Let me note Jed Deppman's influential reading of this poem as well as his work on Dickinson as a poet of "weak thought" and the importance of purposeless, a-teleological movement in her play poems. See his *Trying to Think with Emily Dickinson* (Amherst: University of Massachusetts Press, 2008), 184–204.

17. Jim von der Heydt, "'Perfect from the Pod': Instant Learning in Dickinson and Kierkegaard," in *Emily Dickinson and Philosophy*, 105.

18. Emily Dickinson, *The Letters of Emily Dickinson*, ed. Thomas H. Johnson, vol. 3 (Cambridge: Harvard University Press, 1958), 691.

19. Thomas Wentworth Higginson, "Letter to a Young Contributor," *Atlantic Monthly* (April 1862); quoted in Alfred Habegger, *My Wars Are Laid Away in Books: The Life of Emily Dickinson* (New York: Random House, 2001), 452.

20. Thomas Wentworth Higginson, "My Out-door Study," *Atlantic Monthly* (September 1861); quoted in Harding, *The Days of Henry Thoreau*, 455.

21. Gary Lee Stonum, "Dickinson's Literary Background," in *The Emily Dickinson Handbook*, ed. Gudrun Grabher, Roland Hagenbüchle, and Cristanne Miller (Amherst: University of Massachusetts Press, 1998), 53.

22. Dickinson, *Letters*, 2:404.

23. Dickinson, *Letters*, 2:403.

24. It's possible that Dickinson created a second anthology for publication in the short-lived Brooklyn paper *Drum Beat*, although that's far from certain. Karen Dandurand makes the argument that Dickinson selected the poems for this debut. See her "New Dickinson Civil War Publications," *American Literature* 56, no. 1 (March 1984): 17–27. Habegger disputes that claim in *My Wars Are Laid Away in Books*, 402–3.

25. Schiller, *The Aesthetic Education*, 30.

26. See his *Playing and Reality* (1971; repr. London: Routledge, 2005), 58.

27. Elisa New, *New England Beyond Criticism: In Defense of America's First Literature* (Chichester, West Sussex: Wiley Blackwell, 2014), 39.

28. New, *New England Beyond Criticism*, 24.

29. John Cotton, *Christ, the Fountaine of Life* (New York: Arno Press, 1972), 121; quoted in New, *New England Beyond Criticism*, 39.

30. See his *The Folly of God*, 17.

31. New, *New England Beyond Criticism*, 30.

32. New, *New England Beyond Criticism*, 34.

33. I am much indebted to Jim von der Heydt's work on this theme in the Higginson anthology, in which epistemological uncertainty dismantles "the engine of

mental progress" and poses an alternative to totalizing forms of aesthetic education. See his "Perfect from the Pod," 105–28.

34. Henry D. Thoreau, *Walden*, ed. Jeffrey S. Cramer (New Haven: Yale University Press, 2006), 187.

35. Suzanne Juhasz, "The Big Tease," in *Comic Power in Emily Dickinson*, 27.

36. Schiller, *The Aesthetic Education*, 49.

37. I have in mind the description of "weak thought" by the Italian philosopher Gianni Vattimo, in his book, *Belief*, as well as the discussion of "weak religion" by Vattimo and Richard Rorty in *The Future of Religion*. Vattimo argues that weak thought responds to the long history of violence in religious and secular fundamentalisms by relinquishing metaphysical claims of truth and practicing a self-consciously "reduced faith" oriented toward philosophical humility and responsive concern. On this, see Gianni Vattimo, *Belief*, trans. Luca D'Isanto and David Webb (Stanford: Stanford University Press, 1999). Vattimo and Rorty extend this line of thought by picturing, in *The Future of Religion*, a weakened or partial faith alert to its own error and so unwilling to participate in systematic theologies and grand religious schemes. The future Vattimo and Rorty imagine involves a transition in religious thinking from power to charity, doctrine to hermeneutics, authority to dialogue, and metaphysics to risk-taking play: "The transition from power to charity," Rorty argues in *The Future of Religion*, "and that from the metaphysical Logos to postmetaphysical thought are both expressions of a willingness to take one's chances, as opposed to attempting to escape one's finitude by aligning oneself with infinite power." See Richard Rorty and Gianni Vattimo, *The Future of Religion*, ed. Santiago Zabala (New York: Columbia University Press, 2005), 56. John A. McClure provides a valuable summary of Rorty and Vattimo in his *Partial Faiths: Postsecular Fiction in the Age of Pynchon and Morrison* (Athens: University of Georgia Press, 2007), 10–17.

38. Although she doesn't consider the implications of Wisdom's play in Proverbs 8, Beth Maclay Doriani notes that Anne Bradstreet often speaks in the voice of female Wisdom in her poems and that Dickinson aligns herself with this prophetic tradition, selecting and using the wisdom literature to portray a feminine divine presence and to set her wisdom against the orthodox codes of Dickinson's religious heritage. See her *Emily Dickinson: Daughter of Prophecy* (Amherst: University of Massachusetts Press, 1996), 25.

39. On this, see Christopher Pramuk, *Sophia: The Hidden Christ of Thomas Merton* (Collegeville, MN: Liturgical Press, 2009), 142–44. Merton's commentary on *multiformis sapientia* in Maximus Confessor and Evagrius' *Kephalaia Gnostica* centers on a series of distinctions between the inner life of Wisdom and its revealed expressions: the spirit rather than the letter of Scripture, for instance; or the *logoi* of created things rather than their materiality. Because that inmost spirit is never fully revealed, the Wisdom of God holds faith and history open, responsive to the creative mystery of what's still to come. On this, see Thomas Merton, *An Introduction to Christian Mysticism: Initiation into the Monastic Tradition 3*, ed. Patrick F. O'Connell (Kalamazoo: Cistercian Publications, 2008), 121–36.

40. Walter Brueggemann, *Reverberations of Faith: A Theological Handbook of Old Testament Themes* (Louisville: Westminster John Knox Press, 2002), 235.

41. Walter Brueggemann, *Theology of the Old Testament: Testimony, Dispute, Advocacy* (Minneapolis: Fortress Press, 1997), 346.

42. Caputo, *The Folly of God*, 27.

43. Dickinson, *Letters*, 3:727.

44. Henry D. Thoreau, *The Journal of Henry D. Thoreau*, gen. ed. John C. Broderick, vol. 1 (Princeton: Princeton University Press, 1981), 1:81.

45. Maxine Sheets-Johnstone, *The Primacy of Movement* (Amsterdam: John Benjamins, 1999), 136. See also Sam Gill's discussion of this idea in *Dancing Culture Religion* (Lanham, MD: Lexington Books, 2012), 16–21.

46. James McIntosh, *Nimble Believing: Dickinson and the Unknown* (Ann Arbor: University of Michigan Press, 2004).

47. Megan Craig, "The Infinite in Person: Levinas and Dickinson," in *Emily Dickinson and Philosophy*, 209.

48. Caputo, *The Insistence of God*, 6.

49. Marilynne Robinson, "Risk the Game: On William James," *The Nation* (November 23, 2010), https://www.thenation.com/article/archive/risk-game-william-james/html (accessed April 12, 2018).

50. Thoreau, *Walden*, 336–37.

51. Thoreau, *Walden*, 336.

52. Thoreau, *Walden*, 336.

53. Thoreau, *Walden*, 211.

54. Raimon Panikkar, *The Rhythm of Being: The Unbroken Trinity* (Maryknoll, NY: Orbis, 2013), 49.

55. On this, see not only *Comic Power in Emily Dickinson* but also Dorothy Huff Oberhaus, "Dickinson as a Comic Poet," in *Approaches to Teaching Dickinson's Poetry*, ed. Robin Riley Fast and Christine Mack Gordon (New York: MLA, 1989), 118–23; Walker, "Emily Dickinson and the Self: Humor as Identity," 57–68; Marlene Springer, "Emily Dickinson's Humorous Road to Heaven," *Renascence* 23 (1971): 129–36; and Karl Keller, *The Only Kangaroo Among the Beauty: Emily Dickinson and America* (Baltimore: Johns Hopkins University Press, 1979).

56. Amherst is named after Lord Jeffrey Amherst, who came up with the idea of using smallpox-infected blankets to eliminate nonbelieving Indians.

57. Thoreau, *Walden*, 237. Someone turned down this page in "Higher Laws," Emily perhaps, in the copy of *Walden* in the Dickinson private library, now in The Emily Dickinson Collection of the Houghton Library at Harvard.

58. Linda Freedman, *Emily Dickinson and the Religious Imagination* (Cambridge: Cambridge University Press, 2011), 4.

59. Dickinson, *Letters*, 3:728.

60. Freedman, *Emily Dickinson and the Religious Imagination*, 7.

61. Charles Darwin, *The Expression of the Emotions in Man and Animals*, 3rd ed. (New York: Oxford University Press, 1998), 310–44.

62. On this, see Christopher Ricks, *Keats and Embarrassment* (Oxford: Clarendon Press, 1974), 25.

63. Erving Goffman, "Embarrassment and Social Organization," *American Journal of Sociology* 62, no. 3 (November 1956): 264–71. Ricks comments on this essay in *Keats and Embarrassment*, 2.

Chapter 3

Play and Improvisation
Jack Kerouac's Singing Theology

So far, I've argued that Thoreau and Dickinson accent the insecurity of play to excite a mood of hospitable reception. Not knowing what the loon will do in the game Thoreau plays at the pond or who "Daisy" is in the game she plays with "Sir" opens the self to enigmatic encounter. Thoreau and Dickinson fashion literary idioms responsive to that "quickness" and reconceive play not as a strategy of symbolic mastery but as a shifting relationship of temporary rapport, what Gregory Bateson termed "an evolving system of interaction" between mutually participating partners.

To say that play is blessed, as Dickinson told her cousins, or holy, as Thoreau wrote in his *Journal*, is to reorient the religious life around this shifting center and emphasize a heightened state of spiritual alertness, which Thoreau identified as his "profession" as a religious writer: "My profession is to be always on the alert to find God in nature, to know his lurking-places, to attend all the oratorios, the operas, in nature."[1] If this responsiveness is a faith stance, then its hero is less like the imperial subject Thoreau satirizes in *Walden* ("I have, as it were, my own sun and moon and stars, and a little world all to myself") and more like the "Faith" of "This World is not conclusion": a light-spirited, light-footed, endlessly adaptive subject who can slip and rally amid the rolling insecurity of a changing world. "The most uncommon and yet only viable response to the sacred is to play fully," Robert E. Neale writes in his psychology of religion, *In Praise of Play*, and to "allow ourselves the nimbleness of spirit to dance on [life's] revolving surface."[2]

No one was better suited to that kind of rolling faith, Jack Kerouac believed, than a jazz musician. In his 1957 novel, *On the Road*, Kerouac foregrounds a series of improvisational skills in the life of faith and raises the question of how we might learn to live "in time," surrendering preconceived scripts to the evolving flow of thought and experience. Kerouac's risk-laden view of religious "rolling," the key word in his religious vocabulary, galls the back to normal mood of most churches and synagogues in the 1950s (as well as the back to normal longing of Kerouac's ghost-haunted narrator) and gives voice to a modern example of the religious experiments we've seen in Dickinson and Thoreau, a jazz version of their holy play.

I'd like to begin, though, not with a jazz scene but in a chili joint in Wyoming, which sets a context for the playful wisdom of *On the Road*. The scene takes place near the beginning of the first road trip and raises a question about the age of the novel's narrator, Sal Paradise. Kerouac provides half a dozen clues that Sal is in his mid-twenties at this point. He's served in the military, been married and divorced, and attended and dropped out of college. When the novel begins, he's grieving the death of his father (in the 1951 scroll draft of *On the Road*) and the break-up of his marriage (in the published text) and is feeling weary and miserable (in both).[3] Sal's childhood is long past, but there's still something boyish about him as he heads west for the first time. A Mexican-American waitress in the Wyoming restaurant spots it immediately. When Sal writes a flirtatious poem on the back of his bill and invites her to see the town with him, she replies, "I'd love to, Chiquito, but I have a date with my boy friend."[4]

Sal cultivates his Chiquito persona deliberately in *On the Road*. He dresses in ragamuffin clothes and strange "sprouting" Huaraches. He eats apple pie and ice cream every chance he gets and drinks huge milkshakes for his upset stomach. Even his sexuality seems childlike. He calls Terry, his California lover, a little girl, and describes their sexuality as the play of "little lambs" (90). Responding in kind, Terry calls Sal her baby, her kid, a nice boy, a nice college boy. And their brief life together has the enchanted quality of a childhood game: playing dress-up together in Los Angeles, playing house together in the Bakersfield tent.

On the Road appears to be a boyish celebration of innocent wonder and liberated love, but behind the games and play is the very grown-up reality of World War II. We tend to think of *On the Road* as a 1950s (and even 1960s) novel, the back-pocket Bible of an emerging counterculture more than happy to wear those sprouting sandals. But Kerouac set off on his first road trip with Neal Cassady, the inspiration for Dean Moriarity in *On the Road*, in July 1947, when Kerouac was twenty-five. By that point, Kerouac had been married and divorced; survived the death of his father; attended and dropped out of Columbia; and served a stint in the Merchant Marine. In July 1942, Kerouac enlisted as a scullion on the *S. S. Dorchester*, a massive transport ship headed for Greenland on one of the most dangerous shipping routes in the Atlantic. The *Dorchester* was attacked twice by German U-boats, escaping both attacks unharmed, but the experience in combat took a toll on Kerouac, whose hands trembled uncontrollably for months afterward. Unlike the dozens of narrators in the early drafts of *On the Road*, Sal is a military veteran returning from a war that killed half the men in Kerouac's high school class, including his best friend, Sammy Sampas, and nearly everyone on board the *Dorchester*, which was torpedoed and sunk three months after Kerouac's discharge. "As we binged and banged in dusty bloody fields," Kerouac wrote later, looking back at his football playing days in Lowell, "we didnt [*sic*] even dream we'd all end up in World War II, some of us killed, some of us wounded, the rest of us eviscerated of 1930's innocent ambition."[5]

Sal Paradise is one of Kerouac's eviscerated survivors. He doesn't talk about it very much, but he has all the signs of post-traumatic stress disorder, including the inability to talk about it.[6] He can't sleep. He drinks too much. He sees ghosts. He plays incredibly dangerous drinking games with Marylou, based on scenes from *Gone with the Wind*, and equally dangerous gunfighter games with Remi, based on scenes from *The Mark of Zorro*. The war created a profound sense of insecurity for Kerouac, who shows how people play with the things that frighten them to regain some measure of control, as Freud theorized. According to his biographer, Gerald Nicosia, fantasy play was how Kerouac dealt with his own losses. He simply denied them, preferring to live in a state of "fairyland detachment."[7] But if we pull back the veil of kicks and fun Sal uses to disguise the pain—"Ah, it's all right," he tells Marylou in the midst of a party turning ugly, "it's just kicks. We only live once" (125)—what we discover are traumatized, violent, and suicidal young people. Carlo Marx, a character based on Allen Ginsberg, contemplates jumping off a ship on an ocean journey from Dakar. Remi draws a gun on his girlfriend, Lee Ann. Dean forms a suicide pact with Marylou. A young woman kills herself by jumping off the Algiers ferry and drowning in the Mississippi. Another woman shoots her husband, serves a jail sentence, and then comes home and shoots him again. The damage is so widespread that Sal starts referring to young people by their disabilities: Tom, the clubfooted poolshark (59); Alfred, the crippled hitchhiker (165); Tony, the spastic saint (221). Everyone in *On the Road* is touched by trauma, including Sal. His mind keeps going "haywire," as he says, and it scares him (83). A "goof of terror" haunts his dreams, and he sometimes sees "a strange Arabian figure" who pursues him across a desert and catches him just before he can reach "the Protective City"—a fortress tabernacle that could wall out the demons and provide some peace for Sal's restless soul (83, 124).

On the Road doesn't offer *Peace of Soul*, Fulton Sheen's 1949 bestseller. Nor does it provide *A Guide to Confident Living* (1948) or a tribute to *The Power of Positive Thinking* (1952), as Norman Vincent Peale sought to do. *On the Road* doesn't satisfy "the craving for adjustment and conformity" Will Herberg identified as the primary religious impulse of the 1950s.[8] Like Thoreau and Dickinson, Kerouac's vision of sacred encounter is wilder and more turbulent than that. It's "trouble" to settled forms, as Dean said to Sal:

"Troubles, you see, is the generalization-word for what God exists in" (120). Kerouac tells a story of sacred trouble in *On the Road* as a counter-narrative to the mind-cure revivals of postwar America, its guides to confident living, as well as the mind-cure longings of the novel's traumatized narrator, who wouldn't mind shambling after a halfway decent life guide if he could find one. What he finds instead is Dean, who's a world of trouble just standing there, an Angel of Terror with a huge ragged thumb who will reveal the half-rotten spots in Sal's character and open them up for change. "Open your belly as we drive into it," he urges Sal (161). This kind of openness is difficult for Sal, war veteran and pretend-Chiquito. Sal is change-phobic and risk-averse, and he guards his damaged heart with a dozen tripwire defenses, none of which work with Dean. The minute Sal steps into his car, all bets are off. Sal's dreams don't come true. His plans don't materialize. Dean's not his roommate, soul mate, or long-lost brother. He's his adversary, his Moriarity, the *anti* to Sal's plots and dreams.[9] Dean's not a shelter from the storm; he *is* the storm. His "pious frenzy" burns up cars, marriages, friendships, promises, life plans—sacred canopies of all sorts (247). It takes him a weekend to burn through his marriage to Inez. It takes him three days to turn a bulletproof Cadillac into a pile of wreckage cast off in the streets of Chicago. And he wrecks Sal too, leaving him washed up on a broken-down river pier in New Jersey wondering what just happened.

But how is any of that *pious*? How can a road trip with Dean Moriarity be a sacred journey, what Allen Ginsberg termed "a hotrod Golgotha," rather than the suicidal thrill ride of two dopehead nihilists, as many early readers of *On the Road* believed? The answer to that question will suggest a view of the sacred as mobile and transgressive, a divine "rolling" Kerouac associates with rivers, cars, rain, jazz, Jesus, and Thoreau. "Thoreau was right; Jesus was right," Kerouac wrote to Allen Ginsberg in 1949. "It's all wrong and I denounce it and it can all go to hell. I don't believe in this society; but I believe in man, like Mann. So roll your own bones, I say."[10] The phrase "roll your bones" occurs so often in Kerouac's writing that it becomes a kind of signature mantra, gathering associations of risk, change, chance, music, and sexuality—all elements of his thinking about religious play. One of Kerouac's key beliefs was that thought and feeling are not settled but transient, changing by the moment, which put him at odds with the religious foundationalism of the 1950s, what H. Richard Niebuhr called "getting down to bedrock and finding a foundation on which life can rest unmoved."[11]

This distinction between a beat spirituality of improvisational rolling and more secure theologies of bedrock belief is misleading, however, if it ignores the deeply conservative streak in Kerouac's narrator, who ends each road trip by returning to the status quo and whose character seems static even to his friends: "Same old Paradise," Jane Lee notices, seeing Sal again after a long time (142). For all his talk about the spirituality of bebop jazz—George Shearing's godlike piano playing or Slim Gaillard's godlike drumming—Sal is not an improvisational artist tuned to the flow of the moment: this set of players, in this place and time, interacting concretely and directly with one another (rather than with their ideas about one another). Sal doesn't think in concrete particulars. He experiences the world through a scrim of abstraction and generality preformulated for him by books and films. Despite all the traveling, Sal is only partially or occasionally on the road, preferring to keep one foot firmly planted in the myths and ideologies he learned at home. If Kerouac is using Sal to teach us something about improvisational faith, then perhaps he's showing us a photographic negative of that faith, a lesson on what not to do or an example of how not to live (just as Dean offers several lessons on how not to drive).

Maybe, but *On the Road* does more than that. Like Dickinson and Thoreau, Kerouac is a devotee of uncanny "neighboring," the sudden flare-up of faces and meanings hidden in plain view. Kerouac allows life to tear Sal's scrim from time to time and turn him toward the embodied presence of another human being, usually someone in just as much pain as he is. In those moments, Sal stops following a preconceived script and responds to what's happening right in front of him, interacting with people rather than archetypes and making on-the-spot choices in reply to the choices they press on him. When that occurs, he's improvising. He's "open to what is happening," which is how Jacques Lecoq defines improvisation (*disponible à l'événement*).[12] This kind of responsiveness is playful not because it's easy but because it's risky and because it frees Sal from a special kind of "quiet desperation"—the postwar kind, the sort of thing young people feel when half the students in their schools are dead and the rest are eviscerated and they'd give almost anything for a little protection. What Sal does to protect himself is killing him, as he knows, killing his spirit. Sacred encounter is playful because it surprises Sal out of himself, out of his protective fantasies, and helps him experience a world that's stranger and wilder than he thought. The sacred is playful because Sal *didn't* think of it. He didn't write its script, and so it opens possibilities of meaning and relationship that are different and deeper than the limits of his own mind. Most of all, sacred encounter is playful because Sal doesn't know how it will end. A sacred future is open-ended and still rolling, and so it frees Sal from trying to stop time in perpetual Chiquito-hood and gives him a glimpse of the person he might yet be.

THEOLOGY AND IMPROVISATION

Before examining several scenes of scrim tearing in *On the Road*, let me align Kerouac with two recent theologies of play and improvisation: Jean-Jacques

Suurmond's *Word and Spirit at Play: Towards a Charismatic Theology*; and Jeremy S. Begbie's *Theology, Music and Time*.[13] I hope to establish this theological context with some care not only to suggest the internal complexity of both works but also to avoid jumping quickly to post-secular accounts of beat spirituality and thus ignoring how theologians working within a Christian tradition explore the questions of play and alterity so important to *On the Road*.[14]

For Suurmond, playful wisdom means religious ecstasy. Suurmond begins *Word and Spirit at Play* with the Pentecostal revivals led by William J. Seymour in a storefront church on Azusa Street in Los Angeles in 1906. Seymour believed that the Spirit of Pentecost could release people from the rigid boundaries of sexual, racial, and national identities and so achieve the reconciliations of the ancient church: "neither Jew nor Greek, slave nor free, male nor female" (Gal. 3:28). These reconciliations depended for Seymour on the ecstatic possibilities of charismatic spirituality, the ability to stand "outside" oneself in worship and prayer. With no worship programs, church hierarchy, prayer books, or prepared sermons—spontaneity reigned supreme in the Azusa Street revivals, which were marked by collective outbursts of drumming, singing, dancing, prophesy, and glossolalia, the gift of tongues. Glossolalia was central to Seymour's vision of restored community because it refuses to "capture" God in human signs and concepts and so resembles what John Panteleimon Manoussakis calls the "anti-word quality of music," its ability to express meanings we could not otherwise think or say.[15]

Although the Azusa Street revivals ended in 1909, they had a profound effect on world religion (nearly a quarter of all Christians now identify as charismatic); the leadership of the American civil rights movement; and the individual careers of several jazz musicians, including one of Kerouac's heroes, Slim Gaillard. Gaillard owned a record store not far from Azusa Street in the 1940s; spoke a polyglot language he called *vout*, a playful version of glossolalia; and adapted elements of the black Pentecostal tradition to jazz performances that sometimes seemed like worship services, as they did to Dean.[16] When Dean approached Gaillard, "he approached his God," Sal says; "he thought Slim was God" (177). Gaillard is a kind of jazz trickster in *On the Road*, an enigmatic figure of musical and religious transformation. He's hard to find or follow, "Nobody knows where Slim Gaillard is," and he presides over one of Kerouac's most important scenes of gender fluidity, when Dean dreams that he's a pregnant mother lying on the grass with Gaillard beside him, speaking his *vout* version of Pentecostal tongues: "There you go-orooni" (177).

Suurmond doesn't mention Gaillard or Kerouac, and the hero of his book isn't a jazz musician but the Jewish theologian Martin Buber. Buber argued that our relationship with God is mediated through concrete encounters with one another, "I-Thou" relationships of mutuality and rapport (*tegeninnig* in Suurmond's Dutch). I-Thou relationships are not functional or utilitarian, turning the other into an extension of the ego. Nor are they controlled by one side or the other, depending instead on a liminal space between both partners Buber calls love or the Spirit.[17] Suurmond uses Buber's model to contrast a false, ego-centered self, which "constantly aims to preserve itself and therefore opts for routine and predictability," with a charismatic subject open to the spontaneous play of an ever-creative God.[18] "God's creation principle is playful Wisdom," Suurmond argues, commenting on the scene of divine play in Proverbs 8 and coining the same phrase that occurred to Thoreau.[19] Responding to such play requires an attitude of spiritual "lightness" and ad hoc attunement for Suurmond. In play, we sacrifice "rigid idols" for living relationships, static models for I-Thou encounters, and so meet "the other in the now which is always open and unpredictable."[20] Suurmond draws a direct line from the playful wisdom of Proverbs 8, the logos-child playing beside God, to the playful wisdom of Christ's parables, which reframe religious teaching according to the demands of the moment (rather than a predetermined and so atemporal code). For Suurmond, Christ is a frame-shifter and "model breaker," an improvisational artist who deconstructs fixed forms and responds "spontaneously to any new, concrete situation."[21] Christ's situational teaching honors the diversity of his listeners by offering different stories and images of faith on different occasions and in response to the needs of different people. Thus, faith in the gospels is like a shepherd searching for a lost sheep or a woman searching for a lost coin. But faith is also like threading a camel through the eye of a needle or being born again. The parables keep coming, one after another, as if the point of such teaching is to pull the pins holding faith to a single definition and so make possible critical perspectives for change and growth.

For Suurmond, the enemy of playful religion is not only dullness or inattention but also habits of symbolic abstraction that "imprison the other in a picture" based on past experiences and thus create an "it-world" of preformulated response.[22] In these relationships, the other becomes self-confirming and stereotypical, easily assimilated to the ego's needs because no longer a person or neighbor but merely "a repetition of a previously privately coordinated understanding," as Alistair McFadyen has argued.[23] Reacting spontaneously, as Christ does, means approaching the other without these preconceptions, the way a visual artist might respond to a blank canvas or a jazz musician to an interacting ensemble. "Begin not from preconceived idea of what to say about image," Kerouac writes in his prose manifesto, "Essentials of Spontaneous Prose," "but from jewel center of interest in subject of image at *moment* of writing" (original emphasis).[24] Kerouac tends to call this unscripted openness "improvisation or spontaneity." Suurmond uses the Pauline word *charism*, a gift of grace, which makes possible "an exodus from my own, self-confirming presuppositions" and so a revelation of "the totally other in the neighbour."[25] This exodus isn't something we can choose or control, which only deepens our preoccupation with ourselves, but comes to us as a gift of divine love playing itself out in time.

As an example of Suurmond's "it-world," consider Dean's pack of pornographic playing cards, a form of play that turns sex into a stylized routine of poses and partners. Dean plays this game not only with his cards but also with his lovers, shuffling and reshuffling the deck: Marylou, Camille, Inez, Camille again, Marylou again. And all the lovers without names: the woman in the restaurant parking lot, the woman behind the pool hall, and so on. Neal Cassady's sexual play seemed almost mythic to the Beats, a godlike liberation from middle-class norms. In the N.C. (Neal Cassady) section of *Howl*, for instance, Ginsberg begins by celebrating Cassady as the "secret hero of these poems," the "cocksman and Adonis of Denver," a "joy to the memory of his innumerable lays of girls." But there's little joy or liberation in these encounters, which begin to look increasingly compulsive and solipsistic as the stanza continues: "on mountaintops in caves or with gaunt waitresses in familiar roadside lonely petticoat upliftings & especially secret gas-station solipsisms of johns, & hometown alleys."[26] The Whitman-like ampersands just make things worse, pointing up the difference between the sexual mutuality of many of the *Calamus* poems and whatever's happening in those johns and alleys. We're not in heaven with this kind of play, no matter what Sal says. We're in an "it-world" of fungible exchange, this girl for another girl, this trick for another trick, until the gaunt waitresses blur into one another.

What's missing from such play is the particularity of improvisational encounter, the *frisson* of a unique event. Drawing on Suurmond, the Anglican theologian Jeremy Begbie accents this particularity as a key feature of Christian theologies of response, eschatology, ecclesiology, and time. Like many theologians, Begbie seeks to understand what music can offer theology as a way of thinking about God. What's distinctive about Begbie's approach is that he doesn't adduce religious themes from a musical composition, exploring what we might learn about faith or spirit from a Bach chorale, but stresses instead the "musicality" of theology itself, imagining what it would mean to think and live in a musical mode.[27] For Begbie, this means acknowledging the role time plays in music and using that temporality to critique theology's drift toward essentialism and metaphysics. Unlike Hellenic and Augustinian theologies of music, which associate music with the eternal, music is an art of the passing moment for Begbie, time-saturated all the way through. Music is temporality shaped and made tangible—time signatures we can feel and sing.

Learning to "sing" theology, Begbie suggests, means learning a series of music lessons that can help theology do its work. In the chapter "Time to

Improvise," his discussion of improvisational jazz, Begbie argues that jazz teaches us the virtues of delay and patience, waiting for resolutions that may or may not come and living for long stretches in the "meanwhile" of unresolved tension (and learning to cherish that tension). Moreover, jazz can teach us something about polyphonic thinking, being at home with the simultaneous interaction of multiple voices, a form of conversational theology I'll develop more fully in chapter 6. But jazz teaches other lessons as well: unlike musical traditions that emphasize score over performance, jazz improvisation casts a gentle eye on failure and shows people how damaged things can be "taken up" into an evolving whole, made beautiful again, like the rag rug Sal's aunt creates from scraps of old clothes (107).[28] In addition, jazz embodies the wisdom of "contingency" for Begbie, who uses the word to mean non-necessity and newness: "Contingent things do not have to be and contingent events do not have to happen. Applied to musical experience, along with regularity and consistency, we sense (even if we do not articulate) that much of what we hear *might have been otherwise*, and the psychological force of this contingency is *newness*" (original emphasis).[29] Contingency means that there's never only one way to get from "here" to "there" in a jazz performance, which is exactly what Sal learns when his plans break down at Bear Mountain: "It was my dream that screwed up, the stupid hearthside idea that it would be wonderful to follow one great red line across America instead of trying various roads and routes" (11).

Finally, Begbie helps us see that musical theologies live peacefully with constraint. On the earth-bound side of things, music doesn't occur in a temporal vacuum, Plato's *apeiron*. It takes place in specific circumstances and so bumps up against limits no one controls: the quirks and resistances of saxophone reeds, concert halls, guitar strings, and the personalities of different audiences and performers.[30] There are built-in limits to how a human hand can move over a keyboard or how an ensemble can move on stage. There are sounds a human voice can produce and others it cannot (and sounds a voice can produce on this day and not another). These limits interact in various ways to shape the resulting performance, which emerges in dialogue with the alterity of a balky world. Sometimes the constraints are invisible because the performance fits seamlessly within its context and tradition. But jazz musicians often court the constraints to make the resistance stand out. Don Cherry played a miniature pocket trumpet. Slim Gaillard played piano with the backs of his hands. In "Shanghai Shuffle" Louis Armstrong used a plunger mute to create an eight-bar improvisation based on the repetition of a single note. For Begbie, jazz freedom emerges not by mastering resistance but by working within it. For many performers and listeners, the excitement of a jazz concert comes from knowing that what we're hearing is fleeting and occasional, constrained by the specific circumstances of a one-time performance. Begbie's point is that improvisational musicians are often more alert to those circumstances than performers accustomed to written scores and note-for-note rehearsal. In this sense, improvisation favors a special form of situational awareness—what Lecoq calls *disponibilité* and what Thoreau described as his "profession" as a religious writer: being on the alert, being attuned to a changing locale.

This jazz-like self-tuning is uniquely suited to the "rolling" theology of *On the Road*, with its emphasis on flux and process, but it also suggests for Begbie a relational account of Christian spirituality. Improvisation might seem to imply the singular brilliance of an individual performer, as in Keith Jarrett's *Solo Concerts*. But jazz improvisation is more like the give and take of a conversation for Begbie (with the "conversation" including composers and performers in the past).[31] Where the French composer Pierre Boulez sees only private psychodrama in jazz improvisation, "not the slightest scope for anyone else to join in,"[32] Begbie sees a "gift exchange" of interactive community, individual performers passing ideas back and forth and making musical choices based on what's happening around them.[33] This call-and-response pattern resembles the charismatic traditions Suurmond studies and reinforces his notion that play is "ecstatic" or self-transcending.[34] But the word "play" can be misleading if improvisation seems childlike or untutored. The "play" Begbie has in mind depends on a long apprenticeship in music, where repertory and experience count as much as natural sensitivity and where the skills that emerge from a lifetime in jazz constitute a spiritual discipline as well as a creative practice: giving space to the other through alert responsiveness; accepting and benefiting from conflict; accepting and reframing failure; receiving other people's gifts in humility; and listening and replying to those gifts in turn.[35] These are church skills for Suurmond and Begbie, the tool kit of Christian community, just as they are ethical and spiritual skills for Kerouac, who explores what it means to experience the sacred in a jazz idiom and thus "play" or "sing" theology in *On the Road*. For all three writers, what matters is immediacy, tuning in to the uniqueness of a contingent occasion and living gracefully "in time." Which is just how Kerouac puts it in the Slim Gaillard scene in *On the Road*:

> Slim Gaillard is a tall, thin Negro with big sad eyes who's always saying, "Right-orooni" and "How 'bout a little bourbon-orooni." In Frisco great eager crowds of young semi-intellectuals sat at his feet and listened to him on the piano, guitar, and bongo drums. . . . Dean stands in the back, saying, "God! Yes!"—and clasping his hands in prayer and sweating. "Sal, Slim knows time, he knows time." Slim sits down at the piano and hits two notes, two Cs, then two more, then one, then two, and suddenly the big burly bass-player wakes up from a reverie and realizes Slim is playing "C-Jam Blues" and he slugs in

his big forefinger on the string and the big booming beat begins and everybody starts rocking and Slim looks just as sad as ever, and they blow jazz for half an hour. (176–77)

This is an unusual rendering of "C-Jam Blues." The New Orleans' clarinetist Barney Bigard wrote the melody for "C-Jam Blues" in 1941, and Duke Ellington arranged and performed the piece the following year. (Bigard was a member of Ellington's orchestra.) By the time Kerouac heard Gaillard perform in San Francisco in 1947, "C-Jam Blues" had been adapted to several different musical styles: Ellington's swing orchestra, Louis Armstrong's New Orleans jazz, Charlie Parker's bebop, and others. None of that comes into view here. What Kerouac explores instead is a different notion of jazz creativity, one based not on individual changes within an aesthetic tradition but on the interactions occurring within a group of improvising musicians and between the musicians and their audience. Thus, Kerouac brings forward the situational rapport Ingrid Monson terms "ensemble responsiveness" in her study of improvisational jazz.[36] It's common in jazz history to distinguish between Ellington's carefully orchestrated swing jazz in the 1930s (which involved big bands, big dance halls, and relatively few opportunities for soloing) and Parker's bop jazz in the 1940s (which featured smaller ensembles and venues and the solo improvisations of a star performer). Jazz scholars usually place Kerouac on the Charlie Parker end of the spectrum and stress the "individualism" of his jazz scenes, solos above all.

It's different here. Kerouac blends two unique jazz styles, by having Slim Gaillard play a Duke Ellington tune. And he focuses not on the virtuosity of a solo performer but on the way different people *answer* Gaillard's opening invitation: the bass player's beat; Dean's prayers and shouts; the audience's dancing; and eventually Kerouac's reworking of the scene in alliterative, drum-like prose. The first eight notes of "C-Jam Blues" are a simple blues riff in C major, four pairs of two notes each with the tonic at the end: GG GG GG GC. But that's enough to draw the bass player out of himself, out of his private reverie, and create a moment of collective interplay and nonidentical reply, again like the call-and-response tradition of charismatic worship. In the music criticism of the 1930s and 1940s, jazz was often associated with a "primitivist" myth of unconscious inspiration.[37] The vitality of jazz creativity was thought to be intuitive and "racial," something African-American musicians do better than white performers: descend to a place below conscious thought, academic training, or musical technique. In *Jazz: From the Congo to the Metropolitan* (1944), the jazz critic Robert Goffin argued that black musicians like Louis Armstrong, Charlie Shavers, and Leo Watson possessed a uniquely racial ability to enter that unconscious space, which he called "the trance."[38] Kerouac's jazz scenes often mirror the primitivist assumptions of his contemporaries, but in this scene the beat begins when people *wake* from trance and interact consciously and deliberately with one another.

Such moments are intensely sacred in *On the Road*, as suggested by Dean's spontaneous prayer. If this scene suggests what theology might learn from jazz, a snapshot of its playful wisdom, then Kerouac's focus is on the delicacy of these situational interactions, what John Clellon Holmes called "the tenuous, hair-breadth rapport of improvisation."[39] The point is not to ignore other people and trust the intuitive rightness of one's own ideas, a formula that leads to several scenes of failed jazz in *On the Road*. Nor is the point to imitate Gaillard note for note and follow lockstep behind his lead. What matters is the ability to put oneself in dialogue with Gaillard, adding new gifts to the conversation he begins: cries, yesses, sweat, bass beats, dance moves, prayers, and prose. If Dean, the bass player, the audience, and even Kerouac are all included as co-performers in the improvisation, then what happened that night isn't fungible at all but keyed instead to the specific shape of a singular occasion. Others will certainly play "C-Jam Blues" in the future, including Gaillard, but it won't be *this* "C-Jam Blues"—because the mood, setting, ensemble, instruments, audience, and even Gaillard himself will all be different. "Jazz music lives and dies in the moment of performance," Ted Gioia said, and to know that, Kerouac suggests, is to know time.[40]

WAKING UP IN TIME

It may seem odd to bring *Walden* into a discussion of jazz at this point, but the bass player's disrupted reverie may owe something to Kerouac's lifelong fascination with Thoreau.[41] Waking up from sleep or dream is the beginning of spiritual wisdom in *Walden*, the first step in knowing where we are in the world. As Mitchell Breitwieser has argued, the place Thoreau wakes up to is not "reality at large, in some abstract sense, but to 'the snow lying deep on the earth dotted with young pines, and the very slope of the hill on which my house is placed,' this place, here, a world, the neighborhood, the locale that also holds, in its other crevices, precisely these objects (though they are subjects now), just these species of animals, though there is little interest in species of animals any more."[42]

There are dozens of these scenes in *Walden*: "I found myself suddenly neighbor to the birds," Thoreau writes in "Where I Lived, and What I Lived For." "I found myself suddenly in the shadow of a cloud," he says in "Baker Farm."[43] Thoreau doesn't wake up to "C-Jam Blues" of course but to bird song or cloud shadow, and yet the results are nearly the same: Thoreau finds himself in the midst of an active present, interacting with others who loom suddenly out of the fog. These others were there the whole time but hidden until now by sleep, fretfulness, reification, prejudice, inattention—all the ways we fail to notice where we are and who is there beside us. Thoreau stresses the uncanny "nextness" of these awakenings, what McFadyen calls "the along-sidedness" of relational theologies in which we discover ourselves and others at the same time.[44] The place Thoreau wakes up to is both home and not home. It's exactly where he was before—only wilder, louder, busier, and more fully inhabited (and so not at all where he was before). Each sudden self-finding in *Walden* reveals Thoreau's place in a dense milieu, surrounded by birds and clouds he hadn't noticed before, birds and clouds he now calls his neighbors. As Stanley Cavell points out, Thoreau reserves the title of "traveler" to those who accept this new orientation, this emplacement in a changing locale, and recognize that waking up to the true scope of our relations is a continuous activity and conscious discipline. It is in fact what spirituality means in *Walden*.[45]

Sal resists that kind of "traveling." He protects himself from enigmatic encounter by withdrawing from an active present and falling back on preformulated racial, sexual, and religious clichés—that is, by *not* improvising. When Gaillard's performance becomes increasingly "charismatic" in the San Francisco nightclub for instance—"Slim goes mad and grabs the bongos and plays tremendous rapid Cubana beats and yells crazy things in Spanish, in Arabic, in Peruvian dialect, in Egyptian"—Sal stabilizes the scene by primly sorting the heteroglossia into component languages, none of which he speaks, and by emphasizing the craziness and foreignness of an experience he does not share: "Every time Slim said, 'Orooni,' Dean said, 'Yes!' I sat there with these two madmen. Nothing happened. To Slim Gaillard the whole world was just one big orooni" (177).

I mention this not to criticize Sal but to suggest where he is in his journey. Kerouac picks up the story of Sal's spiritual formation near its beginning, when Sal is still a little boy, a Chiquito. And he uses Sal's failures and prejudices not to judge his character, which is still evolving, but to help us see what blocks or delays improvisational play: Sal's unwillingness to open himself to other people and "surrender" some measure of control, a key word for many improvisational performers.[46] Like Thoreau, Sal often wakes up to find himself in a place he's never been before, interacting with neighbors he barely knows, but the improvisations that result are fragile and brief, sometimes lasting only a few seconds. And then the doors of perception swing shut again, and we're back in "fairyland," a movie-inspired fantasy playing privately in Sal's mind.

This is what makes the scene with Terry in the Los Angeles hotel room so important: Sal accepts the gift of her presence and vulnerability and interacts with her spontaneously and specifically, without the help of a preformulated code. There's nothing musical about the scene, unless we count the sound of Terry's shoes hitting the bathroom door as the opening beat. But that's enough to wake Sal from his private reverie and disrupt the script he'd been following since the day they met. On the bus ride from Bakersfield to Los Angeles, a few pages earlier, Sal began playing an imaginary game in which he assumes the role of Joel McCrea, from Preston Sturges' film *Sullivan's Travels* (1941), and Terry becomes Veronica Lake as she sleeps on his lap. Sal plays versions of this movie game several times in *On the Road*. His mind is basically a machine for turning life into a movie: a Preston Sturges film, starring Sal and Terry; a *Mark of Zorro* film, starring Sal and a .32 automatic; a Mexican pornographic film, starring Sal and several teenage prostitutes; and so on. But Sal's film machine breaks down in the Los Angeles hotel room, when he sees something so utterly unexpected, so "wild" to his frame of reference, that it feels almost sacred:

> In reverent and sweet little silence she took all her clothes off and slipped her tiny body into the sheets with me. It was brown as grapes. I saw her poor belly where there was a Caesarian scar; her hips were so narrow she couldn't bear a child without getting gashed open. Her legs were like little sticks. She was only four foot ten. I made love to her in the sweetness of the weary morning. (85)

Sal's references to Terry's "little silence" and "tiny body" are important not because they sustain the childish play he typically prefers—Terry's belly is marked by unmistakable signs of adulthood and trauma—but because her physical body deflates Sal's high-blown fantasies and brings him back down to earth. *This* earth, scarred and gashy. The fairyland "Terry" starring in Sal's movie is not the migrant mother now lying in his bed; and that deflation acts as a *charism* for Sal, an exodus from his self-confirming presuppositions. Kerouac draws out nonidentical qualities in Terry—her scars, her emaciated legs—to distinguish her from the blown-up doll-women Sal prefers and to accent a fierce particularity so important to Kerouac's vision of the sacred that he coins an unusual phrase: "riotous angelic particulars" (209). If Sal is allowing that particularity to disrupt his reifying fantasy, then this is indeed a scene of improvisational dialogue and sacred play, what Sal calls the communion of "two tired angels," "the closest and most delicious thing in life" (85).

This kind of improvisation occurs rarely in *On the Road*. After this, Sal's erotic encounters are fast and faceless, and he won't allow himself to particularize poverty, femininity, tenderness, or the sacred quite this way again. Like many male American writers, Sal is more comfortable with the sublime than the particular. He cherishes the generalizing tendencies of his imagination and refuses to see or believe in things that contradict his preconceived "picture" of life, as Kerouac once said about himself.[47] To build and sustain that picture, Sal uses universals and long shots—rooftops, mountaintops, panoramas, horizons—that gobble up individualizing difference in a wide-angle Emersonian gaze. To Sal's usual way of thinking, individual women are more or less stylized and interchangeable, like Dean's playing cards. After Sal leaves Terry in Bakersfield and takes a bus back to New York, for instance, Sal "made the acquaintance of a girl and we necked all the way to Indianapolis. She was nearsighted. When we got off to eat I had to lead her by the hand to the lunch counter" (103). The vulnerability of Terry's "poor belly" fades away almost immediately and we're back in Dean's deck of cards: this girl for another girl, this trick for another trick—which is what Sal thought when he first met Terry, that she was a prostitute turning a trick. Sal mentions that the busgirl is "nearsighted"—but that description fits him more than her, his tendency to blur out particularizing differences and so legitimate racial and sexual clichés.[48]

These self-protective clichés return long before Sal steps on the New York bus. When Sal and Terry return to Bakersfield to build a new life for themselves and Terry's son, Johnny, Sal reverts to the racial and class fantasies he'd abandoned briefly in Los Angeles. As Sal describes his experience picking cotton, for instance, he doesn't see that work as a farm laborer would, as Terry would. He sees it like a filmmaker, Preston Sturges perhaps, who had a gift for making rural poverty seem in the end rather beautiful. "We bent down and began picking cotton. It was beautiful," Sal says, glancing toward and then beyond two African-American farmworkers laboring nearby. "My back began to ache. But it was beautiful kneeling and hiding in that earth. If I felt like resting I did, with my face on the pillow of brown moist earth" (96). There's plenty of work going on in this scene, but none of it has to do with picking cotton. As Mark Richardson has argued, this scene suggests the racial and ideological work of a white writer dreaming himself past the actual lives of Mexican-American and African-American migrant workers.[49] To that end, Sal adopts a telescopic gaze that moves from the fields and tents of the workers in the foreground, to the foothills in the middle distance, and from there to the mountaintops of the Sierras and a high morning sky. Whatever's prickly or disagreeable in the scene—the prick of cotton thorns that make Sal's fingers bleed—is softened by this long-angle lens. The "pillow of brown moist earth" is the giveaway. This is dream work, a kind of postwar, post-traumatic world-building that replaces lethal fact with harmonizing myth. Sal hungers for the raw and the real—that's what draws him to Dean and the road in the first place—but he also longs for the sleepy security of a prewar America immune to time and loss.

Sal starts in on the work of redreaming that America almost immediately. When Sal sees Dean for the first time in New York, he can't believe his luck. Dean's different from his friends in New York: not "arty," "sulky," or "cynical" (which are the worst things one can be in a Jack Kerouac novel), but terrifically exciting and naive. He's a teenage ode to joy, "a sideburned hero of the snowy West," and best of all, he's *exactly* like the boys Sal grew up with in Paterson (the stand-in for Kerouac's hometown of Lowell). "[H]e reminded me of some long-lost brother," Sal says. "I heard again the voices of old companions and brothers under the bridge, among the motorcycles, along the wash-lined neighborhood and drowsy doorsteps of afternoon where boys played guitars while their older brothers worked in the mills" (7).

This is an unusual thing to say in 1951, given that so many of Kerouac's childhood companions did not return from the war. So again, the sleepiness is the key. The "drowsy doorsteps" in Paterson suggest that Sal is using Dean to recreate a wished-for space of pastoral dreaming. This would be Dean's job description, if Sal had anything to say about it: to be their dream weaver and tambourine man; their gold-hatted, high-bouncing lover, as Fitzgerald said of Gatsby. And it's worth noting that whatever music the boys are playing on their guitars, it's probably not jazz. Like Fitzgerald, Kerouac uses jazz not to sustain atemporal dreaming but to expose and critique it, so that we might rouse ourselves from drowsy doorsteps and live again in the beat of time.

Let me consider one more scene of improvisational awakening in *On the Road*, where once more the call Sal responds to is not exactly musical, it's a baby's wail, and yet that cry creates the same sense of waking up "in time" Kerouac associates with jazz spirituality. The scene takes place on Sal's last road trip, where he ends up in a Mexican whorehouse playing a violent game of competitive sexuality. "We made the bed bounce a half-hour," Sal tells us, measuring his performance by the clock and resecuring an imperiled masculinity (287). Sal is profoundly troubled by the depth of his feelings for Dean, which do not fit any of the scripts he inherited, and so part of what Sal's doing in Gregoria is reaffirming his heterosexuality as publicly and aggressively as possible, with the help of several Mexican and Venezuelan women. Except for Sal, these aren't actually "Mexican and Venezuelan women," but convenient stand-ins for the Ali Baba and the Courtesans film playing in his head. There's a religious icon in a corner of the bed-bouncing room, which distracts Sal briefly with a reminder of how far things have fallen. But the film really jumps the sprockets when a crying baby tears the scrim and wakes Sal up to where he actually is in the world: "I heard a baby wail in a sudden lull, remembering I was in Mexico after all and not in a pornographic hasheesh daydream in heaven" (289).

It seems strange to call this scene an "improvisation" or to think of it as being somehow sacred. And yet Kerouac is drawn to exactly those moments when the in-breaking presence of another person pierces Sal's fairyland detachment and rehabilitates an awareness drifting toward sleep. Kerouac rightly calls that interpersonal sleep "pornography," which fetishizes single traits and reduces people to easily assimilated sexual and racial clichés, "white legs protruding from the silk." The crying child fractures that familiar script and introduces the possibility of new awareness, another sudden self-finding where Sal wakes up to his true locale: not in an Ali Baba daydream but in the company of other suffering people. Sal calls that new locale *Mexico*—"I was in Mexico after all"—which is confusing, because Sal also calls his fantasy place *Mexico* and peoples that place with all sorts of movie characters and stereotypes. One of the last things Sal sees in Mexico are beggars "wrapped in advertising posters," but that world-wrapping impulse is in place from the beginning (301). Sal and Dean have never been to Mexico and confess, at the border crossing at Laredo, that they have "no idea what Mexico would really be like" (273). This "No Idea Zone" is dangerous and uncomfortable, like all border crossings, and so Sal and Dean get right to work building a fairyland "Mexico" out of bits and pieces of cultural lore. The remapping happens fast, within a few moments, so that when Sal and Dean cross the Rio Grande, they're surprised that they're not surprised. Mexico looks like itself: "To our amazement, it looked exactly like Mexico" (274). That's what "staying home" means in *On the Road*. Sal often comes into a place for the first time and feels like he's been there before—precisely because he pre-built that place in his imagination.

The baby's cry interrupts this synthetic menu of pre-thought thoughts. It opens a gap in Sal's preconceptions and draws him in to a completely different "ensemble"—one in which the people he interacts with have names, scars, histories, children. That improvisation lasts only a few seconds, however, and then the traveling ends, the clichés return, and Sal retreats to safer ground, showering in "an ordinary American-type bathhouse" and putting as much distance between himself and that revelation as he can (290). Sal glances back as they drive away and notices "a sad kiddy park" growing smaller behind them, a reminder of the crying child, and then he lets his thoughts scatter under a fading sun.

Spiritual insight is temporary and fleeting in this way in *On the Road*, yet this is what "traveling" means for Kerouac, spiritual traveling rather than the sex tourism Sal and Dean are doing in Gregoria. Kerouac imagines spiritual growth as an improvisational "exile" where whatever superstructure of religious ideas his characters use to orient themselves breaks apart and they suddenly find themselves outside, on the road, where the wild things are. This is the hard gospel of Kerouac's novel. It's "good news" for a character slowly closing out the world to protect his troubled heart, the situation we saw in Dickinson's "I dreaded that first Robin, so." But it's not the news Sal hoped to hear when he started his journey. Nor is it what most people expect from a novel that seems to validate a narcissistic gospel of self-fulfillment and syncretic whim. Kerouac never drifted far from his Catholic roots, and the goal of traveling in *On the Road* is not self-fulfillment but self-emptying, a kenosis so profound that it strips Sal of nearly everything he holds dear: his dreams, his plans, his ideas about Dean, his ideas about God—whatever would shelter him from what Kerouac calls "the raw road night" (11). Coming into that night without evasion or defensiveness is the difficult work of spiritual growth for Kerouac, a journey that leaves the traveler homeless, exhausted, undefended, *beat*. And thus receptive, available, submissive, *beatific*.[50]

A different writer might hide these closure-wrecking gaps and protect whatever recuperating structures she or he needs to organize the real. In Kerouac, the gaps always show. He doesn't let us forget that behind the famous madness myth—"the only people for me are the mad ones, the ones who are mad to live, mad to talk, mad to be saved"—is a particular person, Jane Lee, wandering through Times Square with her baby daughter in her arms and ending up in Bellevue mental hospital (5). Or that behind the pastoral myth of boys and their guitars are soldiers and sailors who aren't coming home. Or that behind the beat myth of erotic liberation are teenage prostitutes and their children. There are bodies in Sal's beloved Mississippi, the suicide at the Algiers ferry, and all the beautiful ideas in the world can't hide that damage. Kerouac's response, theologically, is to recognize the damage to his ideas as a *charism*, a redemptive exodus, and to cherish a rawness or rupture at the heart of human experience that disables conceptual structures and returns people to a world outside their minds.[51]

This return doesn't happen all at once. Our dreams are tough and resilient, Kerouac shows. They're not made of fairy dust; they're made of fear. We build them to withstand the strangeness of the world and so protect our lives from the rolling insecurity of time and change. "The years have rolled severally behind us," Dean tells Sal just before the Mexico trip, his speech coming apart like his damaged body, "and yet you see none of us have really changed, that's what so amazing, the dura—the dura—bility—in fact to prove that I have here a deck of cards" (262). Then Dean shows Sal the porno pack, his charm against change. Sal has his own protective charms, and he's not giving them up without a fight—not because he's afraid of the world but because he's afraid of being disillusioned with the world; afraid that if he loses his dreams, compromised as they are, he'll lose the best part of himself: his faith, his ecstasies, his sense of a world lit with wonder. Thus, Kerouac suggests that we may need angelic myths just as much as we need angelic particulars—not to insulate our lives from change but because myth is our only way of imagining the presence of God in the world and to lose that, for Sal, is to lose everything. "Simply to renounce illusion," John Leland argues, "would be to renounce Dean, the West, the road and the clarion call of Whitman's America. It is the dullest and most reductive form of secularism. If *On the Road* is a spiritual quest, it cannot love only the factual. Myth has truth, too."[52]

Kerouac lets the world roll hard against the sea wall of his narrator, but he doesn't disillusion him. Even at the end of *On the Road*, after all he's been through, Sal is still capable of astonishing naivete—the sentence "God is Pooh Bear" comes to mind—not because Kerouac wants us to smirk at Sal's innocence but because he wants us to cherish it. But cherish it *wisely*. Cherish the religious myths (or beat myths or childhood myths) knowing that they won't last long and that they shouldn't last long. Even our best moments are streaked with delusion, and bleaching *it* out is the equivalent to bleaching *us* out, bleaching the human part out, in the colorless atheism of the void, which Kerouac in his later books was increasingly willing to do. But not here. In *On the Road*, Kerouac is tender with the human part. He's tender with naivete—even as he leads Sal back to a state of beatific submission, not once but continually, repeatedly, in a kenotic surrender of his dreams to the cockeyed strangeness of the world.

TRUE AND SINCERE TRAVELING

Thoreau had a good, simple word for that strangeness. He called it "wildness," and he thought that living in the wilderness of things as they are (rather than things as they should be or as we want them to be) was the hardest and most fulfilling spiritual discipline in life. It's almost impossible to imagine Thoreau ever reading *On the Road* much less recognizing his work filtering into the urban infernos of Kerouac's novel. But when Thoreau looks at the young people of his generation, what he sees is not so different from what Kerouac sees: quietly desperate young people playing trauma games to hide their despair: "A stereotyped but unconscious despair is concealed even under what are called the games and amusements of mankind."[53] When Thoreau goes on to say, in the same passage, "There is no play in them, for this comes after work," I think the "work" he has in mind is also what Kerouac explores in *On the Road*: the work of wise dreaming. And the "play" he imagines is close to the spiritual vision of *On the Road*: a responsiveness of spirit constantly adapting to new perspectives and revising its mythologies in the light of riotous, angelic particulars.

Thoreau called this kind of religious play "living in the present" and thought of it as a "newer testament," as he said in "Walking," "the gospel according to this moment." Kerouac both believed and disbelieved in that newer testament. In his writing practice, which was also a spiritual practice for Kerouac, he tried to open himself to the play of ideas as they were happening in time. He believed that truth could not be stated in doctrines or formulas but in the movement "from moment to moment incomprehensible, ungraspable, but terribly *clear*" (original emphasis). Kerouac tried to tune himself to that living instant like a jazz musician or action painter, living in the now, "danc[ing] on the edges of relative knowledge."⁵⁴ But he also recognized the extraordinary cost of that responsiveness and the dura-dura-bility of our preformed ideas. Kerouac explores this tension with great care. If Thoreau rejects any hint of religious conservatism in himself and his culture, Kerouac sticks closer to the middle, and he allows his novel to fluctuate, then, between two moods: traveling and staying home, waking and falling asleep, looking forward and glancing back. It's not that God is incomprehensible in *On the Road* and our attempts to understand the sacred deform a pure alterity, as Thoreau sometimes believed. Instead, the sacred is *almost* incomprehensible, a phrase Kerouac uses in *Visions of Cody*, teasing us with what's just beyond the limits of our vision and so drawing out our capacity for change and trust.⁵⁵ It's exhausting to try to control the world, as Sal learns, and so he tries sometimes to take his hands off the wheel and allow the world to flow according to the pattern of its own intentions. Sal is part of that intention, not watching from a safe distance but hip deep in the mud and flow, rolling with the same currents, here and then gone just like everything else—but not as frightened by that passing because this is how we experience the sacred in time: not God in a temple but God passing by, as the biblical writers say.

Thoreau felt that sacred play in the roll of the seasons and the melting of the sandbank and in the physical changes of his own body. Dickinson felt it in an "Aptitude for Bird" that rose in her to answer the in-breaking call of an astonishing world. Kerouac felt it in the roll of taped-up tracing paper flying off his typewriter, when he could stop prescribing his work and allow the book to be what *it* wanted to be, as if the typewriter had its own divine intentions. Sal experiences sacred play in the flow of the Mississippi; in the sweaty, heart-piercing music he loved; and in the roll of a car on a long American highway. This kind of rolling reminds Sal of loss and death, but Sal didn't always fear that traveling, because sometimes the rolling of a car is like a love song, a three-chord lullaby played through the hum of the tires. And it says, keep going and open your belly to it. It says, keep rolling under the stars and take care of the children as best you can.

This takes us to the end. I wish I could point to a passage that shows how far Sal's traveled as a person, but the fact is Sal doesn't change all that much, even sitting on the broken-down pier in the novel's last paragraph—except that he hears something different in that scene, hears it and sings it back to us: "So in America when the sun goes down and I sit on the old broken-down river pier watching the long, long skies over New Jersey and sense all that raw land that rolls in one unbelievable huge bulge over to the West Coast, and all that road going, all the people dreaming in the immensity of it, and in Iowa I know by now the children must be crying in the land where they let the children cry" (307).

There's much to say about this scene, but I want to close by thinking about the children. Listening to crying children is the last thing the old Sal would ever do. *On the Road* is bursting at the seams with children in trouble: Terry's child, Victor's child, Jane's children, Dean's children, the child in the brothel, and many others. Sal barely gives those children a glance much less a mythical heartland an "Iowa," where their suffering emerges full voice: "I know by now the children must be crying in the land where they let the children cry."[56] This is a small but important step in Sal's spiritual growth. It's hard for Sal to hear the crying children because he's one of those children, a twenty-something Chiquito hurt by the war. Facing their suffering would be a step toward facing his own. Sal takes that step now—and when he does, he's traveling. The cosmos Sal glimpses at the end of *On the Road* is a world in motion, just as it was for Thoreau. Sal is sitting still on the river pier and yet nothing is still. The approaching night "cups," "folds," "darkens," and "blesses"—as if it were a living creature (307). The stars aren't fixed points of light but "drooping" and "shedding" in cycles of disappearance and return that echo the ending of *Walden*. Even "America" is glimpsed in passing, not as a city on a hill but as a huge raw rolling: "all that raw land that rolls." It takes Sal a long time to get here, but when he does it's like watching a young writer find his voice, fumbling for it, reaching for it, and getting it wrong and still wrong. And then it's there, an American blues song of loss and change. This is the feeling Melville associated with the rolling of the whale in *Moby-Dick* and Whitman associated with the rolling of the tides in "Crossing Brooklyn Ferry." Kerouac's achievement in *On the Road* is to blend the voices of the older American prophets with the jazz musicians of his own era and so transmute private grief into shared pain and shared healing.

That kind of healing doesn't come cheap. Thoreau was crystal clear about the "work" of spiritual transformation: we have to die and be born again. That is, the old self has to die, the old Sal, the one starring in a movie he'd written about himself. Here's how Thoreau put it in *A Week*:

> True and sincere travelling is no pastime, but it is as serious as the grave, or any part of the human journey, and it requires a long probation to be broken into it. . . . The traveller must be born again on the road, and earn a passport to the elements, the principal powers that be for him. He shall experience at last that old threat of his mother fulfilled, that he shall be skinned alive. His sores shall gradually deepen themselves that they may heal inwardly, while he gives no rest to the sole of his foot, and at night weariness must be his pillow, that so he may acquire experience against his rainy days. —So was it with us.[57]

Kerouac doesn't say much about inward healing in *On the Road*, or in any of his books—not because he doesn't believe in it but because he stresses the "long probation" preceding spiritual growth and because he had a special genius for showing young men skinning themselves alive. Thoreau helped Kerouac see how to turn that suffering into a journey narrative and adapt the religious imagery of crucifixion and rebirth to a rolling theology of rivers and time. In 1949, Kerouac borrowed a copy of *A Week* from a local library and never returned it. That copy is now in the Berg Collection of the New York Public Library. On page 227 of *A Week*, Kerouac underlined the sentence "The traveller must be born again on the road" and placed a small neat check mark beside it in the margin. And then wrote a book about it all, and called it *On the Road*.

NOTES

1. Henry D. Thoreau, *The Journal of Henry D. Thoreau*, gen. ed. John C. Broderick, vol. 4 (Princeton: Princeton University Press, 1992), 55.

2. Robert E. Neale, *In Praise of Play: Toward a Psychology of Religion* (New York: Harper and Row, 1969), 125, 31.

3. The publication history of *On the Road* is complicated but important—and there are several versions. The one Kerouac favored was that he wrote the book from scratch in a three-week burst of white-hot creativity in April 1951 in the Chelsea apartment at 454 West 20th Street that he shared with his second wife, Joan Haverty. Kerouac typed the manuscript on strips of Japanese tracing paper that allowed him to keep writing for long periods of time without interrupting his narrative flow. When he finished the manuscript, Kerouac taped these strips together into a 120-foot scroll, now called "the scroll manuscript," and presented it to his editor, Robert Giroux. The pure spontaneity Kerouac stressed in his writing theories and in this story of *On the Road's* composition is misleading. Kerouac had been drafting ideas and scenes for his road book since 1948, and the scroll manuscript incorporates passages from journals and letters that stretch back for several years. After Giroux refused the novel as unpublishable in that form, Kerouac spent the next six years trying to place *On the Road* with a new publisher as well as finish an expanded version of his road book, *Visions of Cody*. Matt Theado reviews the publication history of the novel in "Revisions of Kerouac: The Long, Strange Trip of the *On the Road* Typescripts," in *What's Your Road, Man? Critical Essays on Jack Kerouac's "On the Road,"* ed. Hilary Holladay and Robert Holton (Carbondale: Southern Illinois University Press, 2009), 8–34.

4. Jack Kerouac, *On the Road* (1957; repr. New York: Penguin, 2003), 32. Subsequent references to *On the Road* will refer to this edition and be cited in the text by page number.

5. Jack Kerouac, *Vanity of Duluoz: An Adventurous Education, 1935–46* (1968; repr. New York: Penguin, 1994), 16.

6. On this, see Gladys Foxe, "'And Nobody Knows What's Going to Happen to Anybody': Fear and Futility in Jack Kerouac's *On the Road* and Why It Is Important," *Psychoanalytic Review* 95, no. 1 (February 2008): 45–60.

7. Gerald Nicosia, *Memory Babe: A Critical Biography of Jack Kerouac* (1983; repr. Berkeley: University of California Press, 1994), 93.

8. Will Herberg, *Protestant, Catholic, Jew: An Essay in American Religious Sociology* (1955; repr. Garden City, NY: Anchor Books, 1960), 59. Several religious historians discuss the conservatism of 1950s spirituality and its reconciliation with middle-class values, including Sydney E. Ahlstrom, *A Religious History of the American People* (New Haven: Yale University Press, 1972); Robert Wuthnow, *After Heaven: Spirituality in America Since the 1950s* (Berkeley: University of California Press, 1998); and Stephen R. Prothero, "On the Holy Road: The Beat Movement as Spiritual Protest," *Harvard Theological Review* 84, no. 2 (1991): 205–22. In addition, several social critics in this period view the preoccupation with personality adjustment within a stable work group as the secular equivalent of religious experience. On this, see William H. Whyte, *The Organization Man* (1956; repr. Philadelphia: University of Pennsylvania Press, 2002), 6, 32–46.

9. Gerald Nicosia recognizes an allusion to Sherlock Holmes' nemesis, "Professor Moriarty," in Dean's family name, and Hilary Holladay notices the Latin root: *morior*—to die. See Nicosia, *Memory Babe*, 347; and Holladay, "Parallel Destinies in *The Bell Jar* and *On the Road*," in *What's Your Road, Man?* 113.

10. *Jack Kerouac: Selected Letters, 1940–1956*, ed. Ann Charters (New York: Viking, 1995), 194.

11. H. Richard Niebuhr, "On Our Conservative Youth," *Seventy-Five* (anniversary publication of the *Yale Daily News*, 1953), 90; quoted in Herberg, *Protestant, Catholic, Jew*, 71.

12. On this, see Anthony Frost and Ralph Yarrow, *Improvisation in Drama* (Basingstoke: Macmillan Education, 1990), 152.

13. Jean-Jacques Suurmond, *Word and Spirit at Play: Towards a Charismatic Theology*, trans. John Bowden (Grand Rapids: Eerdmans, 1995); and Jeremy S. Begbie, *Theology, Music and Time* (Cambridge: Cambridge University Press, 2000). On improvisation and the sacred, see also Stephen Nachmanovitch, *Free Play: Improvisation in Life and Art* (New York: Jeremy P. Tarcher/Putnam, 1990); Bruce Ellis Benson, *The Improvisation of Musical Dialogue: A Phenomenology of Music* (Cambridge: Cambridge University Press, 2003); and Nathan Crawford, *Theology as Improvisation: A Study in the Musical Nature of Theological Thinking* (Leiden: Brill, 2013). I'm also grateful to Nathan Crawford for email exchanges about theology and improvisation in the course of writing this chapter.

14. Let me note that the approach I'm taking here does not exhaust the complexity of Kerouac's thinking about religious play. A more comprehensive treatment would include several topics I set to the side: Catholic theologies of clowning and carnival; Buddhist traditions of spontaneity and *wu wei*; the Sufi practice of *sama*, dancing oneself into ecstasy; and the Zen delight in holy laughter, sly enemy of religious pomposity. What I address instead could be called a charismatic theology of jazz improvisation in *On the Road*, a form of ecstatic spirituality with deep roots not only in the literary tradition of Thoreau and Dickinson but also in the worship practices of African-American Pentecostalism and the jazz musicians who opened that practice to the Beats.

15. John Panteleimon Manoussakis, *God After Metaphysics: A Theological Aesthetic* (Bloomington: Indiana University Press, 2007), 103.

16. On Gaillard's relation to African-American Pentecostalism and the Azusa Street revivals, see R. J. Smith, *The Great Black Way: L.A. in the 1940s and the Lost African-American Renaissance* (New York, Public Affairs, 2006), 172–75.

17. Suurmond, *Word and Spirit at Play*, 174.

18. Suurmond, *Word and Spirit at Play*, 77.

19. Suurmond, *Word and Spirit at Play*, 38.

20. Suurmond, *Word and Spirit at Play*, 137, 176.

21. Suurmond, *Word and Spirit at Play*, 50. Bruce Ellis Benson makes a similar claim about Jesus' adaptation of Old Testament symbolism and narrative: "Thus, Jesus—a master improviser on Old Testament texts—inscribes a new reading within an old one, affirming both but transforming the old so that it can no longer be read in the same way." See his "Improvising Texts, Improvising Communities: Jazz, Interpretation, Heterophony, and the *Ekklēsia*," in *Resonant Witness: Conversations Between Music and Theology*, ed. Jeremy S. Begbie and Stephen R. Guthrie (Grand Rapids: Eerdmans, 2011), 309.

22. Suurmond, *Word and Spirit at Play*, 176, 177.

23. Alistair I. McFadyen, *The Call to Personhood: A Christian Theory of the Individual in Social Relationships* (Cambridge: Cambridge University Press, 1990), 26.

24. Jack Kerouac, "Essentials of Spontaneous Prose," in *The Portable Beat Reader*, ed. Ann Charters (New York: Penguin, 1992), 58.

25. Suurmond, *Word and Spirit at Play*, 183.

26. Allen Ginsberg, *Howl*, in *The Portable Beat Reader*, 65.

27. Victor Shepherd makes this point in his review of *Theology, Music and Time* in the *International Journal of Systematic Theology* 5, no. 2 (July 2003): 241–47.

28. Ingrid Monson cites several jazz performers who cherish the expressive potential of musical mistakes. According to Monson, "The repair of those moments—having the poise to take problems and make aesthetic virtues of them—is one of the most highly prized skills of an improviser." See her *Saying Something: Jazz Improvisation and Interaction* (Chicago: University of Chicago Press, 1996), 176. See also Leonard B. Meyer, *Emotion and Meaning in Music* (Chicago: University of Chicago Press, 1956), 197–232; and Nachmanovitch, *Free Play*, 88–93.

29. Begbie, *Theology, Music and Time*, 184.

30. On this, see Nachmanovitch's chapter "The Power of Limits," in *Free Play*, 78–87.

31. Monson also stresses the collaborative quality of improvisation and notes that jazz musicians often use the metaphor of "conversation" to describe their musical interactions. See her *Saying Something*, 8, 32.

32. Pierre Boulez, *Conversations with Célestin Deliège* (London: Eulenburg, 1976), 65; quoted in Begbie, *Theology, Music and Time*, 180.

33. Begbie, *Theology, Music and Time*, 247–55.

34. Suurmond, *Word and Spirit at Play*, 180, 181. On how call-and-response worship traditions take shape in jazz performance, see Daniel Belgrad, *The Culture of Spontaneity: Improvisation and the Arts in Postwar America* (Chicago: University of Chicago Press, 1998); and Monson, *Saying Something*, 95–96.

35. Begbie, *Theology, Music and Time*, 206.
36. Monson, *Saying Something*, 29.
37. On this, see Jon Panish, "Kerouac's *The Subterraneans*: A Study of 'Romantic Primitivism,'" *MELUS* 19, no. 3 (Fall 1994): 107–23.
38. Robert Goffin, *Jazz: From the Congo to the Metropolitan* (New York: Doubleday, 1944), 167; quoted in Ted Gioia, *The Imperfect Art: Reflections on Jazz and Modern Culture* (New York: Oxford University Press, 1988), 30.
39. John Clellon Holmes, *The Horn* (New York: Random, 1958), 36.
40. Gioia, *The Imperfect Art*, 83.
41. Kerouac makes this leap in a notebook entry from January 1942: "Henry Thoreau's passion for the woods and some colored Blues saxophone player in a smoky Harlem cell are one and the same—both come under the heading PASSION FOR LIFE." Quoted in Isaac Gewirtz, *Beatific Soul: Jack Kerouac on the Road* (New York: The New York Public Library; London, in association with Scala Publishers, 2007), 52. Kerouac thought of Thoreau as an American Jesus; identified with him as a fellow French-Canadian writer; planned to write film scripts based on Thoreau's life; and savored the purity and self-discipline of Thoreau's example as an antidote to his own accelerating addictions. In *The Subterraneans*, Kerouac explored the idea that the writers and artists of the beat movement were "urban Thoreaus" carrying out their own *Walden* experiments on the streets of Denver and New York. On the influence of Thoreau on Kerouac and the Beats, see John Tytell, *Naked Angels: Kerouac, Ginsberg, Burroughs* (New York: Grove Press, 1976); Ronald J. Bartnik, "Autobiographical Fiction: The Fusion of Art and Life in Henry David Thoreau's *Walden* and Jack Kerouac's *On the Road*" (PhD diss., Kent State University, 1986); and Rod Phillips, *"Forest Beatniks" and "Urban Thoreaus": Gary Snyder, Jack Kerouac, Lew Welch, and Michael McClure* (New York: P. Lang, 2000). The phrase "urban Thoreaus" occurs in Kerouac's *The Subterraneans* (New York: Grove Press, 1958), 15.
42. Mitchell Robert Breitwieser, "*Walden* and the Spirit of Capitalism: Presence, Damage, and Cultural Revival," unpublished manuscript.
43. Henry D. Thoreau, *Walden*, ed. Jeffrey S. Cramer (New Haven: Yale University Press, 2006), 91, 222.
44. McFadyen, *The Call to Personhood*, 26.
45. Stanley Cavell, *The Senses of Walden*, expanded ed. (Chicago: University of Chicago Press, 1992), 54.
46. "Faithfulness to the moment and to the present circumstance entails continuous surrender," Nachmanovitch writes. "As an improvising musician, I am not in the music business, I am not in the creativity business; I am in the surrender business." See his *Free Play*, 21.
47. "When you knew me," Kerouac wrote to Neal Cassady in 1948, "I was so locked up in a rigid 'picture' of life that I refused, I absolutely refused to participate or believe in anything that did not fit in that picture." Kerouac, *Selected Letters*, 166.
48. This is an important theme in the revisionist criticism of Kerouac and the Beats, which recognizes not only how beat writing challenges hegemonic sexual and

racial codes but also how it supports them, legitimizing the "master narratives" that it seeks to undo, as Robert Holton argues. See his "Kerouac among the Fellahin: *On the Road* to the Postmodern," *Modern Fiction Studies* 41, no. 2 (Summer 1995): 265–83.

49. See Mark Richardson, "Peasant Dreams: Reading *On the Road*," *Texas Studies in Literature and Language* 43, no. 2 (2001): 207–31.

50. Isaac Gewirtz provides a helpful summary of how Kerouac used the word "beat" to mean not only exhaustion but also relinquishment and blessing: "'Beat' had long been an American slang synonym of 'down and out,' not only in the financial sense, but physically and emotionally; in 1960, recalling his own research into the word, Kerouac dated this sense of it to 1910. But for him, as well as for Allen Ginsberg and William S. Burroughs . . . 'beat' always had a positive as well as a negative connotation, in the sense that only at the most desperate moments could one see honestly and speak truthfully. Still, when Kerouac joined 'beatific' to 'beat' in a 1948 journal, he made explicit the spiritual dimension of a goal that he and his friends had been seeking." See his *Beatific Soul*, 11.

51. In the same notebook where he outlined his original plans for *On the Road*, Kerouac wrote an essay called "God as the Should-Be," which begins this way: "The most beautiful idea on the face of the earth is the idea the child has that his father knows everything, knows what should be done at all times and how one should live always. This is the idea men have of God." This is one of several "beautiful ideas" Sal will come to surrender on the road. Gewirtz reprints this journal page in *Beatific Soul*, 153.

52. John Leland, *Why Kerouac Matters: The Lessons of "On the Road"* (New York: Penguin, 2007), 22.

53. Thoreau, *Walden*, 7.

54. Kerouac to Ed White, May 9, 1949, "Letters from Jack Kerouac to Ed White, 1947–68," *The Missouri Review* 17, no. 13 (Nov. 3, 1994): 130.

55. Jack Kerouac, *Visions of Cody* (New York: Penguin, 1972), 394.

56. Kerouac had been working on this ending for years. He wrote a first draft of the "So in America when the sun goes down" paragraph in January 1951 and used it as the opening paragraph of the last English-language draft of his many road manuscripts, entitled the "Ben Boncoeur' Excerpt." Sometime between January and April, Kerouac changed his mind about how to begin *On the Road* as well as how to end it, and he used the "So in America" passage as the last paragraph of the scroll manuscript as well as the published text. But there's no mention of the crying children in either the Ben Boncoeur notebook or the scroll manuscript. Kerouac added that passage in 1956, very late in the composition process of the novel, where it shows up in the first of the two extant post-scroll typescript drafts. Kerouac resisted nearly all post-scroll editorial changes in *On the Road*, which makes his inclusion of the crying children even more significant. On this, see Gewirtz, *Beatific Soul*, 99; 145; 196n30.

57. Henry David Thoreau, *A Week on the Concord and Merrimack Rivers*, ed. H. Daniel Peck (New York: Penguin, 1998), 247–48.

Chapter 4

Play and Nonsense
Thomas Merton's Last Poem

THE FATAL CHILDREN

Cables to the Ace is the first of two book-length poems Thomas Merton wrote at St. Mary of Carmel, the cinderblock hermitage in Nelson County, Kentucky, where he lived from August 1965 until his death in Thailand in 1968. The hermitage is less than a mile from Gethsemani, still within range of the monastery bells, but the symbolic distance seems greater. In his essay "Merton's Hermitage," Belden Lane describes how Merton's writing became more subversive and playful after the move to St. Mary of Carmel. The hermitage was "a protective enclosure for the imagination," Lane argues, freeing Merton from his public role as the bestselling author of a spiritual autobiography, *The Seven Storey Mountain*, and the most famous Catholic writer in the world. "He began to play the fool more creatively than ever," Lane writes, "and to make mistakes which would free him from the weight of the contrived self he had nurtured for so long."[1]

The author of *Cables to the Ace* is not afraid to play the fool. Composed in spontaneous verse paragraphs Merton calls "cantos," *Cables* challenges most everything we know about how to read poetry, including the idea that a poem should progress from start to finish. The eighty-eight cantos of *Cables* can be shuffled into different patterns like a deck of cards, one sense of the "ace" in its title. Readers can enter the poem anywhere—reading from back to front or from the center out, as if plot is less important than experiencing the poem from all sides, like a cubist painting or surrealistic montage. Merton was a friend of the Chilean surrealist Nicanor Parra and was one of the American translators of Parra's *Poems and Antipoems* (1967). Merton develops his own version of "anti-poetry" in *Cables* by marrying elements of French and Latin American surrealism with images and ideas from key works in American literature, including *Walden* and *On the Road*. Announcing that his "poetics are on vacation" in *Cables*, Merton celebrates unintended or non-purposeful actions, like the experimental walking of the French surrealists or the holy sauntering of Thoreau. Similarly, the verbal debris of *Cables*—quotations from corporate memos, gossip columns, love letters, and Catholic mystics—resists unifying generalities, like the *objet trouvé* of a Robbe-Grillet novel. He moves back and forth between French and English. He slips in and out of the subversive anti-language he had used for years in his correspondence with his friend, Robert Lax, a language of parody, ambiguity, and word play Merton called "anti-letters."[2] The poem rotates through dozens of voices and perspectives: sometimes straight-ahead first person, sometimes a disembodied omniscience disconnected from any particular character or context. It changes moods: playful, angry, surreal, apocalyptic. It changes genres: from lyric poetry to science fiction; from film and radio scripts to parodies of news broadcasts; from a quote by Meister Eckhart to something Merton picked up from *Esquire* magazine.[3] In the course of writing *Cables*, Merton had asked his friend, W. H. Ferry, to mail him some "good, gaudy, noisy *ad* material," and Ferry had sent him, among other things, copies of *Playboy*, *Fortune*, and *Esquire*. Merton wrote back to say in effect, enough is enough: "for petesake no tearsheets from Playboy. . . . It was all I could take. Am still retching. Weak stomach. Getting old. Too long in the woods. Can't handle Esq. Old gut won't hold it."[4]

Playing the fool means many things to Merton. It suggests a deeper capacity for creative risk and emotional vulnerability, as Lane argues. It expresses Merton's interest in avant-garde aesthetic practices that fracture preconception and reduce the power of rational mind. As a student of Buddhism, Merton enjoyed the paradoxical turns of Zen humor, which reframe life from a different center and reveal the artifice of our conceptual grids. As a student of *Walden*, Merton cherished Thoreau's "idleness" as a form of spiritual protest and nonparticipation.[5] And as a Trappist monk, Merton embraced his calling to be a fool for Christ, a "jester" or "tumbler" whose sacred play upends the reigning wisdom of the day. "For what else do worldlings think we are doing but playing about," the founder of Merton's Cistercian order, St. Bernard of Clairvaux, wrote in one of his pastoral letters, "when what they desire most on earth, we flee, and what they flee, we desire? We are like jesters and tumblers, who, with heads down and feet up, exhibit extraordinary behaviour by standing or walking on their hands, and thus draw all eyes to themselves. But ours is not the play of children or of the theatre. . . . No ours is a joyous game."[6]

Merton loved that game. The famous stories of the monk doing yoga headstands in the Gethsemani chapel or singing Bob Dylan songs in the hermitage or falling in love with a student nurse half his age—all express a more joyous and permissive spirituality in Merton's last years, a wild streak of countercultural play existing squarely and firmly within the institutional history of the Catholic church.[7]

But playing the fool is also a response to power for Merton and an intervention in a mass culture that left him sick at heart: "It was all I could take. Am still retching." This kind of play acts like a Brechtian "estrangement effect" in *Cables*, causing us to question social conventions we'd otherwise take for granted and revealing toxic or sinister aspects of everyday life so grooved into the cultural unconscious we barely notice they're there.[8] "The right fragrance," a voice whispers in the poem, "is so right it is not noticed" (28). The "nonsense" makes us notice. Merton defamiliarizes the "right fragrance" (or voice or gesture or perspective). He demythologizes social constructs that seem so natural and inevitable that we don't really think of them as "constructs," not something we learn but something we are, and so beyond the reach of conscious thought and revision. Merton had no illusions about the liberating effects of popular games and amusements, which seemed to him like bread-and-circus diversions from the violence of American life. Instead, Merton cherished the ancient examples of holy fools and Cistercian tumblers for the vantage point they occupy in relation to hegemonic power, just off-center enough to pry open a fresh perspective. Moreover, he thought that American literature provided two important examples of that off-center perspective in Thoreau and Dickinson, who were for him monastics without the cowl or cloister, hermit-poets whose withdrawal from society conveyed a special kind of neighborly love.[9]

In *Cables*, Merton expresses that love as social critique. Merton peoples his poem with a host of characters who are being extinguished by subtle manipulations of power, half-conscious, often childlike "trainees" who are internalizing cultural scripts that are killing them (24). In one canto, we see a woman learning to hate her own face under the narcotic influence of an advertising campaign (30). In another, we witness a man in a behavioral lab trying to overcome his melancholy by pressing pleasure buttons while being wired to a rat's brain (13–14). In others, we find a girl burlesquing her disability in a carnival show; a boy with a knife in his side being turned into a tree; a wounded football player being turned into a building. These dehumanizations seem normal enough as they're happening—once the man in the rat lab sheds his humanness he "met and talked with normal / Minds" (14)—which leads Merton to subvert "normal mind" in *Cables* and jolt us from stories and habits we'd never think to question. Merton calls the damaged people in his poem "fatal children," and when he looks closely, he sees blue flame in their mouths:

Lenses discover blue flame
In the mouths
Of fatal children

Parades and takeovers
Follow the parable
Wherever normal. (11)

Merton deconstructs the American "normal" (and the parades and takeovers that support it). From his *Walden*-like position outside the mainstream, Merton shuffles the "lenses" we use to manage experience and so helps us glimpse neurotic or compulsive norms obscured by tradition, inattention, indifference, and the common sense.[10] Those norms comprise what Merton calls the "habit frequency" of American culture, a set of ready-made stories and sounds playing like a radio station in the minds of his characters (13). Disrupting that frequency—by expanding the bandwidth of his poem to include dozens of outlaw voices, perspectives, communications, "cables"— Merton recovers sacred elements of verbal and spiritual play and offers his poem as a pastoral letter to the fatal children of the 1960s.

ONE DIMENSIONALITY

When Merton describes himself as an American transcendentalist, as he does in a letter to his friend, Henry Miller, or pictures the trainees "Swimming in Walden Pond" in *Cables* (51), or praises Thoreau's leisure as a holy practice, he has this dimension of Thoreau's project in mind, *Walden* as dialectical critique.[11] Like Merton, Thoreau analyzes modernity as the inability to question commonsense norms or think against the grain of conventional wisdom and he construes "play" and "idleness" as a response to that moral dilemma. As Stephen John Mack points out, the idea that literature has a moral (rather than purely aesthetic) function has a long history in Western criticism, beginning with Aristotle.[12] Unlike Aristotle, however, Merton and Thoreau do not see that purpose in terms of edifying models, aesthetically pleasing examples of the good life or the good person (which comes off as just another kind of salesmanship in *Cables*). What matters instead is the writer's ability to defamiliarize cultural constructs that permeate the life of a society and shape the subjectivity and needs of its people—constructs, both Merton and Thoreau stress, which serve the historical interests of power. Literature of course is one of those constructs, and Merton uses the cranky voice of an "author" giving advice and instructions to his readers to demystify literary power and make the book's designs on us more apparent. Thus, literature serves a moral purpose by making ideology visible and helping readers glimpse cultural practices that normalize violence and turn human beings into uncritical, unthinking machines, like the man in the rat lab.

Thoreau calls that passivity "quiet desperation" to evoke the feelings of dread and entrapment people experience in deeply engineered environments. That melancholy is not inherent to human experience as a kind of existential malaise. It's not fated or fatal, Thoreau stresses. Instead, the desperation of modern life is produced by historical circumstances that make people feel powerless, not the authors of their own existence but passive consumers in industrial economies they feel helpless to change. In his political writings, Thoreau pictures this conformity as the transformation of people into things: citizens into "wooden men," neighbors into "machines."[13] In *Walden*, Thoreau responds to that alienation by fracturing normative views and experiencing the pond from different angles and perspectives, often by "walking" or "sauntering" around an object to recover its multiplicity and visual depth.

I've described this dimensional seeing as a consequence of Thoreau's interest in the framing effects of play, which yards or brackets everyday experience and reveals the provisionality of any single perspective. Ludic thinking stimulates our awareness of multiple meanings and dialectical perspectives and so stirs thought from routinized perception. To borrow a term from Alfred Schutz, play "possibilizes" things, including itself, like the manifold vision of the *Gita* or the compound planes of the ice mirrors. Thoreau drew inspiration for this view of play not only from the Hindu scriptures he took to heart but also from the moment-by-moment changes he experienced at the pond and sought to answer in a daily practice of spiritual attunement, as we saw in chapter 1.

All this depends, however, on being able to free thought from socially constructed habits and create leverage points of estrangement and critique. For Thoreau, the conditions of modern life demand not less but *more* estrangement, rupturing or dissonant styles of thought and writing that break apart smooth-running modern logics and preserve a realm of ideas and images outside the dominant mode, what later theorists will call *anti-myths* (Victor Turner) or *anti-languages* (M. A. K. Halliday) or *anti-environments* (Marshall McLuhan). And which Merton explores in the anti-poetry of *Cables*. Merton stresses this contrastive or dialectical dimension of play. He embraces his identity as a Cistercian tumbler whose upside-down unwisdom reveals an alternative point of view. The disconcerting task of modern hermits, Merton argues in "Notes for a Philosophy of Solitude," is to show "that underneath the apparently logical pattern of a more or less 'well-organized' and rational life, there lies an abyss of irrationality, confusion, pointlessness, and indeed of apparent chaos."[14] The monk's role is to face and name that chaos. From his outsider position as an "idle" or "inconsequent" person, the monk sees from the margin what's hidden at the center: that the seemingly rational practices of modern life are in fact killing the children. The monk's role is to misunderstand those practices, the subtitle of *Cables* is "Familiar Liturgies of

Misunderstanding," and thus subvert and reframe what his culture identifies as the real or the sacred.[15]

In one of his major essays on Thoreau, "Rain and the Rhinoceros," Merton explores this reframing by looking at "rain" from two different points of view. In one, rain is a *utility*—that is, something we might profit from as a commodity or resource (including a resource for writing and thinking). From the other, Thoreauvian, perspective, rain is a *festival*—that is, wholly gratuitous and free. From festival's perspective, rain exists in itself, separate from whatever advantage we might hope to gain from it. It's simply raining—and we're in it. Listening to the rain thus becomes an act of contemplative attention for Merton, as listening to the drumming of the partridges was for Thoreau, a reminder of human limits in a world that includes us but is not us, not bound by our notions of value.

Even as he listens to rain's festival, however, Merton senses that this other perspective is quickly collapsing into a single totalitarian point of view:

> Let me say this before rain becomes a utility that they can plan and distribute for money. By "they" I mean the people who cannot understand that rain is a festival, who do not appreciate its gratuity, who think that what has no price has no value, that what cannot be sold is not real, so that the only way to make something *actual* is to place it on the market. The time will come when they will sell you even your rain. At the moment it is still free, and I am in it. I celebrate its gratuity and its meaninglessness. (original emphasis)[16]

In this passage, the distinction between "I" and "they" is relatively stable, as the monk takes a position outside the market economies he intends to oppose. A remnant remains to celebrate rain's festival, an "I" not part of the general collective. At other points in the Thoreau essay, however, Merton wonders whether *they* might also include *him*, his books and writing, as if the distinction between center and margin had already collapsed.

In this sense, Merton's thinking about social and religious dissent was powerfully influenced not only by *Walden* but also by the Frankfurt School theorist Herbert Marcuse, whose 1964 book, *One-Dimensional Man*, makes the unsettling argument that there's no real difference between center and margin in advanced industrial societies and that the attempt to stand on the "outside," in the monk's position, is easily recuperated into the status quo.[17] Merton believed that religious contemplatives were the true "outlaws" of American society, its freaks and fools.[18] For Marcuse however, mass culture specializes in turning outlaws into product lines, Beats into beatniks, monks into celebrities, and thus using countercultural examples to affirm rather than negate the existing order. That order appears then as a *monism*, Marcuse's term for the way technological cultures absorb and cancel alternative points of view, making it almost impossible to envision any other mode of existence, any reality different from this one. One-dimensionality doesn't mean sameness or uniformity for Marcuse, the mechanical reproduction of vanilla-bland consistency. Modern capitalism creates a material surface of extraordinary diversity and manipulates consumer tastes by creating ever-new sensations and pleasures. The dimension modernity lacks is dialectic, what Marianne DeKoven calls the "other-dimensionality" of social critique, "where terms (ideas, social and political formations, structures of feeling, lifeworlds) opposed and in contradiction to those that exist have a palpable reality."[19] In one-dimensional societies only what exists is real, and the Archimedean lever Merton needs to create a vantage point of religious dissent looks wishful and naive. There's no "place" to set that lever, as several postmodern theorists point out, no ethical or religious standpoint outside those market norms.

Merton understood this completely. He was a spiritual superstar in the 1960s. His books sold millions. It bothered him that Gethsemani was becoming a commercial factory that manufactured bacon, smoked ham, cheese, alfalfa pellets, and fruitcakes—all contributing to the wealth of a militaristic nation at the height of the Vietnam War. But the main business at Gethsemani was "Thomas Merton," who was given a silver key to the Merton Archive at Bellarmine University and whose writing and artwork stood at the center of a burgeoning academic and religious publishing industry. So, when Merton writes "they" in "Rain and the Rhinoceros," he hints at a theme he'll face directly in *Cables*: the collapse of any meaningful distinction between margin and center, monastery and factory, sacred and secular, festival and utility. To foreground the moral dilemma of modern monks in one-dimensional societies, Merton compares his situation at Gethsemani with Thoreau's perspective at the pond and wonders if Thoreau realized the extent of his own complicity: "Thoreau sat in *his* cabin and criticized the railways. I sit in mine and wonder about a world that has, well, progressed. I must read *Walden* again, and see if Thoreau already guessed that he was part of what he thought he could escape" (original emphasis).[20]

There's no real escape in *One-Dimensional Man*. The subtitle of Marcuse's book is "Studies in the Ideology of Advanced Industrial Society," and Marcuse saw little hope of resisting that *advance*. Where earlier forms of totalitarianism had depended on high-profile spectacles of brute force, like the mock trials and public executions Marcuse witnessed in Nazi Germany, modern totalitarianism is "quieter" and more efficient. It operates at the level of needs and appetites. In Marcuse's view, we're trained from childhood to desire what's on the industrial menu, a taste for certain kinds of food, friendship, music, clothing, reading, and religion (and not others). This is the way ideology enters the body for Marcuse, *sticks* to the body—not as concepts or theories, those develop later, but as the almost unconscious instinct to turn the dial of a car radio or savor a particular brand of perfume. The conclusion Marcuse draws from this analysis is that people raised in one-dimensional societies are not the best judges of their own well-being, a version of the Frankfurt School (and Marxian) question of whether indoctrinated consciousness can change itself.[21] If consumer desires are installed so far down in the primal hardpan of human personality that they don't feel false any more, not artificial constructs but natural preferences, what hope is there for change? The thesis of *One-Dimensional Man* is that people can be taught to desire whatever they're offered, craving the very things an industrial economy uses to maintain itself, the brands and gadgets, so that society no longer *denies* our instincts, the repression Freud theorized as the "reality principle" of modern consciousness, but instead *fulfills* them, satisfying the appetites it created in the first place and thus perpetuating a consumer loop Marcuse calls *mimesis*: a point-by-point coordination of inner consciousness and outer environment so perfect we mirror industrial capitalism all the way down, recognizing "ourselves" in the things we buy and love: "The people recognize themselves in their commodities; they find their soul in their automobile, hi-fi set, split-level home, kitchen equipment. The very mechanism which ties the individual to his society has changed, and social control is anchored in the new needs which it has produced."[22] As this happens, the world ground closes around us like a torture scene in a Poe story, and we find ourselves swallowed up by our own alienation: "There is only one dimension," Marcuse declares, in the classic voice of 1960s apocalypse, "and it is everywhere and in all forms."[23]

Marcuse's colleague, Theodor Adorno, was less pessimistic. The aesthetic theory of the Frankfurt School emphasized the way art cultivates a yearning for "otherness"—lifeworlds, social orders, states of thought and feeling—*not* manifest by the status quo. As modern life becomes increasingly solipsistic, mirroring only itself, art sustains what Adorno called a promise of future happiness, *une promesse de bonheur*, a promise art keeps by breaking covenant with a problematic status quo and exposing its contradictions.[24] People are suffering, no matter what the ads show, and that "negative" aesthetic sustains our desire for something other or something more, things that we sense are true, or at least potentially true, but don't see anywhere around us. Even at his most despairing, Adorno believed that art could reveal the quiet desperation of modern society, what he called its "damaged life," and so inspire people to imagine other ways of being in the world.

Marcuse popularized the social theory of the Frankfurt School and adopted many of its key terms—instrumentality, execution, management—but he did not share Adorno's faith in the artist's ability to negate the ersatz happiness of modern life and free thought from a damaged but self-replicating status quo. Marcuse includes a half-hearted final section called "The Chance of the Alternatives," but *One-Dimensional Man* offers little promise of future *bonheur*. Rather, Marcuse predicts an ideological encroachment so profound it leaves nothing untouched, an air-conditioned nightmare of "total administration" in which our deepest aspirations and needs, including our need for God, are created and then satisfied within the closed universe of manufactured desire.[25] Moreover, "play" is no exception to that encroachment. It too is an administered commodity, Marcuse argues, something structured for us by "fun managers" and "leisure experts" who bottle play's anarchic energies in economically profitable ways. In his early essays on the philosophy of pleasure, Marcuse stressed the liberating possibilities of play and leisure as instruments of social change. In *Eros and Civilization*, for instance, he disputed the Marxian idea that labor is the center of human existence and claimed instead that only in play are we fully human, able to bridge the divide between reason and sensuality and live a more fully integrated life. (This was Friedrich Schiller's view.) That integration, Marcuse argued in *Eros and Civilization*, changes everything. Where Freud located the origin of modern consciousness in toil and renunciation, Marcuse argued that play exists outside that "reality principle" and so represents a potentially new life principle based on freedom and self-fulfillment, people who sing, as Orpheus did, by choice rather than command. Little of that survives in *One-Dimensional Man*, where play is simply work by another means, work disguised as leisure, and all of it saturated with the cool managerial logic Marcuse saw wherever he turned, drenching the steeples and soaking the woods like the rain that day at Gethsemani.

SUPERABUNDANT NONSENSE

Merton attacks that managerial logic at the level of language. During his Asian journey in 1968, Merton was rereading *One-Dimensional Man* as he prepared the lecture "Marxism and Monastic Perspectives," which he delivered in Bangkok on the day of his death. Marcuse was on Merton's mind in Asia because he'd just completed his own response to one-dimensionality in *Cables* and saw in Marcuse a kindred spirit and fellow monastic:

> Marcuse has shown how mass culture tends to be anticulture—to stifle creative work by the sheer volume of what is "produced," or reproduced. In which case, poetry, for example, must start with an awareness of this contradiction and *use* it—as anti-poetry—which freely draws on the material of superabundant nonsense at its disposal.(original emphasis)[26]

Merton drew heavily on Marcuse's analysis of modern alienation, but he did not share his pessimism. In his more oracular moments, Marcuse makes critique seem impossible—"There is only one dimension, and it is everywhere and in all forms"—which begs the question of how Marcuse could actually *know* that in a world with only one dimension or how his book could have been written in the first place, as Marcuse's critics point out.[27] For Merton, nothing's that closed or complete, not God, discourse, technology, the church, the future. Or for that matter, cultural *monism*. Merton exposes the discursive boundaries of one-dimensional worlds by making the dominant culture declare itself, name its symbols and stories (which then become "symbols" and "stories" rather than passive descriptions of an indisputable real). The experimental zaniness of *Cables* is a leverage point of religious dissent not because it speaks a higher language of mystical unmeaning but because its nonsense reveals what the common sense keeps hidden: the relative nature of interpretation and the incompleteness of any single voice or view. As Susan Stewart argues, nonsense creates the conditions of critique by causing the common sense to declare itself, to say what it's *not* (wastefulness, foolishness, frivolity, impiety), whatever exists "outside" that particular social construction. Once the zone of the not-real or the not-important appears, cultures become less one-dimensional and our relationship with them less literal or unaware. The common sense works best when we don't have to think about it very much, when its precepts are implicit or preconscious, not something we "know" but something we do instinctively, do because we've always done it that way. Nonsense doesn't offer an alternative model or recipe for anything (how to work, pray, write poems, take care of children). It's not in competition with the common sense. Instead, nonsense yields the field to its more productive and powerful partner and accepts its designation as idle or foolish. But it does make the "field" visible, as Stewart stresses.[28] The moment we say, *Knock off the silliness* or *Stop playing around*, a border appears and suddenly there are lines and limits, foregrounds and backgrounds. There are different ways to exist in that language field and different subject locations from which to speak, some in the power position up front and others further back or off to the side, where the silliness lives. What may have seemed one-dimensional a moment ago is now fenced or constructed, "yarded" as Thoreau would say. "What before was considered to be a matter of course," Stewart points out, "now becomes a matter of discourse, subject to ongoing, ragged-edged interpretation."[29] In terms of the story Marcuse tells, "ongoing, ragged-edged interpretation" is the exact *opposite* of what totalitarian ideologies need to stay in business: it's better if we don't see behind the curtain (or realize there are curtains in the first place). Like Batesonian play, nonsense reveals the artifice of communication systems as *systems*, which could be constructed differently. Both play and nonsense introduce contradictory (and thus ironic) voices not wholly assimilated by the everyday lifeworld. Both cause an "anti" to appear, something the common sense is not. Merton uses the anti-poetry of *Cables* to subvert the managerial monotone that terrified Marcuse and so create a discursive field crisscrossed with different idioms, accents, cables, and codes—all speaking at once, all vying for our attention. And that, to Merton, seemed splendid: "a splendid confusion of cries" (30).

I'll consider several examples of splendid confusion in a moment, but first let me quote one of the most Marcusean scenes in *Cables*, a passage in which the social conditioning is nearly complete and something Merton calls "the monogag," the no-nonsense voice of modern power, sweeps the field clean:

> Approved prospect of chairs with visitors to the hero. Temperature is just comfortable for a variety of skins. It is with our skins here that we see each other all around and feel together. We are not overheated, we smell good and we remain smooth. No skin needs to be absolutely private for all are quiet, clean, and cool. The right fragrance is so right it is not noticed. The cool of the whole area is like that of a quiet car and presences. No one is really ailing and no one is quite that tired. See the pictures however for someone elsewhere who is really tired. Hear the sound of the music for someone who is relaxed (with an undercurrent of annoyance). She is glad to be sitting down with her limbs as if her long legs were really hers and really bare. This year the women all worry about their skirts. But she is well arranged. Whether they walk or sit they manage to be well arranged. In any case all is springlike with the scent of very present young women which with all our skin we recognize. Nothing is really private yet each remains alone and each pretends to read a magazine. But each one still smuggles a secret personal question across the frontiers of everybody: the skin of the body and the presence of the scent and the general arrangement. Nothing is out of place or disapproved. One by one each skin will visit the hero. (28–29)

It's hard to tell where we are in this scene, although the chairs and magazines suggest a doctor's office or hospital waiting room. But the location matters less to Merton than the social pressures causing people to conform in this space, to seek approval. Merton reveals those pressures through stark imperatives—*hear the sound of the music*—which control attention and close off other avenues of awareness. Those other possibilities are still present in the scene as undercurrents and cross-pressures, an important layering of language that embeds critique within the construction of an everyday lifeworld, a point I'll return to in a moment. But the dominant forces in the waiting room are toward enforced conformity, the construction of a fully intersubjective lifeworld where people see and feel the same things in the same way. The pressures are constant because the framing is constant, offering no access to a worldview outside the air conditioning. (Even that "elsewhere" looks scripted: "See the pictures however for someone elsewhere.") If this is how one-dimensional worlds are created, by privileging an approved set of shared sensations, then we have indeed lost our "senses," as Thoreau points out, not because we've gone numb or insane but because our senses are no longer ours. Instead, they're constructed for us by the manipulation of feelings and sensations within managerial societies, exactly the area Marcuse investigates in *One-Dimensional Man*.

The path toward recovery in *Walden* involves a sensory re-education within the natural world: listening to birdsong, for one thing, or listening to the click of bones in a whippoorwill's throat, the sound below the sound, as we saw in chapter 1. In this spirit, Merton lets loose dozens of dissonant voices that overwhelm the orchestrated calm of the waiting room. Among other things, *Cables* is an atonal sound experiment, a Panasonic broadcast of squawks, sobs, echoes, whispers, laughter, nursery rhymes, a bird song, a rock song, a doorbell, the sound of someone being called back to consciousness ("Bernstein! Can you still hear me? Are you conscious?"); the sound of "ten thousand crickets in the deep wet hay of the field"; and the "nine even strokes" of the monastery bells calling the monks to prayer.[30] When T. S. Eliot hears the nine strokes of the church bell at Saint Mary Woolnoth in *The Waste Land*, it sounds like the Babel of an Unreal City and a reminder of how far we've fallen: "And each man fixed his eyes before his feet. / Flowed up the hill and down King William Street, / To where Saint Mary Woolnoth kept the hours / With a dead sound on the final stroke of nine." When Merton brings the Gethsemani bells into *Cables*, it's a canticle of morning, a wake-up call to his sleepy and half-conscious neighbors: *Can you still hear me? Are you conscious?*

No one hears much of anything in the waiting room, where the desperation is "quiet" and the physical sensations are depersonalized and abstract: "She is glad to be sitting down with her limbs as if her long legs were really hers and really bare." If this is one of the fatal children of *Cables*, Merton pictures her distress as a progressive dissociation. At this moment, she remains partly connected to her physical self: she sits *with* her limbs, as if they were hers. But even that modest feeling of sensory companionship is moving toward a more complete separation. By the end of the scene, physical sensations are wholly reified and impersonal: *the* skin of the body (not ours or hers), *the* scent of the general arrangement. Sensations come from nowhere now, they come from utopia, and the trick Odysseus played on Cyclops has become a language game of infinite substitution: her skin is anyone's skin and so her pain belongs to "no one": "No one is really ailing and no one is quite that tired." There are more violent dehumanizations in *Cables*, the man wired to a rat's brain comes to mind, but few that are this complete or depend so fully on our own cooperation. The women in the waiting room surrender themselves to "the general arrangement" as a redemptive ritual of cleansing and comparison. That surrender resecures the common sense, "saving" it as Merton says in the next canto, but it does great harm in the process (29). We tend to think of one-dimensional worlds as operational and scientific, at least Marcuse did, but surrendering to the general arrangement looks quasi-religious in *Cables*, a willing suspension of disbelief that drives doubt and distrust downward, into secret undercurrents, as an act of professed communion.

PLAY AS THE PRESENTATION OF ALTERNATIVES

Ludic genres reverse that downward thrust by revealing what the common sense keeps hidden: that the rules for organizing the flow of life are constantly changing, which renders them less secure. Religious reframing occurs in many sacred traditions, as we've seen, and inspires several theologies of play, attunement, imagination, secularity, inter-faith dialogue, and religious community in this period.[31] In *Cables*, Merton offers a distinctively Trappist and literary contribution to these theologies of play, not as a way of staying in step with the countercultural mood of the 1960s but more as a Burkean or Thoreauvian "strategic answer" to what Merton saw as the source of its despair: the ascendancy of instrumental reason as the unquestioned paradigm of the age, the only wisdom that makes any sense.

Merton attacks that sense-making with puns, inversions, travesties, comedy, word play, and nonsense—a radical departure from his previous poetry. As George Woodcock points out, "the old Merton has vanished":

> The poetry of the choir, with its joyous noisy psalms, has gone completely, and even the poetry of the desert, with its clear simplicity, hardly exists in a recognizable form. Metrical form, except as parody, is banished, and so, as Merton tells us in the anti-prologue to *Cables to the Ace*, are "rhythms, melody," and "pictures," by which he means his old stock-in-trade of religious and nature imagery.[32]

Reinventing himself as an anti-poet, Merton explores the expressive and religious possibilities of spontaneous nonsense. In canto 27, for instance, a midget pops up out of nowhere and shouts "Hats off to the human condition!" In canto 6, Shakespeare's Caliban suddenly appears, raining down red curses. Bakhtin describes similar disruptions in Dostoevsky as the "carnivalistic drawing-out of man from the usual, normal rut of life, out of 'his own environment,' his loss of his hierarchical place."[33] In *The Dialogic Imagination*, Bakhtin noted how unexpected word-linkages in Rabelais "are aimed primarily at destroying the established hierarchy of values, at bringing down the high and raising up the low, at destroying every nook and cranny of the habitual picture of the world."[34] Merton doesn't write or think that violently. Nor does he turn his back on his ordination and abandon orthodox forms of Catholic piety. Instead, Merton reclaims a dialectic at the heart of that piety, the foolishness at the core of Christian wisdom, and presents the splendid confusion of nonsense as a precondition for spiritual growth, "the ruins" in which Christ appears (55). The frame-rattling instrument of that growth is language, the very thing Marcuse saw as the root of the whole problem. Marcuse's chapter on modern language is called "The Closing of the Universe of Discourse" where he explains how instrumental reason disables dialectic through propagandistic repetition and thought-numbing cliché.

Merton answers that situation by subverting its base. The anti-language of his poem is mobile, doubled, ironic, slippery, self-mocking, and completely unpredictable, like the French and Latin American surrealists he admired. ("What happens next escapes me almost entirely," André Breton wrote in "Soluble Fish.") Discourse remains *discourse* in *Cables*, constantly deferring and rearranging meaning. The key word "waiting," for instance, which feels like a kind of soul death in the waiting-room scene, is reframed as *Gelassenheit* in canto 84, the contemplative waiting of the faithful heart. Or the body alienation we've just considered, where people no longer feel their legs, is reframed as ecstatic transcendence in canto 62, abandoning the body in a mystical experience of pure light. In this sense, there are no "terminal declarations" in *Cables* (3), no final word or final thought about anything, which means there are also no "fatal children," no lives beyond the reach of mercy and change. *Grace*, *soul*, *waiting*, and *letting* are profoundly unstable terms in Merton's poetic vocabulary. Just as *vineyard*, *garden*, *bread*, and *faith* are unstable terms in Jesus' parables. It's impossible to "close" the universe of discourse, as Marcuse claimed, and that instability is Merton's pastoral gift to the children of the 1960s, tutored since birth in one-dimensional thought. If the Dick-and-Jane plainness of the waiting-room scene—*see the pictures, hear the music*—conveys Merton's sense that what's happening there is a kind of "primer," an elementary pedagogy of one-dimensional consciousness, then the roots of dissent are there as well: in underground feelings that don't fit the norm; in the ludic possibilities of seeming and pretense; in religious possibilities of grace and reversal; and in the mere fact that whatever's learned can be *unlearned*, as Catholic theologians have often stressed about religious play, the wisdom of the age exposed and parodied by Mock Queens, Boy Bishops, and the Lords of Misrule. This is what "festival" means to Merton: access to another point of view, like the unthinking drums of the crickets or the nonsense voices of the rain.

I draw two conclusions from this. First, the playful wisdom of Merton's poem suggests that "no norm is necessary" (12). What seems terminal or fatal from one point of view is constructed and provisional from another. In his role as Cistercian tumbler, Merton brings the norms into focus and compels the common sense to draw its boundaries, to say what it is and what it's not, and thus make manifest what would otherwise remain hidden or implicit. As that happens, we learn something about what lies "outside" the boundaries, where faith and play abide. By its very nature, faith breaks the rules of instrumental reason and points beyond them, as Harvey Cox argues in *The Feast of Fools*, published the year after *Cables*.[35] Faith doesn't exist within the limits of our present condition, Cox stresses, but in the other-dimensionality of dreaming, imagining, pretending, and playing. Both faith and play draw a line in the sand and then step across it, to a place where all things are possible. To pray for forgiveness is to act "as if" change can still happen and that we can be different from what we've been before. To pray for others is to see life from someone else's perspective, nothing short of a miracle for Thoreau, and believe that the past doesn't predetermine the present or future. To believe in God's mercy is to believe against logic and common sense, as St. Paul argued, and embrace the unwisdom of Christ-crucified, which looks like "insanity" (*moria*). Divine love is not the necessary term in a logical sequence or the inevitable effect of a causal chain. Merton believed that reality is consistent only if we factor God out of the equation and let the wheels roll unchecked. The wild card in a deterministic universe is unmerited love, as he argued in *Raids on the Unspeakable*. It's impossible to account for that love within a hard-block universe of fixed result. God's mercy is caused by nothing and answers to nothing and so it seems blessedly "comic" and "inconsistent" to the existing order, a wild love out of bounds.[36]

My second conclusion is that "there is a revolt everywhere," as Merton said in one of the anti-letters.[37] Resistance to modernity's damaged life does not depend on a super group of contemplative outlaws leading the way toward social change. Nor does it depend on privileged sites like Gethsemani and Walden, no-fly zones beyond the influence of cultural norms. Rather, critique remains partial, embedded, egalitarian, and textual in Merton, what postmodern theorists term "complicitous critique" or "resistance from within."[38] There are innumerable leverage points for this critique, every perfume ad is a leverage point, and the tools of social and religious dissent are not precious or elitist but small acts of ironic refusal that "misunderstand" the everyday liturgies of modern life, turning its wisdom upside down.

Merton stages this critique in several ways. In canto 34, for instance, he returns to the "trainee" level of consciousness and shows how the common sense is constructed through media routines of confessional intimacy. This too is a scene of linguistic coercion where people are receiving instruction in the "base" grammar of social consciousness. The tone is different from the waiting-room scene, the sorrow closer to the surface, but the goal is the same: to produce a monologic like-mindedness in the way we experience and express our inner lives:

> The sweetgum avenue leads to a college of charm
> Where nubile swimmers learn to value
> The exercise of pendulums
> And join a long line
> Of unreliable dials
> For a nominal fee one can confide in a cryphone
> With sobs of champagne
> Or return from sudden sport to address
> The monogag
> The telefake
> The base undertones of the confessional speaker
> Advising trainees
> Through cloistered earphones. (23–24)

Sometimes we hear the "monogag" by itself in *Cables*, as an advertisement or newscast. Sometimes a media voice is positioned against older discourses in the poem: the voices of Plato, Christ, Eckhart, Blake—often presented as "(Plato)" in the soft whisper of the parentheses. If it's a competition, however, the media voice is winning, choking off competing idioms and translating the intimate language of subjectivity and spirit into the same bureaucratic dialect: "You wake and wonder / Whose case history you composed / As your confessions are filed / In the dialect / Of bureaux and electrons" (4). There's a great deal at stake here. The confessional programs humming through media cables are not a distraction from the real, Merton suggests. Rather they produce and organize the real, blueprinting in people the deep pattern of feelings and fears that constitute humanness in a particular time and place: what it means to be a woman, a man, a poet, a Christian. In this sense, the "base undertones" of television and advertising represent a novitiate for "cloistered" "trainees"—a catechism in a certain kind of social doctrine. The undertones are *base* not because they're venal or crass but because they're *basic*, so fundamental to a certain way of organizing the world.

The "wild hope" of *Cables* is that these blueprints are incomplete (38). If religious faith sometimes requires "a presentation of alternative and deeper views," as Merton said in his *Journal*,[39] then priest and poet share the same goal: to dispute the finality of a damaged status quo and hold open the promise of future transcendence, *une promesse de bonheur*. In canto 11, Merton connects that vision of open-ended process with a heightened sense of verbal difference and dialogue, not monism but the interaction of multiple voices.

This again is a teaching scene, like the waiting room and the cryphone, but what we're learning in Merton's classroom is more like the jazz lesson of heteroglossia than the monologic creed of the telefake:

What do you teach me
Mama my cow?
(My delicate forefathers
Wink in their sleep)
"Seek advancement
Then as now
And never learn to weep!"

What do you want of me
Mama my wit
(While the water runs
And the world spins)
"All the successful
Ride in their Buicks
And grow double chins"

What do you seek of me
Mama my ocean
(While the fire sleeps
In well baked mud)
"Take your shotgun
And put it in the bank
For money is blood." (6–7)

The scene is composed in at least two idioms, something aggressive and instrumental: *seek advancement, put it in the bank*. And something below or beside that voice, a softer discourse of nursery rhymes and childhood dreams: *Mama my cow*. It's hard not to gender the two voices: a father tongue that's rule-bound and prescriptive; and a mother tongue that's playful, funny, dreamy, and surrealistic. The interaction of the voices creates the call-and-response rhythm of a church service or a jazz improvisation, where one voice asks questions—What do you teach me? What do you seek of me?—and the other answers. The answers are sharp and somewhat violent: they have to do with banks, Buicks, shotguns, and blood. But the answers don't silence the questions. Rather, they seem to provoke and enable them, creating the back and forth of a conversation, which Merton pictured in the cryphone canto as "the exercise of pendulums"—first one side and then the other. It's tempting to privilege one side of the dialogue as better, more humane, and read the canto as an advertisement for mother wit, which would silence the father tongue and turn the violence in the other direction. But it may be that the content of either side is less important than the rhythm of the whole, the to-and-fro motions of a swinging pendulum: sense and silliness; utility and festival; father tongue and mother wit; question and then answer and then another question.

Emerson thought that this is what an active, self-correcting mind looks like up close, like a pendulum swinging between two poles. Likewise, Hans-Georg Gadamer believed that the back-and-forth rhythm of games and play provides a model for ethical dialogue and philosophical conversation. If that's true, then Merton may be teaching us to think dialogically in this canto, think in more than one voice. In this sense, nonsense doesn't *conquer* the reigning ideology, what Merton might call the father tongue, but instead *reveals* it, bringing its codes and instructions into conscious awareness, into quotation marks, where we can see them for what they are and decide for ourselves whether or not they're true. This may be play's "anti" function: not to judge or defeat a culture's base ideas but rather to expose them as *ideas*, rooted in society rather than nature or necessity.[40] In a time of rampant militarism, consumerism, and an escalating Asian war, shotguns and blood money seem like terrible ideas. But Merton leaves that decision up to us, refusing to deepen the uncritical passivity his poem as a whole critiques. Thus, play doesn't offer a new doctrine (of idleness or nonsense). Instead, it restores an imperiled dialectic, the pendulum swing between poles, which preserves the perspectival structure of two-dimensional thought.

THE FACE OF CHRIST IN DISGUISE

Let me turn now to the most important scene of religious dissent in *Cables*, the appearance of the "nameless rebel" in canto 66, and then close with a comment about figure/ground reversals as a way of illustrating the playful wisdom of Merton's poem. Canto 66 begins with a proto dialogue between *yes* and *no*, another pendulum swing, but that prime mobility slows and stills as the "right" perspective takes hold:

Oh yes it is intelligence
That makes the bubble and weather of "Yes"
To which the self says "No."

Science when the air is right says "Yes"
And all the bubbles in the head repeat "Yes"
Even the corpuscles romp "Yes"

But lowdown
At the bottom of deep water
Deeper than Anna Livia Plurabelle
Or any other river
Some nameless rebel
A Mister Houdini or somebody with fingers
Slips the technical knots
Pops the bubbles in the head
Runs the vote backwards
And turns the bloody cooler
All the way
OFF. (42)

Merton's notion of "depth" here, at the bottom of deep water, suggests an intriguing connection to Thoreau. "Depth" is a spiritual as well as a spatial figure for Thoreau, as J. Heath Atchley has argued. Against the reduction of life to surface habits (from Latin, *habere*, to have or hold), reality has multiple levels and dimensions in *Walden*. There's always "more" in play than thought can process for Thoreau, a depth that exceeds his measurements. Viewed in this way, depth is a sign not only of our spiritual hope, Atchley points out, but also of our spiritual disappointment (and the styles of thought and perception stimulated by that disappointment).[41] Depth thus stands for all the things we can't grasp, possess, measure, or master. It's the anti-commodity in *Walden*, what thought cannot "have." Thoreau calls attention to the hidden depths of God, the pond, himself, his book, in order to provoke and sharpen that disappointment, to bring it forward, so that we might learn to tolerate that loss, even savor it, as the condition of continual rebirth. When Thoreau measures and remeasures the depth of the pond in *Walden*, drilling over a hundred holes in the ice, he's calling attention both to the disappointment and the incentive of deep-water thinking. In the end, he doesn't know how deep the pond is. Its depth is not a solvable problem or answerable question, which would place the pond among the array of objects available to that kind of thinking, that kind of acquisition. Disciplining thought's need to have and acquire, Thoreau cultivates a mood of fertile disappointment in his writings. He tries in fact to *live* in that mood, "I wanted to live deep," he says, and so create a space open to the unsounded mysteries of God.

This is how I interpret the deep water of Merton's canto. At the point in *Cables* when everything seems to be saying the same thing, the same *yes*, flattening thought toward Marcuse's monism, Merton points to another dimension, a watery medium below conscious intelligence and scientific technique. Marcuse worried that the one-dimensional monologue of contemporary discourse had erased the pivot points of critique even at the level of the sentence, absorbing the *and yets* and *but thens*, which might disrupt harmonizing consciousness and turn thought in a different direction.⁴² Merton builds his canto around that kind of linguistic pivot: "But lowdown / At the bottom of the deep water." The interruption seems potentially redemptive, something bloody and mechanical is turned OFF by the end, but the technique of that redemption, the sort of thing instrumental reason would like to know, remains uncertain, just as the deep-water rebel remains unnamed. It may be then that the mere presence of this other dimension is what matters to Merton, the existence of a realm deeper than primers and poems, deeper even than Anna Livia Plurabelle, the dream river of James Joyce's *Finnegans Wake*.⁴³ That realm does not depend on our cognitive preferences, our *votes*, as if the sacred were something we could simply choose or set aside, like any other commodity. This of course is how market culture frames and compartmentalizes religion (and sustains the acquisitive subject on which that kind of culture depends). The rebel's critique may be deeper than that, the irruption of a sacred presence from outside those frames of reference, an "elsewhere" not pictured in the waiting-room magazines and not assimilated to the logic of our desires. What gets untied, then, is the knot of appetites and inclinations formed strand by strand in the Marcusean economy. And what emerges in its place is something Merton calls at different times *communion*, *stillness*, *emptiness*, and *contemplation*—the ability to open ourselves to the mystery of God, to abide in the deep waters, without trying to acquire that depth as an object of thought. "In this water cavern I easily live," Merton wrote in this mood.⁴⁴

How exactly we do that is an open question. When a speaker steps up in the next canto to explain what just happened, pairing the capitalized OFF of the deep-water canto with the answering HOW of this one, the explanation breaks down in stammered uncertainty:

This is how to
This is with imperatives
I mean models
If you act
Act HOW. (42)

As the syntax collapses, we're left with another scene of splendid confusion, where the shift from instrumental reason to deep-water rebel disables "models" and "imperatives," indeed seems to disable language itself, as if again it's the disappointment that matters, the not being able to say. In its stuttering and emendations, the Act-HOW canto resembles an Emily Dickinson poem, where something familiar (a robin, the daffodils in their yellow gowns) bursts the seams of syntax and leaves a trail of cuts and dashes in its wake. Merton thought of Dickinson as his "flesh and blood" and uses her poetic rhythms in *Cables* to evoke the mind's rebellion against literary and religious cliché.[45] The world is deeper than consciousness for Dickinson just as consciousness is deeper than the thinking mind, so the tools and terms she uses to span those depths are often bent or broken in the process. Stammering is the natural voice of religious witness for Dickinson, faith's true tongue, and Merton contrasts that halting rhythm with the easy fluency of a one-dimensional world, where the air says *yes* and the head says *yes* and even the corpuscles repeat the same refrain.

The deep-water rebel interrupts that smooth consensus and restores the dimension of otherness missing from the rat labs and waiting rooms. That nameless rebel, it seems, is Christ, but Christ disguised as fish or *fin* (*Finnegans Wake*), Christ as the culmination of Merton's many images of water, rivers, oceans, and rain. At times, *Cables* evokes a science-fiction dystopia of human life as *wiring*: cultural stereotypes wet-ported into people by cryphones and the telefake. But we may yet unlearn that circuitry in response to a deep-water savior not bound by hegemonic norms and indifferent to the reigning standards of taste, profit, utility, and value. Indeed, that kind of divinity may be profoundly *unprofitable*, especially if what we lose in this redemption is a strong version of ourselves: the bounded, buffered, acquisitive, market-ready version industrial societies are determined to create.

This may take us back to the bottom, the redemptive lowdown. If the deep-water canto suggests a resurrection rather than a burial (Finnegans *Wake*), it's an Easter moment that emerges when life is nearly wrung out. George Kilcourse points out that the "ace" in a deck of cards is both high and low and that if Christ is the "ace of freedoms," the high point of all creation, he's also at the bottom of the scale, a self-emptying savior who identifies with the bankrupt moments of human life.[46] This is one of the ironies of the Easter story and part of the nimble play of Merton's Christology. To join that play, Merton suggests, involves an ability to abstract and reframe, allowing the sacred to disrupt established patterns and wake us from dormitive thinking and spiritual sleep. In accord with the negative aesthetic of his anti-poetry, Merton explores the failure of that double vision in canto 80, where a sleepy disciple mistakes the light of Christ for an unremarkable harvest moon:

Slowly
Comes Christ through the garden
Speaking to the sacred trees
Their branches bear his light
Without harm

Slowly
Comes Christ through the ruins

Seeking the lost disciple
A timid one
Too literate
To believe words
So he hides

Slowly
Christ rises on the cornfields
It is only the harvest moon
The disciple
Turns over in his sleep
And murmurs:
"My regret!" (55)

Once again, the bloody cooler is turned off for a moment and we glimpse a peaceable kingdom free from harm: the "branches bear his light / Without harm." To the sleepy disciple, however, the sacred light is only the harvest moon, as if that too counts for nothing, which leaves his worldview unchanged. When Christ appeared at the empty tomb in John's gospel, as I mentioned in the Introduction, Mary doesn't recognize him at first, mistaking him not for the moon but for the gardener—or *only* the gardener as the sleepy disciple might say. When Christ calls her by name, however, the perspective changes and Mary sees him for the first time. John's story is a teaching scene, like many of Merton's cantos (Mary uses the Aramaic word for "teacher" when she recognizes Christ), and the theme of Christ's teaching at the tomb parallels his "song of the vineyard," which invites us to see and think differently, in more than one way:

> He asked her, "Woman, why are you crying? Who is it you are looking for?" Thinking he was the gardener, she said, "Sir, if you have carried him away, tell me where you have put him, and I will get him." Jesus said to her, "Mary." She turned toward him and cried out in Aramaic, "Rabboni!" (which means "Teacher"). (John 20:15–16 NIV)

Let me close with a thought about this turn or trope in Mary: she turned toward him and cried out. The frame shift from *gardener* to *Rabboni* in the gospel narrative, or from the harvest moon to the light of Christ in Merton's canto, resembles the figure/ground reversals of gestalt illusions: stairs that go up and then down and then up again. Or the white image of a vase, which becomes two black faces in profile silhouette, so close their lips nearly touch. The gestalt psychologists describe this change as a "depth effect"—"When one sees the white figure, the black ground is *behind* it"—so that what appeared flat and static a moment before, now exists dynamically in three dimensions.[47] Once we see the second image, the picture becomes both deeper and more active. To achieve that depth, however, what the therapists call "insight," we have to spontaneously reorganize the vase by letting go of our first impression and allowing the background figures to come forward (rather than *causing* them to come forward as an act of will). This kind of visual "play" fascinated Annie Dillard, as I'll say more about in the next chapter. In *Pilgrim at Tinker Creek*, Dillard explores styles of perception that release the sacred from preformed judgments and create a space for the self-presentation or self-disclosure of the natural world. Dillard calls this negative aesthetic *unpeaching* and associates it not only with the gestalt puzzles she enjoyed as a child but also with the "insight" parables of Christianity and Judaism, the stories of recovered vision.

Something like this unpeaching may have been on Merton's mind when he subtitled *Cables*, "Familiar Liturgies of Misunderstanding," and introduced Houdini as a figure of Christ, "a Mister Houdini or somebody with fingers" (42). Stewart notes that many of Houdini's tricks depended not only on his physical dexterity but also on the kind of figure/ground reversals the gestalt psychologists studied in the Rubin vase.[48] This is why Houdini's tricks seem like "magic" at first: the key was there all along, disguised not by the occult but by the audience's preconceptions about foreground and background, their sense of what's important and what's not. The pleasure of magic tricks is the sudden reversal of those fields, the "jump" or "shock" of a frame shift. But to experience that reversal we must accept the inadequacy or incorrectness of our first impression, just as we must "misunderstand" the vase to allow the faces to come forward and "misunderstand" the moon to glimpse Christ's light in the trees.

The frame shift in the gospel account seems to follow a similar logic, bringing *gardener* and *Christ* together in the same figure, the same person. If Christ is indeed both triumphant and self-emptying, just as the "ace" is both high and low, then Merton's poetry may help us loosen perceptual frames and experience the sacred not only with Mary at the Easter tomb but also with the women in the waiting room and the children on the cryphone, making their despair less fatal. Such seeing exalts the lowest levels of human life, what's "lowdown / At the bottom," even as it contradicts the reigning wisdom of shotguns and power. This ultimately is the playful wisdom of Merton's poem and his prayer for a quietly desperate age: more folly, more dancing, more tumbling, more nonsense—until the ligatures we use to bind the world "give" a little and we glimpse the stairs ascending or the lovers kissing or the face of Christ in disguise.

NOTES

1. Belden C. Lane, "Merton's Hermitage: Bachelard, Domestic Space, and Spiritual Transformation," *Spiritus* 4, no. 2 (Fall 2004): 127, 125. For other accounts of spiritual play in Merton, see Belden C. Lane, "Merton as Zen Clown," *Theology Today* 46, no. 3 (October 1989): 256–68; and Christopher Pramuk, *Sophia: The Hidden Christ of Thomas Merton* (Collegeville, MN, Liturgical Press, 2009), 11–17, 133–48, 191–212. For Merton's reflections on how Trappist discipline and liturgy constitute forms of sacred play, see Patrick Hart and Jonathan Montaldo, eds., *The Intimate Merton: His Life from His Journals* (San Francisco: HarperOne, 1999), 29.

2. Thomas Merton and Robert Lax, *A Catch of Anti-Letters* (Mission, KS: Sheed and Ward, 1994).

3. Thomas Merton, *Cables to the Ace; or, Familiar Liturgies of Misunderstanding* (New York: New Directions, 1968), 28. Subsequent references to *Cables to the Ace* will refer to this edition and be cited in the text by page number.

4. Letters to W. H. Ferry, September 17 and October 4, 1966; quoted in Ross Labrie, *The Art of Thomas Merton* (Fort Worth: Texas Christian University Press, 1979), 137–38.

5. Merton argued that Thoreau's "idleness" was in fact a contemplative model of detachment and non-conformity, and thus a pastoral "gift" to an advanced technological society: "Thoreau's idleness (as 'inspector of snowstorms') was an incomparable gift and its fruits were blessings that America has never really learned to appreciate. (Industrious and affluent America, busy making more money than ever, has little time for him. At best he was a beatnik who came a hundred years early!) Yet Thoreau proffered his gift nevertheless, though it was not asked for, and he knew it would be neglected." See *Conjectures of a Guilty Bystander* (Garden City, NY: Image Books, 1968), 249.

6. *The Letters of St. Bernard of Clairvaux*, trans. Bruno Scott James (London: Burns Oates, 1953), 130; quoted in John Saward, *Perfect Fools: Folly for Christ's Sake in Catholic and Orthodox Spirituality* (Oxford: Oxford University Press, 1980), 58.

7. On this, see Romano Guardini, "The Playfulness of the Liturgy," in his *The Church and the Catholic and the Spirit of Liturgy*, trans. Ada Lane (New York: Sheed and Ward, 1953), 171–84; Hugo Rahner, *Man at Play*, trans. Brian Battershaw and Edward Quinn (New York: Herder and Herder, 1967); and Saward, *Perfect Fools*.

8. Derived in part from the Russian Formalists' concept of "defamiliarization," Bertolt Brecht's *Verfremdungseffekt* or *V-effekt* disrupts an audience's passivity. Making the artifice of his plays as high profile as possible (through disruptive commentaries, jarring scene shifts, and sudden outbursts of song), Brecht encourages his audience to see through the illusions on stage and recover self-conscious critical distance.

9. Thomas Merton, "Notes for a Philosophy of Solitude," in *Disputed Questions* (New York: Farrar, Straus and Cudahy, 1960), 177.

10. In his review of Roland Barthes' *Writing Degree Zero*, Merton describes the political purpose of literature this way: "[The writer] does something to society not

by pushing against its structures—which are none of his business—but by changing the tune of its language and shifting the perspectives which depend on the ways words are arranged. He systematically de-mythologizes literature." See his *The Literary Essays of Thomas Merton*, ed. Patrick Hart (New York: New Directions, 1981), 144. Despite the either/or phrasing, Merton intervenes in the social crises of his culture in *both* ways: "pushing against its structures" in countless works of political and social advocacy as well as "shifting the perspectives" through the kaleidoscopic anti-poetry of works like *Cables to the Ace* and *The Geography of Lograire*.

11. The reply to Henry Miller can be found in Thomas Merton, *Cold War Letters*, ed. Christine M. Bochen and William H. Shannon (Maryknoll, NY: Orbis Books, 2006), 167–70. Previous studies of Thoreau and Merton include Gilles Farcé, "Different Drummers: Thomas Merton and Henry Thoreau," *The Merton Seasonal* 10, no. 2 (1985): 2–6; John Albert, OCSO, "Lights Across the Ridge: Thomas Merton and Henry David Thoreau," *The Merton Annual* 1 (1988): 271–317; Ross Labrie, "Merton and the American Romantics," *The Merton Annual* 9 (1996): 34–54; and Patrick F. O'Connell, "Keeping Pace With His Companion: Thomas Merton and Henry Thoreau," *The Concord Saunterer* N. S. 7 (1999), 115–48.

12. Stephen John Mack, *The Pragmatic Whitman: Reimagining American Democracy* (Iowa City: University of Iowa Press, 2002).

13. Henry D. Thoreau, "Resistance to Civil Government," in *The Higher Law: Thoreau on Civil Disobedience and Reform*, ed. Wendell Glick (Princeton: Princeton University Press, 2004), 66–67.

14. Merton, *Disputed Questions*, 179.

15. My emphasis on play as the presentation of alternatives builds on a theological foundation Christopher Pramuk develops in *Sophia: The Hidden Christ of Thomas Merton*, especially Pramuk's interpretation of Merton's sapiential poem, *Hagia Sophia*. Merton wrote *Hagia Sophia* in 1962 in response to a series of dreams he experienced based on the Wisdom child of Proverbs 8. In the first of those dreams in 1958, Wisdom appeared to Merton as a Jewish girl he named "Proverb" and in later dreams as a Chinese princess and an African-American mother (whose dancing inspired the closing scene of *New Seeds of Contemplation*). Merton interpreted those dreams as redemptive, in-breaking alternatives to the hegemonic logic of the day, what the New Testament calls "worldly wisdom" (*sarx*, 2 Cor. 1:12), and which Merton believed had led the world to the brink of destruction. *Hagia Sophia* wakes the poet from that sleep of death, Pramuk argues, and helps him recover a view of life as responsiveness, playfulness, spontaneity, and spiritual trust. See Merton, *Hagia Sophia*, in *Emblems of a Season of Fury* (New York: New Directions, 1963), 61–69; and Pramuk, *Sophia*, 193–212.

16. Thomas Merton, "Rain and the Rhinoceros," in *Raids on the Unspeakable* (New York: New Directions, 1966), 9.

17. Several Merton scholars call attention to the importance of *One-Dimensional Man* to Merton's social advocacy and late poetry, but I'm especially indebted to David D. Cooper's reading of *Cables to the Ace*. See his *Thomas Merton's Art of Denial: The Evolution of a Radical Humanist* (Athens: University of Georgia Press, 1989), 251–69.

18. Merton, *Raids on the Unspeakable*, 14.

19. Marianne DeKoven, *Utopia Limited: The Sixties and the Emergence of the Postmodern* (Durham: Duke University Press, 2004), 29.

20. Merton, *Raids on the Unspeakable*, 12.

21. On this, see Martin Jay, *The Dialectical Imagination: A History of the Frankfurt School and the Institute of Social Research, 1923–1950* (Boston: Little, Brown, 1973), 59.

22. Herbert Marcuse, *One-Dimensional Man: Studies in the Ideology of Advanced Industrial Society*, 2nd ed. (Boston: Beacon Press, 1991), 9.

23. Marcuse, *One-Dimensional Man*, 11.

24. Jay develops the importance of this phrase for the writers of the Frankfurt School in *The Dialectical Imagination*, 178–80.

25. Marcuse, *One-Dimensional Man*, 50.

26. Thomas Merton, *The Asian Journal of Thomas Merton*, ed. Naomi Burton, Patrick Hart, and James Laughlin (New York: New Directions, 1973), 327, 118.

27. See, for instance, Alasdair MacIntyre, *Herbert Marcuse: An Exposition and a Polemic* (New York: Viking Press, 1970), 70.

28. Susan Stewart, *Nonsense: Aspects of Intertextuality in Folklore and Literature* (1978; repr. Baltimore: Johns Hopkins University Press, 1989), 3–20.

29. Stewart, *Nonsense*, 20.

30. Although it's unlikely that Merton knew Adorno's work directly, it's worth noting how Adorno's 1938 essay, "On the Fetish-Character in Music and the Regression of Listening," anticipates Merton's atonal attack on the "habit frequency" of managed listening. The Freudian language in Adorno's title attests to what he saw as the inability of modern audiences to tolerate difficult or experimental music, like children who only enjoy food they've eaten in the past. The regressed listener narrows the bandwidth of acceptable sound to the fetishized repetition of familiar music and so robs music of its "negative" function, its ability to inspire meaningful change. See Theodor W. Adorno, *Essays on Music*, ed. Richard Leppert; with new translations by Susan H. Gillespie (Berkeley: University of California Press, 2002), 288–317. See also Martin Jay's commentary on Adorno's essay in *The Dialectical Imagination*, 189–91.

31. A small sampling would include Robert E. Neale's *In Praise of Play: Toward a Psychology of Religion* (1969); Sam Keen's *To a Dancing God* (1970); David LeRoy Miller's *Gods and Games: Toward a Theology of Play* (1970); Josef Pieper's *In Tune with the World: A Theory of Festivity* (1965); and William F. Lynch's theologies of fantasy and the imagination: *Christ and Apollo: The Dimensions of the Literary Imagination* (1960) and *Images of Hope: Imagination as Healer of the Hopeless* (1965). In addition, the death-of-God movement took the study of sacred play in two directions. In works like *The Gospel of Christian Atheism* (1966) and *The Descent into Hell* (1970), Thomas J. J. Altizer revered Nietzsche's Zarathustra as the embodiment of a fully secularized, fully pagan human joy, liberated at last from transcendental notions of judgment and guilt. And in an essay that first appeared in *Theology Today* in 1966, "The New Optimism: From Prufrock to Ringo," William Hughes Hamilton, another of the 1960s radical theologians, announced not only the

death of God but also the death of modernism, with its gloomy synthesis of existential anxiety and neo-orthodox dread. What rises to take its place, Hamilton argues, is a new era of spiritual lightness, playfulness, and goofball wit, more like Ringo Starr than J. Alfred Prufrock. Among the many theologies of inter-faith dialogue in this period, Dom Aelred Graham's *Zen Catholicism* (1963) and Alan Watts' *Beyond Theology: The Art of Godmanship* (1964) brought Western and Eastern spiritualities together around the concept of holy play. Merton's friend and correspondent, Rosemary Radford Ruether, wrote widely on feminist models of post-Catholic community, including *The Church Against Itself: An Inquiry into the Conditions of Historical Existence for the Eschatological Community* (1967), which pictures the church as a temporal "happening," created and reformed moment by moment through improvisational encounter. Harvey Cox offers a useful survey of several strands of 1960s theology (aesthetic theology; neo-mysticism; the death-of-God movement; the theologies of hope) and aligns those trends with theologies of play and festival. See his *The Feast of Fools: A Theological Essay on Festivity and Fantasy* (Cambridge: Harvard University Press, 1969). For a more comprehensive history of 1960s spirituality, see Robert S. Ellwood, *The Sixties Spiritual Awakening: American Religion Moving from Modern to Postmodern* (New Brunswick, NJ: Rutgers University Press, 1994).

32. George Woodcock, *Thomas Merton, Monk and Poet: A Critical Study* (New York: Farrar, Straus, Giroux, 1978), 173–74.

33. Mikhail Bakhtin, *Problems of Dostoevsky's Poetics*, ed. and trans. Caryl Emerson (Minneapolis: University of Minnesota Press, 1984), 292.

34. M. M. Bakhtin, *The Dialogic Imagination: Four Essays*, ed. Michael Holquist; trans. Caryl Emerson and Michael Holquist (Austin: University of Texas Press, 1981), 177.

35. Cox, *Feast of Fools*, 146.

36. Merton, "To Each His Darkness," in *Raids on the Unspeakable*, 27–33.

37. Merton, *A Catch of Anti-Letters*, 43.

38. See, for instance, Linda Hutcheon, *The Politics of Postmodernism* (London: Routledge, 1989).

39. Merton, *The Intimate Merton*, 202.

40. Stewart, *Nonsense*, 49.

41. J. Heath Atchley, "Sounding the Depth of the Secular: Tillich with Thoreau," *Implicit Religion* 15, no. 2 (June 2012): 153–66.

42. Marcuse, *One-Dimensional Man*, 226–27.

43. Anna Livia Plurabelle is the mother-source in *Finnegans Wake*, the free-flowing matrix of all waters and a profound image of the sacred for Joyce: "In the name of Annah the Allmaziful, the Everliving, the Bringer of Plurabilities, haloed be her eve, her singtime sung, her rill be run, unhemmed as it is uneven!" See James Joyce, *Finnegans Wake* (1939; repr. New York: Viking, 1976), 104. Merton alludes to Anna Livia Plurabelle not only in this canto but also in the "Mama my ocean" scene and develops a similar set of associations linking water, plurality, maternity, music, and the sacred.

44. Merton, *The Intimate Merton*, 87.

45. See, for instance, this passage from Merton's *Journal*: "Emily Dickinson, my own flesh and blood, my own kind of quiet rebel, fighting for truth against catchwords and formalities, fighting for independence of the spirit." *The Intimate Merton*, 149.

46. George Kilcourse, *Ace of Freedoms: Thomas Merton's Christ* (Notre Dame: University of Notre Dame Press, 1993), 178. I'm also grateful for personal correspondence with George Kilcourse on an earlier draft of this chapter.

47. Frederick Perls, Ralph F. Hefferline, and Paul Goodman, *Gestalt Therapy: Excitement and Growth in the Human Personality* (New York: Delta, 1951), 27.

48. Stewart, *Nonsense*, 89–91.

Chapter 5

Play and Risk
Annie Dillard's Daredevil Faith

YES AND NO TOGETHER

Let me begin this chapter by reviewing my argument so far. As I mentioned in the Introduction, play thrives in a mixed zone of competing perspectives and contradictory claims. This is play's natural domain, as Gregory Bateson argues in "The Message 'This is Play'" and "A Theory of Play and Fantasy." In play, rote phrasing opens in the presence of paradox and the interactions between people loosen and evolve. In Bateson's view, human beings are hardwired against social and psychological change. People are perceptually conservative, he believed, pre-equipped with governing loops and rebalancing tactics that neutralize disturbance and maintain the equipoise of homeostatic systems. This is what troubled Thoreau about market capitalism: its special genius for disarming competing systems of value so that everything appears in the same way and through the same uniform and intersubjective lens: calculable use. Thoreau's emphasis on perspectival knowing and provisional value in *Walden* causes a zone of strangeness or otherness to appear, a discursive space not subject to one-sided or one-dimensional utilitarian regimes.

This is what the writers of *Playful Wisdom* share with Bateson and with one another: an emphasis on multiple viewpoints and interactive framing. Bateson and his colleagues were interested in how play reorganizes the boundaries of discourse, creating what he called "a cut or slash" in our experience of the real and heightening our sense that the everyday lifeworld harbors multiple angles, niches, dimensions, and planes.[1] In play, things are no longer singular or self-consistent. As he puts it, "A falling leaf, the greeting of a friend, or a 'primrose by the river's brim' is not 'just that and nothing more.'"[2] Meaning depends instead on yards and contexts and on our being able to move through different interpretative domains (rather than being trapped within one set of procedures). Like metaphor, play is transgressive and metaxic. Bateson's word is "transcontextual." Play mixes things that wouldn't normally intersect and so exposes the "normal" to revision and difference, which is exactly what Thoreau reveals at the sandbank: a leaf that's not "just that and nothing more" but the prototype for feathers, trees, ice crystals, lungs, livers, ova, and blood vessels. Thoreau is more explicitly religious about this reframing than Bateson; transcontextual play is the *līlā*-sport of *Walden*'s God, but like Bateson he studies the impact of play on human thought and language. When *a leaf* is also *not a leaf* in Thoreau or *a bite* is also *not a bite* in Bateson, something profound happens: communication sequences open and disseminate, admitting a wider range of possibility and tone. As that occurs, a different kind of learning comes to the fore, what Bateson called deutero-learning, which exchanges stylized messages, subject to rigid rules, for impromptu or improvisational messaging, subject to the give and take of a live encounter.

Bateson is especially helpful for play theory because the "other" in his play scenes plays back. There's a kinetic "mobility" at the heart of Batesonian play—something nervy, twitchy, muscular, and alive. When Freud and Erikson think about play, cotton reels and steamboats come to mind, children in full command of their microenvironments and so actively rehearsing what Erikson called the hallucination of mastery.[3] The cotton reel doesn't have a life or mind of its own. It's *ours*, incorporated into the drama of our subjectivity, an object we can use. When Bateson considers play, cats, otters, wolves, puppies, dolphins, monkeys, and jackdaws come to mind, a free-wheeling animal ecology that is absolutely not us, not ours to command. Other creatures play with us or against us in Bateson, which puts "us" (our rote sequencing, our commonsense modes of thought and interaction) at considerable risk, as we've seen many times in *Playful Wisdom*.

Bateson foregrounds this conceptual impasse. We simply can't "think" play with any kind of logical consistency. Every time he tries to define it, he hits a wall, as if play were comparable to the Epimenides paradox, an unassimilable *anti* that exposes the limits of our categories. Thus, Bateson seizes on the idea of limits and boundaries and stresses the way *this is play* and other metamessages cause a space of subjunctivity, fantasy, and figurality to appear. In play, the scene at hand is never self-contained nor is the player herself merely "self-surrounded" (as Eudora Welty once said about Dillard). On the contrary, play remains relative to what stands apart from it, relative to what it's *not*, which makes one-dimensional thinking and communication less secure. This fictional element of play—"the messages or signals exchanged in play are in a certain sense untrue or not meant" and "that which is denoted by these signals is nonexistent"[4]—brings forward a mode of double-voiced discourse that simultaneously affirms and denies its own reality, linking "absence and presence together," as Stephen Nachmanovitch has argued about this aspect of play, "yes and no together."[5]

We've seen a version of this idea in various Catholic, Jewish, and radical theologies of play. For Hugo Rahner, for instance, religious faith requires a person who can "say 'Nay' along with his 'Yea,' and . . . say it without demur or hesitation."[6] For Michael Fishbane, the call of God "is the primal claim of Yes and No," an invitation to affirm the positivity of existence and yet deny that *this* existence is in any way sufficient or complete.[7] For John Caputo, "Radical theology is a delicate art that requires the equipoise of being able to say in one breath, 'yes, yes, but perhaps not,' of being something as if not."[8] Like Caputo, Bateson responds to the core paradox of play, "being something as if not," with modal qualifiers like "perhaps" or "almost" or "sort of" as if to shade his concepts with what they're not, causing them to stand both in and out of the light, half-revealed and half-concealed by what he can and cannot say. A discourse of partial glimpses and almost-guesses keeps thought open for Bateson, keeps it playful, ever alert to the nonsense at the edge of speech or the darkness on the verge of insight.

For the writers in my study, play is a Batesonian mood signal or context marker that accents the *not really* or *not entirely* aspects of religion, the way a life of faith operates in a halfway zone of conviction and doubt, presence and absence, yes and no—all bundled together and co-constituting one another like the play of shadow and light. The metamessage *no* at the heart of ludic communication thus foregrounds the provisionality of play and religion and blocks more appropriative or presumptive modes of thought. For Bateson, play depends on that implicit negation, a productive *no* within communication sequences that protects the revisability of the message, its basic open-endedness.

In faith, we're asked to accept that open-endedness in our relationship with God, which safeguards a space of gift, grace, event, and mystery—all the things that are not ours to calculate and control. Because we don't control those possibilities, anything can happen: the gift may turn out to be a disaster (and then the "disaster" may prove to be a "gift" and so on)—which leads Jürgen Moltmann to describe faith as "this game of all-reversing grace."[9] A core phenomenon of the religious life is exactly this chance for reversal and change, the hope that things can be different than they are today, that *we* can be different, and so the die is not yet cast. But there's no endpoint to the all-reversing process, no final state or master key that cancels grace and ends the game. As Bateson would put it, the message can always be reframed: "What exists today are only messages about the past which we call memories, and these messages can always be framed and modulated from moment to moment," which creates "slipping and sliding meanings."[10]

This kind of slippery hermeneutics is "trouble" to our religious and ethical narcissism, as we saw in Kerouac—"Troubles, you see, is the generalization-word for what God exists in"—but the writers I've gathered *choose* that interpretive trouble as the underlying condition of a religious life. Knowing full well that answering the call of an enigmatic God will put an end to egocentric regimes, the "little world" Thoreau satirizes in *Walden*, the writers of *Playful Wisdom* accept that insecurity and respond to divine invitation with a variable grammar of assent: Merton's hallelujahs, Kerouac's yesses, Thoreau's trembling, and Dickinson's raised pen. It's call and response all the way through, which is also the way Jesus imagined the life of faith, as a cry in the wilderness or a knock at the door.

For many postmodern writers play happens on its own. Play is something language does to itself, something it does without us. The trace is an inherent feature of linguistic and cultural systems, built in to how those systems operate, and so always-already hidden within ordinary discourse. (Bateson shared this view.) But for the writers in my study, play is more like a choice or a covenant, something we can accept or reject, which is what makes it truly playful, non-compulsory. When the gospel writers make room for our refusal—"We sang to you, and you did not dance" (Matt. 11:17)—they frame our participation around that covenantal freedom and invite us to imagine what the dance-play of faith might mean.[11]

DARK PLAY

This strikes me as the kind of covenant Annie Dillard explores in her 1974 book, *Pilgrim at Tinker Creek*, a spiritual and ecological memoir published two years after *Steps to an Ecology of Mind*. When Dillard senses "something powerful playing over me" and turns to join that play undefended, or when she describes her spirituality as "a fierce game" she can't win and doesn't need to win because its possibilities are beyond her reach, or when she compares the life of faith to riding a bucking horse or being pummeled by a play-fighting tomcat, she hints at what it might mean to accept the invitation of divine play and raise her pen to a possible God.[12] Dillard shares Bateson's emphasis on continuous reframing, messages that can be modulated moment by moment, but she turns that idea to a more explicitly religious purpose than he does, exploring the "slipperiness" of the sacred in the manner of her two most important literary mentors: Dickinson and Thoreau. Beginning with her undergraduate honors project on Dickinson, "The Merchant of the Picturesque," and continuing into her master's thesis on *Walden*, and then into *Pilgrim at Tinker Creek*, Dillard explores a mode of ludic faith unbound by rigid codes and agile enough to accommodate the shifting light of the divine. This isn't an implicit or occasional feature of Dillard's writing. It's her declared purpose. When she says, "I am above all an unscrupulous observer" (33), she announces her intention to face upstream, face whatever the creek might bring, without preformed scruples or prejudicial conditions.[13] This means that what's coming down the creek is what's coming down the creek. Gift or disaster, blessing or poison—she bears witness to each in turn.

Dillard develops the implications of this open stance through the idea of "hosting" or "hospitality," letting the other arrive according to the terms of its own self-disclosure (rather than the terms she would set for it). As Richard Kearney points out in regard to postmodern ethics and religion, such "letting" is more complicated than it sounds, precisely because it runs up against the problem of the abject (Julia Kristeva) and the monstrous (Slavoj Žižek)[14]—possibilities Dillard examines in miniature in her scenes of insect predation, parasitism, cannibalism, and "hosting." This is the Darwinian inflection of Dillard's fierce game. Like play, evolution runs on chance and change. It too serves a God of the possible, whose creativity is expressed through mutation, deformity, experimentation, and difference. And whose communion cup, Dillard notes, is filled with blood. If that's true, then the hospitality Dillard explores in *Pilgrim* opens the religious imagination to "hostis" or "hostility," what Derrida called "hosti-pitality" in a famous essay, so that receiving the other means welcoming the one whose face is benign, welcoming the one whose face is terrifying: hosting Jesus, hosting parasites, hosting the tree with the lights in it, hosting its galls and leeches. She opens the door either way.

For this reason, I've chosen to call the playful wisdom of *Pilgrim* "dark play"—a phrase Richard Schechner uses to discuss the play theologies of classical Hinduism, where Siva's dancing decreates existence at the end of each era and Krishna's flute sends shock waves through life, rattling the world down to its core components and building it back up from there.[15] The *līlā* of the Hindu scriptures is dark, like Krishna, whose name means "blue-black," the color of a thundercloud, and who reveals himself to his mother, Yashoda, in the *Bhāgavata Purāna* as a universe-devouring mouth, a scene Dillard quotes in *For the Time Being*.[16] If "horror" is one of the names we give to the precariousness of human experience, then "play" is another name for that insecurity, what Schechner calls "the unsteadiness, slipperiness, porosity, unreliability, and ontological riskiness of the realities projected or created by playing."[17] Dark play draws on both sets of associations. It refuses to rule out the possibility of the monstrous in our relationship with the divine, which threatens at times to turn *Pilgrim at Tinker Creek* into *Night of the Living Dead* (in which Dillard's father played a small role). But it also refuses to allow the monstrous to have the last word. It refuses the idea of the last word. Dark play substitutes ontological riskiness for ontological security and so opens a space for innovation and growth. When Dillard quotes from the Advent psalm in *Pilgrim*, "Our God shall come" (263), she possibilizes the present from out of the future without making any claims about what that advent might mean or which "God" may be coming (there are several in *Pilgrim*). What matters to Dillard is the "may be"—the structural openness of the subjunctive. The intelligibility of hope in *Pilgrim* does not depend on doctrinal creeds or propositional claims (I know my God is merciful, I know my God will save me), but on the possibilities of a God who is always arriving and always on the way, like the flow of Tinker Creek. This view of the sacred threatens onto-theologies of sameness, logos, and divine presence, just as it threatens the buffered, imperial, self-secure Western subject made in the image of that God. In place of that security, Dillard explores a religious milieu where everything floats and drifts, congealing-and-dissolving, not only in large-scale scenes of flooding and decreation but also on the much smaller scale of what she sees through the lens of her microscope: "I see the amoebae as drops of water congealed," she writes, "bluish, translucent, like chips of sky in the bowl" (26). This kind of thinking is disturbing, sky-breaking, but it's also profoundly hopeful—as if even the sky is fragile, deconstructible, revealing who knows what on the other side.

My argument is that Dillard chooses this position of precariousness and religious risk as a sacred office or holy calling, a way of being faithful to "that Diviner thing" now coming, as Dickinson said. Accepting a covenant with a God who may be, Dillard enters a religious milieu that's changing right before her eyes, changing even as she writes about it: "A fish flashes, then dissolves in the water before my eyes like so much salt" (18). *Fish, light, water, salt*: these are ancient religious symbols reincarnated and recombined in Tinker Creek. Faith for Dillard means choosing this incarnational fluidity, accepting and turning toward it in gratitude and love and so joining the danceplay of an ongoing creation.

ALMOST BUT NEVER QUITE PRESENT

At first glance "The Merchant of the Picturesque: One Pattern in Emily Dickinson's Poetry," Dillard's 1967 honors project at Hollins College, offers few hints that the twenty-two-year-old Dillard would eventually become one of America's most celebrated religious writers. It seems more likely that Dillard would become a literary scholar, like her college classmates Lucinda Hardwick MacKethan and Anne Goodwyn Jones; or a metaphysical nature poet, like her writing mentor at Hollins, Julia Randall Sawyer. If anything, the tone of iconoclastic critique in "Merchant" sounds more like Annie Doak than Annie Dillard—the Pittsburgh wild child who despised the cotton-glove conservatism of her family's church, Shadyside Presbyterian, and writhed in teenage agony at the sight of a watercolor Jesus hanging in the church's Sunday school classroom. Dillard wanted nothing to do with that religious tradition ("I hated it so passionately," she wrote in *An American Childhood*), and she knew even as a teenager that her faith journey would take her outside the bounds of the institutional church and beyond the role of the dutiful daughter. Which raises the question of what that faith might look like in 1967 and what sources of empowerment and affiliation might bring it to voice. These are the questions Dillard's friend, Lucinda Hardwick MacKethan, later raised in her study of southern women writers, *Daughters of Time: Creating Woman's Voice in Southern Story*:

> My study concerns the possibilities for reversal, for empowerment, that southern women seized upon when they moved beyond the role of daughter and into the role of storyteller. Central to my exploration of this direction are certain questions: what does the entity of Daughter entail? what "veiled" strategies does a woman bring to the mission of voicing herself in male gardens? can she take possession of her own garden, a place where she is free to imagine, to design, to produce creations that bear her distinctive personality and purpose? how, ultimately, does she speak a story out of the condition of voicelessness?[18]

MacKethan's work may help us remember that *Pilgrim at Tinker Creek* emerges not only in dialogue with Thoreau, as a great deal of commentary emphasizes, but also and initially in dialogue with Dickinson—a writer who also rejected the role of the dutiful daughter (when she was nearly the same age as Dillard) and explored the possibilities for carnivalesque reversal in the male gardens of her family's church.[19]

Dillard brings the carnivalesque front and center in "Merchant" by choosing Dickinson poems that personify God as "The Showman," the "Juggler," and "The Merchant of the Picturesque"—a trickster-figure who creates liminal spaces of shimmering instability.[20] The "play" in these poems is related to beguilement, illusion, duplicity, and sleight-of-hand, a theme Dillard will later develop through the "carnival magician" in the opening chapter of *Pilgrim*. Dickinson tends to confront divine tricksters with cold scorn, exposing their games of hide and seek not as play but as cruelty, like the wanton gods of *King Lear*. Dillard's trickster is milder than that, an abracadabra con man who makes clouds, rabbits, trees, and an entire mountain range disappear into his black hat. But even though the tone is lighter in *Pilgrim*, the possibility that God is toying with our pain is never far from view in Dillard's religious writings, *Holy the Firm* and *For the Time Being* in particular, and so the theodicy questions are never far behind.[21]

In "Merchant," however, Dillard sets theodicy questions aside to examine how Dickinson configures the sacred as present in absence, the category paradox Bateson and the play theorists study. And she explores how we might have a relationship with a God who appears and disappears in the same ambiguous moment. That "disappearance" takes two forms in "Merchant." First, it means loss, plain and simple, an enveloping darkness surrounding Dickinson's visual field. Various small, precious, airy things (butterflies, birds, bees, rays of sunlight) become visible briefly in Dickinson's nature poems before dropping into the darkness of sudden death, which Dillard calls Dickinson's downbeat, or rising into the darkness of sudden transcendence, her upbeat. Both beats amount to the same thing and create the same trope: *watching things go away*. Here's how Dillard expresses that preliminary insight: "The pattern is, quite simply, one of description and disappearance. The poet describes something—usually something good or beautiful—then 'kills it off' in a variety of ways. It dies, or, more frequently, it is translated into a vague 'beyond,' a beyond that holds both death and all the unattainable secrets of life."[22]

When God appears in this version of the pattern, his face is monstrous and his play is cruel: "And so the pattern repeats itself. The unconscious things of the natural world move away from the poet towards death, the sea, or the skies as though pulled by some jealous hand. The natural world is a beautiful and cruel peep-show, a burlesque directed by a half-malicious God who turns out the lights just as the fans are about to part."[23] It's a complicated image, one that simultaneously feminizes nature, an idea with a long history in American literature, and carnivalizes God, turning him (always him in "Merchant") into an erotic trickster who provokes and merchandizes our longing, creating a sadistic economy of spiritual desire.

We could contextualize the theme of "watching things go away" from several perspectives. It's the elegiac voice of Dickinson and Thoreau for one, writers who were acutely aware of their estrangement from a natural world that hid or withdrew from them. Moreover, "watching things go away" is about as close as we might come to a four-word summary of *On the Road*, a book Dillard adored. The primal scene of that novel is Sal watching the people he loves grow smaller as he drives away from them, grow smaller and then disappear. Watching things go away may also evoke the death of God theologians of Dillard's era, writers like Thomas J. J. Altizer and William Hamilton, whose project centers on a Nietzschean reading of divine maliciousness as well as a cultural reading of the 1960s as the moment when that God disappeared. Finally, it's worth remembering that many of the Dickinson poems Dillard studies were written at the height of the Civil War and that "Merchant" itself was written at the height of the Vietnam War. Both the poems and their analysis are drenched in death, although neither writer historicizes her thought quite that way, as if framing the losses around war would make them seem exceptional, even avoidable, where the wave-like fluctuations of presence and absence are deeper and more organic than that, like the rhythms of time and motion, as Dillard stresses, the rhythm of "ultimate," rather than conditional, "annihilation."[24]

But there's another way to look at these disappearances. Dillard calls her project "one pattern in Emily Dickinson's poetry," but there are actually two. It's possible to read the darkness as pure loss and imagine a God who designs that kind of world as a half-malicious trickster, like the various horror theophonies in *Pilgrim* (God as a divine malevolence, an archer in hiding, a deranged manic depressive, an idiot engineer, and so on). But it's also possible to read the darkness as a *boundary*, what both Dillard and Dickinson call a *circumference*, which establishes a space outside our frame of reference. To draw a boundary is to admit the possibility of difference and create a place for that difference to dwell, what Dillard calls a place for "secrets": "a beyond that holds both death and all the unattainable secrets of life." In this reading, darkness makes things possible. It marks a domain beyond human consciousness where a certain kind of "presencing" can begin—the free life of strangers, animals, divinities, secrets. This may be what Heidegger had in mind with this sentence from "Building Dwelling Thinking": "A boundary is not that at which something stops but, as the Greeks recognized, the boundary is that from which something *begins its presencing*" (original emphasis).[25] Commenting on this passage in reference to Thoreau, Joseph G. Kronick points out that if the Heideggerian boundary "is the site where presencing begins, it is also the site where presence remains almost, but never quite, present."[26]

This strikes me as the second pattern in Dickinson's nature poems, that of *the never quite present*, which is where religious reflection begins, as Dillard notes: "In some of the pattern poems, a basis of communication—of communion—is almost established."[27] These disappearances are just as vivid; our losses are still our losses. But Dickinson responds to those losses differently, Dillard argues, by allowing them to open into an experience of partial communion, ghostly and almost there, like a stranger who approaches, comes closer, and then withdraws. Thus in "A curious Cloud surprised the Sky," another Dickinson poem in "Merchant," a cloud comes slowly into focus, taking shape as a sheet with horns, then more clearly as a blue sheet with gray antler horns, and then just at the point of comprehension and contact, the moment when "It almost touched the Lawns," the cloud withdraws in regal disdain, refusing to wear our sheets and antlers, refusing to be for us anything but itself.[28]

Dickinson was fascinated by these refusals, when nature shies away from whatever antler-and-blue-sheet costume she'd selected for it to wear that day.

Self-presencing depends on this kind of dispossession for Dickinson, the loss of what we thought we knew, which gives disappearance a different, more promising, more playful, and ultimately more religious tone. Disappearance can mean dead lack, the "ultimate annihilations" of Dillard's first pattern, but disappearance can also mean the promise or possibility of what's still coming, like the darkness before dawn or the death that brings forth life. Thus, darkness can be both empty and fertile for Dillard, illegible and yet full of meaning: "Even the simple darkness of night whispers suggestions to the mind," as she says in *Pilgrim* (21).

The problem Dillard explores in "Merchant" is how Dickinson frames these paradoxes around the sacred, which may have been exactly what Dillard needed in 1967, when the radical theologians of her generation tended to explore the problem of divine alterity through binary categories of transcendence or immanence, a God who is either "above" or "below" us (with the radical theologians choosing *below*, an immanent God of the here and now).[29] Kearney argues that much contemporary thinking about God splits along the same vertical axis: a hyper-ascendant deity of apophatic unknowing, so far above us that whatever we might say about God seems like idolatry (as in the negative theologies of Levinas and Derrida). Or a monstrous deity of abyssal abjection, so far below us that whatever we might say seems like self-protective denial (as in the horror theologies of Joseph Campbell and Slavoj Žižek).[30] In Dickinson's nature poems, Dillard found a middle ground, a site where "presence remains almost, but never quite, present," as Kronick suggests, and where thought is provoked by something that's outside consciousness but not outside awareness. "God immanent and transcendent," as Dillard says in *For the Time Being*, "God discernible but unknowable, God beside us and wholly alien."[31]

How can we be aware of something that we can't know? Even vague words like "whispers" and "suggestions" frame our encounters with the divine in human terms and confirm at least some measure of conceptual control. In the never-quite-present poems, however, Dickinson encounters various strangers who "shake" her conceptual frames, setting off tremors she can feel but not read back to their source. Dickinson is especially alert to the impact of the trace on smooth-running religious and discursive systems, which causes them to vibrate a little, like the play of a ball bearing. (Derrida calls this effect *ébranler*, the wavering or trembling of play.) When the trace doesn't rest easily in its categories, it sets off vibrations Dickinson tunes her poems to record. Sometimes the frameworks are human constructs, *our* thoughts, but sometimes nature surprises itself, rattles its own frames, as when the curious cloud surprised the sky. In both cases, we sense the presence of the other by what it does, by the shivers and shock waves it sets off, which leaves thought surprised, stirred, ajar—and so alert to what it does not know, as in this poem about a rainstorm:

Like Rain it sounded till it curved
And then we knew 'twas Wind -
It walked as wet as any Wave
But swept as dry as Sand -
When it had pushed itself away
To some remotest Plain
A coming as of Hosts was heard
That was indeed the Rain -
It filled the Wells, it pleased the Pools
It warbled in the Road -
It pulled the spigot from the Hills
And let the Floods abroad -
It loosened acres, lifted seas
The sites of Centres stirred
Then like Elijah rode away
Opon a Wheel of Cloud -[32]

Dillard's commentary on this poem is brief, only a few sentences, but we're moving toward the watery milieu she'll later develop in *Pilgrim*, where the turbulent force of nature seems almost religious, or at least something we could ride toward the religious, like Elijah. This is another poem about misreading or misnaming, where the storm disturbs the poet's centering intelligence: "the sites of Centres stirred." Indeed, that's what makes *it* appear—when the storm curves away from what she thought it was: "like rain it sounded till it curved." The curve suggests a counter-rotation to the poem's natural trajectory, as if the storm exists as something angled or athwart, crossing the grain of initial perception. What follows in the poem is a playful hermeneutic of partial-glimpses and almost-guesses which fail to arrest the decentering mobility of the scene. Like a cloud that is not a cloud or a God who is not a God (or at least not *our* God), the storm exists at the disappearing point where interpretations loosen in the face of what we do not comprehend, provoking the "almost contact" of natural and divine self-presencing. The heavenly Hosts are there not to stabilize the counter-rotations and pin things down to a doctrinal interpretation, as in a more orthodox typological poem. On the contrary, the allusions to the coming of the Hosts and Elijah in his chariot create an analogy between the way we experience the rain and the way we experience the sacred: both are present as they escape us, both are present as they pass by: "So it shall be, while My glory passes by" (Exod. 33:22).

In developing this idea, Dickinson models the congealing-and-dissolving trope Dillard will later explore at the creek. The acre-loosening power of the storm is both natural and textual in Dickinson, a statement about the weather and a statement about the poem. Both are unstable. Both are changing right before our eyes, as the speaker sees something at her window and declares it for half a second and then *undeclares* it just as fast. As if to say: *It's the rain. No, it's a dry wind. No wait, it really is the rain. Or maybe it's not a storm at all but the coming of the Hosts or Elijah in the whirlwind.* As the poem tropes and turns its way through the storm, the micro-adjustments of Dickinson's language coincide with the movements of the storm itself. Which Dickinson imagines first as walking and then as singing, *warbling*, and which she tries to match note for note in the language of the poem. Thus, nature's pleasure is shared now, open to the vibrant sensibility of the attending poet. In place of comprehension, nature offers attunement and rapport: the possibility of singing or writing in responsive accord with what the poet can discern but not direct. In a different poem, this instability would be terrifying, an experience of abjection or sublimity that might come across like drowning. But nature finds the shape-shifting pleasing—"it pleased the Pools"—just as Dickinson finds it sacred, drawing the aesthetic and the religious into dialogue. As the poem builds toward its crescendo, the storm pulls a plug and lets loose a cleansing flood that sweeps the world like a huge wet broom—loosening landscapes, lifting seas—until, in the last lines, the anchor-hold in this world breaks loose and the storm sweeps upward, toward infinity, like Elijah riding the clouds.

All of this comes back in *Pilgrim*: the flooding; the vibrant attunement; the apophatic declaring and undeclaring. And most of all, the almost-contact with something that's both here and not here, both immanent and transcendent. The fish and muskrats in *Pilgrim* are also "almost impossible to see" or "almost impossible to observe," self-presencing along Heidegger's boundary. Like Dickinson, Dillard's nature descriptions are a series of near misses that call attention to the "slipperiness" of living creatures moving in and out of her visual field. And in that free movement we experience a quality of alert loss or fertile sorrow both Dillard and Dickinson call a sacrament. Hinduism locates that sacramental sorrow in the fluctuating rhythm of divine incarnations that succeed one another in time, like waves breaking on the sand. Christianity evokes that sorrow through theologies of paradoxical presence in which Christ exists at the disappearing point of the here and now, as Harvey Cox points out about Jürgen Moltmann's theology of hope: "the New Testament really knows of no Christ who is present for us in the 'here and now.' Christ is always present at the disappearing point where the future impinges on the present and is therefore never fully here or now."[33] Dickinson helped Dillard locate this paradox in nature, in her response to the transience of living creatures who move in and out of her visual field, "unraveling" even as she watches them: the starlings "seemed to unravel as they flew, lengthening in curves, like a loosened skein" (41).

There's nothing we can do to control or comprehend these almost-encounters, but we can prepare our hearts for divine self-presencing by studying nature, as Dickinson's Puritan ancestors believed. The practice of reading nature typologically, reading it as a second scripture, trains the Christian in a religious hermeneutics that slides up and down the scale of being, wasp to sinner, risen sun to risen Son, natural fact to spiritual law, "emblem" to "interpretation"—again and again, like a child learning to read. This is the theme of Edward Taylor's prayer at the end of "Upon a Wasp Child[34] with Cold":

> Lord cleare my misted sight that I
> May hence view thy Divinity.
> Some sparkes whereof thou up dost hasp
> Within this little downy Wasp
> In whose small Corporation[35] wee
> A school and a schoolmaster see
> Where we may learn, and easily finde
> A nimble Spirit.[36]

Here again the wasp is "more" than itself: a literal creature but also a symbol for the stagnant soul chilled with sin and warming now to the presence of divine light. This spiritual double-mindedness textualizes the world, which is why the transcendentalists found it so appealing. Typology reimagines nature as a picture book of divine symbols, which turns the theologian into a literary theorist, as Dillard once remarked.[37] Moreover, nature's "theory" is surprisingly playful, not only for the Puritans but also for Dickinson, as Elisa New has argued. Learning to release the wasp from its literal meaning requires what Taylor calls "a nimble Spirit" responsive to the turns and tropes of divine presence.

For Dillard, the full expression of this hermeneutics would have to wait for *Pilgrim*, but its outline is present in her Dickinson essay and comes most fully into view in her commentary on "A Light exists in Spring." Once again, the light disappears into a surrounding darkness, the first pattern of the "Merchant" poems. But this time the darkness seems more fertile than fatal as loss opens toward religious mystery: "Nature slips from man's grasp and enters a realm to which the poet assigns the vague label 'infinity.'"[38] The light that almost speaks to us in Dickinson's poem is an earthy, earth-bound thing. That kind of light *exists*, Dickinson says, "A Light exists in Spring": "It waits opon the Lawn, / It shows the furthest Tree / Opon the furthest Slope you know / It almost speaks to you."[39] But that light is also not earth-bound, not yarded by the lawns we know. Instead, it's a transcendent light, or somehow immanent and transcendent at the same moment, which makes it seem like a "sacrament" to Dillard: "This light is a kind of sacrament, bringing eternity almost within man's apprehension."[40] Moreover, Dickinson's willingness to receive or attend that sacrament seems to Dillard like an act of religious faith (although different enough that she sets the word in quotation marks): "That 'faith' is important, for certainly the encounters with beauty seem accidental; the light shifts, and the feeling is gone. Yet Emily Dickinson begins to insist on the spiritual validity of the encounter."[41] This brings us closer to the playful wisdom of *Pilgrim*. In Dickinson, Dillard found a powerful validation of her belief that life and thought are constantly changing, constantly in flux, and that faith's fluctuations bear witness to that difficult truth. Doubt renews and recreates faith for Dickinson. These are complementary rather than self-canceling spiritual states. "Faith is *Doubt*," Dickinson said to her sister-in-law, Susan Gilbert Dickinson, as if in place of constancy or orthodoxy Dickinson cherished a capacity for spiritual modulation and expressive range, as we saw in chapter 2.[42]

In her master's thesis on *Walden* the following year, Dillard returned to these themes of quickness, vibration, plasticity, and faith and discovered an expressive symbol for her own religious art. "All of nature is somehow organic, plastic, and fluid," she writes about *Walden*. "It moves, guided by its own secret impulses, and is moved, a vast Aeolean harp on which the winds of heaven play."[43] Dillard tries out several images to describe nature's sensitivity—harp, mirror, thermometer—before hitting on the idea of an oscillograph: "The pond itself is like a stylus on the most sensitive recording oscillograph."[44] When Dillard returns to this image to describe her own faith in *Pilgrim*—tuned to the divine "like a running chart, a wildly scrawling oscillograph on the present moment" (79)—she offers the basic outline of her project: to record fleeting moments of divine encounter that come and go in time and to discover forms of religious thought and writing sensitive to those shifting states. Against theological traditions that imagine faith as unyielding or rock-like, Dillard presents something altogether different: a religious subjectivity as light and nervy as an oscillograph needle. In this way, Dillard articulates a spiritual practice devoted not to preserving faith's witness in unchanging amber but to recording the wave-like fluctuations of divine spirit in the unscrupulous witness of her art: presence and absence, praise and protest, God as savior and God as showman. Moving back and forth like the swing of a needle, Dillard addresses these alternatives in turn—because each is true in turn, true "for the time being," and so worthy of a religious witness that remains faithful to the unfolding play of living experience, faithful to the flow of living waters, and so nimble enough to accommodate a woman's experience of the divine.

DANCING IN SHADOW CREEK

Many of these themes converge in the famous and controversial opening story of *Pilgrim*. Sometimes a religious hermeneutic develops in situations of thinness or aridity, the loss of meaning John Caputo studies in Derrida and Heidegger (and calls "cold hermeneutics").[45] Nothing really makes contact, and so we cast our poems and prayers into the void, like Whitman's noiseless patient spider. But sometimes interpretive systems open or become playful in the face of too much meaning, the semiotic excess Paul Ricœur and Stephen Webb stress, where "more" is in play than thought can handle, an extravagant surplus that overtops our conceptions and reveals their limitation.[46] When that happens, the contact can feel like being overwhelmed by something or pummeled by something: a hard muscular energy that thought has trouble handling because the provocation is so *unlike* thought, not abstract or conceptual at all. This is one reason why Bateson was drawn to the play-fighting of monkeys in his original work on play in the 1950s. His thinking about the distancing effects of play, the way it rises out of its categories as a flexible metalanguage, reflects thought's attempt to come to terms with what threatens to engulf it, an urgent physicality it can't process in any other way. The play-fighting in the opening scene of *Pilgrim* evokes a similar pattern: something intensely embodied rattles Dillard's frame, literally leaps through her open window, and sets off a whole series of interpretive reactions:

> I used to have a cat, an old fighting tom, who would jump through the open window by my bed in the middle of the night and land on my chest. I'd half-awaken. He'd stick his skull under my nose and purr, stinking of urine and blood. Some nights he kneaded my bare chest with his front paws, powerfully, arching his back, as if sharpening his claws, or pummeling a mother for milk. And some mornings I'd wake in daylight to find my body covered with paw prints in blood; I looked as though I'd been painted with roses.
>
> It was hot, so hot the mirror felt warm. I washed before the mirror in a daze, my twisted summer sleep still hung about me like sea kelp. What blood was this, and what roses? It could have been the rose of union, the blood of murder, or the rose of beauty bare and the blood of some unspeakable sacrifice or birth. The sign on my body could have been an emblem or a stain, the keys to the kingdom or the mark of Cain. I never knew. I never knew as I washed, and the blood streaked, faded, and finally disappeared, whether I'd purified myself or ruined the blood sign of the passover. (3–4)

The possibilities Dillard uses to process the event—murder, birth, sex, sacrifice—are clearly extravagant, wildly out of proportion to what just happened, which prompts various critics to dismiss the scene as "overwrought and overwritten," an inexperienced writer's purple prose.[47] But purple prose is play's natural voice. This is how we know we're in the domain of the *as if*. Play aims "beyond" its literal target or "past" its actual referent. Essential to transformative thought is "an element of exaggeration," Theodor Adorno argues, "of over-shooting the object, of self-detachment from the weight of the factual, so that instead of merely reproducing being it can, at once rigorous and free, determine it. Thus every thought resembles play, with which Hegel no less than Nietzsche compared the work of the mind."[48]

It's easy enough to imagine non-playful thoughts of course, actions of mind geared toward the indicative or bound by the common sense, which is what prompted Thoreau's thinking about play in the first place. But it's quite difficult for Dillard to imagine non-playful or non-rhetorical thoughts about *nature*:

> If the landscape reveals one certainty, it is that the extravagant gesture is the very stuff of creation. After the one extravagant gesture of creation in the first place, the universe has continued to deal exclusively in extravagances, flinging intricacies and colossi down aeons of emptiness, heaping profusions on profligacies with ever-fresh vigor. The whole show has been on fire from the word go. (11)

To open writing to that profligate vigor is to risk appearing foolish, weak, immature—a writer not fully in command. But Dillard accepts that risk in order to tune her prose to the extravagance of the natural world and so fully inhabit Tinker Creek. The figurative excess of Dillard's writing coincides with the mobility she senses in nature—which shifts, springs, pivots, and pummels with the wild muscularity of the tomcat. Dillard's metaphoric extravagance corresponds to that wildness, as Nathalie Cochoy has argued, revels in it, mirroring its burgeoning vitality and creative excess in the figurative lushness of her prose.[49] When Dillard changes her mind about what happened that morning, declaring and then undeclaring her meanings Dickinson style (it's the rose of beauty, it's the blood of murder, and so on), her turns and tropes match the extravagance of the material world, as if this is how nature "thinks," in heaves and pivots (rather terminations and still points). Moreover, by weaving scriptural references into the scene (to Cain, the Passover, the scapegoat, Jesus' keys to the kingdom, and so forth), Dillard raises the possibility that this is how God "thinks" too: rhetorically, playfully, in rapid shifts of meaning and frame that curve away from the last thing we thought *it* was, exactly like Dickinson's rainstorm. "The spirit seems to roll along," Dillard writes, in a sentence Jack Kerouac would enjoy. "It rolls along the mountain ridges like a fireball, shooting off a spray of sparks at random, and will not be trapped, slowed, grasped, fetched, peeled, or aimed" (77).

A religious sensibility geared to that rolling will sacrifice indicative realities for the possibilizing extravagance of the *as if*. It will aim "beyond" its literal target, as Adorno argued about ludic thought (and Dillard said was the best way to chop wood). Thus, Dillard's opening scene is intensely and self-consciously rhetorical, like Thoreau's sandbank, another bloody field of interacting and contradictory tropes. But Dillard's body is rhetorical too—cat-marked, written-on—as if to deny any stable or sufficient ground. Trying to establish that strong ground (in nature, scripture, science, reason, the body) contradicts the heaving of the world and the rolling of the spirit, thus freezing what God and nature set in motion. Dillard resists that trap by making her metaphors as purple as possible—just as she'll later make her framing perspectives as strange as possible, reading the world through a butterfly wing at one point, lest we mistake her angle of vision for a necessary or compulsory point of view. There's more to life than we can see through a butterfly wing of course. And if that's not obvious, Dillard tells us, in almost the exact words Thoreau used in *Walden*: "The world is wilder than that in all directions, more dangerous and bitter, more extravagant and bright" (274).

Subjunctive theologies are "weak" in this way, as I argued in chapter 2, aware of their inadequacy, which also means they're endlessly correctable, perfect for the spiritual and material encounters of *Pilgrim*. Dillard deploys the ancient trope of religious awakening in her opening scene—"I'd half-awaken"—but adapts that figure to her needs as a religious pilgrim whose every thought, claim, vision, metaphor, truth, revelation, and standpoint is subject to continual revision and restatement, what the play theologian Hugo Rahner called a life of "indefatigable tinkering."

This is what it means to live at Tinker Creek. Cat, body, scripture, literature: all of it purrs and trembles, like the shaking of a rainstorm or the vibrations of an oscillograph. Even the chapter title's a little wobbly, "Heaven and Earth in Jest." Which seems to be exactly what's happening here, until the narrator tells us a few pages later that this is in fact a rhetorical question in the Koran—"The heaven and the earth and all in between, thinkest thou I made them *in jest*?"—where the answer should be obvious: God is *not* jesting. This is followed by Einstein offering his supporting opinion that God is not cruel or cunning (and later, that God does not take chances or roll dice). And then the carnival magician arrives, with his tricks and beguilement. Thus, we encounter a book that's jesting and then not jesting and then maybe jesting again. As if "play" itself is unstable, not a privileged or consistent perspective but just as slippery as everything else. Margaret Loewen Reimer stresses exactly this oscillating movement in Dillard's thinking about the divine: the world is "meticulously created" and yet also a "mindless stutter" (136, 163). "Divinity is not playful" and yet "the creator loves pizzazz" (275, 139). God works in "solemn incomprehensible earnest" and yet "the whole creation is one lunatic fringe" (275, 146). Like Merton's "exercise of pendulums," Dillard's dialectical vision swings back and forth between opposed terms. "Given the gift of acute sight," Reimer says, "she has dared to look at both sides and to accept them both at the same time."[50]

I'm sure I'm missing some of the vibrations in Dillard's scene, but the point should be clear: play thrives on instability, paradox, and interpretive risk. It may be difficult to say precisely what "play" is, as Gregory Bateson and Victor Turner stress, but it's not difficult to see what it does: play dissolves and reforms things. It creates carnivalesque reversals in indicative situations. It proliferates meanings, traces, tremors, storms. In play, what was closed now opens, disseminates. What was tame grows wild, anticipating what Dillard will later call the "wild scrawl" of her oscillograph. And in the conditions of horror Dillard presents to the religious imagination, where "the wonder is that all the forms are not monsters, that there is beauty at all" (148), play is also a domain of hope, the promise of an open future, *une promesse de bonheur*.

Dillard cultivates that possibilizing ground by continually shifting her point of view in *Pilgrim*, changing the lenses she uses to make sense of experience and welcoming the inadequacy of any single perspective. Looking at the creek through a dozen different frames—a window, a microscope, a telescope, a camera lens, a butterfly wing, a sheet of ice, the view formed by the brim of her hat, the view formed by her thumb and forefinger—Dillard runs perception through a yoga-like exercise of nimble reframing. It's impossible to dispense with frames altogether, of course, and experience the world naturally or nakedly (impossible for us but not impossible for a cerebral-cortex lacking amoeba, as Dillard points out). So the next best thing is to multiply frames of reference rapidly, almost kaleidoscopically, and thus stretch perception across several different positions: sheet-of-ice-pose; butterfly-wing pose; hat-brim pose. Again and again in graceful, dance-like succession. In this way, Dillard rehearses in the text, as an act of reading and thinking, the "quickness" she experienced first-hand at the creek. In this sense, reading a *Pilgrim at Tinker Creek* and being the Pilgrim at Tinker Creek come down to the same thing: releasing nature from prestructured viewpoints and "letting" the other appear in its own way and for its own sake:

> But there is another kind of seeing that involves a letting go. When I see this way I sway transfixed and emptied. The difference between the two ways of seeing is the difference between walking with and without a camera. When I walk with a camera I walk from shot to shot, reading the light on a calibrated meter. When I walk without a camera, my own shutter opens, and the moment's light prints on my own silver gut. When I see this second way I am above all an unscrupulous observer. (33)

Letting go of the light is more difficult than it sounds—precisely because our perceptions are already stylized, as Bateson and Merleau-Ponty have argued, pre-equipped with default practices and sensorimotor schemata that reconstitute the objects of sensation to fit what we already know, the light we've seen before and recognize (as *light* rather than something else). Thus, we reassemble this "moment's light" within a remembered anthology of prior scenes, which confirms and stabilizes our sensory world, making it knowable. (Merleau-Ponty calls this the constancy hypothesis.) Dillard explores dozens of strategies to delay or disrupt this constancy effect and free nature from her preformed judgments, a process she calls "unpeach[ing] the peaches" (32). In "Seeing," for instance, Dillard tells a story of how newly sighted people see everyday objects as shifting patches of color and light, so that a human hand, unrecognized, becomes "something bright and then holes." And a cluster of grapes, ungraped, becomes "dark, blue, and shiny. . . . It isn't smooth, it has bumps and hollows" (31). "Dillard is not yearning for a world devoid of meaning," Colleen Warren argues about this passage; instead she cherishes "the ability to see unhindered by preconceptions, by categories of knowing that constrain a broader vision. The color patches represent a preculture sight, even a precreation sight freed from established meaning."[51] To be able to see this way is nothing short of a miracle, which Dillard prays for in an allusion to Christ's healing of a blind man in Mark 8:24 and Saul's restored sight in Acts 9:18: "The scales would drop from my eyes," she says; "I'd see trees like men walking; I'd run down the road against all orders, hallooing and leaping" (32).

Although Dillard can't ultimately unpeach the peaches and free herself from stylized preconceptions, she continues to explore creek-side versions of *upekṣa* and *Gelassenheit*, the ancient exercises of "unseeing" or "unknowing" she studied in Meister Eckhart, Thomas Merton, and the *Bhāgavata Purāna*. Thus, she shuffles the perceptual lenses she uses to frame her subjects by retelling the same story from different perspectives or at different times of the day. Like Thoreau, she often walks around an object to recover its dimensionality and visual depth: "We walk around; we see a shred of the infinite possible combinations of an infinite variety of forms. Anything can happen; any pattern of speckles may appear in a world ceaselessly bawling with newness" (147). To sustain that perceptual variety, she changes her focal points, from cosmic to microscopic and back to cosmic again. She reverses field and ground, causing the implicit to leap forward and the explicit to fall back, like the gestalt puzzles she played with as a child (19). She practices "child seeing," where a row of Lombardy poplars becomes a fluttering patch of "silver and green and shape-shifting blue" (32). She often looks at things in the "wrong" way, inside out or upside down, like Krishna holding the universe in his mouth or Thoreau fishing in the stars. "The dark is overhead and the light at my feet," she writes in a typical upending; "I'm walking upside-down in the sky" (45).

And then sometimes Dillard stops "looking" altogether and relies on kinesthetic forms of perception based on touch, movement, pressure, and rhythm—so that whatever she's touching touches back. Bodies becomes "reversible" in this way, as Merleau-Ponty has argued, co-dependent and co-constituted within an intersubjective field that runs deep in *Pilgrim*. Dillard feels the "flings and pulls" of groundwater under her feet (98). She lifts a finger to the wind and touches the "now" (99). She tastes the weather with her tongue and lets the butterflies taste her (42, 259). Dillard attributes "bodies" to things that seem immaterial—shadows, spirit, wind, time—in order to create a space where structural oppositions can be held together without reduction or resolution. If time walks like a Slinky, it might be possible to match its loopy gait (77). If shadows pool and thicken, it might be possible to dance with them, as Dillard does in the last scene of *Pilgrim*. Dillard's emphasis on the body of both world and spirit allowed her to think about forms of movement and interaction that arise in difference. The various forms of play in *Pilgrim*—dancing, stalking, playing catch, playing Red Rover—all depend on oscillating movements that are impossible without the other and that endure only as long as the other endures, as Hans-Georg Gadamer has argued about play, creating a ludic "structurality" in which opposing forces interact without being absorbed into either side, which ends the dance or stops the game.[52]

In this sense "letting go" doesn't mean withdrawal or reticence, as it often does for Thoreau, but participation and consent, giving in to a world of astonishing mobility and "riding" its physical and spiritual energies, like Elijah riding the clouds. Our bodies "know" things we can't always say, which suggests a change in religious thinking from doctrinal propositions and rational proof to bodily ways of knowing that abide in our muscles and skin, as many theologians have explored.[53] Dillard invites this change by stressing the tactile movement of nearly everything she considers. Thought, dream, prayer, and spirit are all like animals in motion in *Pilgrim*. Which is also how Dillard describes her faith: "I ride a bucking faith while one hand grips and the other flails the air, and like any daredevil I gouge with my heels for blood, for a wilder ride, for more" (275).

In this spirit, a single winged seed whistles with animate purpose and rides the wind "like a creature muscled and vigorous" (273). Even light has a physical body: "There is a muscular energy in sunlight," Dillard says, and a corresponding muscularity in our perception of light (119). Sometimes vision is passive in *Pilgrim*, and the eye is like a photographic plate receiving an imprint. But sometimes vision is active and embodied, reaching into the world with a corresponding physicality, as if vision could touch the objects it perceives. The analogy between eye and camera encourages an illusion of visual autonomy and objectivity that isolates the viewer from the world. The analogy between sight and touch dissolves that isolation by connecting us to the world with a visual "hand," as if we could feel the jerk or buck of living contact through our eyes as well as our fingers.[54] And if perception pulls on the world like a reaching hand, the world pulls *back*, resisting our attempts to hold and control it. When Dillard describes her faith this way—"I ride a bucking faith"—she ascribes the same muscular energy to the life of the spirit that she discovers in herself and in wild nature. It's the *same* spirit, as the transcendentalists believed, the same springy torque running through loons, squirrels, ponds, books, bodies, mountains, and God. When Dillard quotes from Ps. 68:16—"Why leap ye, ye high hills?"—as she does in "Spring," she discovers the same energetic transformations in scripture that she witnessed first-hand at the creek: salmon leaping up fish ladders, water leaping over stones, a cat leaping into her bed, a mole leaping out of her open hand. Everything feels it—the moles, the hills, King David—"a tremendous heave" of spirit that stirs the centers and sets things dancing: "King David leaped and danced naked before the ark of the Lord" (96, 97).

Hugo Rahner argues that David's dancing before the arc of the covenant resonates with the logos-child "playing" before God in Prov. 8. If David's dancing manifests holy covenant, Rahner suggests, making it more fully embodied in the world, then his dancing co-accomplishes God's promise in the same way the playing child in Prov. 8 cocreates God's wisdom. For Rahner this means that the world is not a hard-block system of remorseless law and that we are not pawns or victims in that system. Instead, we become co-fashioners with God in the unfolding possibilities of divine love, embodying that love in human form.[55] The Hebrew scriptures picture this artistic co-fashioning with many of the same images Dillard uses in *Pilgrim*: leaping, dancing, wrestling, singing together, playing together. Indeed the Hebrew word for David's dancing in 2 Sam. 6:16, *pazaz*, gives Dillard the word she uses to describe the playful wisdom of God: "the creator loves pizzazz" (139).

It's common to stress the solitude and even solipsism of Dillard's writing and to see *Pilgrim* as a table set for one. "Annie Dillard is the only person in her book," Eudora Welty wrote in an early review of *Pilgrim*, "substantially the only one in her world. . . . Speaking of the universe very often, she is yet self-surrounded."[56] On the contrary, what's striking about religious play in *Pilgrim* is how it creates rhythmic conditions of intersubjective rapport. That rapport extends to the stars, in a passage Dillard quotes from Arthur Rimbaud immediately before the scene of David's dancing: "I have stretched cords from steeple to steeple, garlands from window to window, chains of gold from star to star, and I dance" (97). Moreover, these connections are buried underfoot in the microscopic dance of roots and cicada nymphs, which

Dillard describes immediately after the David passage: "The insects and earthworms, moles, muskrats, roots and fungal strands are not all. An even frailer, dimmer movement, a pavane, is being performed deep under me now. The nymphs of cicadas are alive" (97). Dillard invites us to make connections between sacred history and natural history in scenes like these and to see that spirit exists as expenditure and passage: not trapped by local habitations but leaping from star to steeple to window to nymph. And all of it hardwired to *move*, right down to the root tips, the blind threads reaching in the dark.

The lushness of Dillard's dance conceit helps carry this idea. The prose is itself a conductor, a transit point. It leaves nothing inert. Moles, hills, steeples, subsoil, a Hebrew king, a French surrealist: we have to catch and release to keep up, letting the passage create meaning through unlikeness, as metaphor does, through the movement from known to unknown. Dickinson's Puritan ancestors cherished the rhetorical turns and tropes of scripture for exactly this reason, as we've seen. The figurative extravagance of scripture trains the reading mind to be nimble, playful, and alert to the passage of spirit through unlikely things: chilled wasps, burning bushes. The known is shocked into motion by divine inspiration, transformed into something else. Dillard develops this idea by exploring a kinesthetic theology of movement and touch. In *Pilgrim*, the dance-play doesn't exist as a special category, the "sacred" or the "aesthetic." It's everywhere: present underfoot, present in the stars, but also present in the lush figurality of Dillard's prose, as if writing too is mobile and cat-quick, more tendon and tissue than dead flat text.

This strikes me as the opposite of being self-surrounded, as Eudora Welty argued. Dialogue and intersubjectivity are not moral choices in *Pilgrim* but inescapable facts, as they are in *Walden*, something inherent to lived experience. To be fully awake is to know this, to find ourselves in a busy, noisy, crowded, pre-existing habitat and so accept what Thoreau called "the infinite extent of our relations" (and the responsibility that acceptance entails). When Dillard develops this idea in *For the Time Being,* she stresses how the presence of the sacred brings the human and nonhuman into complex rapport, causing them to tremble in vibrant attunement:

> Sometimes the Baal Shem Tov trembled at prayers. Once, a disciple touched his robe at the shoulder and trembled himself. Once, the Baal Shem Tov leaned against the east wall of a house, and by the west wall the grain in open barrels trembled. A water trough in a room where he was praying trembled. When he stood to pray, the fringes of his prayer robe trembled.[57]

It's hard to mark the limits of the sacred here, which opens to include not only other people but also houses, grain, water, barrels, and the fringes of a robe. When Dillard dances in the "fringes" of Shadow Creek at the end of

Pilgrim, it too becomes a prayer robe. Her dancing joins company with the old saints and surrealists to sustain the ongoing play of creation, co-fashioning the sacred through the dance-like medium of her art.

There's nothing compulsory about any of this, as the gospel of Matthew acknowledges in the divine invitation—"We sang to you, and you did not dance"—and as the Hebrew scriptures attest when Michal turns away from her husband with contempt: she "saw King David dancing and playing; and she despised him in her heart." Dillard stresses the same freedom of refusal. We're not forced to dance and tremble. We can retreat instead into any number of safe spaces Dillard stakes out at the creek: abstract thought, picturesque nature writing, method-driven science, and Gnostic spirituality, among others—all of which break the animal tension of live contact, the felt heave of creatures in motion. For Dillard, the surprise of divine play is that God *needs* our heaving—summons it, yearns for it—as if the dance of creation is incomplete without us and both God and the world are diminished by our refusal. This is Dillard's version of postmodern theology's wounded, kenotic, or self-limiting God: not a "Newtonian God" sitting on the throne of judgment; nor a "Deuteronomic" God intervening in human history; nor an omnipotent God "blinding people with glaucoma," as Dillard says in *For the Time Being*.[58] Rather, Dillard emphasizes "God the Semipotent"—a God who needs us, who calls to us, and whose advent depends on our participation, on the tiny "heaves" we feel in the presence of the sacred, "that heave in my wrist when I saw the tree with the lights in it" (94).

Dillard was fascinated by various versions of this "weakened" God. She saw it in Teilhard de Chardin's belief that we're called to aid God in the work of redemption, which charged human life with meaning and value.[59] She was interested in Hasidic theologies of divine exile, in which God is scattered or estranged like holy sparks trapped in matter and who needs us to release and reunite the holy.[60] She was drawn to the Baal Shem Tov's idea that we are syllables from God's mouth, God's voice revealed through us. Moreover, she incorporated into *Pilgrim* a version of the Baal Shem Tov's teaching that our heaves of spirit restore divinity to itself, co-creating or co-accomplishing God's presence in the world: "By a tremendous heave of his spirit, the devout man frees the divine sparks trapped in the mute things of time; he uplifts the forms and moments of creation, bearing them aloft into that rare air and hallowing fire in which all clays must shatter and burst" (96)

When Dillard says "all clays must shatter," she means, among other things, *us*—our physical bodies at some point but also our perceptual frames and sensory schemata, the set or cast of our ideas. Richard Kearney's example of the dance-play of creation, the *perichoresis*, is shapely and limited, the three members of the Trinity moving together in a holy circle of loving consent.[61] The dance-play of *Pilgrim* is more dangerous than that, not the *perichoresis* but a tarantella: "Someone has piped, and we are dancing a tarantella until the sweat pours. I open my eyes and I see dark, muscled forms curl out of water" (23–24).

Taking her cue from the creek, Dillard sought to fashion a literary and religious aesthetic attuned to that wild mobility. If it's right to call this aesthetic *playful*, it seems closer to Siva's dark play than the child play of Prov. 8, which is play detached from risk, exactly the connection Dillard stresses. Nature's aesthetic is a self-consuming art of decreation and rebirth. Nature tears its paintings and "eats" its texts. When Dillard tells the story of the praying mantises emerging from an egg case in a Mason jar, for instance, the insect bodies form a kind of sacred language, like Edward Taylor's chilled wasp: "I watched the newly hatched mantises emerge and shed their skins; they were spidery and translucent, all over joints. They trailed from the egg case to the base of the Mason jar in a living bridge that looked like Arabic calligraphy, some baffling text from the Koran inscribed down the air by a fine hand" (56–57). The static or "eternal" quality of a printed book serves Dillard less well than the air-writing of the praying-mantis scripture or the skywriting of Dave Rahm's plane. She's drawn toward spiritual messages that self-destruct or self-erase even as she's reading them, which invests the sacred with the symbolic evanescence she admired in Dickinson. But the baffling part of the praying-mantis scripture is not that it disappears but that it's self-consumed, as the insects eat each other over the course of several hours until all that's left are tiny legs kicking from the mouths of the survivors: "The two survivors grappled and sawed in the Mason jar; finally both died of injuries. I felt as though I myself should swallow the corpses, shutting my eyes and washing them down like jagged pills" (57). Dillard's scene may be a retelling of the ant battle Thoreau describes in *Walden*, but Thoreau holds himself apart from that scene, watching the violence through the lens of a glass. There's no protective lens here. When Dillard feels as if she should swallow the corpses, it's not that she experiences a predator thrill of old evolution but that she seeks to take to heart the dark play of the creek, which has nothing to do with purity or stasis and everything to do with spiritual and ecological transformation: leaves into subsoil; ants into snail castings; praying mantises into one another (and into her); Arabic calligraphy into Catholic communion—and from there to something else.

Modeling her writing on this porousness and insecurity, Dillard combs vivid shapes out of the flux before releasing that shape to the ongoing flow of the next thing coming, and the next after that. This is how the sandbank "thinks" in *Walden* and how the creek "thinks" in *Pilgrim*: its free flow congealed for a moment into "frog" or "sycamore," but just for the moment, as the heave or push of the living water flows on in wave-like fluctuations of decay and rebirth. Sometimes those fluctuations are almost impossible to bear, when what's dissolving is utterly necessary and precious: the life of a loved one dissolving in death or the face of a seven-year-old girl burned in a plane accident. But we do bear those losses, everything does, as the congealing-and-dissolving action of the creek draws us back to the rolling heart of creation itself: "The death of the self of which the great writers speak is no violent act. It is merely the joining of the great rock heart of the earth in its roll" (262–23).

Dillard chooses to end her journey by joining the earth in its dance-like roll, just as "Faith" does in "This World is not conclusion" and Sal does in *On the Road*. Nothing is really solved at the end of *Pilgrim*: "I am not washed and beautiful, in control of a shining world in which everything fits" (245). If anything, she understands *less* at the end than she did at the beginning, senses the gaps in her understanding even more vividly, because the point is not to perfect human habits of comprehension and control but to sacrifice those habits on the altar of the real: "I am a sacrifice bound with cords to the horns of the world's rock altar" (246). In an older or more orthodox religious tradition, such self-sacrifice would be called "obedience" or "relinquishment." But those words are so gummed over with secondary messages about female submission and religious conformity that they are less useful to Dillard to describe her spirituality. So she describes her faith as a letting-go seeing or unscrupulous witness, in order to pull faith's surrender away from those gendered contexts. And further, to pull faith's surrender away from religion altogether, as so many of the visionary heroes of Dillard's book are entomologists, astronomers, botanists, and bench scientists who practice this surrender with great devotion: letting go of explanatory constructs when they no longer fit a changing real, sacrificing those constructs as they collide with a world that shreds scientific theories as easily as it splits a snakeskin. This surrender marks the vitality of scientific discovery as it confronts a world it cannot fully comprehend, just as it marks the vitality of faith's journey into the wilderness of God. We may desire this wildness because we sense, as Thoreau did, that in wildness is the preservation of the world. Or we may desire that wildness because we sense, as Dickinson did, a corresponding wildness in ourselves, made in the image of God.

This is how *Pilgrim* answers the quiet desperation of its historical moment. In the massively commodified and engineered landscapes of modern America, Dillard encounters a God who hides in leafy nature, half in shadow, half in sunlight, "never quite disclosed / And never quite concealed."[62] For Dillard, God is never really *here*, fully revealed in the present moment; and yet never *not here* either, fully withdrawn into what would then become a final or actual darkness. And what might "faith" in that kind of God look like? as a religious writer would need to know. Not like a man girded for battle with the breastplate of righteousness and the sword of the spirit. But more like a woman dancing in the shadows of a creek, as Dillard shows in her last scene, and her feet aren't shod with the armor of anything. She's written "Amen" and "Glory" on her shoes, and so she's shod with prayer, she's shod with expectancy, moving in and out of the shadows and light exactly as God does, exactly as everything does, "exultant, in a daze, dancing, to the twin silver trumpets of praise."

NOTES

1. Gregory Bateson, *Steps to an Ecology of Mind* (1972; repr. Chicago: University of Chicago Press, 2000), 413.
2. Bateson, *Steps to an Ecology of Mind*, 272.
3. Freud argued that children come to terms with their fears of being abandoned by their mothers by re-invoking those feelings in games of loss and recovery, making the "mother" disappear and reappear on command and thus strengthening the imperiled illusion of ego control. In Freudian play, children engage contingency under safe conditions—hiding a doll under a blanket and then finding it again or throwing a wooden reel into a crib curtain and then retrieving it—until loss feels safe and familiar. This is what makes play pleasurable for Freud: it brings disorder under the mind's control and compensates for renunciations of instinct (not having or being the mother), with the symbolic substitutions of the game. In "Toys and Reasons," Erikson extends this Freudian theme into a developmental model of human agency. For Erikson, the purpose of play is for children to hallucinate mastery over their own developing bodies. Erikson's prime example is Mark Twain's character, Ben Rogers, who gains power and efficiency the moment he turns himself into an imaginary steamboat, the *Big Missouri*. Where Freudian play rehearses the hallucination of mastery in a child's microsphere, a manageable world of toys and objects, Eriksonian play extends that mastery into the child's physical life. Erikson's discussion of agonistic mastery begins not with disorienting feelings of loss in the child's relationship with its mother, as in Freud, but with the unruliness of the child's physical self, which play brings under control. Erikson saw this childhood accomplishment not as a temporary victory but as the basis for subsequent attempts to master reality through rational planning and experimental control. On this, see Sigmund Freud, *Beyond the Pleasure Principle*, trans. and ed. James Strachey (New York: Norton, 1961), 8–11; and Erik H. Erikson, *Childhood and Society,* 2nd ed. (New York: Norton, 1963), 209–22.
4. Bateson, *Steps to an Ecology of Mind*, 183.
5. Stephen Nachmanovitch, "This is Play," *New Literary History* 40, no. 1 (Winter 2009): 2.
6. Hugo Rahner, *Man at Play*, trans. Brian Battershaw and Edward Quinn (New York: Herder and Herder, 1967), 40.
7. Michael Fishbane, *Sacred Attunement: A Jewish Theology* (Chicago: University of Chicago Press, 2008), 35.
8. John D. Caputo, *The Insistence of God: A Theology of Perhaps* (Bloomington: Indiana University Press, 2013), 81.

9. Jürgen Moltmann, *Theology of Play*, trans. Reinhard Ulrich (New York: Harper and Row, 1972), 24.

10. Bateson, *Steps to an Ecology of Mind*, 233.

11. On this, see Richard Kearney, *The God Who May Be: A Hermeneutics of Religion* (Bloomington: Indiana University Press, 2001), 106–11.

12. Annie Dillard, *Pilgrim at Tinker Creek* (1974; repr. New York: HarperPerennial, 2007), 4, 14, 275, 3. Subsequent references to *Pilgrim at Tinker Creek* will refer to this edition and be cited in the text by page number.

13. On this, see Julia A. Ireland, "Annie Dillard's Ecstatic Phenomenology," *Interdisciplinary Studies in Literature and Environment* 17, no. 1 (Winter 2010): 23–34.

14. Richard Kearney, *Strangers, Gods and Monsters: Interpreting Otherness* (London: Routledge, 2003), 83–108.

15. Richard Schechner, "Playing," *Play and Culture* 1 (1988): 5.

16. Annie Dillard, *For the Time Being* (New York: Vintage Books, 2000), 96.

17. Schechner, "Playing," 15.

18. Lucinda H. MacKethan, *Daughters of Time: Creating Woman's Voice in Southern Story* (Athens: University of Georgia Press, 1990), 5. Nancy C. Parrish calls attention to the importance of MacKethan's study of female creativity for understanding the work of several writers associated with Hollins College in the 1960s. See her *Lee Smith, Annie Dillard, and the Hollins Group: A Genesis of Writers* (Baton Rouge: Louisiana State University Press, 1998), 82.

19. The scholarly commentary on *Pilgrim* reflects this imbalance. Critical studies stressing the influence of Thoreau on *Pilgrim* include Mary Davidson McConahay, "'Into the Bladelike Arms of God': The Quest for Meaning through Symbolic Language in Thoreau and Annie Dillard," *Denver Quarterly* 20, no. 2 (Fall 1985): 103–16; Gary McIlroy, "*Pilgrim at Tinker Creek* and the Social Legacy of *Walden*," *South Atlantic Quarterly* 85, no. 2 (Spring 1986): 111–22; Marc Chénetier, "Tinkering, Extravagance: Thoreau, Melville, and Annie Dillard," *Critique: Studies in Contemporary Fiction* 31, no. 3 (Spring 1990): 157–72; Donna Mendelson, "Tinker Creek and the Waters of *Walden*: Thoreauvian Currents in Annie Dillard's *Pilgrim*," *The Concord Saunterer* 3 (Fall 1995): 50–62; James A. Papa, Jr., "Paradox and Perception: Science and Narrative in *Walden* and *Pilgrim at Tinker Creek*," *Weber Studies: An Interdisciplinary Humanities Journal* 14, no. 3 (Fall 1997): 105–14; Alan D. Hodder, "The Gospel According to this Moment: Thoreau, Wildness, and American Nature Religion," *Religion and the Arts* 15, no. 4 (2011): 460–85; and many others. To my knowledge, only one scholar, Nancy C. Parrish, takes up the question of Dillard's relationship with Dickinson and considers the importance of Dillard's formative essay, "The Merchant of the Picturesque." See her *Lee Smith, Annie Dillard, and the Hollins Group*, 147–49.

20. Annie Dillard, "The Merchant of the Picturesque: One Pattern in Emily Dickinson's Poetry," *The Hollins Symposium: An Undergraduate Learned Journal* 3, no. 1 (May 1967): 41.

21. Dillard develops this view of play in *Holy the Firm* with phrasing that echoes Gloucester's despair in *King Lear*. "The gods in their boyish, brutal games bore you

like a torch"—she writes, addressing Julie Norwich, a seven-year-old girl whose face was terribly burned in an airplane accident. See her *Holy the Firm* (New York: Harper and Row, 1977), 74.

22. Dillard, "Merchant," 33.
23. Dillard, "Merchant," 42.
24. Dillard, "Merchant," 33.
25. Martin Heidegger, *Poetry, Language, Thought*, trans. Albert Hofstadter (1971; repr. New York: HarperPerennial, 2013), 152.
26. Joseph G. Kronick, *American Poetics of History: From Emerson to the Moderns* (Baton Rouge: Louisiana State University Press, 1984), 31.
27. Dillard, "Merchant," 38.
28. Emily Dickinson, *The Poems of Emily Dickinson*, ed. R. W. Franklin (Cambridge: Harvard University Press, 1999), #509.
29. On this, see Thomas J. J. Altizer and William Hamilton, *Radical Theology and the Death of God* (Indianapolis: Bobbs-Merrill, 1966), 9–21.
30. Kearney, *The God Who May Be*, 7.
31. Dillard, *For the Time Being*, 164.
32. Dickinson, *The Poems of Emily Dickinson*, #1245.
33. Harvey Cox, *The Feast of Fools: A Theological Essay on Festivity and Fantasy* (Cambridge: Harvard University Press, 1969), 129.
34. Taylor spells chilled as "child" here.
35. That is, the wasp's body.
36. Edward Taylor, "Upon a Wasp Child with Cold," in *The Harper American Literature*, 2nd ed. (New York: Harper and Row, 1987), 239.
37. Karla M. Hammond, "Drawing the Curtains: An Interview with Annie Dillard," *Bennington Review* 10 (April 1981): 34. Several scholars address the question of typology in *Pilgrim*, but I find Stephen H. Webb's discussion of spiritual extravagance especially helpful. According to Webb, Dillard "does share with the Transcendentalists the idea that the natural is always symbolic of the spiritual, but nature is not simply God's book. . . . If Dillard 'reads' nature at all, it is as a meditation on that which challenges and resists our interpretations, not because of a deficiency of human intellectual power but because of the enormity and complexity of the object at hand." See his "Nature's Spendthrift Economy: The Extravagance of God in *Pilgrim at Tinker Creek*," *Soundings* 77, nos. 3–4 (Fall/Winter 1994): 433.
38. Dillard, "Merchant," 39.
39. Dickinson, *The Poems of Emily Dickinson*, #962.
40. Dillard, "Merchant," 39.
41. Dillard, "Merchant," 41.
42. Emily Dickinson, *The Letters of Emily Dickinson*, ed. Thomas H. Johnson, vol. 3 (Cambridge: Harvard University Press, 1958), 830.
43. Annie Dillard, "Walden Pond and Thoreau" (master's thesis, Hollins College, 1968), 19.
44. Dillard, "Walden Pond and Thoreau," 18.
45. John D. Caputo, *Radical Hermeneutics: Repetition, Deconstruction, and the Hermeneutic Project* (Bloomington: Indiana University Press, 1987), 187–206.

46. Commenting on the "much more" of Rom. 5:16–17 and the "all the more" of Rom. 5:20–21, Ricœur points out that the superabundance of divine gifting is opposed to the proportional logic of economic equivalence ("the wages of sin is death"). Ricœur describes this extravagance as a "passion for the possible," which answers with hope "all Nietzschean love of destiny" and "worship of fate." See his *Figuring the Sacred: Religion, Narrative, and Imagination*, trans. David Pellauer; ed. Mark I. Wallace (Minneapolis: Fortress Press, 1995), 206. See also, Stephen H. Webb, *Blessed Excess: Religion and the Hyperbolic Imagination* (Albany: SUNY Press, 1993).

47. Robert Detweiler, *Breaking the Fall: Religious Readings of Contemporary Fiction* (New York: Harper and Row, 1989), 128. Although Detweiler locates the religious imagination in "communities of play" devoted to innovation and risk, he drops that argument in his reading of *Pilgrim*, somewhat surprisingly, and emphasizes instead how Dillard appropriates the shamanistic imagery of body inscription. The bloody paw prints in the opening of *Pilgrim* remind Detweiler of the erotic skin-mutilations in Franz Kafka and Pauline Réage (the pseudonymous author of *Story of O*).

48. Theodor Adorno, *Minima Moralia: Reflections from Damaged Life*, trans. E. F. N. Jephcott (1974; repr. London: Verso, 2005), 126–27.

49. Nathalie Cochoy, "The Imprint of the 'Now' on the Skin of Discourse: Annie Dillard's *Pilgrim at Tinker Creek*," *Revue Française d'Études Américaines* 106 (December 2005): 33–49.

50. Margaret Loewen Reimer, "The Dialectical Vision of Annie Dillard's *Pilgrim at Tinker Creek*," *Critique: Studies in Contemporary Fiction* 24, no. 3 (Spring 1983): 190.

51. Colleen Warren, *Annie Dillard and the Word Made Flesh: An Incarnational Theory of Language* (Bethlehem, PA: Lehigh University Press, 2010), 72.

52. Hans-Georg Gadamer, *Truth and Method*, trans. ed. Garrett Barden and John Cumming (New York: Seabury Press, 1975). I'll return to this theme in some detail in chapter 6.

53. On this, see David Brown, *God and Grace of Body: Sacrament in Ordinary* (New York: Oxford University Press, 2007); Karmen MacKendrick, *Word Made Skin: Figuring Language at the Surface of Flesh* (New York: Fordham University Press, 2004); and Marcia W. Mount Shoop, *Let the Bones Dance: Embodiment and the Body of Christ* (Louisville: Westminster John Knox Press, 2010).

54. Teresa Brennan makes this point in her essay, "'The Contexts of Vision' from a Specific Standpoint," in *Vision in Context: Historical and Contemporary Perspectives on Sight* ed. Teresa Brennan and Martin Jay (New York: Routledge, 1996). Malcolm Clemens Young explores the interplay of active and passive modes of vision in Thoreau's *Journal* and considers Thoreau's notion that the eye "touches" the world. See his *The Spiritual Journal of Henry David Thoreau* (Macon: Mercer University Press, 2009), 155–85.

55. Rahner, *Man at Play*, 20.

56. Eudora Welty, "Meditation on Seeing," *New York Times On the Web*, March 24, 1974. https://archive.nytimes.com/www.nytimes.com/books/99/03/28/specials/dillard-tinker.html.

57. Dillard, *For the Time Being*, 115.
58. Dillard, *For the Time Being*, 165, 167.
59. Dillard, *For the Time Being*, 127.
60. Dillard, *For the Time Being*, 51, 138, 141, 173.
61. Kearney, *The God Who May Be*, 109–10.
62. Dickinson, *The Poems of Emily Dickinson*, #1140.

Chapter 6

Play and Understanding
Marilynne Robinson's Religious Hermeneutics

PLAY IS AT THE HEART OF EVERYTHING

Religious play isn't the first thing that comes to mind when thinking about Marilynne Robinson. If the essays collected in *The Death of Adam* and *Absence of Mind* are any indication, Robinson's on a moral crusade to attack the caricatures of traditional piety in contemporary discourse and expose literature's disconnection from religious and literary traditions that once gave it elegance and scope. Cut off from those traditions, modern literature grows small, Robinson argues, amusing itself with the easy allure of whatever's trending and ignoring the higher purpose of its work. Others have written similar jeremiads—T. S. Eliot's "Tradition and the Individual Talent" comes to mind—but when we stop to consider *which* tradition Robinson wants to reclaim, the neo-Puritanism of John Calvin and Jonathan Edwards, she's facing a difficult challenge, especially where play is concerned. As I mentioned in the Introduction, renouncing play in one form or another was a central feature of early Protestant conversion narratives. The games change in different versions of the story—"cat" for John Bunyan but bowling, fiddling, or dancing for others. And sometimes it's not a game that calls down the thunder but a loose mood or dreamy desire: "a desire to keep company with other wild boys" (Joseph Pike); a longing "to play and to run out without my fathers consent and againe his command" (John Dane); a "vain and frothy Lightness" (Samuel Blair).[1]

Frothy or not, "lightness" is a good way to describe the graced soul in Robinson's fiction, a religious subject undefended by fortress theologies of dogmatic conviction and open to the play of Holy Spirit in the world. Robinson's very clear about this in her essays and interviews: "I think one of the most poignant things about human beings is that they're so undefended," she said in an interview with Thomas Gardner. Robinson calls this unguarded subject "the famished I, the I stripped to its marrow," in talking about Emily Dickinson, and she cherishes the vulnerability of that frail self as the source of so much good: a "fierce humanness of feeling" in the face of the unknown and a "brave experiment" in religious trust.[2] Robinson pictures this experimental bravery not as by-the-book religious observance but as the spiritual choreography of spontaneous movement, like Ruth and Sylvie waltzing in the flood water in *Housekeeping* or John Ames waltzing in his study in *Gilead*. The spirit's true state is flight and transposition in Robinson's fiction, a lightness of being experienced in moments of ecstatic buoyancy and spiritual lift. What will *death* feel like? Ames wonders. It will be like an "ecstatic pirouette" into pure being, he imagines. And what will *that* be like? Like stretching out to catch a long line drive when we're too young to fear the risk.[3] Robinson's God loves baseball as much as Bunyan loved playing "cat."

Thus, I wasn't completely surprised to find this sentence in an unpublished notebook in the Robinson papers at Yale: "Play is at the heart of everything," she wrote. The undated notebook comes from the beginning of Robinson's career, when her children were still young. (Her sons' drawings of spaceships and stick-figure knights occur on the flipside of many notebook pages in this folder.) Moreover, Robinson's thinking about universal play, present in everything, surfaces at an odd moment, just after a long passage of self-examination where she gives herself a stern talking to about her productivity and social value. "Look at me," she writes, "educated beyond any decent use, and it has made me unruly, discontent, libelous, and slovenly in my habits! A well-ordered society would never have let a being of no use attain such unmanageable proportions!" Unruly, discontent, libelous, slovenly—all sound like Puritan words, slovenly in particular, so that it looks like we're edging toward the kind of introspective soul-thrashing the Puritans practiced in their notebooks. But in this case, Robinson stops herself mid-harangue and reflects on the value of idleness, prodigality, and spiritual play, which becomes for her the true message of the Christian gospels: "Play is at the heart of everything. Work is a mime of play. It is in every parable—be the prodigal, come to the vineyard at the eleventh hour. Anyone's true work is idleness."[4]

This is an unusual way of thinking about Christian faith, one that's closer to the playful wisdom of *Walden* or the blessed play of Dickinson than the workhouse piety of the Puritans. Yet Robinson sees the nineteenth-century Americans as standing in a line of direct descent stretching all the way back to Calvin. Thoreau would never admit it, but when he declares that play is holy, he doesn't set a transcendental theology of spiritual play against church history so much as recover from within early Protestantism an antinomian spirituality present from the start: in the mystic literature of Jacob Boehme; in the inner-light practices of Quakers, Seekers, Anabaptists, and Familists; in the central place of spiritual mirth within Puritan pietism; and in the theology of religious affection in Jonathan Edwards and Benjamin Colman.[5] In these sources, grace can't be earned or possessed but is instead the prodigal gift of a divine love that's unwise (by the wisdom standards of the age), unformulaic (as static doctrine), and unearthly (from the point of view of *this* earth, this arrangement of power). Grace has no relation to human notions of time and causality or human standards of comprehension and value. Thus, it favors a mind that holds such standards loosely, playfully, in responsive readiness to a spirit on the move.

Robinson names this practiced readiness "ecstatic discipline," when she talks about Dickinson and self-transforming "gracefulness" when she talks about Melville and Thoreau.[6] And she tends to call it "Calvinism" when she urges her readers to reclaim the forgotten roots of this tradition in the religious history of the West. Whether or not Calvin would in fact recognize his ideas as the source of Robinson's Christian humanism (or accept his place as the inspiration for abolitionism, women's suffrage, and higher education, as Robinson argues at various points)—all that's an open question.[7] What comes through clearly however is that the religious tradition that interests Robinson has nothing to do with what she calls "the entrapments of scrupulous piety" and everything to do with a flexible stance toward the unknown: "There is something about certainty that makes Christianity un-Christian," she writes in her religious manifesto, "Credo." "Therefore, because I would be a good Christian, I have cultivated uncertainty, which I consider a form of reverence."[8]

What better way to present this tradition to modern readers than with an aging pastor writing letters of love and instruction to his seven-year-old son, letters whose express purpose is to pass on the father's wisdom before it's too late. That wisdom, however, is not what we might expect. There's almost no life-guiding advice in *Gilead*. No solutions to theological problems or answers to the questions of existence. "I really can't tell what's beautiful anymore," Ames says. "I do not understand one thing in this world" (5, 164). The pastor's as bewildered as everyone else—except that Ames comes to cherish bewilderment as a religious disposition. Much that's good and beautiful in Ames' life came to him as a complete surprise, blown in from the wilderness like the strange bird that flew into his house during a storm, as Ames tells his wife in *Lila*. And Lila is that strange bird, or at least one of them, not speaking Ames' theological language or sharing all that much of his religious faith. But she is grace to him nonetheless, and he can sense the wild blessing when she's nearby. "It left a blessing in the house," Ames says of the storm-tossed bird. "The wildness of it. Bringing the wind inside."[9]

If "bringing the wind inside" names a faith practice for Robinson, a way of bringing difference near, then Christian piety has little to do with church structures or theological beliefs—Lila for one believes almost nothing of what Ames preaches—and much to do with remaining open to these wild incursions. This kind of religious practice means remembering that we live in a world of astonishing complexity and having the good sense to hold our judgments lightly in the face of what we don't understand: the presence of God, surely, but also the mystery of the wild creature sharing our bed or standing on the porch or looking back at us from the mirror. Brute neighbors one and all, as Thoreau would say. In every way that matters we're strangers to one another and mysteries even to ourselves, and learning to welcome the stranger with humility and trust is the natural extension of our reverence for God, who is for Robinson wild above all. Thus, Ames tells his son stories of everyday astonishment in *Gilead*: the play of sunlight caught in the willows near the river, for instance, or a girl sweeping rainwater from her shining hair. This is the religious pedagogy of Ames' letters, a catechism of wonder. And of course, his son is part of that wonder, a blessing so wild it turns the pastor's world upside down. If the older traditions of Protestant theology can help us accept these mysteries and cherish the grace of so much turning, then we may feel less alone in the wilderness and gladly share faith's journey. And if it's right to call that tradition *playful*, then we would do well to place such play at the heart of everything, as Robinson said, and embrace the plurality of religious experience as faith's true wisdom and grand laughter as our proper praise.

PLAY AS A MODEL OF UNDERSTANDING

The play theorist who comes closest to this view is Hans-Georg Gadamer, a writer fully committed to the universal theory of play Robinson explored that day in her journal. In *Truth and Method*, Gadamer presents play as a model of human understanding in all its forms, so that we're "playing" every time we try to understand something strange or difficult: giving it a name, framing it, interpreting it (step one). Then allowing the other to "correct" our misperceptions, revealing our mistakes and prejudices and inviting us to think again and think differently (step two). Indeed, that's how Gadamer recognizes real "understanding" when he sees it: understanding changes things, changes us. It makes a practical difference in our values and lives: "It is enough to say that we understand in a different way, if we understand at all."[10]

Gadamer uses "play" to express this transformative, difference-producing dimension of human understanding. He's not giving us tactics for reading and interpreting texts, which is what one might expect from his emphasis on hermeneutics. Instead, he's exploring the nature of human understanding itself: the conditions that support it, the prejudices that block it, and the practical value of understanding as an applied art, Aristotle's *phronesis*. The back-and-forth rhythm of play struck Gadamer as the engine of this cognitive process: provocation, reply, correction, restatement. All of which goes on in a recursive movement that's open-ended and inexhaustible, each experience of understanding corrected and deferred by an endless supplementarity. Conversation, preaching, reading, interacting with other people, interacting with traditions, playing catch, playing with animals: all evoke this model of mind for Gadamer, the to-and-fro movement of interactive play.

If that's all it is, however, just back and forth and back and forth, like a cradle endlessly rocking, it's hard to see what's transformative about play, how it moves things *forward*. Gadamer replies by stressing experiences of mutuality and agreement in our relationships with others, what he calls a "fusion of horizons," when we come to understand one another, at least for a moment, and make meaningful progress in the pursuit of truth. That progress sounds vaguely Hegelian in *Truth and Method*, a dialectical advance, except that Gadamer's dialectic has no final goal or comprehensive synthesis, no *aufgehoben*. Gadamerian play creates a dialectic of the *bad* infinite, as he said about his work, where singularity and strangeness are the lifeblood of understanding, as Monica Vilhauer has argued.[11] When alterity stops, understanding stops, and thought collapses into a complacent and unchanging present.

Thus, what matters to Gadamer isn't the rule-bound configuration of any particular game but rather the "structurality" of play, the oscillating interaction between poles, which holds sway for whatever we're trying to think about.[12] Something looms out of the fog that we can't get a grip on, can't easily assimilate or control, and we respond to that provocation by trying to understand it, drawing a meaning out of what just happened. When Thoreau and Dillard tell the story of interpretative encounter, they often stress the hiddenness or secrecy of the other, the way it retreats as we move forward, slipping back into water, mist, forest, camouflage. They accent the "shyness" of the other, so that the game of understanding in Dillard and Thoreau can be like playing hide and seek, stalking something that remains hidden. The scene of interpretation is more violent and provocative than that for Gadamer: something surprises us, knocks us off-kilter. We feel solicited by the encounter (*sollicitare*: shaken, disturbed), so that we're drawn outside ourselves, outside the circle of our expectations, in a process Nicholas Davey calls the "ex-stasis of the aesthetic subject."[13] That ex-stasis is disruptive at first, "a prodigal departure" from what we thought we knew,[14] and it thus resembles what I described as learning in its deconstructive phase in reference to Emily Dickinson in chapter 2. Gadamer sees this shock-of-the-new displacement most clearly in our relationship with works of art, but he extends his hermeneutic model to include our encounters with nature, tradition, scripture, God, and other people. Thus, Gadamer reverses the typical model of understanding as grip or grasp, thought as a way of comprehending something, by stressing the way a work of art *takes hold of us*, coming out of the fog with force and intention:

> When a work of art truly takes hold of us, it is not an object that stands opposite us which we look at in hope of seeing through it to an intended conceptual meaning. Just the reverse. The work is an *Ereignis*—an *event* that "appropriates us" to itself. It jolts us, it knocks us over, and sets up a world of its own, into which we are drawn.(original emphasis)[15]

All this jolting and jostling isn't an end in itself for Gadamer. Instead, being bowled over by a work of art is the preliminary condition of dialogic understanding in *Truth and Method*, a way art has of making us drop our shields, our protective prejudices, and opening us to an encounter we don't yet understand. Like virtually all postmodern play theory, Gadamerian play is open-ended and "interminable" (*die Unabschliessbarkeit aller Erfahrung*), an ongoing process of making a claim or taking a position and then being corrected by the work itself, jolted once more into attention and dialogue—and again and again after that. Thus, Gadamerian play resembles what Calvin might call prevenient grace, that is, a preparatory experience that leaves us stunned, unguarded, ungrounded—and thus ready to receive what we don't expect or control. Gadamer's not exactly a religious thinker, but when he writes about *that* kind of understanding he moves closer to the language of faith: "To reach an understanding with one's partner in a dialogue is not merely a matter of total self-expression and the successful assertion of one's own point of view, but a transformation into a communion, in which we do not remain what we were."[16]

Admittedly, Robinson would be surprised to see herself mentioned in the same paragraph with *Truth and Method* and would find the terminology of postmodern play theory—deferral, structurality, supplementarity, event—averse to her literary imagination and alien to the Calvinist roots of her faith. And yet Robinson's emphasis on ecstatic discipline and receptive poise in her essays and interviews resembles Gadamerian hermeneutics, transposes those hermeneutics into a different key, as in this passage from "Credo":

> So this is what I believe. More precisely, this is some small part of what I believe, or rather of the way in which I believe, at this point in my life, allowing for the certainty that I am in error in ways that are significant and unknown to me—there is a special Calvinist peace that comes with learning to make that concession. I am confident that I have been and will be instructed, knowing that instruction means correction, the discovery of error.[17]

Gadamer could have written that paragraph, except for the part about Calvinist peace, which doesn't mean that Robinson is a Gadamerian moral philosopher or that Gadamer is a closet Calvinist but rather that there are surprising points of intersection among religious and philosophical traditions that seem to have nothing in common. One such point is the notion of dialogic understanding. For Gadamer, meaning doesn't exist in itself, like a truth nugget waiting to be uncovered by a scrupulous hermeneut—which was the original model of biblical hermeneutics, a method for determining the correct interpretation of scripture. The "method" in Gadamer's title, *Truth and Method*, is wry and subversive. His method is enigmatic encounter, exactly as it is for the six writers of my study. Truth for Gadamer doesn't mean presence, certainty, actuality, or correspondence with the real. Truth isn't something we can grasp, uncover, bank on, build from, or possess. Truth is something we experience in dialogic moments of genuine understanding that leave us different than we were before. Being prepared for those transformations—attuned to them as in Thoreau or poised for them as in Dickinson—is the real method of *Truth and Method*.

But this is also the method of many of the key scriptures in *Gilead*—Paul's letter to the Romans, Jesus' Parable of the Prodigal Son, the Genesis stories of Balaam's Ass, Hagar and Ishmael, and Jacob wrestling with the Angel, among others—as well as the method of one of Ames' favorite theologians, Karl Barth (whose notion of "integral hermeneutics" anticipates the philosophical hermeneutics of *Truth and Method*).[18] One reason Robinson shows little interest in postmodern theory is that she discovers key elements of philosophical hermeneutics within her own religious tradition, just as Thomas Merton did. Robinson didn't need to read *Truth and Method* to see that play is a model of religious understanding: it's in the Wisdom literature of Proverbs, the subject of one of Robinson's sermons, and Zechariah's vision of *shalom*, children playing together in the streets, the subject of one of Ames' final letters.[19] I stress this point to suggest that the core themes of postmodern hermeneutics—lightness, readiness, alterity, the ability to change mental perspectives—are available to practicing Christians within their own confessional histories, which makes the straw-man attacks on traditional piety in contemporary theory a little hard to take. When John Caputo pictures his project as "Spooking the Faithful," for instance, he assumes that practicing Christians are one big thing, the Faithful, and that their faith needs a good spooking—as if traditionally religious people are somehow immune to feelings of haunting and doubt, which his rogue theology will now supply.[20] Robinson's piety *cultivates* haunting and doubt; that's how she knows her beliefs are in fact Christian. Her religious tradition is one long reminder that no one knows the day nor the hour and that God comes to us like a thief in the night—and so be *ready*.

This stance of responsive readiness emerges in much the same way for Gadamer as it does for Robinson: not from a rogue position outside historical tradition—Gadamer wonders how that position could actually exist or where we'd find a place to set its Archimedean fulcrum—but rather from inside an intellectual history in constant debate with itself. Gadamer is interested in the transformative possibilities of that kind of tradition, which he imagines not as a monolithic canon of established truths but as a living chorus of competing voices, a loud and layered conversation, which comes at us from the past, jolts us from the past, and invites us to fashion a response. In *Gilead*, Robinson builds that choral voice into the family history of three congregational pastors, who share the same name but disagree about nearly everything else. Tradition is not one thing here, a dominant voice or authoritative perspective, and thus the enemy of meaningful change. (This was Jürgen Habermas' critique of Gadamer.) Instead, tradition is "conservative" exactly to the degree that it conserves the conflicts and controversies, the multiple perspectives people of faith have taken on the "same" thing.[21]

Thus, Gadamer would undoubtedly cherish the perspectival knowing Robinson builds into her three Iowa novels, where the same experiences and relationships are explored from multiple points of view: Ames' in *Gilead*, Lila's in *Lila*, and Glory's in *Home*. And surely this cubistic perspectivism could multiply indefinitely, compelling us to hold *every* stance and perspective in abeyance, ready for the moment when the frames change or the center shifts and something else comes into play. This seems close to the "truth" of *Truth and Method*. Understanding for Gadamer means understanding differently, not assimilating new information to a pre-existing grid, what he calls a pre-judgment or fore-understanding (*Vorurteil*), but instead allowing the event to take hold of us, to appropriate us, and so inspire a fresh, ad hoc reply. Gadamerian hermeneutics thus requires the same lightness of mood and stance Robinson stresses in Ames' ecstatic pirouette, what we might call the ex-stasis of the religious subject, as well as the cultivated uncertainty she emphasizes in her own religious manifesto, the conviction that whatever she might say about Christian faith will be significantly and inadvertently wrong.

Before turning to *Gilead*, let me mention that *Truth and Method* is the minority report of postmodern play theory, which is tipped more strongly toward Derrida than Gadamer. Gadamer's thinking about hermeneutic play (*Spiel*) resembles Derrida's notion of deconstructive play (*jeu*)—but only up to one key point: what play actually accomplishes, what changes or transformations it produces. Both writers are interested in play and transformation, those moments when "something is suddenly and as a whole something else," but they differ in how and where those changes occur.[22] For Gadamer, transformation is *intersubjective*, occurring in the liminal space of dialogue and interaction between players. For Derrida, transformation is *intra-linguistic*, occurring within texts, in the ephemeral play of language endlessly deferring. For Derrida, reading and writing are like play not because we lose ourselves in the game and discover new possibilities of meaning and truth, Gadamer's view. Reading and writing are like play because they're inexhaustible and ultimately meaningless, like playing chess on a bottomless chessboard.[23] Such play is an endless series of moves and countermoves, interpretations and corrections, but nothing is actually gained or advanced that way. Derridean play offers no *phronesis* that I can see, no practical wisdom we might apply to our own lives, something Gadamer insists on: "Understanding always involves something like the application of the text to be understood to the present situation of the interpreter."[24]

In his early work on play, Derrida had little use for that kind of application and even less for the redemptive note Gadamer often struck to describe these experiences: our "redemption and transformation back into true being."[25] Deconstructive play is "free-floating" in the sense that language isn't anchored by notions of knowledge or truth. It's not tied to any specific situation, author, intention, or audience. Nor is it bound by the interpretive protocols we use to understand it, the limits we might set to how and what it means. Instead, language is produced by a linguistic system of differential spacing. Things "mean" by contrast and opposition. They mean by what they're not. Each piece of the linguistic code, each sign, is meaningful only in relation to the code as a whole, the differential oppositions that produced it. "Play" is the word Derrida chooses to describe the slippage and dissemination that occur within this system, not as an accidental by-product of the linguistic code, and thus something we might correct, but as an exact consequence of the way language works. Thus, play produces and reproduces endless transformations within texts: always deferring a final interpretation, always meaning differently or meaning otherwise, and in that way remaining true to itself, true to the linguistic structure that produced it. It's not fair to say that this model of play is sterile or unproductive. Indeed, deconstructive play is extraordinarily fertile in producing more of itself, that is, more language and writing, as Richard Rorty notes approvingly: "For Derrida, writing always leads to more writing, and more, and still more."[26]

What Gadamer helps us see in *Gilead* is a different notion of knowledge and truth: not the bottomless chessboard of deconstructive play, nor the unspooked dogmatism of Caputo's Faithful, but something halfway in-between, something I'm tempted to call wild knowledge (thinking of the wild bird in *Lila*) or prodigal truth (thinking of Ames' prodigal godson). In this mode of thought and encounter, we experience the other in relationships of intimate mystery and kinetic touch, something Ames experienced as a child playing with half-wild cats, feeling their arched power under his own small hand (and experienced again in rituals of blessing and baptism in his life as a pastor). "There is a power in that," he says about the cats. "I have felt it pass through me, so to speak. The sensation is of really knowing a creature, I mean really feeling its mysterious life and your own mysterious life at the same time" (23). If this constitutes the playful wisdom of *Gilead*, such wisdom is fleeting, practical, relational, and surprisingly hard. Playful wisdom comes at a price for Ames, the sacrifice of prejudices and presuppositions that block wild knowing and frame the other from a self-serving point of view. Robinson shows that much of Ames' thinking about Lila, scripture, his church, his town, and his godson and namesake Jack Boughton is significantly and inadvertently wrong, as she said about her own faith. But revealing the prejudices of the pastor, as I intend to do now, is only half the story. What also matters are the transformations that may follow those losses, breakthrough moments of understanding when Ames comes to know the mysterious life of another person and his own mysterious life as well. This is Lila's position in the theological discussion between Jack and the pastors in *Gilead* and her answer to Jack's implicit questions about predestination: Are people doomed to a predetermined future? Can they be different from what they've always been? "A person can change," she says, predicting the course her husband's life will take. "Everything can change" (153). This strikes me as the hermeneutics of hope in *Gilead* and its balm for a suffering world.

PLAY AND PREJUDICE

Genuine understanding doesn't come easily for most people, precisely because it disrupts the self-protective prejudices we use to feel safer in the world. Who wants a wild bird in the house? Certainly not the speaker of Dickinson's poem, "I dreaded that first Robin, so," who'd do almost anything to keep the birds outside. John Ames knows all about traumatic incursions, and so for much of his life he builds a world every bit as dimmed by dread as the speaker in Dickinson's poem. If one theme in Ames' letters is a catechism of everyday wonder, another is a litany of intimate loss (and the self-defensive prejudices that form as a result). The bullet holes in the weathervane of Ames' church memorialize a social history of trauma and violence re-enacted in the family story of its three pastors. Ames' grandfather fought with John Brown in the Free Soil movement of the 1850s and may have murdered a U.S. soldier to protect Brown's retreat from Gilead, an act he commemorates by wearing a bloody shirt in the pulpit. Ames' grandmother died a terrible death of cancer, while her children and grandchildren watched helplessly nearby. Both his sisters and one brother were killed by diphtheria within two months of one another. Ames' first wife, Louisa, died giving birth to their daughter, who lived only long enough for Robert Boughton to baptize her and give her the name "Angeline." Ames' godson and namesake, John Ames Boughton, called Jack, fathered (and then abandoned) a child who cut her foot on a piece of metal and died of the infection when she was three. Life turns on a dime in *Gilead*, in "the twinkling of an eye" (53). And when Ames watches his young son blowing soap bubbles in the yard, he feels how precious and fleeting it all is.

Ames responds to this insecurity by building a fragile shelter of protective retreat, what Robinson calls "the dear ordinary" in *Housekeeping*. Not ecstatic pirouettes but "somnolence" and "dull habit"—and thank god for it (20). In a world where soldiers drown in their own blood and children walk barefoot on rusty metal, the church can settle things down a little. At least that was Ames' view for much of his ministry. Religion can add some reassuring weight to all that famished longing and help us rest easier in the world. Ames doesn't sleep particularly well, and at one point in *Gilead*, he remembers, years before, waking up in his armchair at home, walking to his church in the pre-dawn darkness, and listening there to "an obliging, accommodating sound," the creak of the old building settling into itself:

> In those days, as I have said, I might spend most of a night reading. Then, if I woke up still in my armchair, and if the clock said four or five, I'd think how pleasant it was to walk through the streets in the dark and let myself into the church and watch dawn come in the sanctuary. I loved the sound of the latch lifting. The building has settled into itself so that when you walk down the aisle, you can hear it yielding to the burden of your weight. It's a pleasanter sound than an echo would be, an obliging, accommodating sound. You have to be there alone to hear it. . . . After a while I did begin to wonder if I liked the church better with no people in it. (70)

The world outside that church is far from quiet. *Gilead* takes place in 1956, two years after the Supreme Court ruled in Brown v. Board of Education of Topeka, Kansas that public school segregation was unconstitutional. A year later, Emmett Till, a Chicago teenager visiting his family in Mississippi, was kidnapped, beaten, shot, and dumped in the Tallahatchie River. Soon after Till's murder, Rosa Parks refused to give up her seat in the "colored section" of a Montgomery, Alabama bus, triggering a bus boycott led by the newly elected president of the Montgomery Improvement Association, the Reverend Martin Luther King, Jr.

Ames doesn't mention any of this in his letters to his son, Robby, who will grow up in the boiling heart of it all soon enough. Ames doesn't mention Korea or the House Committee on Un-American Activities or the Cold War. He doesn't mention the rise of the Klan in nearby Des Moines or ask questions about de facto housing segregation in Iowa and the upper Midwest. All this despite the fact that Jack and his African-American wife, Della, have endured exactly this kind of racism in St. Louis. Ames has never been to St. Louis to visit his godson. He hasn't met Della or her child. He doesn't know very much about the African-American pastor in Gilead or bother to find out what happened to him after his church was vandalized in a hate crime. Except that Ames doesn't call it "a hate crime" but just a small fire, as he says several times, just some brush stacked against a back wall (36). Ames doesn't literally turn off the television when stories from the civil rights movement come on the news, as Jack's father does in *Home*. But Ames isn't engaged by these concerns, which are crucial to Jack and his family. Unlike his fire-breathing grandfather—who preached with a gun in his belt and had mystic visions of Jesus in chains—Ames lives at some remove from that violent world, living on a religious island of quiet pleasures and solitary retreat.

It doesn't stay that way for long. As Ames looks back over the history of his family in *Gilead*, a pattern of sacred disruption emerges: moments when Ames experiences something that he cannot fully understand or represent, something outside himself and his mental categories that shocks him into a new perspective, snatching him out of his character, his calling, and his reputation. All of which fall away like a dry husk (205). Sometimes Ames calls that something grace. Sometimes extravagance or bewilderment. But Ames often calls that something *Jack*—Jack Boughton, his "godson, more or less" (92). A prodigal son on the margins of Gilead culture, Jack unsettles the pastor's quiet world, exposing his prejudices and opening the older man to growth and change. When that happens, Ames grows younger. He feels, even in the midst of aging and angina, recreated.

This insight will prompt a different notion of religious belief in *Gilead*. Not a home-grown piety of nativism or nostalgia but something wilder than that. Like the honeysuckle in the cemetery where Louise and Angeline are buried in *Gilead* or the wild bird blown in by the storm in *Lila*, the sacred comes from elsewhere. It's not native born. Or maybe as Gadamer would say, the sacred is both native and non-native at the same time, existing within a familiar horizon (and so something we could potentially understand) and yet standing at the outer limit of that horizon (and so potentially transformative).[27] Ames experiences the sacred in his midst, within his own family and community, but that discovery is still unsettling, triggering a prodigal departure from what he thought he knew.[28] Which is how Ames knows it's sacred rather than the homespun product of his own imagination, what he calls his "magical thinking" (188).

When Robinson writes about her own spirituality in "Psalm Eight," one of *The Death of Adam* essays, she also stresses the insecurity of her faith in the face of a sacred presence that pre-dates and exceeds any of the categories she can use to describe it.[29] She sensed God's presence before she learned to call it "God's presence," which even now doesn't sound quite right to her any more than it did to Thoreau. "I was so distinctly made aware of the presence of something kindred to me," he says cryptically in *Walden*.[30] And then leaves it at that, refusing to align this "something kindred" with what Emerson called "the dear old doctrines of the church" and so feel more at home with these spiritual sensations. For Thoreau the point is *not* to feel at home. Thus, he insists on a desirable vagueness (often rendered as a faint sound or fragrance) whenever he writes about religious experience: "The words which express our faith and piety are not definite; yet they are significant and fragrant."[31] The significance of such undefined piety is political as well as personal for Thoreau: religious experience should draw us out of ourselves, out of our nativism, and pull against provincial habits of self-protecting enclosure. The faithful soul dwells in possibility, as Dickinson would say. It lives "laxly" in front, as Thoreau puts it in *Walden*, turning an implied critique of indefinite piety (too easy or lax) into an heroic emblem of the pilgrim's unguarded heart: "In view of the future or possible, we should live quite laxly and undefined in front, our outlines dim and misty on that side."[32]

This is the signature of Thoreau's religious style, as we've seen, dim and misty every time, precisely because the moment we ignore or tame that kindred "something" things begin to settle inward, falling into themselves like Ames' accommodating church. Only that sinking center isn't soothing in *Walden*; it's stagnant and dying: "Our village life would stagnate if it were not for the unexplored forests and meadows which surround it. We need the tonic of wildness."[33] By "tonic," Thoreau means soul medicine, a stimulating counter-agent to thought's self-protecting calm. And by "wildness," he means not only wild nature but also wild spirit, a sacred presence that's kindred but unfamiliar, *next* to him but *not* him, and so capable of resisting faith's solipsistic collapse. Responding to that sacred otherness will require new modes of thought and expression for Thoreau, a religious writing that remains somewhat cryptic and obscure. Further, it will require a tolerance for religious transgression: "We need to witness our own limits transgressed, and some life pasturing freely where we never wander."[34] Whatever's pasturing out there is still indefinite, "some life." But the cost of living in relationship with that neighboring presence is clear: the boundary-crossing bravery of spiritual exploration and the ego-shattering bravery of spiritual kenosis. In both cases, the *Walden* self remains undefended, the key word in Robinson's notion of reverence. Not wearing a breastplate of righteousness but living "quite laxly and undefined in front."

Robinson loves the old doctrines of the church as much as anyone, but when she writes about her own faith she stresses the same fugitive sensation of wild neighboring, the sense of being close to something that's dear to her but not her, a stranger in the house not subject to her language and control:

"In my childhood, when the presence of God seemed everywhere," she writes in "Psalm Eight," "and I seemed to myself a mote of exception, improbable as a flaw in the sun, the very sweetness of the experience lay in that stinging thought—not me, not like me, not mine."[35] It's natural to feel proprietary toward that sacred presence and do whatever we can to take the sting out of our religious thought. The challenge Robinson poses is to abide in that prickly intimacy, which seemed to Thoreau like trying to sleep with wasps in his bed, and to see in the end that the proximity and the danger are part of the same thing, the same uncanny neighboring. As Robinson develops this idea around Jack Boughton, the prickliest character on earth for Ames, she suggests that loving one's neighbor without being able to change or control him, indeed loving one's neighbor without being able to understand him very well, is a version of our love for God and keyed to the same emotional pitch: sweet but stinging, fragrant but wild, kindred to me but not me, not like me, not mine. Moreover, by having a Congregational pastor tell this story (rather than a religious outsider like Thoreau), Robinson helps us see that these experiences aren't exceptional in the history of the church and that feeling these things doesn't make us improbable and flawed. This is the Protestant tradition, Robinson suggests, or at least part of it. These are the doctrines most dear.

What makes Jack's presence so prickly to Ames isn't his atheism but his suffering, the fact that he condenses a history of trauma that's been present in Gilead for as long as people can remember but that Ames and others would rather forget. Jack can't forget. He's a walking advertisement of loss. He didn't create the diphtheria that killed Ames' brother and sisters or the influenza that left soldiers drowning in their blood. But he reminds people of lost and abandoned children. He didn't create the racial segregation and shame still burning under the surface of small towns in the Midwest. But he stirs those memories. In this sense, what's uncanny about Jack is not only his difference from Ames but also his similarity. Like Jack, Ames lost a child and a wife and sees traces of that grief mirrored back to him in his godson. Like Jack, Ames understands the fugitive sorrow of not being entirely at home in Gilead. He felt that way for forty years. He hasn't been literally homeless, like Jack and Lila, but before meeting Lila he spent many nights peering through closed windows at brightly lit scenes of domestic happiness he could not share.

Isn't this what Jack felt in St. Louis and Memphis? And again in Gilead?—where playing catch with Ames' son would surely remind him of his own faraway child. The resemblances go on and on. Ames hasn't married a woman beyond the pale of Gilead culture, as Jack did with Della, but Lila comes close. She's much younger than Ames and from a different background and social class. Lila feels the difference sharply from time to time, and Ames does too, especially when Jack points it out: "unequally yoked and so on"

(230). Ames isn't an alcoholic as Jack is, but Ames has a "reptilian self" of his own to deal with, a sullen ego he's ashamed of but feels helpless to reform. Most importantly, Ames hasn't abandoned his child as Jack did when he turned his back on Annie Wheeler and their daughter, but Ames knows that Lila and Robby will experience his death as an abandonment. And he feels ashamed of that too. Just as the "ashy bread" of Ames' childhood evokes a complex history of love, fatherhood, pastoring, and communion, all present in the touch and taste of the bread, Jack condenses and activates an equally complex history of loss, trauma, injustice, and shame.

There's a prescient logic in Boughton's decision to name his son after his best friend. They mirror one another. And for most of the novel Ames hates and fears what that mirror reveals: the stay-at-home elder brother—"I myself was the good son," Ames says (238)—doubled and demonized in the prodigal son. To make things worse, this prodigal son has a special genius for religious parody. Jack can "do" the Gilead pastors almost perfectly—their walk, their pocket handkerchiefs, their voices—which sound precious and tinny when he does it. Not the transparent expression of a genuine self, which is what Ames tries to pour into his writing and preaching, but theatrical and "pulpitish" (29). When that happens, the idea of native eloquence or expressive style goes straight out the window. Which is the last thing John Ames wants to hear.

So he doesn't. Ames doesn't allow himself to hear the voice and story of his godson. He can barely tolerate the two minutes Jack spends with him in the kitchen. The flatness of Ames' writing and thinking about Jack—dumbed down to an all-purpose explanation of "meanness"—is a clue that there's something blocking the lens and keeping Ames from seeing Jack with open and compassionate eyes. When Ames writes about Jack's childhood, for instance, he doesn't see Jack's games with anything like the resonance he sees in the soap bubbles and catting pole of his own son at play. Jack speaks an incredibly subtle dialect of his own. He talks with his hands and his posture and his cigarettes. He talks with silence. He talks with where he stands in a room and what he touches (the fringe of a lampshade, the shoulder of a chair) and what he refuses to touch. He's always done this. As a child, Jack spoke with pranks and vandalism the way some children speak with toys or drawings and others speak with self-bruising and cutting, articulating a coded but legible dialect of loneliness and rage.

Jack's been speaking this dialect his whole life. When he was ten, he filled Ames' mailbox with wood shavings and set it on fire. He painted the front steps of Ames' porch with molasses. He found a way to break the windows of Ames' study so that the whole pane shattered at once. He stole a Greek New Testament, a picture of Louisa, and a penknife made from a shell casing—right off Ames' desk. Then brought them all back, one by one, re-positioned just enough for Ames to notice, as if a fifteen-year-old Poltergeist had swept through the house. When Ames found the penknife, it was stuck through the heart of an apple and left on his kitchen table. "I found that disconcerting," Ames says (183). Who wouldn't? It's hard not to think about the emotional complexity of these pranks—which look like messages, warnings, nightmares, koans, cries for help, cries for attention, and who knows what else. But which Ames tends to see as *meanness*, plain and simple. "He's just mean," Ames says (184). End of story.

This is not how Ames' mind usually works. None of the pastor's stories snap shut like this. He can do three pages on the ashy bread, not once but several times. Moreover, each detail of Robby's beloved presence—his "skinniness and boy strength," his drawings, the way he plays on a tree swing—each is worthy of deliberate witness. Each is a miracle of grace. "There's a shimmer on a child's hair, in the sunlight," Ames writes in this mood. "There are rainbow colors in it, tiny, soft beams of just the same colors you can see in the dew sometimes. They're in the petals of flowers, and they're on a child's skin" (52). This is a remarkable scene, as if we're watching Pentecost in the pastor's backyard. As Ames dials the lens of his writing so far down he can see the color of light, "there are rainbow colors in it," he places his son in a rich field of associations and memories, naturalizing him in the physical landscape of his town. Skin, hair, dew, rainbows, sunlight, flower petals—all merge and interlock to hold the beloved child within a cupped and sheltering space. This child is *home*. He belongs in exactly this place, mirrored not only in the loving eyes of his father but also in the incandescent light of flower petals and dew.

There's nothing like that in Ames' writing about Jack. Ames leaves the article indefinite in the rainbow passage—"there's a shimmer on a child's hair"—as if this way of seeing were infinitely replicable, as if every child were haloed and sacred. But of course it's not all that replicable. Ames can see some children this way but not others—precisely because the suffering of outcast children opens him to the shame of not being able to provide for his family after he's gone. He can see the girl shaking rainwater out of her luminous hair and his son dancing in the iridescent water of a backyard sprinkler and the young mechanics so full of spark and laughter they look ready to burst into flame. But it's hard for Ames to see the boy who set his mailbox on fire or the African-American children in Selma and St. Louis with anything like this generosity of spirit.

If it's right to call that blocked lens a prejudice, as Gadamer would, then it's possible to see the same prejudicial distortion in the way Ames reads scripture. Like any reader, he sees what he's able to see and been taught to see, not reading scripture as a disruptive event, an *Ereignis*, but as a confirmation of what he already knows and needs to know, the confirmation of a bias that protects him. For instance, you have to read fairly selectively to believe, as Ames does, that "nowhere in Scripture is there a father who behaves wickedly toward his child" (135). You have to ignore that bitter business with Lot and his virgin daughters for one thing. And not look too closely at the biblical history of Gilead for another, including the part where Gilead's son Jephthah murders his only child as a blood sacrifice to God.[36] The rainbow of light passage is a counter spell to *that* Gilead. As Ames narrows the focus of his gaze to see the light on his son's hair all the rest goes dark, as it's meant to. For here is the magic that will this time and for this family shelter the angel-child within a circle of light that looks like god's own mantel, woven from the whole cloth of a father's love. When Ames thinks about Jack as a child, he can't make the writing shimmer and doesn't want to. He doesn't see in Jack "that little incandescence" of possibility and excess he sees in the members of his church (53). And no wonder. Jack's not a member. His sign is not a nimbus of light but an apple with a knife through it. Until Ames accepts how powerless he is to protect his child playing in the sunlight and how powerless we all are to build magic gardens around those we love—until then, Jack will remain a blank cipher of "pure meanness" (157). So overloaded with prejudice and projection he's barely a person at all.

Gilead swings back and forth between these two views. The novel is built around binary pairs and structural oppositions: home and away, inside and outside, member and non-member, the luminous angel-child and the dark meanness of his twin. Moreover, in that vacillation Robinson suggests an emblem for Ames' thinking mind and the roots of a "nimble piety" that will, in time, allow Ames to welcome the stranger in his midst, welcome and bless his godson, and face the world undefended.[37] That change doesn't happen all at once but develops slowly from a style of religious thinking Ames has been practicing for years. Its image is the porch swing where Ames rests in the afternoons and the tree swing where his son plays outside. Ames tends to live and work in dialectical rhythms of back and forth: conversing, preaching, writing letters—in short, oscillating between different poles, the game-play structurality we saw in Gadamer. This is the rhythm Ames enjoys in his own gentle play, the to and fro of rocking chairs and porch swings, and this is also a tendency he notices in his own thinking: "There is a tendency, in my thinking, for the opposed sides of a question to cancel each other more or less algebraically—this is true, but on the other hand, so is that, so I discover a kind of equivalency of considerations" (140). Ames' mind works in these dialectical rhythms of *this side* and *that*, on the *one hand* but on the *other*. "No doubt that is true," he says at one point, thinking about how life will end abruptly and without memory, ending as dreams do. "But that cannot be true," he thinks a moment later: "I can't believe we will forget our sorrows altogether" (104). Ames looks at scripture in the same manner, often on long walks with Boughton where their theological conversations recreate the back-and-forth rhythm they enjoyed while playing catch together as boys.

This dialectic bothers Ames sometimes (because it feels like deadlock), but it also opens the prospect that there are "opposed sides" to any question or person, a structural polarity or implicit perspectivism that evokes the *movement* of thought rather than its stalemate. Somewhat ironically, Ames' access to that opposed side is present at the scene of his own writing, present in the very letter he's using to think through the question of Jack's character. That opposed side of course is his son's side, an implied and unvoiced alternative to Ames' interpretation of Jack's meanness. Robby has a structural role to play in *Gilead* as the future audience for his father's writing, a reader whose subsequent response is impossible to predict. Thus, Robby occupies a unique hermeneutic position. He both *experiences* (in the moment) and *reads about* (years later) the "same" events: drawing in his father's study, playing with Lila, playing with Soapy, and so on, which creates a parallax effect of temporal displacement. In Gadamer's vocabulary, Robby's "horizon" is a moving target, changing in time as everything does, which prevents historical understanding from caving in on itself, like the settling church.[38] Ames thinks about this all the time, how his letters will be received by Robby someday, how in effect he's performing his writing in the presence of his future son, who will at some point *reply*—by amending, accepting, criticizing, or cherishing his father's words and so turning the letters into a dialogue, a conversation with his past. In his Preface to the First Edition of *The Epistle to the Romans*, Karl Barth describes historical understanding in just this way, as "an uninterrupted conversation between the wisdom of yesterday and the wisdom of tomorrow."[39] Robinson frames the playful wisdom of *Gilead* around a similar dialectic: the wisdom of *yesterday*, Ames' letters, and the wisdom of *tomorrow*, Robby's future reply, which may take a completely different form. If we were to substitute Paul's letter to the Romans for Ames' letters to his son, we would find ourselves in the situation Barth explores in *The Epistle to the Romans*: participating in a dialectical conversation with the past.

What Gadamer would call the game-play rhythm of that conversation, its back and forth, is more than apparent to Ames as a working pastor. The "game" Ames often has in mind is baseball—"I listened to thousands of baseball games, I suppose" (44)—but it's not the box score that matters as much as the movements of the game, which he enjoys reviewing and rehearsing in his mind: the circular pattern of base runners; the tactical feints and shifts of the defensive players; and the long slow arc of a fly ball (which Ames compares to planetary motions). In this scene, those game-play rhythms also remind Ames of the pastoral conversations he's had with members of his church, where the movement is less circular, like the path of a base runner, and more dialectical, like the back and forth of playing catch:

And I would think back on conversations I had had in a similar way, really. A great part of my work has been listening to people, in that particular intense privacy of confession, or at least unburdening, and it has been very interesting to me. Not that I thought of these conversations as if they were a contest, I don't mean that. But as you might look at a game more abstractly—where is the strength, what is the strategy? As if you had no interest in it except in seeing how well the two sides bring each other along, how much they can require of each other, how the life that is the real subject of it all is manifest in it. (44)

This view of pastoral care and conversation may also be a metacognitive comment about the letter itself, evoking Ames' implicit awareness that Robby is part of a game they're playing together, one side of a conversation, where the aim isn't to win the contest and end the game, but to keep it going, keep it moving, so that through their shared play something new comes into being, what Ames calls "the life that is the real subject of it all."

Ames preaches with this conversational model very much in mind. His sermons are one half of an ongoing dialogue, as every preacher knows. Whatever she might say from the pulpit is being "answered" by people in the pews—received, rejected, modified, celebrated, mocked by audiences who often reply the same way Jack does: with how they move and sit; with where they look or refuse to look; with a sophisticated vocabulary of attention and disinterest. "A good sermon is one side of a passionate conversation," Ames says. "It has to be heard in that way" (45).

Surely letters do too. We don't have access to Robby's side of the conversation, but Ames knows that his son experiences a very different Jack. When Robby catches sight of Jack coming down the road, he doesn't hesitate or withdraw, fearful of the bullet knife and the burning mailbox. Instead, he rushes off the porch to meet Jack, to play catch with him. Ames' "Jack" connotes atheism, prodigality, bad fathering, and pure meanness. Robby's "Jack" means companionship, acceptance, play—and maybe liberation from the solitary bent of his own personality, his deep shyness. When Ames describes Jack as his "godson, more or less," it's a distancing gesture, a way of not acknowledging the affectional bonds he owes Jack as a member of his family and community (and thus affirming by contrast the real son, the luminous child). But the slippage in that formulation can also be a space-clearing gesture, an implied negation, especially if it suggests the alterity of a person not fully revealed by our judgments, a person we more or less get wrong. As I mentioned in the last chapter, Gregory Bateson tends to add *sort-of* prefixes to even his most basic claims for the same reason: a swan is a "sort-of swan" in a key father–daughter metalogue in *Steps to an Ecology of Mind*. Caputo favors modal qualifiers to accomplish the same purpose: *perhaps* this is God (but on the other hand, perhaps *not*). If Robby's implied presence brings forward this loosening effect for Ames, this structural perspectivism, then the performative dimension of letter writing corresponds with what Ames seeks to teach his son about the mystery of *being*, how it too is different from whatever concepts and categories we might use to understand it.

Thus, the to-and-fro structurality of conversation and preaching suggests a hermeneutics of play and understanding that applies to people as much as to texts. In both cases, we don't think in a void. Our experiences with others, exactly like our experiences with scripture, are inflected by pre-existing assumptions that make understanding possible in the first place (possible but prejudicial as Gadamer stresses; possible but inevitably and significantly wrong as Robinson argues in "Credo"). No one in the Iowa novels speaks from a place of interpretative innocence and self-clarity, a place purged of prejudice and so protected from the back and forth of the hermeneutic circle. What Gadamer helps us see is that the performative dimension of play and understanding, playing *for* someone—Robby in the letters, Lila in the porch-swing conversations, Boughton on the preaching walks, church members at the sermons—*exposes* those prejudices and presuppositions, puts them in play, where we can realize and revise them.[40]

At one point, Ames extends this performative hermeneutics to his relationship with God—"Calvin says somewhere that each of us is an actor on a stage and God is the audience" (124)—which makes the "opposed side" of dialogic understanding more or less permanently available.[41] Who could ever fuse with that horizon? Ames doesn't have access to God's response to his performance any more than he has access to Robby's reply to his letters, as if the specific *content* of the reply is less important than the metacognitive *framing*, Ames' sense that he's performing for someone who doesn't see or think the same way he does. In Bateson's theories of play and fantasy, this metacognitive framing changes the way we use language. Signals become "signals" (which can be trusted, denied, expanded, interpreted), thus introducing an element of free variability into communication sequences. For Thoreau, play's metacognitive framing changes the way he sees himself; Thoreau becomes "Thoreau," an actor in a role: "I only know myself as a human entity; the scene, so to speak, of thoughts and affections; and am sensible of a certain doubleness by which I can stand as remote from myself as from another."[42] Thoreau was aware that part of his mind always stood apart from his thoughts and actions, even in moments of intense involvement. That internal audience, Thoreau watching Thoreau, also introduces elements of free variability by presenting consciousness as multiple and mobile, staged rather than frozen in place.

Robinson develops this metacognitive theme somewhat differently. First, by exploring polarities that exist outside the self, outside Ames' thinking mind (and in God's case, *way* outside). And second, by *withholding* the other's response, the actual content of God's judgment or Robby's reply. The communication sequences Bateson examines in his play studies are actual give-and-take dialogues, self-aware creatures playing with and off one another. Robinson's communication sequences are sometimes like that, face-to-face encounters in real time, as I'll explore in a moment, but she's also interested in how a *silent* auditor changes things, introducing the kind of metacognitive awareness Ames experiences through writing and prayer, the sense that he's performing or auditioning his life in the presence of someone else, even when he's alone. The moment he frames his experience that way, and the whole book is framed that way, he's in the middle of a conversation, which for Gadamer is the hermeneutic condition of understanding and growth.

This implicit perspectivism strikes me as the Archimedean lever of critical difference in *Gilead*, which is built into a Calvinist theology of divine alterity and stands directly under Ames' hand as he writes his letters to his son. And of course those "levers" are everywhere. Ames' "Jack" differs from Robby's (as well as Lila's, Boughton's, Glory's, Della's, and Jack's own self-understanding and presentation), which reveals the inadequacy of any stable, definitive point of view. Ames builds this metacognitive awareness into his preaching and theology, he knows that understanding is a passionate conversation, but he has yet to fully apply that practical wisdom to his own life, which is the key step for Gadamer, the *phronesis*: "Understanding always involves something like the application of the text to be understood to the present situation of the interpreter."[43]

Ames knows all this, at least in part. Ames considers his ideas and experiences from different angles and points of view in a way that creates increasing levels of complexity around a small imagistic vocabulary: water, ash, bread, tree swings, the trees themselves. Ames often refers to an extravagant fullness in the world, "an excess of being," which leads him to hold his judgments in abeyance, knowing that his perception of a thing is inadequate to that manifold fullness and so subject to corrections and adjustments (which will themselves fall short). This means that he's going to be wrong most of the time and feel a gap open between the works and thoughts of man, as Calvin would say, and the Creation itself.

Ames cherishes that gap as a corrective to faith's tendency to mistake its view for an adequate conception of the whole. Keeping the errors and misjudgments front and center may seem like Puritan soul-thrashing and weeping for one's sins, but it's really an exercise in epistemological humility and spiritual attention for Ames. As Robinson points out in "Credo," no one pays much attention to a God "he or she presumes to know sufficiently already, by dogma or by rote."[44] Thus, religious dogmatism feels impertinent to Ames, claiming "for God a place within our conceptual grasp" (179). But it also feels irreverent, a way of draining the sacred of mystery and substituting rote dogma for responsive attention, the qualities Robinson admires in Dickinson and Thoreau. When Thoreau thinks about the extravagance of a world that is greater than his comprehension, he tends to picture that difference in terms of blocked vistas and partial views: "The universe is wider than our views of it."[45] When Ames experiences these excess-of-being moods, he drops into the language of sacramental theology, the language of Calvin and Barth, savoring the fullness of symbolic objects that are always "more" than themselves. Water but more than water. Bread but more than bread. And always more than *his* bread, more than whatever meaning he attributes to the symbolic object in that letter on that day. The world's mysterious abundance defeats his best conceptions, which keeps things dim and misty up front, not predetermined along a fixed course but subject instead to continual change.

This sounds at first like a theoretical problem worth discussing on a long walk with Boughton, but Ames stresses the practical wisdom of this sort of understanding for the people in his church: "People talk that way when they want to call attention to a thing existing in excess of itself" (28). Ames talks that way all the time. Things hum a little in his writing, as if he can hear the sounds of vibrancy and growth. He loves the word *susurrus*, with its suggestion of rippling echoes. He's often drawn toward material things that taper off toward a live wavering edge, like the worn sofa in Boughton's living room. When someone sits down there, a tiny feather puffs out; *wafts*, as Glory remembers, a word she first learned from Jack. This active edge is where soul and body comingle for Ames, a visible emblem of a material world converting into spirit like a couch changing into feathers. Or a bank of trumpet vines tapering into hummingbirds. Or the flickering "incandescence" that hovers like a candle flame over the old saints of the church, the Mirabelle Mercers and Lacey Thrushes sitting in the pews. They too are "more" than themselves, more than their knuckle bones and Easter hats. The point isn't to sheer off from the material world in transcendental flights of pure abstraction but to rock back and forth along this continuum from couch to feather, hummingbird to trumpet vine, until wonders reveal themselves in the everyday, *Mirabelle* Mercer; and we sense the wild birds nearby, Lacey Thrush.

Something like this wild knowledge begins to emerge for Ames when Jack tells the story of his wife, Della, and their son, Robert Boughton Miles. If Ames becomes different to himself in the course of the novel, if he experiences a religious "ex-stasis," then that transformation owes much to his face-to-face conversations with Jack, which foreground and reframe many of the prejudices Ames uses to feel secure in the world (and so *not* change). One of their last conversations, held in Ames' church, brings many of these issues into clear focus. As Jack recounts the suffering he endured with Della because of segregated housing practices and anti-miscegenation laws in St.

Louis, for instance, Jack's poverty and prodigality appear in a different light, not the result of a dishonorable character, pure meanness, but the result of racial and religious prejudices Ames tolerated in Gilead and so helped maintain (blurring the line between Iowa and Missouri). Protecting himself from all that, Ames rehearses the old story of the "little nuisance fire" at the Negro church, not a hate crime at all, and points out that Iowa has never had anti-miscegenation laws. "Yes, Iowa, the shining star of radicalism," Jack replies (220). And immediately the self-protections sound insincere, "pulpitish," undercut by what Jack has actually endured.

Prejudice is revealed as prejudice within these conversational events, brought to light by the fact that Jack's history and perspective differ from his godfather's—which changes the way Ames sees himself. When Jack tells the story of being preached at by Della's father in the Memphis church, for instance, turned into a "whited tomb" of uncleanness and a "ravening wolf" of deceit, even as he sits there in the pew, Jack foregrounds what Ames did to him in his sermon on Hagar and Ishmael: interpreting Jack's character for him and weaponizing scripture as an instrument of judgment (and an exact example of the unkindness Ames was preaching *against*). Moreover, when Jack shows Ames the portrait of Della and Robert and shares the grief he's endured in their absence, Ames sees that Jack has his *own* wife and child, which exposes the pettiness of the usurper narrative, Ames' fear that Jack is trying to take his place. And finally, when Jack says that Della's father thinks that all white men are atheists, the remark accents Ames' own fondness for blanket pronouncements—that "dishonorable people," Jack included, "never really repent and never really reform," which makes the whole idea of pastoral ministry more or less moot (156).

There's a powerful bracketing or ironizing effect in play here, which mirrors the sacramental excess at the heart of Ames' theology, where ash and rain are "more" than themselves (and thus subject to ongoing correction). The implicit perspectivism Robby provides in the letters becomes explicit and immediate in these face-to-face conversations with Jack, so that the foundational narratives Ames uses to organize his life—his goodness, for one, his position as the "good son" of Gilead—become suddenly less secure, as if spooked now by haunting and doubt. Words that were stable before, words Ames had used a dozen times in his conversations and sermons—*home*, *marriage*, *Reverend*, *Christian*—take on different meanings when Jack uses them. "I thought maybe things were improving," Jack says when Della's family brings him supper one evening in Memphis, "but they were all just being Christian" (228). Being Christian means being courteous now, practicing a surface civility (while who knows what rages underneath). Like irony and satire, Jack's verbal gifts, tone is everything here. By merely adding one word, *just* being Christian, Jack frames the whole matter in a different way.

Let me close then by stressing the cumulative or eventual nature of hermeneutic understanding in Robinson, where our prejudices are revealed and worn away over time (rather than being dispelled in a single shining moment). There are shining moments in *Gilead*, of course, when Ames turns to his godson in the bus station, for instance, placing his hand on Jack's brow, exactly as he did with the half-wild cats, and experiencing the genuine mystery of another person, someone he'd known for years and yet never known. In that moment, Ames doesn't see pure meanness, which is the story he'd been telling himself about Jack for years. Instead, he sees "John Ames Boughton, this beloved son and brother and husband and father" (241). And yet even here, a fusion of horizons if there ever was one, understanding remains clouded and incomplete. The moment Jack replies, "Thank, you, Reverend," Ames realizes that Jack experiences each term in the blessing as an attack—*son, brother, husband, father*—not an affirmation of the person Jack has become but a reminder of everything he's lost: "'Thank you, Reverend,' he said, and his tone made me think that to him it might have seemed I had named everything I thought he no longer was, when that was absolutely the furthest thing from my meaning, the exact opposite of my meaning" (241-2).

A NUPTIAL YES

It doesn't seem like there's any alternative to this, as if human understanding *inevitably* misunderstands itself and so our conversations never really conclude. Or if there is such an alternative, it's one Robinson rejects out of hand: *not* participating, *not* joining the back and forth of the hermeneutic game (an alternative Ames had explored for years). Jack's blessing to the pastor, if it's right to call it that, is that he draws Ames back into the world, as Ames realizes at the end: "I think I'll put an end to all this writing. I've read it over, more or less, and I've found some things of interest in it, mainly the way I have been drawn back into this world in the course of it" (238). The passive voice seems right here, *I have been drawn back*, precisely because this is not something Ames achieves by himself, within what Huizinga termed the "play-ground of the mind."[46] Understanding doesn't happen all at once, and it doesn't happen to the soul alone. Lila helps by teaching Ames to cherish the blessing of the wild birds, which prepares him for a life of surprise. Robby helps by being an audience for Ames' writing and turning his diary into a dialogue. Boughton helps by teaching Ames that doing theology can be like playing catch with your friend (and you both win). Calvin helps by reminding Ames that being wrong most of the time doesn't make him evil; it makes him human. And of course Jack helps by calling Ames back into the world, like the bees and robins of an Emily Dickinson poem. Jack's presence is a solicitation for Ames, an invitation to come out of that closed study, out of the magical world Ames built to protect himself and re-enter the buzzing blooming raw heart of the thing, for this is what we're called to love.

"Let us love the country of here below," Simone Weil writes, in a passage Annie Dillard quotes in *Pilgrim at Tinker Creek*. "It is real; it offers resistance to love. It is this country that God has given us to love. He has willed that it should be difficult yet possible to love it."[47] Weil imagines such love as an act of practiced *consent*—a "nuptial yes"—repeated again and again, in sickness and in health, for better or for worse, until it marries us to life.[48] Marries us to *this* life, as Ames says: "I have been drawn back into this world." Robinson's Iowa novels take place in this nuptial terrain. She adapts elements of the playful wisdom she discovered in earlier American literature but locates that play within the noise and stir of living families: cats squalling, windows breaking, and that woeful boy standing on the pastor's porch. Robinson has an eye for the way families work and worry one another. How they wear us down and rub us the wrong way, knowing exactly which buttons to push to disintegrate and disconcert us. Until it all feels like so much "devilment," as Ames says at one point. It's not. For Robinson, all that button-pushing is the deep action of grace in human life. A divine friction that works (and works and works) to soften the edges of a walled-in life. That's how we know it's real—"it offers resistance," as Weil says—and that's how we know it's working: it gives off some heat in the kitchen. Ames senses the effect of all that friction one morning when he takes a good look at himself in the mirror and sees that "the irises of my eyes have begun to melt at the edges a little" (167).

Perhaps this is the live action of grace in Robinson's fiction: it melts people at the edges a little and helps them recover a thin active margin, electric as hummingbirds, where their lives make contact with the world. Lila and Robby and Jack and many others contribute to this deep melting in Ames, which is gradual and cumulative, a sum of small things adding up over time. If there's a kind of divine friction in *Gilead*, there's also a kind of divine mathematics. But it's less like the algebraic stalemate Ames worries about in his own writing and more like Robby doing "a page of sums" in the morning: counting things over, adding them up (8). What's adding up over the course of the novel is a series of spiritual affirmations that marry Ames to the country of here below: a nuptial *yes* to Lila and the friction of living families and a *yes* finally to Jack. Until the defensiveness Ames had hugged close for so long—"Why must I always defend myself against this sad old youth?" (180)—falls away like an old husk and something else takes its place, what Ames calls a wild gesture of love: "The thing I would like, actually, is to bless you," Ames says to Jack. "We all love you, you know" (241, 242).

What the blessing means to Jack is an open question. Even after all this time, he's hard to read. At the end of the scene, Jack laughs a little, gives

Ames that cryptic look of irony and longing, then tips his hat, and disappears down the road. Will the touch of Ames' hand on his forehead be a kind of divine melting for him? Jack's not saying, and he may not know. But not knowing is a blessing too. It's the assurance that Jack's life is still dim and misty ahead, not predetermined from the beginning of time to be the sad thing it is now.

What the blessing in the bus station means to Ames is clearer. It's the culmination of a long history of consent that melts his religious defensiveness and allows him to recover the grand laughter of an unguarded life. I think he owes this joy to Jack, who draws him back into the world, as the boy's been trying to do since he was ten: breaking the closed windows of the pastor's study, sticking him to the floor with a thin coat of molasses. And when Ames takes that lesson to heart it changes not only his relationship with his godson but also his relationship with his God. At the end of the novel the candle flame Ames sensed above the heads of the old saints begins to spread outward into a "great and general incandescence" on the faces of all God's children—Mirabelle and Lila and Della and Jack. All part of the membership. All precious beyond counting. This strikes me as Ames' nuptial *yes* not only to this world but also to what exists beyond the scope of his understanding, a future he can't see and doesn't need to see, which is also what the wedding vow promises: *yes* to this moment and this person but also *yes* to people as they change, as Lila would say, a promissory welcome to whatever's coming.

Let me end then with Lear's prayer, which offers a particularly vivid example of what Gadamer saw as the ex-stasis of the religious subject. Ames often quotes a line from the storm scene in Act 3 of *King Lear*: "I'll pray, and then I'll sleep." But Ames usually flips Lear's line, in that pendular way of his, and puts the sleeping first: "Now I'll pray. First I think I'll sleep" (131). As Jack leaves Gilead, Ames swings back the other way and recites Lear's sentence word for word. The scene in *King Lear* is the end product of a different kind of mathematics, a series of subtractions that strip the wide margin of privilege protecting Lear from the storm. When the play begins, he's thick with it, surrounded by a retinue of knights more than a hundred strong. Then it's fifty, then twenty, then just the fool. As Lear stands shivering on the heath, he sees the fool beside him and urges the boy to take shelter. At that moment Lear prays for the first time in the play and maybe the first time in his life for the poor souls huddled nearby, neighbors who've been present but invisible until then. This is the perfect place to end *Gilead*. Jack's been Ames' fool for years, testing his patience, wracking his nerves, parodying his theology until it sounds broken and weird. Yet in that broken place Ames discovers a different call. Not just to his church or the dear boy of his old age but a call to the dispossessed and downtrodden, all the "poor naked wretches, whereso'er you are, / That bide the pelting of this pitiless storm." And Jack is among them, and we are among them, and none of us is alone.

NOTES

1. The passages from Joseph Pike, John Dane, and Samuel Blair are quoted in Michael Oriard, *Sporting with the Gods: The Rhetoric of Play and Game in American Culture* (Cambridge: Cambridge University Press, 1991), 361, 362.

2. Thomas Gardner, "Interview with Marilynne Robinson," in *A Door Ajar: Contemporary Writers and Emily Dickinson* (New York: Oxford University Press, 2006), 68, 69.

3. Marilynne Robinson, *Gilead* (New York: Picador; Farrar, Straus and Giroux, 2004), 142. Subsequent references to *Gilead* will refer to this edition and be cited in the text by page number.

4. Marilynne Robinson Papers. Yale Collection of American Literature, Beinecke Rare Book and Manuscript Library.

5. On this, see Oriard, *Sporting with the Gods*, 363–64.

6. Gardner, *A Door Ajar*, 68, 59. Robinson also discusses the influence of Dickinson and Thoreau on her work in Thomas Schaub, "An Interview with Marilynne Robinson," *Contemporary Literature* 35, no. 2 (1994): 231–51.

7. On this, see Todd Shy, "Religion and Marilynne Robinson," *Salmagundi* 155/156 (Summer–Fall 2007): 251–64; Christopher Leise, "'That Little Incandescence': Reading the Fragmentary and John Calvin in Marilynne Robinson's *Gilead*," *Studies in the Novel* 41, no. 3 (Fall 2009): 348–67; Thomas Gardner, "Keeping Perception Nimble," *Christianity Today* 54, no. 2 (February 2010): 32–35; Thomas F. Haddox, *Hard Sayings: The Rhetoric of Christian Orthodoxy in Late Modern Fiction* (Columbus: Ohio State University Press, 2013), 186–203; and Justin Evans, "Subjectivity and the Possibility of Change in the Novels of Marilynne Robinson," *Renascence* 66, no. 2 (Spring 2014): 131–50.

8. Marilynne Robinson, "Credo," *Harvard Divinity Bulletin* 36, no. 2 (Spring 2008): 25, 23.

9. Marilynne Robinson, *Lila* (New York: Farrar, Straus and Giroux, 2014), 19.

10. Hans-Georg Gadamer, *Truth and Method*, trans. ed. Garrett Barden and John Cumming (New York: Seabury Press, 1975), 264. Gadamer develops his theory of play as a model of understanding in the section, "Play as the Clue to Ontological Explanation," in *Truth and Method*, 91–119; and in "'The Relevance of the Beautiful' and 'The Play of Art'," in *The Relevance of the Beautiful and Other Essays*, trans. Nicholas Walker and ed. Robert Bernasconi (Cambridge: Cambridge University Press, 1986).

11. See Monica Vilhauer, *Gadamer's Ethics of Play: Hermeneutics and the Other* (Lanham, MD: Lexington Books, 2010).

12. Sam D. Gill explores this aspect of Gadamerian play in *Dancing Culture Religion* (Lanham, MD: Lexington Books, 2012), 137–44.

13. Nicholas Davey, "Gadamer's Aesthetics," *The Stanford Encyclopedia of Philosophy*, ed. Edward N. Zalta (Winter 2016), https://plato.stanford.edu/archives/win2016/entries/gadamer-aesthetics/.html (accessed November 8, 2019).

14. Nicholas Davey, *Unquiet Understanding: Gadamer's Philosophical Hermeneutics* (Albany, NY: SUNY Press, 2006), 65.

15. Hans-Georg Gadamer, *Gadamer in Conversation: Reflections and Commentary*, ed. and trans. Richard E. Palmer (New Haven: Yale University Press, 2001), 71.

16. Gadamer, *Truth and Method*, 341.

17. Robinson, "Credo," 23.

18. On this, see Fred Lawrence, "Gadamer, the Hermeneutic Revolution, and Theology," in *The Cambridge Companion to Gadamer*, ed. Robert J. Dostal (Cambridge: Cambridge University Press, 2002), 167–200.

19. See Marilynne Robinson, "Wisdom and Light," *Christian Century* 129, no. 8 (April 18, 2012), 11–12; and *Gilead*, 242.

20. See John D. Caputo, *The Insistence of God: A Theology of Perhaps* (Bloomington: Indiana University Press, 2013), 74–76.

21. Let me note here that feminist responses to *Truth and Method* raise the question of just how open Gadamer is to multiple voices and perspectives. While embracing Gadamer's emphasis on partial and historically situated modes of knowledge and affirming his emphasis on how unacknowledged prejudice both reveals and distorts what we know, feminist theorists also explore which prejudices Gadamer is prepared to acknowledge (religious dogmatism, scientific empiricism, and Kantian subjectivity, among others), and which ones he prefers to ignore (historical privilege and the workings of power). On this, see Lorraine Code, "Introduction: Why Feminists Do Not Read Gadamer" and Veronica Vasterling, "Postmodern Hermeneutics? Toward a Critical Hermeneutics," in *Feminist Interpretations of Hans-Georg Gadamer*, ed. Lorraine Code (University Park, PA: Pennsylvania State University Press, 2003), 1–36 and 149–80. By contrast, Susan Hekman argues that Gadamer's theory of change in *Truth and Method* makes his hermeneutics more compatible with the goals of feminist theory than other strands of philosophical postmodernism. See her "The Ontology of Change: Gadamer and Feminism," in *Feminist Interpretations of Hans-Georg Gadamer*, 181–201.

22. Gadamer, *Truth and Method*, 100.

23. On the play of traces as a "bottomless chessboard," see Jacques Derrida, *Speech and Phenomena: And Other Essays on Husserl's Theory of Signs*, trans. David B. Allison (Evanston: Northwestern University Press, 1973), 154. As Niall Lucy points out, play is a prominent feature of Derrida's early work, especially after the 1967 publication of "Structure, Sign, and Play in the Discourse of the Human Sciences," but Derrida became less interested in play in his later writings, in part because of the way his notion of deconstructive freeplay (*le jeu*) was made to stand for Nietzschean "wildness" by American literary critics. On this, see Niall Lucy, *A Derrida Dictionary* (Malden, MA: Blackwell, 2004), 95–96; and Jacques Derrida, *Limited Inc*, trans. Samuel Weber and ed. Gerald Graff (Evanston: Northwestern University Press, 1988), 115–16.

24. Gadamer, *Truth and Method*, 274.

25. Gadamer, *Truth and Method*, 101.

26. Richard Rorty, *Consequences of Pragmatism: Essays, 1972–1980* (Minneapolis: University of Minnesota Press, 1982), 94. Gary B. Madison discusses this passage in "Beyond Seriousness and Frivolity: A Gadamerian Response to Deconstruction," in *Gadamer and Hermeneutics*, ed. Hugh J. Silverman (London: Routledge, 1991), 127.

27. On this, see Gadamer, *Truth and Method*, 262–63; and Davey, *Unquiet Understanding*, 11–12.

28. Let me mention here how this view differs from Amy Hungerford's work on postmodern belief. Hungerford's reading of *Gilead* is keyed to the notion of "home" not as a place but as a practice, especially a commitment to shared understanding that reconciles individual differences. Belief *is* this shared relationship for Hungerford, this coming together around a common purpose, rather than whatever propositional content about religious faith individual members of that fellowship may espouse: "Difference, then, is encompassed by the family sphere: radical unlikeness is comprehended by 'home.'" Literature enacts this reconciliation both as discourse, through the form of the novel, and as rhetoric, through the figure of the simile. Thus, "home" in Robinson encompasses difference by producing social and rhetorical *kinship*, which enacts a "contentless" form of religious belief: people working together toward mutual understanding under the same discursive roof (again, regardless of what they might actually say or think about God). As will become clear, I stress a contrasting theology of difference in *Gilead*, one in which radical unlikeness is not comprehended by anything and that even in the most transparent moments of kinship, the blessing in the Gilead bus station, for instance, a central scene in Hungerford's argument, difference delays and corrects comprehension, exposing its prejudice. This drives faith *forward*, toward an undisclosed future, rather than inward, toward a family circle. I follow Gadamer (and Thoreau) in arguing that understanding brings difference near, creating relationships of neighboring and proximity, but it does not comprehend or contain that difference, which is the incentive for our next attempt to understand. See Amy Hungerford, *Postmodern Belief: American Literature and Religion Since 1960* (Princeton: Princeton University Press, 2010), 107–21.

29. Marilynne Robinson, *The Death of Adam: Essays on Modern Thought* (1998; repr. New York: Picador, 2005), 228.

30. Henry D. Thoreau, *Walden*, ed. Jeffrey S. Cramer (New Haven: Yale University Press, 2006), 142.

31. Thoreau, *Walden*, 353.

32. Thoreau, *Walden*, 352.

33. Thoreau, *Walden*, 344.

34. Thoreau, *Walden*, 344.

35. Robinson, *The Death of Adam*, 230.

36. See Genesis 19:6-8 and Judges 11:1-40.

37. Although the phrase "nimble piety" sounds Dickinsonian and vaguely postmodern, Robinson discovers a source for this idea in Calvin's *Institutes*: "Manifold indeed is the nimbleness of the soul with which it surveys heaven and earth," Calvin writes, "joins past to future, retains in memory something heard long before, nay, pictures to itself whatever it pleases. Manifold also is the skill with which it devises things incredible, and which is the mother of so many marvelous devices." Such

nimbleness is not an obstacle to a life of faith, Calvin argues, but the very manifestation of God's creative freedom within human thought and imagination. In her Preface, Robinson applies Calvin's notion to "the aesthetics and the metaphysics of classical American literature" and offers a clear example of her own nimble thinking by ending an essay on Calvin with an allusion to Whitman and a quote from Thoreau. See her Preface to John Calvin, *Steward of God's Covenant: Selected Writings*, ed. John F. Thornton and Susan B. Varenne (New York: Vintage Books, 2006), xxiii, xxvii.

38. Gadamer's comments on historical understanding seem especially relevant to the temporal situation Robinson creates through Ames' letters: "The historical movement of human life consists in the fact that it is never utterly bound to any one standpoint, and hence can never have a truly closed horizon. The horizon is, rather, something into which we move and that moves with us. Horizons change for a person who is moving. Thus the horizon of the past, out of which all human life lives and which exists in the form of tradition, is always in motion. It is not historical consciousness that first sets the surrounding horizon in motion. But in it this motion becomes aware of itself." *Truth and Method*, 271.

39. Karl Barth, *The Epistle to the Romans*, trans. from the 6th edition by Edwyn C. Hoskyns (London: Oxford University Press, 1933), 1.

40. Gadamer develops the performative dimensions of play in "Play as the Clue to Ontological Explanation," in *Truth and Method*, 97–99, as well as in the final discussion of "The hermeneutic significance of temporal distance: "In fact our own prejudice is properly brought into play through its being at risk. Only through its being given full play is it able to experience the other's claim to truth and make it possible for he himself to have full play." *Truth and Method*, 266.

41. On theatrical metaphors in Calvin's thought and the performative character of theological reflection, see Belden C. Lane, "Spirituality as the Performance of Desire: Calvin on the World as a Theatre of God's Glory," *Spiritus* 1, no. 1 (Spring 2001): 1–30.

42. Thoreau, *Walden*, 145–46.

43. Gadamer, *Truth and Method*, 274.

44. Robinson, "Credo," 30.

45. Thoreau, *Walden*, 347.

46. Let me note here how the playful wisdom of *Gilead* differs from theories of art and play that stress the isolated subjectivity of the players, as in this passage about poetry as play from Johan Huizinga: "*Poiesis*, in fact, is a play-function. It proceeds within the play-ground of the mind, in a world of its own which the mind creates for it." See his *Homo Ludens: A Study of the Play-Element in Culture* (1950; repr. Mansfield Centre, CT: Martino Publishing, 2014), 119. *Gilead* moves in the opposite direction, as we've seen, not toward private playgrounds—the "little world" of the narcissistic imagination Thoreau satirizes or the dimmed world of traumatized self-protection Dickinson considers—but toward relationship, exposure, conversation, and hermeneutic risk. The mind doesn't create transformative play spaces. We need "Jack" for that.

47. Simone Weil, *Waiting for God*, trans. Emma Craufurd (1951; repr. New York: HarperPerennial, 2009), 114.

48. Weil, *Waiting for God*, 79.

Bibliography

Abbott, Philip. "Henry David Thoreau, the State of Nature, and the Redemption of Liberalism." *Journal of Politics* 47, no. 1 (1985): 182–208.
Adorno, Theodor W. *Essays on Music*. Edited by Richard Leppert; with new translations by Susan H. Gillespie. Berkeley: University of California Press, 2002.
——————. *Minima Moralia: Reflections from Damaged Life*. Translated by E. F. N. Jephcott. 1974. Reprint, London: Verso, 2005.
Ahlstrom, Sydney E. *A Religious History of the American People*. New Haven: Yale University Press, 1972.
Aho, Kevin. "Recovering Play: On the Relationship Between Leisure and Authenticity in Heidegger's Thought." *Janus Head* 10, no. 1 (2007): 217–38.
Albert OCSO, John. "Lights Across the Ridge: Thomas Merton and Henry David Thoreau." *The Merton Annual* 1 (1988): 271–317.
Altizer, Thomas J. J., and William Hamilton. *Radical Theology and the Death of God*. Indianapolis: Bobbs-Merrill, 1966.
Atchley, J. Heath. *Encountering the Secular: Philosophical Endeavors in Religion and Culture*. Charlottesville: University of Virginia Press, 2009.
——————. "Sounding the Depth of the Secular: Tillich with Thoreau." *Implicit Religion* 15, no. 2 (June 2012): 153–66.
Bakhtin, Mikhail. *The Dialogic Imagination: Four Essays*. Edited by Michael Holquist. Translated by Caryl Emerson and Michael Holquist. Austin: University of Texas Press, 1981.
——————. *Problems of Dostoevsky's Poetics*. Edited and translated by Caryl Emerson. Minneapolis: University of Minnesota Press, 1984.
Barbour, John D. *The Value of Solitude: The Ethics and Spirituality of Aloneness in Autobiography*. Charlottesville: University of Virginia Press, 2004.
Barth, Karl. *The Epistle to the Romans*. Translated from the 6th edition by Edwyn C. Hoskyns. London: Oxford University Press, 1933.
Bartnik, Ronald J. "Autobiographical Fiction: The Fusion of Art and Life in Henry David Thoreau's *Walden* and Jack Kerouac's *On the Road*." PhD diss., Kent State University, 1986.

Bates, Catherine. *Play in a Godless World: The Theory and Practice of Play in Shakespeare, Nietzsche and Freud*. London: Open Gate, 1999.

Bateson, Gregory. "The Message 'This is Play.'" In *Group Process: Transactions of the Second Conference*. Edited by Bertram Schaffner, 145–243. New York: Josiah Macy, Jr. Foundation, 1955.

———. *A Sacred Unity: Further Steps to an Ecology of Mind*. Edited by Rodney E. Donaldson. New York: Cornelia and Michael Bessie Book, 1991.

———. *Steps to an Ecology of Mind*. 1972. Reprint, Chicago: University of Chicago Press, 2000.

Bateson, Gregory, and Mary Catherine Bateson. *Angels Fear: Towards an Epistemology of the Sacred*. Toronto: Bantam, 1988.

Beck, Guy L. *Sonic Theology: Hinduism and Sacred Sound*. Columbia: University of South Carolina Press, 1993.

Begbie, Jeremy S. *Theology, Music and Time*. Cambridge: Cambridge University Press, 2000.

Belgrad, Daniel. *The Culture of Spontaneity: Improvisation and the Arts in Postwar America*. Chicago: University of Chicago Press, 1998.

Benson, Bruce Ellis. *The Improvisation of Musical Dialogue: A Phenomenology of Music*. Cambridge: Cambridge University Press, 2003.

———. "Improvising Texts, Improvising Communities: Jazz, Interpretation, Heterophony, and the *Ekklēsia*." In *Resonant Witness: Conversations Between Music and Theology*. Edited by Jeremy S. Begbie and Stephen R. Guthrie, 295–319. Grand Rapids: Eerdmans, 2011.

The Bhagavad Gita. Translated by Eknath Easwaran. Tomales, CA: Nilgiri Press, 1985, 2007.

Bhagvat-geeta; or Dialogues of Kreeshna and Arjoon. Translated by Charles Wilkins. London [n.p.], 1785.

Blake, William. *Letters of William Blake*. Edited by Geoffrey Keynes. New York: MacMillan, 1956.

Boudreau, Gordon V. *The Roots of "Walden" and the Tree of Life*. Nashville: Vanderbilt University Press, 1990.

Breitwieser, Mitchell Robert. "*Walden* and the Spirit of Capitalism: Presence, Damage, and Cultural Revival." Unpublished manuscript, last modified February 24, 2020. Microsoft Word file.

Brennan, Teresa. "'The Contexts of Vision' from a Specific Standpoint." In *Vision in Context: Historical and Contemporary Perspectives on Sight*. Edited by Teresa Brennan and Martin Jay, 217–30. New York: Routledge, 1996.

Bridgman, Richard. *Dark Thoreau*. Lincoln: University of Nebraska Press, 1982.

Brown, David. *God and Grace of Body: Sacrament in Ordinary*. New York: Oxford University Press, 2007.

Brueggemann, Walter. *Reverberations of Faith: A Theological Handbook of Old Testament Themes*. Louisville: Westminster John Knox Press, 2002.

———. *Theology of the Old Testament: Testimony, Dispute, Advocacy*. Minneapolis: Fortress Press, 1997.

Buranelli, Vincent. "The Case Against Thoreau." *Ethics* 76, no. 4 (1957): 257–68.

Burke, Kenneth. *The Philosophy of Literary Form: Studies in Symbolic Action.* Berkeley: University of California Press, 1973.

Caillois, Roger. *Man, Play and Games.* Translated by Meyer Barash. 1961. Reprint, Urbana, IL: University of Illinois Press, 2001.

Calasso, Roberto. *Literature and the Gods.* Translated by Tim Parks. New York: Vintage, 2001.

Caputo, John D. *The Folly of God: A Theology of the Unconditional.* Salem, OR: Polebridge Press, 2016.

——. *The Insistence of God: A Theology of Perhaps.* Bloomington: Indiana University Press, 2013.

——. *Radical Hermeneutics: Repetition, Deconstruction, and the Hermeneutic Project.* Bloomington: Indiana University Press, 1987.

Cavell, Stanley. *In Quest of the Ordinary: Lines of Skepticism and Romanticism.* Chicago: University of Chicago Press, 1988.

——. *The Senses of Walden.* Expanded Edition. Chicago: University of Chicago Press, 1992.

Chénetier, Marc. "Tinkering, Extravagance: Thoreau, Melville, and Annie Dillard." *Critique: Studies in Contemporary Fiction* 31, no. 3 (Spring 1990): 157–72.

Christy, Arthur. *The Orient in American Transcendentalism: A Study of Emerson, Thoreau, and Alcott.* 1932. Reprint, New York: Octagon Books, 1972.

Cochoy, Nathalie. "The Imprint of the 'Now' on the Skin of Discourse: Annie Dillard's *Pilgrim at Tinker Creek*." *Revue Française d'Études Américaines* 106 (December 2005): 33–49.

Code, Lorraine, ed. *Feminist Interpretations of Hans-Georg Gadamer.* University Park, PA: Pennsylvania State University Press, 2003.

Connolly, William E. *Identity\Difference: Democratic Negotiations of Political Paradox.* Ithaca: Cornell University Press, 1991.

Coomaraswamy, Ananda K. "Līlā." *Journal of the American Oriental Society* 61, no. 2 (June 1941): 98–101.

——. "Play and Seriousness." *The Journal of Philosophy* 39, no. 20 (September 24, 1942): 550–52.

Cooper, David D. *Thomas Merton's Art of Denial: The Evolution of a Radical Humanist.* Athens: University of Georgia Press, 1989.

Cox, Harvey. *The Feast of Fools: A Theological Essay on Festivity and Fantasy.* Cambridge: Harvard University Press, 1969.

Craig, Megan. "The Infinite in Person: Levinas and Dickinson." In *Emily Dickinson and Philosophy.* Edited by Jed Deppman, Marianne Noble, and Gary Lee Stonum, 207–26. New York: Cambridge University Press, 2013.

Crawford, Nathan. *Theology as Improvisation: A Study in the Musical Nature of Theological Thinking.* Leiden: Brill, 2013.

Dandurand, Karen. "New Dickinson Civil War Publications." *American Literature* 56, no. 1 (March 1984): 17–27.

Darwin, Charles. *The Expression of the Emotions in Man and Animals.* 3rd ed. New York: Oxford University Press, 1998.

Davey, Nicholas. "Gadamer's Aesthetics." *The Stanford Encyclopedia of Philosophy*. Edited by Edward N. Zalta (Winter 2016), https://plato.stanford.edu/archives/win2016/entries/gadamer-aesthetics/.html (accessed November 8, 2019).

———. *Unquiet Understanding: Gadamer's Philosophical Hermeneutics*. Albany, NY: SUNY Press, 2006.

DeKoven, Marianne. *Utopia Limited: The Sixties and the Emergence of the Postmodern*. Durham: Duke University Press, 2004.

Deleuze, Gilles. *Difference and Repetition*. Translated by Paul Patton. New York: Columbia University Press, 1994.

Deppman, Jed. *Trying to Think with Emily Dickinson*. Amherst: University of Massachusetts Press, 2008.

Derrida, Jacques. *Limited Inc*. Translated by Samuel Weber. Edited by Gerald Graff. 1977. Reprint, Evanston: Northwestern University Press, 1988.

———. *Speech and Phenomena: And Other Essays on Husserl's Theory of Signs*. Translated by David B. Allison. Evanston: Northwestern University Press, 1973.

Detweiler, Robert. *Breaking the Fall: Religious Readings of Contemporary Fiction*. New York: Harper and Row, 1989.

Dickinson, Emily. *The Letters of Emily Dickinson*. Edited by Thomas H. Johnson. 3 vols. Cambridge: Harvard University Press, 1958.

———. *The Poems of Emily Dickinson*. Edited by R. W. Franklin. Cambridge: Harvard University Press, 1999.

Dillard, Annie. *For the Time Being*. New York: Vintage, 2000.

———. *Holy the Firm*. New York: Harper and Row, 1977.

———. "The Merchant of the Picturesque: One Pattern in Emily Dickinson's Poetry." *The Hollins Symposium: An Undergraduate Learned Journal* 3, no. 1 (May 1967): 33–42.

———. *Pilgrim at Tinker Creek*. 1974. Reprint, New York: HarperPerennial, 2007.

———. "Walden Pond and Thoreau." Master's thesis, Hollins College, 1968.

Doriani, Beth Maclay. *Emily Dickinson: Daughter of Prophecy*. Amherst: University of Massachusetts Press, 1996.

Ellwood, Robert S. *The Sixties Spiritual Awakening: American Religion Moving from Modern to Postmodern*. New Brunswick, NJ: Rutgers University Press, 1994.

Emerson, Ralph Waldo. *Ralph Waldo Emerson: Essays and Lectures*. Edited by Joel Porte. New York: Library of America, 1983.

Erikson, Erik H. *Childhood and Society*. 2nd ed. New York: Norton, 1963.

Evans, James H., Jr. *Playing*. Minneapolis: Fortress Press, 2010.

Evans, Justin. "Subjectivity and the Possibility of Change in the Novels of Marilynne Robinson." *Renascence* 66, no. 2 (Spring 2014): 131–50.

Farcé, Gilles. "Different Drummers: Thomas Merton and Henry Thoreau." *The Merton Seasonal* 10, no. 2 (1985): 2–6.

Fishbane, Michael. *Sacred Attunement: A Jewish Theology*. Chicago: University of Chicago Press, 2008.

Fitzgerald, F. Scott. *The Great Gatsby*. 1925. Reprint, New York: Scribner, 2004.

Foxe, Gladys. "'And Nobody Knows What's Going to Happen to Anybody': Fear and Futility in Jack Kerouac's *On the Road* and Why It Is Important." *Psychoanalytic Review* 95, no. 1 (February 2008): 45–60.
Freedman, Linda. *Emily Dickinson and the Religious Imagination*. Cambridge: Cambridge University Press, 2011.
Freud, Sigmund. *Beyond the Pleasure Principle*. Translated and edited by James Strachey. New York: Norton, 1961.
Frost, Anthony, and Ralph Yarrow. *Improvisation in Drama*. Basingstoke: Macmillan Education, 1990.
Gadamer, Hans-Georg. *Gadamer in Conversation: Reflections and Commentary*. Edited and translated by Richard E. Palmer. New Haven: Yale University Press, 2001.
———. *The Relevance of the Beautiful and Other Essays*. Translated by Nicholas Walker. Edited by Robert Bernasconi. Cambridge: Cambridge University Press, 1986.
———. *Truth and Method*. Translation edited by Garrett Barden and John Cumming. New York: Seabury Press, 1975.
Garber, Frederick. *Thoreau's Redemptive Imagination*. New York: NYU Press, 1977.
Gardner, Thomas. *A Door Ajar: Contemporary Writers and Emily Dickinson*. New York: Oxford University Press, 2006.
———. "Keeping Perception Nimble." *Christianity Today* 54, no. 2 (February 2010): 32–35.
Geertz, Clifford. "Common Sense as a Cultural System." 1975. Reprint, *The Antioch Review* 67, no. 4 (Fall 2009): 770–90.
Gewirtz, Isaac. *Beatific Soul: Jack Kerouac on the Road*. New York: The New York Public Library; London, in association with Scala Publishers, 2007.
Gill, Sam D. *Dancing Culture Religion*. Lanham, MD: Lexington Books, 2012.
Ginsberg, Allen. *Howl*. In *The Portable Beat Reader*. Edited by Ann Charters, 62–71. New York: Penguin, 1992.
Gioia, Ted. *The Imperfect Art: Reflections on Jazz and Modern Culture*. New York: Oxford University Press, 1988.
Gleason, William A. *The Leisure Ethic: Work and Play in American Literature, 1840–1940*. Stanford: Stanford University Press, 1999.
Goffman, Erving. "Embarrassment and Social Organization." *American Journal of Sociology* 62, no. 3 (November 1956): 264–71.
Guardini, Romano. *The Church and the Catholic and the Spirit of Liturgy*. Translated by Ada Lane. New York: Sheed and Ward, 1953.
Habegger, Alfred. *My Wars Are Laid Away in Books: The Life of Emily Dickinson*. New York: Random House, 2001.
Haddox, Thomas F. *Hard Sayings: The Rhetoric of Christian Orthodoxy in Late Modern Fiction*. Columbus: Ohio State University Press, 2013.
Hammond, Karla M. "Drawing the Curtains: An Interview with Annie Dillard." *Bennington Review* 10 (April 1981): 30–38.
Harding, Walter. *The Days of Henry Thoreau: A Biography*. 2nd ed. New York: Dover, 1982.

The Harivamsha. Translated by Manmatha Nath Dutt. Calcutta: Elysium Press, 1897.
The Harper American Literature. 2nd ed. New York: Harper and Row, 1987.
Heidegger, Martin. *Poetry, Language, Thought*. Translated by Albert Hofstadter. 1971. Reprint, New York: HarperPerennial, 2013.
———. *The Question Concerning Technology and Other Essays*. Translated by William Lovitt. 1977. Reprint, New York: HarperPerennial, 2013.
Hein, Norvin. "Līlā." In *The Gods at Play: Līlā in South Asia*. Edited by William S. Sax, 13–20. New York: Oxford University Press, 1995.
———. "A Revolution in Kṛṣṇaism: The Cult of Gopāla." *History of Religions* 25, no. 4 (May 1986): 296–317.
Henricks, Thomas S. *Play and the Human Condition*. Urbana: University of Illinois Press, 2015.
Herberg, Will. *Protestant, Catholic, Jew: An Essay in American Religious Sociology*. 1955. Reprint, Garden City, NY: Anchor Books, 1960.
Heydt, Jim von der. "'Perfect from the Pod': Instant Learning in Dickinson and Kierkegaard." In *Emily Dickinson and Philosophy*. Edited by Jed Deppman, Marianne Noble, and Gary Lee Stonum, 105–28. New York: Cambridge University Press, 2013.
Hodder, Alan D. "Concord Orientalism, Thoreauvian Autobiography, and the Artist of Kouroo." In *Transient and Permanent: The Transcendentalist Movement and Its Contexts*. Edited by Charles Capper and Conrad Edick Wright, 190–228. Boston: Massachusetts Historical Society, 1999.
———. "'Ex Oriente Lux': Thoreau's Ecstasies and the Hindu Texts." *Harvard Theological Review* 86, no. 4 (October 1993): 403–38.
———. "The Gospel According to this Moment: Thoreau, Wildness, and American Nature Religion." *Religion and the Arts* 15, no. 4 (2011): 460–85.
———. "In the Nick of Time: Thoreau's 'Present' Experiment as a Colloquy of East and West." *Religion and the Arts* 9, nos. 3–4 (2005): 235–57.
———. *Thoreau's Ecstatic Witness*. New Haven: Yale University Press, 2001.
Holladay, Hilary. "Parallel Destinies in *The Bell Jar* and *On the Road*." In *What's Your Road, Man? Critical Essays on Jack Kerouac's "On the Road."* Edited by Hilary Holladay and Robert Holton, 99–117. Carbondale: Southern Illinois University Press, 2009.
Holmes, John Clellon. *The Horn*. New York: Random, 1958.
Holton, Robert. "Kerouac Among the Fellahin: *On the Road* to the Postmodern." *Modern Fiction Studies* 41, no. 2 (Summer 1995): 265–83.
Hopkins, Gerard Manley. *Poems and Prose of Gerard Manley Hopkins*. Edited by W. H. Gardner. 1953. Reprint, London: Penguin, 1985.
Huizinga, Johan. *Homo Ludens: A Study of the Play-Element in Culture*. 1950. Reprint, Mansfield Centre, CT: Martino Publishing, 2014.
Hungerford, Amy. *Postmodern Belief: American Literature and Religion Since 1960*. Princeton: Princeton University Press, 2010.
Hutcheon, Linda. *The Politics of Postmodernism*. London: Routledge, 1989.

Ireland, Julia A. "Annie Dillard's Ecstatic Phenomenology." *Interdisciplinary Studies in Literature and Environment* 17, no. 1 (Winter 2010): 23–34.
Jackson, Carl T. *The Oriental Religions and American Thought: Nineteenth-Century Explorations*. Westport, CT: Greenwood Press, 1981.
James, William. *The Varieties of Religious Experience*: *A Study in Human Nature*. Edited by Martin E. Marty. 1902. Reprint, Harmondsworth, Middlesex: Penguin, 1987.
Jay, Martin. *The Dialectical Imagination: A History of the Frankfurt School and the Institute of Social Research, 1923–1950*. Boston: Little Brown, 1973.
Joyce, James. *Finnegans Wake*. 1939. Reprint, New York: Viking, 1976.
Juhasz, Suzanne, Cristanne Miller, and Martha Nell Smith. *Comic Power in Emily Dickinson*. Austin: University of Texas Press, 1993.
Kearney, Richard. *The God Who May Be*: *A Hermeneutics of Religion*. Bloomington: Indiana University Press, 2001.
——————. *Strangers, Gods and Monsters: Interpreting Otherness*. London: Routledge, 2003.
Keller, Karl. *The Only Kangaroo Among the Beauty: Emily Dickinson and America*. Baltimore: Johns Hopkins University Press, 1979.
Kerouac, Jack. "Essentials of Spontaneous Prose." In *The Portable Beat Reader*. Edited by Ann Charters, 57–58. New York: Penguin, 1992.
——————. *Jack Kerouac: Selected Letters, 1940–1956*. Edited by Ann Charters. New York: Viking, 1995.
——————. "Letters from Jack Kerouac to Ed White, 1947–68." *The Missouri Review* 17, no. 13 (Nov. 3, 1994): 107–60.
——————. *On the Road*. 1957. Reprint, New York: Penguin, 2003.
——————. *The Subterraneans*. New York: Grove Press, 1958.
——————. *Vanity of Duluoz: An Adventurous Education, 1935–46*. 1968. Reprint, New York: Penguin, 1994.
——————. *Visions of Cody*. New York: Penguin, 1972.
Kilcourse, George. *Ace of Freedoms: Thomas Merton's Christ*. Notre Dame: University of Notre Dame Press, 1993.
Kinsley, David R. *The Divine Player: A Study of Kṛṣṇa Līlā*. Delhi: Motilal Banarsidass, 1979.
Krondorfer, Bjorn. "Play Theology as a Discourse of Disguise." *Journal of Literature and Theology* 7, no. 4 (December 1993): 365–80.
Kronick, Joseph G. *American Poetics of History: From Emerson to the Moderns*. Baton Rouge: Louisiana State University Press, 1984.
Labrie, Ross. *The Art of Thomas Merton*. Fort Worth: Texas Christian University Press, 1979.
——————. "Merton and the American Romantics." *The Merton Annual* 9 (1996): 34–54.
Lane, Belden C. "Merton as Zen Clown." *Theology Today* 46, no. 3 (October 1989): 256–68.
——————. "Merton's Hermitage: Bachelard, Domestic Space, and Spiritual Transformation." *Spiritus* 4, no. 2 (Fall 2004): 123–50.

———. "Spirituality as the Performance of Desire: Calvin on the World as a Theatre of God's Glory." *Spiritus* 1, no. 1 (Spring 2001): 1–30.
Lawrence, Fred. "Gadamer, the Hermeneutic Revolution, and Theology." In *The Cambridge Companion to Gadamer*. Edited by Robert J. Dostal, 167–200. Cambridge: Cambridge University Press, 2002.
The Laws of Manu. Translated by Wendy Doniger with Brian K. Smith. New York: Penguin, 1991.
Leise, Christopher. "'That Little Incandescence': Reading the Fragmentary and John Calvin in Marilynne Robinson's *Gilead*." *Studies in the Novel* 41, no. 3 (Fall 2009): 348–67.
Leland, John. *Why Kerouac Matters: The Lessons of "On the Road."* New York: Penguin, 2007.
Lucy, Niall. *A Derrida Dictionary*. Malden, MA: Blackwell, 2004.
MacIntyre, Alasdair. *Herbert Marcuse: An Exposition and a Polemic*. New York: Viking Press, 1970.
Mack, Stephen John. *The Pragmatic Whitman: Reimagining American Democracy*. Iowa City: University of Iowa Press, 2002.
MacKendrick, Karmen. *Word Made Skin: Figuring Language at the Surface of Flesh*. New York: Fordham University Press, 2004.
MacKethan, Lucinda H. *Daughters of Time: Creating Woman's Voice in Southern Story*. Athens: University of Georgia Press, 1990.
Madison, Gary B. "Beyond Seriousness and Frivolity: A Gadamerian Response to Deconstruction." In *Gadamer and Hermeneutics*. Edited by Hugh J. Silverman, 119–35. London: Routledge, 1991.
Manoussakis, John Panteleimon. *God After Metaphysics: A Theological Aesthetic*. Bloomington: Indiana University Press, 2007.
Marcuse, Herbert. *One-Dimensional Man: Studies in the Ideology of Advanced Industrial Society*. 2nd ed. Boston: Beacon Press, 1991.
McClure, John A. *Partial Faiths: Postsecular Fiction in the Age of Pynchon and Morrison*. Athens: The University of Georgia Press, 2007.
McConahay, Mary Davidson. "'Into the Bladelike Arms of God': The Quest for Meaning through Symbolic Language in Thoreau and Annie Dillard." *Denver Quarterly* 20, no. 2 (Fall 1985): 103–16.
McFadyen, Alistair I. *The Call to Personhood: A Christian Theory of the Individual in Social Relationships*. Cambridge: Cambridge University Press, 1990.
McGregor, Robert Kuhn. "Henry David Thoreau: The Asian Thread." In *Thoreau's Importance for Philosophy*. Edited by Rick Anthony Furtak, Jonathan Ellsworth, and James D. Reid, 201–17. New York: Fordham University Press, 2012.
McIlroy, Gary. "*Pilgrim at Tinker Creek* and the Social Legacy of *Walden*." *South Atlantic Quarterly* 85, no. 2 (Spring 1986): 111–22.
McIntosh, James. *Nimble Believing: Dickinson and the Unknown*. Ann Arbor: University of Michigan Press, 2004.
———. *Thoreau as Romantic Naturalist: His Shifting Stance Toward Nature*. Ithaca: Cornell University Press, 1974.

Mendelson, Donna. "Tinker Creek and the Waters of *Walden*: Thoreauvian Currents in Annie Dillard's *Pilgrim*." *The Concord Saunterer* 3 (Fall 1995): 50–62.
Merton, Thomas. *The Asian Journal of Thomas Merton*. Edited by Naomi Burton, Patrick Hart, and James Laughlin. New York: New Directions, 1973.
———. The Behavior of Titans. New York: New Directions, 1961.
———. *Cables to the Ace; or, Familiar Liturgies of Misunderstanding*. New York: New Directions, 1968.
———. *Cold War Letters*. Edited by Christine M. Bochen and William H. Shannon. Maryknoll, NY: Orbis Books, 2006.
———. *Conjectures of a Guilty Bystander*. Garden City, NY: Image Books, 1968.
———. *Disputed Questions*. New York: Farrar, Straus and Cudahy, 1960.
———. *Emblems of a Season of Fury*. New York: New Directions, 1963.
———. *The Intimate Merton: His Life from His Journals*. Edited by Patrick Hart and Jonathan Montaldo. San Francisco: HarperOne, 1999.
———. *An Introduction to Christian Mysticism: Initiation into the Monastic Tradition 3*. Edited by Patrick F. O'Connell. Kalamazoo: Cistercian Publications, 2008.
———. *The Literary Essays of Thomas Merton*. Edited by Patrick Hart. New York: New Directions, 1981.
———. *Raids on the Unspeakable*. New York: New Directions, 1966.
Merton, Thomas, and Robert Lax. *A Catch of Anti-Letters*. Mission, KS: Sheed and Ward, 1994.
Meyer, Leonard B. *Emotion and Meaning in Music*. Chicago: University of Chicago Press, 1956.
Milder, Robert. *Reimagining Thoreau*. Cambridge: Cambridge University Press, 1995.
Miller, Perry. *Consciousness in Concord: The Text of Thoreau's Hitherto "Lost Journal" (1840–1841) Together with Notes and a Commentary*. Boston: Houghton Mifflin, 1958.
Mitchell, Domhnall. *Emily Dickinson and the Limits and Possibilities of Critical Judgment*. PhD diss., Trinity College, Dublin, 1989.
Moldenhauer, Joseph J. "The Extra-Vagant Maneuver: Paradox in *Walden*." In *Critical Essays on Henry David Thoreau's "Walden."* Edited by Joel Myerson, 96–106. Boston: G. K. Hall, 1988.
Moltmann, Jürgen. *Theology of Play*. Translated by Reinhard Ulrich. New York: Harper and Row, 1972.
Monson, Ingrid. *Saying Something: Jazz Improvisation and Interaction*. Chicago: University of Chicago Press, 1996.
Moser, Paul K. *The Elusive God: Reorienting Religious Epistemology*. New York: Cambridge University Press, 2008.
Nachmanovitch, Stephen. *Free Play: Improvisation in Life and Art*. New York: Jeremy P. Tarcher/Putnam, 1990.
———. "This is Play." *New Literary History* 40, no. 1 (Winter 2009): 1–24.
Nagatomo, Shigenori. *Attunement Through the Body*. Albany: SUNY Press, 1992.

Nancy, Jean-Luc. *Listening*. Translated by Charlotte Mandell. New York: Fordham University Press, 2007.

Neale, Robert E. *In Praise of Play: Toward a Psychology of Religion*. New York: Harper and Row, 1969.

New, Elisa. *New England Beyond Criticism: In Defense of America's First Literature*. Chichester, West Sussex: Wiley Blackwell, 2014.

Nicosia, Gerald. *Memory Babe: A Critical Biography of Jack Kerouac*. 1983. Reprint, Berkeley: University of California Press, 1994.

O'Connell, Patrick F. "Keeping Pace With His Companion: Thomas Merton and Henry Thoreau." *The Concord Saunterer* N. S. 7 (1999): 115–48.

Oberhaus, Dorothy Huff. "Dickinson as a Comic Poet." In *Approaches to Teaching Dickinson's Poetry*. Edited by Robin Riley Fast and Christine Mack Gordon, 118–23. New York: MLA, 1989.

Oriard, Michael. *Sporting with the Gods: The Rhetoric of Play and Game in American Culture*. Cambridge: Cambridge University Press, 1991.

Panikkar, Raimon. *The Rhythm of Being: The Unbroken Trinity*. Maryknoll, NY: Orbis, 2013.

Panish, Jon. "Kerouac's *The Subterraneans*: A Study of 'Romantic Primitivism.'" *MELUS* 19, no. 3 (Fall 1994): 107–23.

Papa, James A., Jr. "Paradox and Perception: Science and Narrative in *Walden* and *Pilgrim at Tinker Creek*." *Weber Studies: An Interdisciplinary Humanities Journal* 14, no. 3 (Fall 1997): 105–14.

Parrish, Nancy C. *Lee Smith, Annie Dillard, and the Hollins Group: A Genesis of Writers*. Baton Rouge: Louisiana State University Press, 1998.

Paul, Sherman. *The Shores of America: Thoreau's Inward Exploration*. New York: Russell and Russell, 1958.

———. "The Wise Silence: Sound as the Agency of Correspondence in Thoreau." *New England Quarterly* 22, no. 4 (December 1949): 511–27.

Perls, Frederick, Ralph F. Hefferline, and Paul Goodman. *Gestalt Therapy: Excitement and Growth in the Human Personality*. New York: Delta, 1951.

Phillips, Rod. *"Forest Beatniks" and "Urban Thoreaus": Gary Snyder, Jack Kerouac, Lew Welch, and Michael McClure*. New York: P. Lang, 2000.

Poetzsch, Markus. "Sounding Walden Pond: The Depths and 'Double Shadows' of Thoreau's Autobiographical Symbol." *American Transcendental Quarterly* 22, no. 2 (June 2008): 387–401.

Pramuk, Christopher. *Sophia: The Hidden Christ of Thomas Merton*. Collegeville, MN: Liturgical Press, 2009.

Prothero, Stephen R. "On the Holy Road: The Beat Movement as Spiritual Protest." *Harvard Theological Review* 84, no. 2 (1991): 205–22.

Rahner, Hugo. *Man at Play*. Translated by Brian Battershaw and Edward Quinn. New York: Herder and Herder, 1967.

Raj, Selva J., and Corinne G. Dempsey, eds. *Sacred Play: Ritual Levity and Humor in South Asian Religions*. Albany: SUNY Press, 2010.

Ray, Robert B. *Walden x 40: Essays on Thoreau*. Bloomington: Indiana University Press, 2012.

Reimer, Margaret Loewen. "The Dialectical Vision of Annie Dillard's *Pilgrim at Tinker Creek*." *Critique: Studies in Contemporary Fiction* 24, no. 3 (Spring 1983): 182–91.
Rhoads, Kenneth W. "Thoreau: The Ear and the Music." *American Literature* 46, no. 3 (November 1974): 313–28.
Richardson, Mark. "Peasant Dreams: Reading *On the Road*." *Texas Studies in Literature and Language* 43, no. 2 (2001): 207–31.
Ricks, Christopher. *Keats and Embarrassment*. Oxford: Clarendon Press, 1974.
Ricœur, Paul. *Figuring the Sacred: Religion, Narrative, and Imagination*. Translated by David Pellauer. Edited by Mark I. Wallace. Minneapolis: Fortress Press, 1995, 2006.
Robinson, Marilynne. "Credo." *Harvard Divinity Bulletin* 36, no. 2 (Spring 2008): 22–32.
———. *The Death of Adam: Essays on Modern Thought*. 1998. Reprint, New York: Picador, 2005.
———. *Gilead*. New York: Farrar, Straus and Giroux, 2004.
———. *Lila*. New York: Farrar, Straus and Giroux, 2014.
———. Marilynne Robinson Papers. Yale Collection of American Literature, Beinecke Rare Book and Manuscript Library.
———. Preface to *Steward of God's Covenant: Selected Writings*, by John Calvin. Edited by John F. Thornton and Susan B. Varenne, ix–xxvii. New York: Vintage Books, 2006.
———. "Risk the Game: On William James." *The Nation*, November 23, 2010, https://www.thenation.com/article/archive/risk-game-william-james/html (accessed April 12, 2018).
———. "Wisdom and Light." *Christian Century* 129, no. 8 (April 18, 2012): 11–12.
Rorty, Richard. *Consequences of Pragmatism: Essays, 1972–1980*. Minneapolis: University of Minnesota Press, 1982.
Rorty, Richard, and Gianni Vattimo. *The Future of Religion*. Edited by Santiago Zabala. New York: Columbia University Press, 2005.
Saward, John. *Perfect Fools: Folly for Christ's Sake in Catholic and Orthodox Spirituality*. Oxford: Oxford University Press, 1980.
Sax, William S, ed. *The Gods at Play: Līlā in South Asia*. New York: Oxford University Press, 1995.
Schaub, Thomas. "An Interview with Marilynne Robinson." *Contemporary Literature* 35, no. 2 (1994): 231–51.
Schechner, Richard. "Playing." *Play and Culture* 1 (1988): 3–19.
Schiller, Friedrich. *On the Aesthetic Education of Man*. Translated by Reginald Snell. 1954. Reprint, Mineola, NY: Dover, 2004.
Schmidt, Leigh Eric. *Restless Souls: The Making of American Spirituality*. 2nd ed. Berkeley: University of California Press, 2005, 2012.
Schwartzman, Helen B. *Transformations: The Anthropology of Children's Play*. New York: Plenum, 1978.

Scott, David. "Rewalking Thoreau and Asia: 'Light from the East' for 'A Very Yankee Sort of Oriental.'" *Philosophy East and West* 57, no. 1 (January 2007): 14–39.

Sheets-Johnstone, Maxine. *The Primacy of Movement*. Amsterdam: John Benjamins, 1999.

Shepherd, Victor. "Review of *Theology, Music and Time*." *International Journal of Systematic Theology* 5, no. 2 (July 2003): 241–47.

Shoop, Marcia W. Mount. *Let the Bones Dance: Embodiment and the Body of Christ*. Louisville: Westminster John Knox Press, 2010.

Shy, Todd. "Religion and Marilynne Robinson." *Salmagundi* 155/156 (Summer–Fall 2007): 251–64.

Smith, R. J. *The Great Black Way: L.A. in the 1940s and the Lost African-American Renaissance*. New York: PublicAffairs, 2006.

Snyder, Gary. *No Nature: New and Selected Poems*. New York: Pantheon, 1992.

Springer, Marlene. "Emily Dickinson's Humorous Road to Heaven." *Renascence* 23 (1971): 129–36.

Stewart, Susan. *Nonsense: Aspects of Intertextuality in Folklore and Literature*. 1978. Reprint, Baltimore: Johns Hopkins University Press, 1989.

Stonum, Gary Lee. "Dickinson's Literary Background." In *The Emily Dickinson Handbook*. Edited by Gudrun Grabher, Roland Hagenbüchle, and Cristanne Miller, 44–60. Amherst: University of Massachusetts Press, 1998.

Sutton-Smith, Brian. *The Ambiguity of Play*. Cambridge: Harvard University Press, 1997, 2001.

Suurmond, Jean-Jacques. *Word and Spirit at Play: Towards a Charismatic Theology*. Translated by John Bowden. Grand Rapids: Eerdmans, 1995.

Theado, Matt. "Revisions of Kerouac: The Long, Strange Trip of the *On the Road* Typescripts." In *What's Your Road, Man? Critical Essays on Jack Kerouac's "On the Road*." Edited by Hilary Holladay and Robert Holton, 8–34. Carbondale: Southern Illinois University Press, 2009.

Thoreau, Henry David. *The Higher Law: Thoreau on Civil Disobedience and Reform*. Edited by Wendell Glick. Princeton: Princeton University Press, 2004.

———. *The Journal of Henry D. Thoreau*. 8 vols. to date. Princeton: Princeton University Press, 1981-.

———. *Letters to a Spiritual Seeker*. Edited by Bradley P. Dean. New York: Norton, 2004.

———. *Walden*. Edited by Jeffrey S. Cramer. New Haven: Yale University Press, 2006.

———. "Walking," In *Walden and Other Writings of Henry David Thoreau*. Edited by Brooks Atkinson, 627–63. New York: Modern Library, 1992.

———. *A Week on the Concord and Merrimack Rivers*. Edited by H. Daniel Peck. New York: Penguin, 1998.

———. *The Writings of Henry David Thoreau*. 20 vols. 1906. Reprint, New York: AMS Press, 1968.

Tippett, Krista. *Speaking of Faith*. New York: Viking, 2007.

Turner, Victor. *The Anthropology of Performance*. New York: PAJ Publications, 1986.

———. "Body, Brain, and Culture." *Zygon* 18, no. 3 (September 1983): 221–45.

Tursi, Renée. "Emily Dickinson, Pragmatism, and the Conquests of Mind." In *Emily Dickinson and Philosophy*. Edited by Jed Deppman, Marianne Noble, and Gary Lee Stonum, 151–74. New York: Cambridge University Press, 2013.

Tytell, John. *Naked Angels: Kerouac, Ginsberg, Burroughs*. New York: Grove Press, 1976.

The Upanishads. Translated by Eknath Easwaran. Tomales, CA: Nilgiri Press, 2007.

Vattimo, Gianni. *Belief*. Translated by Luca D'Isanto and David Webb. Stanford: Stanford University Press, 1999.

Versluis, Arthur. *American Transcendentalism and Asian Religions*. New York: Oxford University Press, 1993.

Vilhauer, Monica. *Gadamer's Ethics of Play: Hermeneutics and the Other*. Lanham, MD: Lexington Books, 2010.

The Vishnu Purāna: A System of Hindu Mythology and Tradition. Translated by H. H. Wilson. 1840. Reprint, Calcutta: Punthi Pustak, 1972.

Walker, Nancy. "Emily Dickinson and the Self: Humor as Identity." *Tulsa Studies in Women's Literature* 2, no. 1 (Spring 1983): 57–68.

Walls, Laura Dassow. *Henry David Thoreau: A Life*. Chicago: University of Chicago Press, 2017.

Warren, Colleen. *Annie Dillard and the Word Made Flesh: An Incarnational Theory of Language*. Bethlehem, PA: Lehigh University Press, 2010.

Webb, Stephen H. *Blessed Excess: Religion and the Hyperbolic Imagination*. Albany: SUNY Press, 1993.

———. "Nature's Spendthrift Economy: The Extravagance of God in *Pilgrim at Tinker Creek*." *Soundings* 77, nos. 3–4 (Fall/Winter 1994): 429–51.

Weil, Simone. *Waiting for God*. Translated by Emma Craufurd. 1951. Reprint, New York: HarperPerennial, 2009.

Welty, Eudora. "Meditation on Seeing." *New York Times On the Web*, March 24, 1974, https://archive.nytimes.com/www.nytimes.com/books/99/03/28/specials/dillard-tinker.html (accessed September 19, 2018).

West, Michael. "Scatology and Eschatology: The Heroic Dimensions of Thoreau's Wordplay." *PMLA* 89, no. 5 (October 1974): 1043–64.

Whicher, George Frisbie. *This Was a Poet: A Critical Biography of Emily Dickinson*. New York: Scribners, 1938.

Whitman, Walt. *Walt Whitman: Complete Poetry and Collected Prose*. Edited by Justin Kaplan. New York: Literary Classics of the United States, 1982.

Whyte, William H. *The Organization Man*. 1956. Reprint, Philadelphia: University of Pennsylvania Press, 2002.

Winnicott, D. W. *Playing and Reality*. 1971. Reprint, London: Routledge, 2005.

Woodcock, George. *Thomas Merton, Monk and Poet: A Critical Study*. New York: Farrar, Straus, Giroux, 1978.

Wright, Edmond. "Gregory Bateson: Epistemology, Language, Play and the Double Bind." *Anthropoetics* 14, no. 1 (Summer 2008), http://anthropoetics.ucla.edu/ap1401/1401wright/.html (accessed May 12, 2018).

Wuthnow, Robert. *After Heaven: Spirituality in America Since the 1950s*. Berkeley: University of California Press, 1998.

Young, Malcolm Clemens. *The Spiritual Journal of Henry David Thoreau*. Macon: Mercer University Press, 2009.

Index

Abbott, Philip, 45
abstraction: as depersonalization, 111, 142; particularity as resistance to, 112, 118–19, 122; perceptual reframing and, 12, 31n27; play and, 4–5, 35, 151, 207; self-protection and, 24, 109, 118–19, 181
Adorno, Theodor W., 138, 156n30, 174
ahamkāra (egocentrism), 41, 48–49, 56, 60. *See also* encapsulated ego, the
Ahlstrom, Sydney E., 127n8
Aho, Kevin, 29n8
Albert OCSO, John, 155n11
alienation. *See* common sense, the
alterity (otherness), 71, 83, 88, 94, 124, 138, 151, 159, 193, 201
Altizer, Thomas J. J., 156n31, 166, 186n29
Aristotle, 21, 134, 193
Atchley, J. Heath, 66n49, 149
attunement: in Bateson, 35, 62n2; in Jewish theology, 18–19; kenosis and, 48–49, 60; as a spiritual practice, 2, 8, 40, 54–55, 65n29, 123–24, 180–81; Thoreau's images for, 36–37, 54; Walden Pond as a symbol for, 2, 13, 37; as a writing practice, 170, 180–81. *See also* responsiveness
aufgehoben (Schiller), 73, 80, 85, 193

awakening as spiritual metaphor, 7, 39, 114, 116–18, 142, 146, 175

Baal Shem Tov, the, 180, 181
Bakhtin, Mikhail, 143
Barbour, John D., 29n13
Barth, Karl, 195, 206
Bartnik, Ronald J., 129n41
Bates, Catherine, 16, 28n4
Bateson, Gregory, 4–8, 13, 28n4, 30n23, 35, 60, 105, 159–61, 173, 177, 207–9
Beck, Guy L., 66n58
Begbie, Jeremy S., 24, 112–14
Belgrad, Daniel, 128n34
Benson, Bruce Ellis, 127n13, 128n21
Bernard of Clairvaux, Saint, 132
bewilderment, 15, 46, 65n41, 73, 80, 83, 191
The Bhagavad Gita, 7, 10, 12–13, 26–27, 30n26, 31n31, 38–39
The Bhāgavata Purāna, 163, 177
Bigard, Barney ("C-Jam Blues"), 115
Blake, William, 25, 146
borderlands or liminal spaces, 22, 57–60, 69–70, 77, 82, 111, 121
Boudreau, Gordon V., 53, 60, 67n67
Brecht, Bertolt, 133, 154n8
Breitwieser, Mitchell Robert, 102n13, 116

Brennan, Teresa, 187n54
Bridgman, Richard, 45
Brown, David, 187n53
Brueggemann, Walter, 82–83
Buber, Martin, 33n65, 110–11
Buranelli, Vincent, 45
Burke, Kenneth, 3, 143

Caillois, Roger, 25, 32n41, 88
Calasso, Roberto, 31n35
Campbell, Joseph, 168
Caputo, John D., 70–72, 78, 83, 91, 101, 161, 173, 195, 207
carnivalesque, the, 69, 133, 143, 165, 166, 175–76
Cavell, Stanley, 33n68, 117
charism (Suurmond), 111–12, 118, 122
Chénetier, Marc, 185n19
Christy, Arthur, 63n17
Cochoy, Nathalie, 174
Code, Lorraine, 216n21
common sense, the: frame play as a response to, 9–11, 143; Geertz's analysis of, 28n6, 67n70; Merton's critique of, 25, 133–34, 139–46; nonsense and, 9, 11, 140, 148; Thoreau's critique of, 3–4, 9–11
Connolly, William E., 48
Coomaraswamy, Ananda K., 24, 63n16, 67n68
Cooper, David D., 155n17
Cox, Harvey, 145, 157n31, 170
Craig, Megan, 23, 89, 98, 99
Crawford, Nathan, 65n29, 127n13

"damaged life" (Adorno), 138, 145
dance, 39–40, 88, 105, 162, 178–82, 190
Dandurand, Karen, 102n24
Darwin, Charles, 8, 100, 163
Davey, Nicholas, 193, 217n27
defamiliarization, 74, 77, 133, 134. *See also* Brecht, Bertolt
DeKoven, Marianne, 137
Deleuze, Gilles, 50–52

Deppman, Jed, 102n16
"depth effect." *See* gestalt puzzles
Derrida, Jacques, 70, 71, 163, 168, 173, 196–97, 216n23
Detweiler, Robert, 173–74, 187n47
deus ludens (a playful God), 2, 8, 20, 38–40, 58, 60
dialogic understanding, 26, 148, 194, 195, 208
Dickinson, Emily: as a comic poet, 97; compared to Thoreau, 23, 71, 74, 77, 86, 90, 91–92, 95–96, 105; figurality in. *See* New, Elisa; gender norming in. *See* "We play at Paste"; growth and learning in, 74–76, 79–80, 84–86, 101; the metaphorics of melting in. *See* "I'll tell you how the Sun rose"; personification of "Faith" in, 71, 72, 80, 99–101, 105; play in, 69–72, 74, 77, 84–87, 97, 105; pluralistic consciousness in, 23, 83, 84–86; Puritanism and, 77–78, 86–87, 89, 90; "quickness" in, 74, 87, 88, 98, 105; Schiller's view of play compared to, 72–74, 77, 85, 86; teasing and, 74, 79–81, 83, 97, 102n13; as a trauma artist, 86–87, 90–91, 94; poems ("A curious Cloud surprised the Sky," 167, 168; "A Light exists in Spring," 171–72; "I dreaded that first Robin, so," 75, 91–96, 121, 198; "I dwell in Possibility," 70; "I'll tell you how the Sun rose," 75, 76–79; "In lands I never saw–they say," 23, 80–84; "I've dropped my Brain–My Soul is numb," 87–90, 124; "Like Rain it sounded till it curved," 168–70; "My period had come for Prayer," 95; "The nearest Dream recedes–unrealized," 75, 79–80; "Safe in their Alabaster Chambers," 75, 79; "She rose to His Requirement," 85; "This World is not conclusion," 71, 80, 90, 99–101; "We play at

Paste," 23, 75, 77, 84–86). *See also* bewilderment; borderlands or liminal spaces; ecstatic, the; subjunctivity

Dillard, Annie: animal play in, 173–74; "dark play" in, 163–64; Dickinson's influence on, 162, 164–72; figurality and, 174–75, 180; "hosting" in, 163; "letting go" in, 176–78, 183; "The Merchant of the Picturesque," 162, 164–72; the monstrous and, 163, 166, 167, 176; a self-limiting God in, 181; Thoreau and, 172, 175, 180, 182, 185n19; as an "unscrupulous observer," 163, 172, 176–77, 183, 185n13; vision in, 178–79. *See also* dance; subjunctivity

Doriani, Beth Maclay, 103n38

"dormitive thinking" (Bateson), 9, 151

doubt, 2, 17, 22, 46–47, 161, 172, 195, 211

ébranler (Derrida), 168

Eckhart, Meister, 25, 132, 177

ecstatic, the, 27, 74, 86–96, 110, 114, 127n14, 144, 190, 191, 193, 194, 196, 214

Eliot, T. S., 142, 189

Ellwood, Robert S., 157n31

embarrassment. *See* Dickinson, Emily, "This World is not conclusion"

Emerson, Ralph Waldo, 8, 17–18, 39, 47, 72, 98, 102n13, 148

encapsulated ego, the, 1–2, 47, 56, 60, 105, 111, 162, 213. *See also ahamkāra* (egocentrism)

Erikson, Erik H., 73–74, 160, 184n3

eutrapelia (Aristotle), 21

Evans, James H., Jr., 17

Evans, Justin, 215n7

faith: as agility or adjustment, 8, 20–21, 37, 41, 71, 105, 172; Christ's teachings and, 111, 144. *See also* attunement; Dickinson, Emily, personification of "Faith" in; doubt; play, as a spiritual practice

Farcé, Gilles, 155n11

Fishbane, Michael, 18–19, 21, 33n65, 161

Fitzgerald, F. Scott, 24, 120

folly (*moria*), 25, 52, 98, 144–45

Foxe, Gladys, 126n6

Freedman, Linda, 98, 100

Freud, Sigmund, 56, 73–74, 107, 138–39, 160, 184n3

Frost, Anthony, and Ralph Yarrow, 127n12

Gadamer, Hans-Georg, 26, 88, 148, 178, 192–98, 200, 205, 206, 208, 209, 216n21, 218nn38, 40

Gaillard, Slim, 109, 110, 113–17

Garber, Frederick, 14, 44, 47

Gardner, Thomas, 190, 215n7

Geertz, Clifford. *See* common sense, the, Geertz's analysis of

Gelassenheit (relinquishment), 28, 41, 49, 144, 177

gestalt puzzles, 152–53, 177

Gewirtz, Isaac, 130nn50, 56

Gill, Sam D., 104n45, 215n12

Ginsberg, Allen, 107, 108, 112

Gioia, Ted, 116

Gleason, William A., 3, 9, 14–15, 59

glossolalia, 110

Goffman, Erving, 100

grace, 20, 24, 77–78, 112, 144, 161, 191, 194, 213

Graham, Dom Aelred, 157n31

Groos, Karl, 16

Guardini, Romano, 154n7

Habegger, Alfred, 102n24

Haddox, Thomas F., 215n7

hallucination of mastery, the (Erikson), 160, 184n3

Hamilton, William Hughes, 156n31, 166, 186n29

Hammond, Karla M., 186n37
The Harivaṃśa, 8, 38–39, 60, 64n21
Hawthorne, Nathaniel, 43, 85
Hegel, Georg Wilhelm Friedrich, 73, 74, 174, 193
Heidegger, Martin, 29n8, 167, 170, 173
Hein, Norvin, 38, 39
Hekman, Susan, 216n21
Henricks, Thomas S., 29n11
Heraclitus, 20, 24, 58
Herberg, Will, 107
Heydt, Jim von der, 74, 102n33
Higginson, Thomas Wentworth, 74–76
The Hitopadeśa, 2, 5, 49
Hodder, Alan D., 14, 31n27, 64n17, 67n64, 185n19
Holladay, Hilary, 127n9
Holmes, John Clellon, 116
Holton, Robert, 129n48
hope, 11, 15, 146, 164, 176, 198
Hopkins, Gerard Manley, 11
Houdini, Harry, 149, 153
Huizinga, Johan, 2–3, 15–16, 32n41, 63n16, 70, 85, 88, 212, 218n46
humor, 5, 12, 23, 72, 97, 99, 104n55, 132
Hungerford, Amy, 217n28
Hutcheon, Linda, 157n38

"implicit spirituality" (Weil), 48, 61–62
improvisation: Christ's teachings as, 111; contingency in, 113–14; as conversation, 114, 128n31; reframing failure in, 27, 99, 113; the sacred and, 127n13; self-surrender as a feature of, 117, 129n46; situational awareness in, 109, 114, 115–16; surprise and, 24, 120; temporality and, 105–6, 112
Ireland, Julia A., 185n13

Jackson, Carl T., 63n17
James, William, 34n78, 91
Jay, Martin, 156n21, 156nn24, 30

jazz, 22, 24, 105–6, 108–16, 120, 123–24, 127n14, 128nn28, 34. *See also* improvisation
Jesus Christ, 11–12, 23, 61, 67n58, 83, 97, 99, 108, 111, 128n21, 129n41, 144, 162. *See also* Merton, Thomas, Christology in
Joyce, James, 150, 157n43
Juhasz, Suzanne, 80–81

Kearney, Richard, 163, 168, 181, 185n11
Keats, John. *See* "negative capability" (Keats)
Keen, Sam, 156n31
Keller, Karl, 104n55
kenosis (self-emptying), 28, 48–49, 60, 121–23, 201
Kerouac, Jack: "beat," meaning of in, 122, 130n50; pornography and reification in, 112, 120–21; religious conservatism of, 108–9, 123–24; "rolling" theology in, 105–6, 108, 114, 124–25, 174; spiritual growth in, 24, 109, 117–18, 120–21, 124–25; suffering children in, 107, 120–22, 124–25, 130n56; temporality in, 24, 105, 109, 114–23; Thoreau's influence on, 108, 116–17, 123–26, 129n41; World War II, influence on, 106–7, 125. *See also* jazz; neighbors and neighboring; self-protective fantasy; traveling as spiritual metaphor
Kilcourse, George, 151
King Lear (Shakespeare), 88, 165, 185n21, 214–15
Kinsley, David R., 17, 32n59, 40, 63n16, 65n29
Kristeva, Julia, 163
Krondorfer, Bjorn, 66n54
Kronick, Joseph G., 167, 168

Labrie, Ross, 155n11

Lane, Belden C., 131, 132, 154n1, 218n41
Lawrence, Fred, 216n18
The Laws of Manu, 37–39, 55, 56, 59, 63n17
Lecoq, Jacques, 109, 114
Leise, Christopher, 215n7
Leland, John, 24, 122
Levinas, Emmanuel, 56, 168
līlā (play), 8, 32n59, 37–38, 39, 63n16, 67n68, 163
Lucy, Niall, 216n23
Lynch, William F., 156n31

MacIntyre, Alasdair, 156n27
Mack, Stephen John, 134
MacKendrick, Karmen, 187n53
MacKethan, Lucinda Hardwick, 164, 165
Madison, Gary B., 217n26
Manoussakis, John Panteleimon, 110
Marcuse, Herbert, 9, 136–44, 149–50
market economies: commodification of religion in, 137, 150–51; play as Thoreau's "strategic answer" to, 3, 42, 53, 143; suppression of alternatives in, 3, 136–37, 159
Mary at the Garden (John 20), 10–12, 152–53
McClure, John A., 66n50, 103n37
McConahay, Mary Davidson, 185n19
McFadyen, Alistair I., 111, 117
McGregor, Robert Kuhn, 64n17
McIlroy, Gary, 185n19
McIntosh, James, 17–18, 44, 88–89, 98
Melville, Herman, 47, 125, 191
Mendelson, Donna, 185n19
Merleau-Ponty, Maurice, 177, 178
Merton, Thomas: anti-poetry in, 131–32, 135, 139–41, 155n10; Christology in, 148–53; dehumanization in, 133–34, 142; depth in, 149–50; dialectical thinking in, 134–35, 147–48; Dickinson and, 133, 150–51, 158n45; nonsense in, 25, 139–41, 143–44; perspectival knowing in, 25, 132, 135–36, 144, 146, 148, 154–55n10; religious and cultural dissent in, 132–35, 139–41, 143–45, 154–55n10; as a sound poet, 142, 156n30; Thoreau and, 133–37, 142, 154n5, 155n11. *See also* common sense, the; gestalt puzzles; Marcuse, Herbert
metacognitive thinking, 4–6, 8–9, 30n26, 49, 100, 207–9
Meyer, Leonard B., 128n28
Milder, Robert, 44
Miller, David LeRoy, 156n31
Miller, Perry, 45
Mitchell, Domhnall, 72
Moldenhauer, Joseph J., 44
Moltmann, Jürgen, 19–20, 161, 170
Monson, Ingrid, 115, 128nn28, 31, 34
Moser, Paul K., 66n48

Nachmanovitch, Stephen, 9, 127n13, 128nn28, 30, 129n46, 161
Nagatomo, Shigenori, 66n54
Nancy, Jean-Luc, 56
Neale, Robert E., 105, 156n31
"negative capability" (Keats), 74, 91, 100
neighbors and neighboring, 10, 12, 19, 23, 27, 50–51, 61, 79–81, 109, 116–17, 201–2, 217n28
New, Elisa, 65n29, 77–78, 86, 94, 98, 171
Nicosia, Gerald, 107, 127n9
Niebuhr, H. Richard, 108
Nietzsche, Friedrich, 156n31, 166, 174, 187n46, 216n23
a "nuptial yes" (Weil), 212–15

O'Connell, Patrick F., 28n7, 155n11
Oberhaus, Dorothy Huff, 104n55
Oriard, Michael, 15, 215n5

Panikkar, Raimon, 40–41, 48, 54, 60, 65n29, 96

Panish, Jon, 129n37
Papa, James A., Jr., 185n19
Parra, Nicanor, 25, 131
Parrish, Nancy C., 185nn18, 19
Paul, Saint, 8, 52
Paul, Sherman, 67n64
Perls, Frederick, Ralph F. Hefferline, and Paul Goodman, 152–53
Phillips, Rod, 129n41
Pieper, Josef, 156n31
Plato, 7, 23, 58
play: Bateson's theory of, 4–9, 13, 22, 29n9, 30n23, 35, 159–62; biblical references to, 19, 82, 162, 179, 195; as communication, 3, 5, 13, 35; Derrida's view of, 196–97, 216n23; early Protestant conversion narratives and, 15, 189; embodiment and, 54–55, 58–59, 66n54, 160, 173, 178; framing as a feature of, 3–22, 29n11, 132, 135, 136, 151; Hinduism and. *See līlā* (play); literality and, 9; as movement, 88–90, 160, 175, 179–80; paradox and, 7, 45, 71, 132, 159–61, 166, 170; philosophical hermeneutics and. *See* Gadamer, Hans-Georg; as the presentation of alternatives, 1, 3–4, 10–11, 25, 85–86, 111, 113, 143–48, 159–60, 175–78; religion and, 24, 154n1, 161; Schiller's "drive theory" of, 72–74; as semiotic surplus, 70, 82; as a spiritual practice, 1–2, 7–8, 13, 77–78, 105, 145, 161–62; social control and, 14–16; "structurality" of, 178, 193, 205–6, 208; symbolic mastery and, 71–72, 184n3; theology and, 18–22, 161. *See also* attunement; dance; metacognitive thinking; subjunctivity
"playful wisdom," 1–2, 5–6, 19–20, 22, 26–27, 49, 73, 81, 86, 97, 100, 110–11
Poetzsch, Markus, 46
Pramuk, Christopher, 103n39, 154n1, 155n15

prayer: as embodied participation, 178, 180; in Kerouac's jazz scenes, 114–15; in *King Lear*, 214–15; the loon's laughter compared to, 42, 51; the performative dimensions of, 208–9. *See also* Dickinson, Emily, "My period had come for Prayer"
Prothero, Stephen R., 127n8

"quiet desperation" (Thoreau), 1, 3, 14, 23, 60, 109, 135. *See also* "damaged life" (Adorno)

Rahner, Hugo, 20–22, 24, 154n7, 161, 175, 179
Raj, Selva J., and Corinne G. Dempsey, 29n16
Ray, Robert B., 41
Reimer, Margaret Loewen, 175–76
responsiveness: Dillard's images for, 172; in jazz, 114, 115; as Thoreau's religious "profession," 105. *See also* attunement; Dickinson, Emily, "quickness" in
resurrection, scenes of, 89, 91–92, 96, 151. *See also* Mary at the Garden (John 20)
Rhoads, Kenneth W., 67n64
Richardson, Mark, 119
Ricks, Christopher, 104nn62, 63
Ricœur, Paul, 70, 173, 187n46
Rilke, Rainer Maria, 26
Robinson, Marilynne: baseball in, 190, 206; Calvinism and, 190–91, 209, 212, 217n37; childhood games and play in, 203–4; Dickinson and, 189–90, 212; Gadamer's view of play and, 26, 192–98, 206, 208, 209, 218n40; letter writing in, 206–9; perspectival knowing in, 196, 208–9; prejudice as a theme in, 198–212; Thoreau and, 191, 201–2, 208, 210; uncertainty in, 191, 195–96; the undefended self in, 189–90, 201, 205, 213–14. *See also* dialogic

understanding; metacognitive thinking; a "nuptial yes" (Weil)
Rorty, Richard, 103n37, 197
Ruether, Rosemary Radford, 157n31
rupture, 18–19, 22, 24, 55–56, 135; biblical references to, 84; nonsense related to, 30n25; stammering as an expression of, 21, 22, 150–51. *See also* bewilderment; wilderness and the wild

Saward, John, 154n7
Sax, William S., 63n16, 64nn20, 29
Schaub, Thomas, 215n6
Schechner, Richard, 163–64
Schiller, Friedrich, 2, 72–74, 77, 81, 85–86, 139
Schmidt, Leigh Eric, 17, 18
Schwartzman, Helen B., 29n11
Scott, David, 64n17
self-protective fantasy, 47–48, 95–96, 107, 109, 117–21, 204–5
Seymour, William J., 110
Sheets-Johnstone, Maxine, 88
Shepherd, Victor, 128n27
Shoop, Marcia W. Mount, 187n53
Shy, Todd, 215n7
sleep as spiritual metaphor, 25, 95, 116–17, 119–20, 142, 151–52. *See also* awakening as spiritual metaphor; "dormitive thinking" (Bateson)
Smith, Martha Nell, 72
Smith, R. J., 128n16
Snyder, Gary, 37
Sophia (Prov. 8), 19, 82, 86, 103n38, 111, 155n15, 179
Springer, Marlene, 104n55
Stewart, Susan, 25, 30n25, 140, 153
Stonum, Gary Lee, 75
subjunctivity, 5, 6, 7, 8, 29n16, 54, 58, 70–71, 160, 164, 175
Sutton-Smith, Brian, 8
Suurmond, Jean-Jacques, 109–12, 114. *See also charism* (Suurmond)

Taylor, Edward, 171, 182
Theado, Matt, 126n3
Thoreau, Henry David: aesthetic and spiritual play in, 1–4, 13, 44–46, 159–60; animal play in, 5–7, 51–53; contemplative listening in, 40, 55–57; critique of organized religion in, 43–47; divine encounter in, 50–53, 95, 200–202; Hinduism and, 2, 5, 12–13, 37–41, 54–56; legacy of, 2, 13–14, 27; personality of, 43; perspectival knowing in, 4, 31n27, 46, 135, 159; rhythmic notions of the divine in, 36, 40–41, 53–54; sacred sound in, 53–60; "slipperiness" of the sacred in, 57–59, 100, 162; spiritual discipline in, 42–43. *See also* attunement; "implicit spirituality" (Weil); metacognitive thinking; neighbors and neighboring; wilderness and the wild
Tippett, Krista, 21–22
transformation: in Derrida, 196–97; in Gadamer, 192–93, 195, 196; Gaillard, Slim, as a figure for, 110; in nature, 46, 164, 166, 179, 182; the spiritual cost of, 125, 198; at Thoreau's sandbank, 57–60. *See also* resurrection, scenes of
traveling as spiritual metaphor, 22, 109, 117, 121–26
Turner, Victor, 29n16, 69, 70, 101n1, 136
Tursi, Renée, 72
typology, 169, 171, 186n37
Tytell, John, 129n41

Vasterling, Veronica, 216n21
Vattimo, Gianni, 81, 103n37
Versluis, Arthur, 63n17
Vilhauer, Monica, 193
The Vishnu Purāna, 8, 13, 38–40, 54, 64n22

vulnerability, 19, 70, 71, 100–101, 117, 132, 190. *See also* "weak thought" (Vattimo)

Walker, Nancy, 72, 104n55
walking as the cultivation of perspective, 135, 177
Warren, Colleen, 177
Watts, Alan, 157n31
"weak thought" (Vattimo), 81, 97, 102n16, 103n37
Webb, Stephen H., 70, 173, 186n37, 187n46
Weil, Simone, 48, 61–62, 213–14
Welty, Eudora, 160, 179–80
West, Michael, 63n13
Whicher, George Frisbie, 71–72
Whitman, Walt, 10, 30n26, 55, 78, 112, 125, 173, 218n37

Whyte, William H., 127n8
wilderness and the wild: as blessing, 191–92; God's otherness expressed as, 19, 41–42, 145, 201–2; as knowledge, a form of, 197–98, 210; as literary style, 174–76; in the loon game, 51–53. *See also* bewilderment; neighbors and neighboring
Williams, William Carlos, 77
Winnicott, D. W., 77, 82
Woodcock, George, 143
Wordsworth, William, 9, 30n23, 67n64
Wright, Edmond, 62n2
Wuthnow, Robert, 17, 127n8

Young, Malcolm Clemens, 14, 187n54

Žižek, Slavoj, 163, 168

About the Author

Robert Leigh Davis is Professor Emeritus of English at Wittenberg University in Springfield, Ohio. An award-winning teacher, Davis has published essays in the *American Transcendental Quarterly*, *Literature and Medicine*, the *Journal of Medical Humanities*, *The Wordsworth Circle*, the *Walt Whitman Quarterly Review* and as book chapters in several edited volumes. His book *Whitman and the Romance of Medicine* is published by the University of California Press.

www.ingramcontent.com/pod-product-compliance
Lightning Source LLC
Chambersburg PA
CBHW050902300426
44111CB00010B/1345